THE COMPLETE
MEAT COOKBOOK

THE COMPLETE
MEAT COOKBOOK

CAXTON

The publishers acknowledge the cooperation of the following during photography for this book: Breville, Crown Corningware, Fred Pazotti Tiles Pty Ltd, Hale Imports Pty Ltd, Kambrook Distributors Pty Ltd, Mikasa Tableware, Peters of Kensington, Roden Products, Sanyo, The Bay Tree Kitchen Group, Westinghouse.

The publishers would like to thank the following for their assistance in compiling this book: Jan Aspinwall, Jean Conil, Douglas Marsland, Jan Wunderlich; for additional photography: Ashley Barber and Norm Nichols; for additional food styling: Voula Kyprianou and Jan Wunderlich.

This edition specially produced for CEEPI/Dealerfield Ltd in 1989
ISBN 1-86256-407-8

Published by Bay Books, 61–69 Anzac Parade, Kensington, NSW 2033
Publisher: George Barber
©Bay Books, Sydney and London. © Illustrations Bay Books.
©Illustrations "Les Cours de la Cuisine A a Z" — "Femmes d'Aujourd'hui". Jacket photo © British Meat
Printed in Singapore

Contents

All About Meat

Meat is a compact package of nutrient, protein and vitamin which not only looks appetising but also tastes superb. It enhances any meal — whether festooned with pastry, adding relish to salads, or providing zesty flavour in soups and stocks.

Some of the finest recipes from throughout the world exploring meat's multitude of uses are collected in this cookbook for your enjoyment. The range of meats has been limited to lamb, pork, beef, veal and fancy meats although some recipes include poultry and game. Most methods of cooking meats are represented and recipes for microwave cooking are gathered at the end of each chapter.

Accompanying the recipes are a selection of tempting photographs which enable you to picture the final goal towards which you are working. Pictorial cooking classes are occasionally included which provide a step-by-step guide as you follow the instructions.

Diet Why should meat feature in our daily diets? The answer is that meat is one of the most valuable sources of iron, zinc, protein and B group vitamins.

Protein is instrumental in repairing damaged tissue, fighting disease and building strong bodies. B group vitamins aid digestion and energy supply, and promote healthy nerves and skin. Iron is essential for oxygen circulation and zinc plays an important role in tissue growth, eyesight and skin health.

Meat's total fat content varies enormously but it can be reduced by removing the fat along the edge of the cut. Much of the fat within the meat muscle is polyunsaturated.

Purchase Aim for leaner cuts and pay close attention to colour and texture.

Sheep meat is termed lamb between the ages of five and 12 months when it then becomes hogget and later mutton. Quality lamb is light pink with firm fat deposits. The colour deepens as the animal ages.

Superior beef is light rosy or cherry red in colour and the fat should be a creamy yellow. A minimum of gristle should be apparent. The most tender cuts, such as sirloin, spring back when touched.

Veal is the meat of the young milk-fed calf of up to three months in age although animals of up to one year may be sold as veal. Look for pale pink veal which is moist, firm and pleasant-smelling. White fat with a pink tinge is preferable and the connective tissue must be gelatinous but not hard or bubbly.

Acceptable pork is pale pink, gristle-free and firm. The meat is slightly marbled with milky-white fat and the outer fat is firm and white.

Uses The variety of cooking techniques for meat appears almost inexhaustible but you must ensure that the correct method is used for each cut.

The most expensive cuts of meat are usually the most tender and can be quick-roasted, fried or grilled. Tougher, cheaper cuts require slower cooking methods to soften them.

You can improve inferior cuts of meat by marinating them for several hours in wine, beer, cider of a mixture of fruit juices and vinegar.

Meat tenderisers are available which break down the indigestible elements of older meat prior to cooking. It is vital to insert the tenderiser deep into the meat with a fork. If the meat is at room temperature begin cooking no longer than 15 minutes after using the tenderiser. If the meat is frozen, or refrigerated after tenderising, commence cooking within the hour.

Cheaper cuts can be potroasted, braised, casseroled or stewed. Stews generally use the least expensive cuts of meat such as chuck steak, oxtail, lamb neck chops or veal knuckles.

A meat thermometer ensures a good result whether the meat is roasted or boiled. Insert the point of the thermometer into the middle of the meatiest part and do not allow it to contact bones or fat. Although the temperature desired is a matter of personal taste, the following figures are commonly used.

Rare	Pink	70°C (158°F)
Medium	Pink-brown	73°C (163°F)
Well-done	Brown	77°C (170°F)

Microwave Microwave meat cooking is a time-saving device and a boon to busy cooks.

When using a microwave meat should be cooked in a heatproof container. A browning dish is ideal as it is especially designed to brown and sear meat. Browning agents include gravy powder, butter, paprika, fruit juice, honey and soy sauce, and are applied to the meat before or during cooking.

Meat should generally be cooked on medium power although initially a higher setting may be used. When cooking sasserole-style cover the meat but leave it open if you are roasting. Allow the meat to stand for about one third of the cooking time once the process is complete.

Storage Meat can be bought in bulk and refrigerated or frozen for later use. The nutritional value is little affected by storage, freezing, thawing or ageing.

Meat must be covered loosely, laced on a rack over a plate and stored in the coldest part of the refrigerator. Do not store in sealed plastic bags.

When freezing, store meat in high density polythene bags. Interleave steaks and chops with plastic filk if more than one piece is intended for the bag. Pack against the coldest surfaces of the freezer, leaving an airspace of 10–15 mm (0.4–0.6 inch) between packages and allow up to 48 hours for meat to freeze.

Do not thaw small joints as they are best cooked frozen. Large joints should thaw slowly in the refrigerator, allowing approximately eight hours per 500 g (1 lb). Loosen the wrap and place on a rack over a dish.

Seasoning Meat's natural flavour is salty and less seasoning will be needed later if you salt and pepper prior to cooking. If you forget the meat will taste flat and bland. Many recipes in this book recommend using a bouquet garni. This term refers to a small bunch of fresh herbs such as thyme, rosemary, basil or any others available which are tied with string and added to the dish. Dried mixtures sold in small muslin bags are another alternative.

WEIGHTS AND MEASURES

DRY INGREDIENTS

Metric	Imperial
15 g	½ oz
30 g	1 oz
60 g	2 oz
90 g	3 oz
125 g	4 oz (¼ lb)
155 g	5 oz
185 g	6 oz
220 g	7 oz
250 g	8 oz (½ lb)
280 g	9 oz
315 g	10 oz
345 g	11 oz
375 g	12 oz (¾ lb)
410 g	13 oz
440 g	14 oz
470 g	15 oz
500 g	16 oz (1 lb)
750 g	24 oz (1½ lb)
1000 g (1 kg)	32 oz (2 lb)

CUP MEASURES

1 cup	=	250 mL
½ cup	=	125 mL
⅓ cup	=	80 mL
¼ cup	=	60 mL

LIQUIDS

Metric	Imperial
30 mL	1 fl oz
60 mL (¼ cup)	2 fl oz (¼ cup)
100 mL	3 fl oz
125 mL (½ cup)	4 fl oz (½ cup)
150 mL	5 fl oz (¼ pt)
185 mL (¾ cup)	6 fl oz (¾ cup)
250 mL (1 cup)	8 fl oz (1 cup)
300 mL (1¼ cups)	10 fl oz (½ pt)
360 mL (1½ cups)	12 fl oz (1½ cups)
420 mL (1¾ cups)	14 fl oz (1¾ cups)
500 mL (2 cups)	16 fl oz (2 cups)
625 mL (2½ cups)	20 fl oz (1 pt)

LENGTHS

Metric	Imperial
5 mm	¼ in
1 cm	½ in
2 cm	¾ in
2.5 cm	1 in
5 cm	2 in
6 cm	2½ in
8 cm	3 in
10 cm	4 in
12 cm	5 in
15 cm	6 in
18 cm	7 in
20 cm	8 in
23 cm	9 in
25 cm	10 in
28 cm	11 in
30 cm	12 in
46 cm	18 in
50 cm	20 in
61 cm	24 in
77 cm	30 in

SPOON MEASURES

1 tablespoon	=	20 mL
1 teaspoon	=	5 mL
½ teaspoon	=	2.5 mL
¼ teaspoon	=	1.25 mL

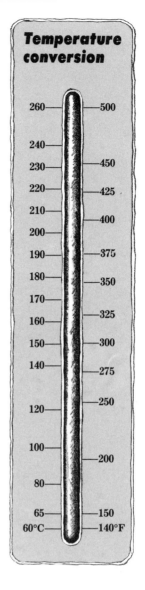

Temperature conversion

°C	°F
260	500
240	
230	450
220	425
210	400
200	
190	375
180	350
170	
160	325
150	300
140	275
120	250
100	200
80	
65	150
60°C	140°F

OVEN TEMPERATURE CHART

	C	F	Gas Mark
Very Slow	110	225	¼
	120	250	½
Slow	140	275	1
	150	300	2
Moderate	160	325	3
	180	350	4
Moderately hot	190	375	5
	200	400	6
Hot	220	425	7
	230	450	8
Very hot	250	475	9

Tempting Appetisers

Ideally appetisers should stimulate the palate, not dull it, so choose ingredients that contrast well in flavour, texture and colour and only serve small portions. Appetisers can be a single ingredient or two, simply served, like Asparagus Ham Rolls or Croque-Monsieur. Or an appetiser can be several ingredients combined together like Spanish Artichokes or Dolmades.

Stuffed Pawpaws, an unusual and exotic dish, make an impressive start to a meal. Lamb in Mint Jelly Mould is a tasty and attractive means of using leftover lamb served in aspic with a cold salad. Try Rabbit and Pork Terrine, a well-seasoned loaf cooked in the oven and served cold.

Cabbage Rolls

Beef Kebabs

225 g (½ lb) beef fillet
2 medium onions, quartered
1 green capsicum (pepper), cut into
  pieces
4 bacon rashers
6 mushrooms
6 bay leaves
30 mL (2 tablespoons) oil
salt and pepper
175 g (6 oz) rice

Marinade
150 mL (¼ pint) (⅔ cup) dry sherry
5 mL (1 teaspoon) vinegar
5 mL (1 teaspoon) Worcestershire
  sauce
1 clove garlic, crushed
15 mL (1 tablespoon) oil
5 g (1 teaspoon) sugar

1 Cut beef into cubes.
2 Make marinade from sherry, vinegar, Worcestershire sauce, garlic, oil and sugar. Marinate the beef for ½ hour.
3 Meanwhile, scald onions and capsicum for 3 minutes.
4 Remove beef and dry on absorbent paper. Impale beef on skewers with rolls of bacon, pieces of capsicum, mushrooms and bay leaves alternately.
5 Place on a baking tray, brush with 30 mL (2 tablespoons) oil and season with salt and pepper.

6 Grill for 4 minutes either side, or longer depending on the meat. Baste with remaining marinade.
7 Meanwhile, prepare rice and serve kebabs arranged on rice on a flat dish.

Serves 3

Tip: Another way of using onions for a kebab is to cut them in half and open up the leaves of the onion. Use each leaf raw curved round a piece of meat on the skewer, in place of the quarters.

Beef Kebabs

Keftedhes Kebab

450 g (1 lb) (2 cups) minced beef
1 onion, chopped
50 g (2 oz) cooked rice
50 g (2 oz) (1 cup) fresh breadcrumbs
1 egg, beaten
salt and pepper
50 mL (2 fl oz) (¼ cup) oil

Barbecue Sauce
15 g (½ oz) (1 tablespoon) sugar
15 mL (1 tablespoon) vinegar
pinch cayenne pepper
300 mL (½ pint) (1¼ cups) tomato
    sauce

1 Preheat oven to 200°C (400°F).
2 Mix beef, onion, rice, breadcrumbs, egg and seasoning together.
3 Divide into 4 and mould on to
short skewers in long oval shapes.
4 Heat oil in frying pan and brown
for 15 minutes covered with a lid.
5 Meanwhile, add sugar, vinegar
and cayenne pepper to the tomato
sauce and boil for 5 minutes.
6 Arrange kebabs in a shallow dish,
pour sauce over and heat in the oven
for 10 minutes.
7 Serve with plain, boiled rice.

Serves 4

Stuffed Pawpaws

Stuffed Pawpaws

3 firm ripe pawpaws
50 g (2 oz) (4 tablespoons) butter
1 small onion, thinly sliced
1 stick celery, finely chopped
1 tomato, skinned, seeded and
    chopped
7 g (1 tablespoon) chopped almonds
350 g (¾ lb) (1½ cups) minced beef
5 mL (1 teaspoon) curry powder
100 mL (4 fl oz) (½ cup) water
salt and pepper
175 g (6 oz) cooked rice
5 g (1 tablespoon) dried breadcrumbs

1 Preheat oven to 200°C (400°F). Peel
and halve pawpaws and scoop out
seeds.
2 Heat half the butter in a pan and
fry onion and celery for 1 minute.
Add tomato and chopped almonds
and fry lightly for a few minutes.
3 Add minced beef, curry powder,
water and seasoning and simmer for
5 minutes. Stir in the cooked rice.

4 Place pawpaw halves on an
ovenproof dish and fill with stuffing
mixture. Sprinkle with breadcrumbs
and the rest of the butter, melted.
Bake in preheated oven for 20 minutes.

Serves 6

Tomatoes with Beef Stuffing

4 large firm tomatoes
salt
225 g (½ lb) cold roast beef
2 onions
25 g (1 oz) (2 tablespoons) butter
pepper
pinch allspice
5 g (1 tablespoon) chopped parsley
30 mL (2 tablespoons) oil

1 Wash and dry tomatoes. Cut off
tops and cut a slice from the bottom
of each.

2 Remove seeds and cores with a
small spoon leaving enough flesh for
the tomatoes to stay firm. Sprinkle
insides with salt and leave upside
down on a rack to drain.
3 Mince the beef and chop onions.
Melt butter in a frying pan and cook
onions over a low heat for 6–7 minutes or until golden.
4 Add minced beef, turn up heat and
cook for 2–3 minutes, stirring constantly. Add salt, pepper and allspice.
5 Remove from heat and stir in the
parsley.
6 Rinse and dry tomatoes. Preheat
oven to 200°C (400°F).
7 Brush the bottom and sides of an
ovenproof dish with oil.
8 Stuff tomatoes and put on their
lids. Place in dish, covered with foil
and bake for 20 minutes. Serve
straight from the oven.

Serves 4

Dolmades

8 cabbage leaves
450 g (1 lb) (2 cups) minced beef
1 medium onion, chopped
50 mL (2 fl oz) (¼ cup) oil
50 g (2 oz) cooked rice
2 g (1 teaspoon) mixed herbs
salt and pepper
300 mL (½ pint) (1¼ cups) tomato
    sauce

1 Preheat oven to 180°C (350°F).
2 Boil cabbage leaves in salted water for 5 minutes. Drain and dry on absorbent paper.
3 Put mince and chopped onion in a saucepan and fry gently in oil until meat is brown, about 10 minutes.
4 Add cooked rice, herbs, and seasoning.
5 Divide filling between the cabbage leaves, roll up and place close together in a baking dish just big enough to hold them. Pour tomato sauce over, cover with a lid, and bake for 40 minutes. Serve hot as an appetiser or as a main dish with plain, boiled rice.

Serves 4

Tip: Traditional Greek Dolmades consist of lamb wrapped in vine leaves, blanched for 5 minutes, and flavoured with mint. Canned vine leaves are available at delicatessens and may be used as an alternative to cabbage leaves.

Tuscan Beef Roll

2 gherkins
2 radishes
1 slice roast beef
2.5 mL (½ teaspoon) made mustard
1 lettuce leaf
1 slice Cheddar cheese
1 bread roll
salt and pepper

1 Slice gherkins and radishes and spread roast beef with mustard.
2 Arrange lettuce, beef, cheese, gherkins and radishes, in that order, inside bread roll and season to taste.

Serves 1

Beef Brunchies

225 g (½ lb) Basic Economy Beef (see
    recipe)
50 g (2 oz) (3 tablespoons) sweet
    pickle or mango chutney
2 hard-boiled eggs, chopped
4 slices toast
50 g (2 oz) (½ cup) grated cheese

1 Make up Basic Economy Beef. Stir in sweet pickle or chutney and the chopped eggs.
2 Make toast and spoon ¼ of the beef mixture onto each slice. Sprinkle grated cheese over and serve garnished with parsley.

Serves 4

Beef Fondue with Dips

300 mL (½ pint) (1¼ cups)
    mayonnaise
5 g (1 teaspoon) curry powder or
    15 mL (1 tablespoon) curry sauce
1 clove garlic, crushed
5 g (1 tablespoon) chopped fresh
    parsley and chives
750 mL (1¼ pints) (3 cups) water
2 beef stock cubes
150 mL (¼ pint) (⅔ cup) dry sherry
bouquet garni
2 fresh mint leaves
salt and pepper
450 g (1 lb) fillet beef, diced

1 Divide mayonnaise between 2 dishes. Mix curry powder or sauce in one to make a curry dip and in the other stir garlic, parsley and chives to make a garlic herb dip.
2 Place fondue pot on the table. Add water and bring to the boil. Add stock cubes, sherry, bouquet garni, mint leaves and season to taste. Each diner places a piece of meat on a fondue fork and leaves it in the stock, which is kept at just below boiling point, until cooked to taste (approx. 2–5 minutes). Meat is then dipped into curry and garlic herb mixture.

Serves 4

Tip: Other fondue sauces include horseradish, tomato, mustard or tartare.

Hungarian Style Cauliflower

1 medium cauliflower

Sauce
50 mL (2 fl oz) (¼ cup) oil
1 medium onion, sliced
10 g (1 tablespoon) paprika
450 g (1 lb) boiled corned beef, cut
    into strips
25 g (1 oz) (2 tablespoons) tomato
    paste
4 tomatoes, skinned, seeded and
    chopped
1 red capsicum (pepper), seeded and
    cut into strips
15 g (½ oz) (1½ tablespoons) cornflour
100 mL (4 fl oz) (½ cup) sour cream
salt and pepper
5 g (1 tablespoon) chopped parsley

1 Remove leaves, wash cauliflower and boil for 20 minutes in just enough salted water to cover. Reserve 300 mL (½ pint) of the cauliflower water. Keep cauliflower hot.
2 Meanwhile, heat oil and fry onion gently without browning. Add paprika, corned beef, tomato paste, tomatoes and red capsicum and cook for 4 minutes. Stir in reserved cauliflower stock and boil for 8 minutes. Mix cornflour with cream and stir into sauce. Boil for 3 minutes until thickened. Season.
3 Sprinkle cauliflower with chopped parsley and serve sauce separately.

Serves 4

Hungarian Style Cauliflower

African Stuffed Avocados

3 avocados
juice ½ lemon
100 g (¼ lb) (⅔ cup) ham, finely
  chopped
50 g (2 oz) (½ cup) chopped
  pineapple
50 mL (2 fl oz) (¼ cup) mayonnaise
salt and pepper
½ green or red capsicum (pepper),
  seeded and chopped
5 g (1 tablespoon) chopped parsley

1 Halve avocados, remove stones
and sprinkle with lemon juice.
2 Mix in a bowl ham, pineapple and
mayonnaise and season with salt
and pepper.
3 Spoon onto avocado halves, and
sprinkle with chopped capsicum and
parsley. Serve as an appetiser.

Serves 4

Ham Logs

6 thick slices very lean ham
½ small celery heart
2 shallots (spring onions, scallions)
handful parsley
small bunch chives
3 portions Demi-sel cheese
juice ½ lemon
5 mL (1 teaspoon) strong mustard
salt
5 mL (1 teaspoon) paprika
pinch cayenne pepper
100 g (¼ lb) chopped walnuts

1 Cut 2 slices of ham into fine strips.
2 Clean celery and chop as finely
possible. Peel and finely chop shallots. Wash, dry and chop parsley and
chives.
3 Mash cheese and beat in the
parsley, chives, shallots, 15 mL (1
tablespoon) lemon juice, mustard,
salt, paprika and cayenne pepper.
4 Stir in chopped ham, celery and
nuts. Beat well until mixture is very
smooth and creamy. Spread onto the
four remaining ham slices and roll
these up to form 'logs'. Serve chilled,
on a bed of lettuce decorated with
sliced tomatoes and a few sprigs of
parsley.

Serves 4

Spanish Artichokes

6 large artichokes
100 g (¼ lb) (¾ cup) long grain rice
2 capsicums (peppers)
1 onion
3 tomatoes
275 g (10 oz) smoked bacon
2 cloves garlic
bunch parsley
75 mL (4 tablespoons) olive oil
pinch saffron
salt and pepper
½ lemon

1 Trim artichokes by cutting the
stalk and leaves 3 cm from the base,
using a serrated knife or scissors for
the leaves. Wash and drain.
2 Boil salted water in a large saucepan. Put in artichokes and boil for 15
minutes.
3 Meanwhile, wash rice until the
water is quite clear.
4 Put rice in twice its volume of boiling salted water, and simmer for 12
minutes.
5 Drain rice, rinse under cold running water, then drain once more.
6 Wash and dry capsicums. Split
them in two, remove seeds and
white fibre and dice the flesh. Peel
and chop onion. Peel tomatoes and
cut into quarters; remove seeds and
dice them also. Dice bacon finely.
Peel and chop garlic cloves. Wash,
dry and chop parsley.
7 Heat 30 mL (2 tablespoons) olive
oil in pan. Put in the diced bacon,
onion and capsicum and fry.
8 When golden-brown, add diced
tomatoes, garlic, parsley, saffron and
rice. Season with salt and pepper and
stir for 3 or 4 minutes over a moderate heat.
9 Drain artichokes, put them in cold
water, then drain and dry. Pull the
outside leaves apart and, with a
small spoon, remove the hairy
centres (chokes) and little leaves. Fill
the artichokes with rice mixture.
10 Heat the rest of the oil in a pan.
Put in artichokes, cover and leave to
finish cooking on a low heat for 40
minutes.
11 Squeeze lemon and add juice and
3 tablespoons hot water to the artichokes halfway through cooking
time. Serve very hot.

Serves 6

Mushrooms Stuffed with Ham

16 large mushrooms
¼ kg (9 oz) (4½ cups) small
  mushrooms
1½ lemons
4 shallots (spring onions, scallions)
60 g (2½ oz) (4 tablespoons) butter or
  margarine
25 g (1 oz) fresh breadcrumbs
30 mL (2 tablespoons) milk
1 bunch mixed herbs (parsley,
  chives)
100 g (¼ lb) cooked ham
15 mL (1 tablespoon) thickened
  cream
salt and pepper

1 Wash and dry mushrooms. Separate the stalks from caps of the large
ones and finely chop the stalks and
the small mushrooms.
2 Squeeze the juice from ½ lemon
over chopped mushrooms. Peel and
chop shallots.
3 Heat 25 g (1 oz) (2 tablespoons) butter in frying pan. Fry shallots until
soft, stir in chopped mushrooms and
cook until liquid has evaporated.
4 Soak breadcrumbs in a little milk,
then squeeze to remove excess
moisture. Wash and dry herbs. Chop
ham and herbs together and mix
with the breadcrumbs. Add cream,
salt and pepper to taste and mix with
the shallot and mushroom mixture
in the frying pan. Heat stuffing
gently.
5 Melt remaining fat in a large saucepan. Squeeze remaining lemon and
add juice to the pan with the mushroom caps. Pour over just enough
water to cover. Cook until mushrooms are just tender, drain and fill
with the stuffing. Arrange on a
heated serving dish and serve hot.

Serves 4–8

Asparagus Ham Rolls

Asparagus Ham Rolls

1 kg (2 lb) fresh asparagus
25 g (1 oz) (2 tablespoons) butter
salt and pepper
2 hard-boiled eggs
15 mL (1 tablespoon) chopped parsley
6 slices ham
30 mL (2 tablespoons) Parmesan cheese

1 Cook asparagus spears for 20 minutes or until tender in boiling salted water. When cooked remove white ends. Coat spears with half the butter seasoned with salt and pepper and cool.
2 Finely dice hard-boiled eggs. In a bowl combine eggs, remaining butter and the chopped parsley. Knead together until finely crumbled.
3 Sprinkle each slice of ham with Parmesan cheese.

4 Divide asparagus spears into 7 equal bundles. Reserve one for later and place each of the others on a slice of ham.
5 Roll ham around asparagus and place, join downwards, on a serving dish. Sprinkle over egg mixture and decorate dish with remaining spears. Serve with a crisp green salad and a vinaigrette dressing.

Serves 6

Croque-Monsieur

8 slices white bread
4 slices ham
8 slices Gruyere cheese
50 g (2 oz) (¼ cup) butter

1 Cut crusts off the bread. Cut ham and Gruyere cheese slices the same size as the bread.
2 Lightly butter one side of each bread slice. Place a slice of cheese on the buttered side, cover with a slice of ham, another slice of cheese, and top with bread. Repeat to make 4 sandwiches. Press lightly to stick the layers together.
3 Heat the rest of the butter in a frying pan and fry the sandwiches for a few minutes on each side, until crisp and golden brown. Drain on absorbent paper. Cut each sandwich into 3 fingers and serve hot.

Serves 4

Ham and Cheese Slice

30 mL (1 fl oz) (1 tablespoon) oil
1 small onion, finely chopped
100 g (¼ lb) (1 cup) mushrooms,
 chopped
100 g (¼ lb) (½ cup) ham, diced
salt and pepper
150 mL (¼ pint) (⅔ cup) white sauce
225 g (½ lb) (2 cups) Gruyere or
 Cheddar cheese, grated
5 g (1 tablespoon) snipped chives
pinch ground nutmeg
450 g (1 lb) flaky pastry
1 egg, beaten

1 Heat oil in frying pan. Gently fry
onion for 3 minutes, until soft but not
coloured. Add mushrooms and cook
for 1 minute, then add diced ham.
Season and cook for another 2 minutes.
2 Stir in the white sauce and bring to
the boil. Crumble in 50 g (2 oz) grated
cheese, stirring until dissolved.
Check seasoning and leave until it is
cold and firm. Stir in snipped chives
and nutmeg.
3 Preheat the oven to 220°C (425°F).
4 Roll out pastry to a little under
½ cm (¼ in). Prick all over with a fork.

Cut into three equal-sized rectangles
and place on a greased baking tray.
Bake for 15 minutes.
5 Place half the sauce on one slice of
pastry, and sprinkle with a little
grated cheese. Place the second slice
on top, and spoon over the rest of the
sauce. Add a little grated cheese.
Place the third slice on top and brush
with the beaten egg. Top with
remaining grated cheese. Return to
the oven for 8 minutes, or place
under the grill. Serve.

Serves 6

Ham and Mushroom Toasts

50 g (2 oz) (¼ cup) butter
450 g (1 lb) button mushrooms,
 trimmed
25 g (1 oz) (¼ cup) flour
300 mL (½ pint) (1¼ cups) milk
225 g (½ lb) (2 cups) grated cheese
salt and pepper
pinch cayenne pepper
225 g (½ lb) ham, diced
6 slices hot toast

1 Melt half the butter in a pan, add
whole mushrooms and cook for 2–3
minutes, stirring. Drain on absorbent
paper.
2 Melt remaining butter in pan and
stir in the flour. Cook over a low heat
for 1 minute, remove from heat and
gradually stir in the milk. Bring to the
boil and simmer for 2 or 3 minutes,
stirring continuously.
3 Add half the grated cheese to the
sauce with the seasoning, mushrooms and ham, and heat through.
4 Arrange slices of toast in a
heatproof dish and spoon on the
mushroom mixture. Sprinkle with
remaining grated cheese. Place under
a hot grill until golden. Serve
immediately.

Serves 6

Ham and Cheese Slice

Ham Whirls

10 mL (2 teaspoons) caster sugar
225 mL (8 fl oz) (1 cup) lukewarm
    water
7.5 mL (1½ teaspoons) dried yeast
350 g (¾ lb) (3 cups) wholemeal flour
5 mL (1 teaspoon) salt
10 mL (2 teaspoons) butter
15 mL (1 tablespoon) yeast extract
100 g (¼ lb) thinly sliced ham
a little milk to glaze

1 Dissolve sugar in water, sprinkle yeast over, and leave in a warm place until frothy.

2 Sift flour and salt into a large bowl and rub in butter. Pour in yeast liquid and mix to a smooth dough. Knead dough on a floured surface until smooth and elastic.

3 Roll out dough to form an oblong, 25 x 30 cm. Spread yeast extract sparsely on the upper surface and lay slices of ham on top. Roll dough up along the longer edge, moisten the end and seal. Place on a greased baking tray, cover with greased freezer wrap and leave in a warm place until it has risen to twice its volume.

4 Preheat oven to 220°C (425°F). Brush the top of the loaf with a little milk to glaze and bake for about 15 minutes. Slice and serve hot or cold with a salad.

Serves 8–12

Spinach and Ham Pate with Salad

3 onions, chopped
75 g (3 oz) (6 tablespoons) butter
450 g (1 lb) (1½ cups) cooked, roughly
    chopped leaf spinach
450 g (1 lb) sliced ham
50 g (2 oz) (1 cup) fresh breadcrumbs
salt and pepper
pinch allspice
grated rind and juice 1 lemon
3 eggs, beaten
150 mL (¼ pint) (⅔ cup) red port
7.5 g (¼ oz) (1 tablespoon) powdered
    gelatine
15 g (¼ oz) (1 tablespoon) butter
1 bay leaf

Salad
225 g (½ lb) (3 cups) cooked rice
4 tomatoes, chopped
4 sticks celery, sliced
1 green capsicum (pepper) seeded
    and sliced
150 mL (¼ pint) (⅔ cup) vinaigrette
    dressing

1 Fry onion gently in butter for 2 minutes. Stir in spinach and cook another 2 minutes.

2 Chop up one slice of ham and stir into the mixture. Remove from heat and add breadcrumbs, seasoning, spice, lemon rind and juice. Finally blend in the beaten eggs to form a thick, smooth mixture.

3 Heat port in a small pan and stir in the gelatine until it dissolves.

4 Preheat oven to 200°C (400°F).

5 Grease the inside of an oblong terrine or ovenproof dish with the butter. Place a bay leaf in the middle of the dish, line the bottom of the dish with 1 or 2 slices of ham and cover with a layer of spinach mixture. Continue in layers of ham and spinach until the dish is full, ending with ham on top.

6 Pour the port over the dish and bake in a bain-marie for 20–30 minutes. Allow to cool, then chill for at least 2 hours before serving.

7 To make salad, place the cooked rice in a salad bowl. Top with tomatoes, celery and green capsicum. Sprinkle the vinaigrette over the top. Serve the pate and salad with hot bread.

Serves 8

Rabbit and Pork Terrine

1 onion
1 clove garlic
2 cloves
1 rabbit, cleaned and skinned
salt and pepper
¾ litre (1¼ pints) (3 cups) dry white
    wine
1 bouquet garni

Forcemeat
liver of the rabbit
125 g (¼ lb) meat from a ham shank
125 g (¼ lb) lean pork
125 g (¼ lb) bacon fat
1 egg
60 mL (4 tablespoons) brandy
grated nutmeg
40 g (1½ oz) (3 tablespoons) butter
1 knuckle of veal
½ calf's foot

1 Peel onion and slice into rounds. Peel garlic clove and stick it with the cloves.

2 Season rabbit with salt and pepper and pour over white wine. Add onion, garlic stuck with cloves and bouquet garni and marinate for 24 hours in the refrigerator.

3 To make forcemeat, wash and finely chop the rabbit liver, ham, pork and bacon and mix well. Break egg and stir into the meat mixture, together with brandy, salt and pepper to taste and a little grated nutmeg. Blend well.

4 Strain off marinade from the rabbit, reserving the liquid, and cut rabbit in half across below the chest opening it up, cutting away and discarding the ribs. Stuff rabbit with forcemeat. Pull over stomach skin to enclose the stuffing and tie securely or sew up with a trussing needle and string.

5 Heat butter in a deep heavy-based pan and brown the rabbit on all sides. Add the knuckle of veal and the ½ calf's foot and brown. Remove pan from heat, pour over reserved marinade, bring to the boil, cover with a lid and cook slowly for about 2 hours. Take veal out of the pan. Remove bones and cut meat into slices. Remove string from the rabbit, take out bones and cut meat strips. Arrange meat slices and forcemeat in a large terrine or loaf tin.

6 Strain cooking liquid through a sieve and pour over meat to cover. Cool and put terrine in the refrigerator overnight till liquid jells. Serve terrine cold with toast or French bread and dill pickles.

Serves 8

Rabbit and Pork Terrine

Chinese Spare Ribs

Chinese Spare Ribs

1½ kg (3 lb) breast of lamb
1 litre (1¾ pints) (4¼ cups) boiling
  water
30 mL (2 tablespoons) vinegar

Sauce
30 mL (2 tablespoons) soy sauce
30 mL (2 tablespoons) clear honey
30 mL (2 tablespoons) plum jam
15 mL (1 tablespoon) white vinegar
5 mL (1 teaspoon) Worcestershire
  sauce
5 mL (1 teaspoon) dry mustard
5 mL (1 teaspoon) tomato paste
juice ½ lemon

1 Remove thin skin and any excess fat from the breast. Cut between each bone.

2 Place meat in boiling water and vinegar and simmer for 15 minutes.

3 Preheat the oven to 180°C (350°F).

4 Mix all the sauce ingredients together, and heat.

5 Drain lamb, and place in a roasting dish. Pour sauce over.

6 Bake for 30 minutes, basting frequently. Increase heat to 200°C (400°F) and cook 20 minutes.

Serves 6

Spicy Lamb Boats

30 mL (1 fl oz) (2 tablespoons) oil
1 onion, chopped
225 g (½ lb) (1 cup) minced cooked
    lamb
pinch allspice
pinch curry powder
(15 g) (½ oz) (2 tablespoons) flour
150 mL (¼ pint) (⅔ cup) pineapple
    juice
50 g (2 oz) (3 tablespoons) mango
    chutney
salt and pepper
75 mL (3 fl oz) (⅓ cup) natural yoghurt
1 cucumber
4 slices processed cheese

1 Heat oil in saucepan and saute
onion until soft. Add minced lamb
and brown for 5 minutes.
2 Add spice, curry powder and flour.
Cook for 2 minutes. Stir in pineapple
juice and chutney and season with
salt and pepper. Cook for 6 minutes,
remove from heat, and stir in the
yoghurt.
3 Peel cucumber, cut in half lengthways and scoop out the seeds. Cut
each piece into 4 chunks.
4 Spoon curried lamb mixture into
each piece of cucumber.
5 Cut each slice of cheese in 2, and
impale on a cocktail stick to resemble
the mast and sail of a boat. Place one
on each cucumber boat and serve.

Makes 8 boats

Kiwi Eggs

450 g (1 lb) (2 cups) minced lamb
1 large onion, grated
25 g (1 oz) (½ cup) fresh breadcrumbs
few drops Worcestershire sauce
salt and pepper
2 eggs, beaten
4 hard-boiled eggs
25 g (1 oz) (⅓ cup) dried breadcrumbs
oil for deep frying

1 Mix in a bowl the minced lamb,
grated onion, breadcrumbs and
Worcestershire sauce. Season with
salt and pepper and bind mixture
with 1 of the beaten eggs.
2 Divide mixture into 4 portions and
mould each around a hard-boiled
egg. Dip in the rest of the beaten egg,
then coat with breadcrumbs.
3 Heat oil in a deep fat fryer and,
when hot, fry kiwi eggs for 5–7 minutes until crisp and golden-brown.
Cool and cut into halves or quarters.
Serve with a green or mixed salad.

Serves 4

Lamb and Pasta Salad

225 g (½ lb) (1⅓ cups) cold roast lamb,
    cut in strips
225 g (½ lb) (1⅔ cups) cooked
    macaroni
50 g (2 oz) (½ cup) thinly sliced
    cucumber
1 stick celery, thinly sliced
½ onion, cut in thin strips
50 g (2 oz) (⅓ cup) ham, cut in strips
1 green capsicum (pepper) seeded
    and cut into strips
225 mL (8 fl oz) (1 cup) mayonnaise
salt and pepper
pinch paprika
8 anchovy fillets
6 black olives

1 Mix all ingredients, except anchov-
ies and olives, in a large bowl. When
they are well coated with mayonnaise, transfer to a serving dish.
2 Arrange anchovy fillets in a criss-
cross pattern across the top and decorate with black olives.

Serves 4

Kiwi Eggs Step-by-step

1 Mix together the minced lamb,
chopped onions and breadcrumbs.
2 Divide into four and mould
around each hard-boiled egg.
3 Dip in beaten egg, coat with
breadcrumbs and deep-fry in hot oil.

Lamb in Mint Jelly Mould

15 g (½ oz) (1 tablespoon) butter
275 g (10 oz) (1⅔ cups) diced leftover cold lamb
100 g (¼ lb) (1 cup) diced, cooked potatoes
salt and pepper
150 mL (¼ pint) (⅔ cup) meat stock
15 mL (1 tablespoon) chopped mint
15 mL (1 tablespoon) sugar
15 mL (1 tablespoon) vinegar
15 g (½ oz) (2 tablespoons) powdered gelatine
50 mL (2 fl oz) (¼ cup) water
4 tomatoes, quartered
1 cos lettuce, shredded

1 Heat butter in frying pan and saute diced lamb for about 5 minutes. Add potatoes and toss gently, remove from pan and season with salt and pepper.
2 Bring stock to the boil; it should be clear and transparent.
3 Mix together mint, sugar and vinegar and add to boiling stock. Remove from heat.
4 Blend gelatine with cold water and stir mixture into the hot stock. Add meat and potatoes, then pour into a 22.5 cm (9 in) ring mould.
5 Cool a little, then allow to set for 2 hours in the refrigerator.
6 When set and firm, turn mint jelly mould onto a dish and decorate the centre with quartered tomatoes. Arrange shredded cos lettuce around sides of the mould and serve.

Serves 4

Lamb in Mint Jelly Mould

Sausage Rolls with Cumberland Sauce

450 g (1 lb) pork sausage meat
15 mL (1 tablespoon) flour, seasoned with salt and pepper
8 bacon rashers
30 mL (1 fl oz) (2 tablespoons) oil
2 oranges
5 mL (1 teaspoon) dry mustard
15 mL (1 tablespoon) brown sugar
pinch salt
pinch cayenne
pinch ground cloves
350 mL (12 fl oz) (1½ cups) red wine
10 mL (2 teaspoons) cornflour
30 mL (1 fl oz) (2 tablespoons) lemon juice

1 Preheat oven to 190°C (375°F). Mould sausage meat into 8 sausage shapes and toss in seasoned flour. Remove rind from the bacon, roll a rasher around each sausage and secure with a cocktail stick.
2 Heat oil in a roasting pan, add sausage rolls and bake for 30 minutes, turning occasionally.

3 Using a potato peeler, peel one of the oranges and cut peel into matchstick-sized strips. Put in a pan with mustard, sugar, salt, spices and wine. Bring to the boil, cover and simmer for 8 minutes.
4 Mix cornflour to a smooth paste with lemon juice, add juice of 1 orange and stir into sauce. Simmer 2 minutes, stirring.
5 Peel remaining orange with a sharp knife removing all pith and slice into rounds.
6 Drain the cooked sausage rolls, remove cocktail sticks and arrange on a heated serving dish. Pour a little of the sauce over and garnish with orange slices. Serve remaining sauce separately.

Serves 4

Tip: For a pleasant herby flavour, add 10 mL (2 teaspoons) chopped fresh sage or 5 mL (1 teaspoon) dried sage to the sausage meat before shaping.

Frankfurts with Gruyere Cheese

20 cocktail frankfurts
50 g (2 oz) Gruyere cheese

1 Preheat oven to 220°C (425°F). Heat the frankfurts for about 7 minutes in simmering water, dry them and make a cut lengthways in each without completely separating the 2 halves.

2 Cut the Gruyere into very thin slices, each the length of a frankfurt, and put a slice in each frankfurt. Close up and secure with a cocktail stick.

3 Put frankfurts on a baking sheet, place in the oven and take out the moment the cheese has melted. Serve hot with a mustard dip.

Serves 10

Sausage Kebabs

450 g (1 lb) sausage meat
1 egg
1 small onion, chopped
25 g (1 oz) (½ cup) breadcrumbs
pinch curry powder
pinch rosemary
salt
8 mushrooms
1 red capsicum (pepper), scalded
6 bay leaves
100 mL (4 fl oz) (½ cup) oil

Rice Pilaf
50 g (2 oz) (4 tablespoons) butter
1 small onion, chopped
175 g (6 oz) patna rice
450 mL (¾ pint) (1⅔ cups) chicken stock

Sauce
25 g (1 oz) shredded ham
150 mL (5 fl oz) (⅔ cup) medium sherry
300 mL (½ pint) (1¼ cups) tomato sauce
pinch oregano and basil
salt and pepper
pinch paprika

Sausage Kebabs

1 Combine sausage meat with egg, onion, breadcrumbs, herbs and salt.

2 Divide into 12 meatballs.

3 Preheat oven to 200°C (400°F).

4 Arrange meatballs on skewers with mushrooms, three-quarters of the capsicum (pepper), chopped, and bay leaves.

5 Heat 25 mL (1 fl oz) (2 tablespoons) oil in the frying pan and brown kebabs on both sides.

6 Bake in oven for 15 minutes.

7 Meanwhile prepare the rice pilaf by heating the butter and 50 mL (2 fl oz) (4 tablespoons) of oil in a saucepan. Fry onion gently for 2 minutes.

8 Add rice and stir for 1 minute until translucent.

9 Add stock. Bring to the boil and transfer to an ovenproof dish covered with a lid.

10 Bake 15–18 minutes until rice is cooked and fluffy.

11 To make the tomato sauce, saute remaining capsicum and ham in 25 ml (1 fl oz) (2 tablespoons) oil for 1 minute.

12 Add sherry and boil for 5 minutes

13 Add tomato sauce, herbs and seasoning. Bring to the boil. Simmer for 10 minutes.

Serves 4

Stuffed Onions

6 large Spanish onions
225 g (½ lb) (1 cup) pork sausage meat
1 egg
50 mL (2 fl oz) (¼ cup) milk
5 g (1 tablespoon) chopped parsley
50 g (2 oz) (1 cup) breadcrumbs
100 mL (4 fl oz) (½ cup) oil

1 Peel onions. Cut off one-third at tip ends, leaving two-thirds of the stem end. Boil in salted water for 15 minutes, then drain.

2 Preheat the oven to 180°C (350°F).
3 Squeeze out the centre of each onion, leaving outer layers to form a case. Chop squeezed-out onion, put in a bowl and blend well with sausage meat, egg, milk and parsley.
4 Fill each onion case with sausage meat mixture. Place onions in a shallow dish, sprinkle with breadcrumbs and pour a little oil over each.
5 Bake in oven 45 minutes. Serve with tomato sauce.

Serves 6

Stuffed Zucchini (Courgettes) with Sausage Meat

4 large firm zucchini (courgettes)
sprig parsley
100 g (¼ lb) (½ cup) butter
15 mL (1 tablespoon) milk
75 g (3 oz) (1½ cups) fresh
  breadcrumbs
5 g (1 teaspoon) chopped chives
pinch dried thyme
150 g (5 oz) (½ cup + 2 tablespoons)
  sausage meat

1 Wash and dry the zucchini. Cut in half lengthways and scoop out the insides. Chop parsley.
2 Using 20 g (¾ oz) (1½ tablespoons) butter, grease an ovenproof dish. Arrange the halved zucchini in the dish.
3 Put the milk, 25 g (1 oz) (½ cup) breadcrumbs and 50 g (2 oz) (¼ cup) butter in a small pan. Add parsley, chives and thyme and cook for a few minutes, stirring.
4 Preheat the oven to 220°C (425°F).
5 Remove pan from the heat and thoroughly mix in the sausage meat. Fill the zucchini shells with stuffing.
6 Sprinkle the remaining fresh breadcrumbs over the zucchini halves. Cut remaining butter into small pieces and dot over the top.
7 Bake towards top of oven for 25 minutes or until topping is golden and the zucchini are tender.

Serves 4

Stuffed Onions

MICROWAVE Appetisers

Lamb Kebabs

500 g (1 lb) lean boneless lamb, cut
    into 24 cubes
1 small can pineapple pieces in juice
10 mL (2 teaspoons) lemon juice
10 mL (2 teaspoons) soy sauce
pinch ground ginger
pinch dried oregano
8 cherry tomatoes
½ green capsicum (pepper) cut into
    eighths
4 wooden sate sticks

1 In a bowl combine ⅓ cup pineapple juice, lemon juice, soy sauce,
ginger and oregano. Stir in lamb and
cover. Marinate overnight in refrigerator. Remove and discard marinade.
2 Thread lamb, tomatoes, capsicum
and pineapple pieces on sate sticks
and arrange on roasting rack. Cook
on medium 10 minutes.

Serves 4

Mexican Tacos

500 g (1 lb) minced beef
1 onion, finely chopped
30 mL (2 tablespoons) oil
75 mL (⅛ pint) (¼ cup) tomato paste
5 mL (1 teaspoon) mixed herbs
pinch chilli powder
1 green chilli, finely chopped
salt and pepper to taste
dash tabasco sauce
dash cayenne pepper
8–10 taco shells
1 lettuce, shredded
2 tomatoes, chopped
50 g (2 oz) (½ cup) grated Cheddar
    cheese
300 mL (½ pint) (1¼ cups) sour cream

1 Place beef, onion, oil, tomato
paste, mixed herbs, chilli powder,
green chilli, salt, pepper, tabasco
sauce and cayenne pepper into shallow dish. Cover and cook on high 10
minutes, stirring twice.
2 Uncover and cook on medium 10
minutes. Set aside.
3 Place 8–10 taco shells upside down
on baking sheet. Cook on high 30
seconds. Serve taco shells filled with
lettuce, tomato, meat mixture,
sprinkled with cheese and a spoonful
of sour cream.

Serves 8–10

Mexican Tacos

Ginger Meatballs

500 g (1 lb) lean minced beef
3 shallots (spring onions, scallions),
 finely chopped
1 egg, beaten
5 mL (1 teaspoon) green ginger, finely
 chopped
pinch garlic salt
150 mL (¼ pint) (½ cup) beef
 consomme
10 mL (2 teaspoons) arrowroot
15 mL (1 tablespoon) soy sauce
5 mL (1 teaspoon) vinegar
15 mL (1 tablespoon) chopped
 parsley

1 Combine mince, shallots, egg, ginger and salt. Form into 24 small balls. Arrange the meatballs around outer edge of a 25 cm pie plate. Cook on high 7 minutes, turning once during cooking. Remove to serving dish.
2 Blend consomme and arrowroot with meat juices in pie plate. Add soy sauce, vinegar and parsley. Cook on high 2–3 minutes until sauce has thickened, stirring twice during cooking. Coat meatballs with sauce and cook 2–3 minutes on high to reheat.

Serves 4–6

Stuffed Capsicum (Peppers)

1 quantity Basic Economy Beef (see
 recipe)
100 g (4 oz) (1¼ cups) cooked rice
250 g (½ lb) tomato paste
2.5 mL (½ teaspoon) chopped basil
 leaves
5 mL (1 teaspoon) sugar
pinch salt
pinch pepper
4–6 large capsicums (peppers)
50 g (2 oz) (½ cup) grated tasty cheese

1 In a 2 litre casserole combine beef mixture, rice, tomato paste, basil, sugar, salt and pepper.
2 Cut tops from capsicums, remove seeds and fill each one with mixture. Place into casserole, cover and cook on high 12 minutes. Top each with cheese during the last minutes of cooking.

Serves 4–6

Cabbage Rolls

12 cabbage leaves, medium-sized
500 g (1 lb) topside, minced
250 g (½ lb) pork, minced
125 g (¼ lb) chopped onion
90 g (3 oz) (¾ cup) cooked rice
1 egg
5 mL (1 teaspoon) thyme
15 mL (1 tablespoon) chopped parsley
1 clove garlic, chopped
15 mL (1 tablespoon) salt
3 mL (¾ teaspoon) pepper
30 g (1 oz) (¼ cup) butter
600 mL (20 fl oz) (2½ cups) fresh
 tomato sauce
2.5 mL (½ teaspoon) cumin powder

1 Place cabbage leaves in 30 mL (2 tablespoons) water in a casserole dish. Cook covered for 8 minutes or until soft.
2 Combine mince, pork, onion, rice, cumin, egg, thyme, parsley, garlic, salt, pepper, and 110 mL (4 fl oz) (½ cup) of tomato sauce. Place 30 mL (2 tablespoons) stuffing on each cabbage leaf and wrap leaves around mixture firmly. Place cabbage rolls in a casserole dish. Spread butter on top of rolls and remaining tomato sauce.
3 Cook, covered, 20 minutes, or until meat is cooked and rolls are tender. Let stand, covered, 10 minutes.

Pork Sate

750 g (1½ lbs) pork meat, cut into
 2 cm cubes
10 mL (2 teaspoons) turmeric
10 mL (2 teaspoons) cumin
rind ½ lemon
5 mL (1 teaspoon) salt
15 mL (1 tablespoon) sugar
60 mL (4 tablespoons) coconut cream
15 mL (1 tablespoon) water

1 Thread pork onto wooden skewers. Blend turmeric, cumin, lemon rind, salt, sugar, coconut cream and water to coat sate. Marinate 1 hour.
2 Drain and place into shallow dish and cook on high 5 minutes. Turn and cook further 5 minutes or finish cooking on barbecue.

Serves 6

Prune and Bacon Rolls

12 pitted prunes
12 blanched almonds
4 bacon rashers
12 cocktail sticks

1 Place 1 almond in each pitted prune. Cut bacon rashers into thirds and wrap 1 strip around each prune. Fasten with a cocktail stick.
2 Heat browning dish on high 6 minutes. Cook bacon rolls on high 1½ minutes, turn and cook a further 1½ minutes. Serve hot.

Makes 12

Veal and Ham Terrine

750 g (1½ lb) veal, minced
6 bacon rashers, rinds removed
1 clove garlic, finely chopped
2 eggs, beaten
pinch dried tarragon
15 mL (1 tablespoon) chopped
 parsley
30 mL (2 tablespoons) brandy or
 sherry
pinch salt
pinch pepper
75 g (3 oz) (¾ cup) soft white
 breadcrumbs
250 g (½ lb) ham, finely chopped
50 g (2 oz) (½ cup) toasted almond
 slivers
50 g (2 oz) (½ cup) drained crushed
 pineapple

1 Line a loaf dish with bacon. In a bowl combine veal, garlic, eggs, tarragon, parsley, brandy, salt, pepper and breadcrumbs. Place ham, almonds and pineapple into a small bowl.
2 Place one-third of veal mixture onto bacon and cover with half ham mixture. Repeat with veal and ham mixtures and cover with remaining veal. Fold exposed ends of bacon over veal and cover with lid or plastic food wrap.
3 Stand terrine on plate to collect spillover and cook on medium — high 20–25 minutes. Let stand 10 minutes, then cool.
4 Remove lid. Place weight on top and refrigerate overnight to prevent crumbling when cut. Serve sliced with salad and toast.

Serves 8–10

Satisfying Soups and Stocks

Clear soups like Beef Consomme are light on the palate and ideal for formal dinner parties. Hearty soups — broths, purees and brews packed with chunks of meat, fish, rice, pasta or vegetables — can be meals in themselves. A full-bodied, flavoursome stock adds zest to soups as well as sauces, gravies and casseroles.

Try Mulligatawny, created in the days of the British in India and basically a rich meat stock flavoured with curry. Dijon Lamb Hotpot hails from France and features lamb cutlets in an unusual wine and mustard flavoured sauce. Also from France is the classic country dish of Hotpot Soup.

Mulligatawny

Beef Consomme Step-by-step

1 Collect the ingredients.

2 Remove any fat from surface of stock.

3 Chop or slice the vegetables and tomatoes. Wash and chop the herbs.

4 Put the prepared vegetables and herbs into a large bowl together with the minced beef. Add the egg whites only.

5 Mix the ingredients together, adding a little cold water to moisten. Add the vegetable mixture to the pan of stock and heat gently, stirring.

6 As soon as it begins to boil, reduce the heat so it is only just simmering. Skim off any fat that rises to the surface — there should hardly be any at all — and cook for 1½ hours without stirring; this will allow a crust to form on top.

7 Scald a cloth and place over a large sieve; put peppercorns on it, then slowly pour soup over vegetable/egg white mixture to clarify.

8 Consomme may be garnished with vermicelli.

9 Chopped tomatoes add to the flavour.

Beef Consomme

2 litres (4 pints) chilled brown stock
1 carrot
1 leek, green part only
2 stalks celery
4 ripe tomatoes, optional
few sprigs chervil and tarragon
2 egg whites
500 g (1 lb) lean minced beef
150 mL (¼ pint) (⅔ cup) cold water
peppercorns
15 mL (1 tablespoon) sherry
    (optional)

1 Remove all fat from surface of stock and turn into a large pan. Peel carrot and chop with leek, celery and tomatoes, if used. Wash, dry and chop herbs.

2 Mix vegetables with the egg whites in a large bowl; stir in beef, tomatoes, chopped herbs and water.

3 Add vegetable mixture to stock, mix together, then bring slowly to the boil, stirring to prevent mixture from sticking. Keep whisking until a thick froth starts to form.

4 As soon as mixture starts to boil, simmer, covered, for about 1½ hours without stirring. Remove any fat which rises to the surface.

5 At the end of cooking time, pour contents of the pan through a scalded cloth over a sieve containing peppercorns, into a bowl underneath. Hold back the egg white crust with a spoon, then let it slip onto the cloth. Pour soup through again and over the egg white filter. Consomme should now be completely clear. Reheat and check seasoning. Sherry can be added to improve the flavour.

Serves 8

Variations:

Consomme Colbert: Add ½ cup port to the above quantity of hot soup; add cooked diced carrots, turnips, peas, as well as a poached egg per serving.

Consomme Julienne: Add cooked matchstick-thin strips of vegetables (carrot, turnip, celery) to hot soup.

Consomme a la Brunoise: Add a mixture of cooked small diced carrots, green beans or celery to the hot soup.

Consomme au Riz: Add a small quantity of cooked long grain rice to the hot soup.

Consomme au Vermicelli: Add vermicelli or other tiny pasta to the soup while reheating.

Quick Consomme

Heat canned consomme gently in a pan and stir in 1 tablespoon sherry or Madeira to taste to boost the flavour. Garnish and serve as for homemade consomme.

Bulgarian Beef Soup

225 g (½ lb) lean beef
4 large onions
40 g (1½ oz) (3 tablespoons) butter
2.5 mL (½ teaspoon) cumin seeds
bouquet garni
1½ litres (2¾ pints) (7 cups) brown
    stock
salt and pepper
45 mL (3 tablespoons) sour cream
1 carton natural yoghurt
15 mL (3 teaspoons) paprika
15 mL (3 teaspoons) ground rice
100 g (¼ lb) cooked ham
sprigs parsley

1 Dice beef finely. Peel onions and cut into quarters.

2 Melt butter in a big saucepan, add beef and onions and fry gently for 20 minutes stirring frequently.

3 Grind cumin seeds in a pepper mill. Wash and dry herbs for the bouquet garni and tie together.

4 Cook beef and onions for 20 minutes, add stock and bouquet garni. Sprinkle with ground cumin. Add salt and pepper to taste and cook for 20 minutes.

5 Put sour cream into a bowl with yoghurt, paprika and ground rice. Mix carefully to avoid lumps and pour into soup. Stir with a wooden spoon over a low heat.

6 Put ham through mincer, wash and dry parsley sprigs and chop finely.

7 Add ham to the soup and cook for 2 minutes over a low heat.

8 Before serving, remove bouquet garni. Taste soup, and if necessary adjust seasoning. Pour into a heated soup tureen, sprinkle with chopped parsley and serve hot.

Serves 6

Minestrone

1 carrot
4 potatoes
1 small white cabbage
½ head celery
100 g (¼ lb) (1 cup) shelled garden
    peas
5 tomatoes
1 clove garlic
175 g (6 oz) bacon
2 onions
30 mL (2 tablespoons) oil
2 litres (3¼ pints) (8 cups) white or
    brown stock
10–15 g (2–3 tablespoons) chopped
    mixed herbs (as available)
salt and pepper
100g (¼ lb) macaroni
grated Parmesan cheese

1 Peel and dice the carrots and potatoes; trim and cut up the cabbage and celery in small pieces. Wash them well. Skin the tomatoes, then cut them in half and scoop out the seeds. Cut the tomato pulp into small cubes. Peel and crush the garlic. Cut the bacon into strips. Peel and chop the onions.

2 Heat the oil in a large pan and when hot fry the bacon, onion, carrots, cabbage, celery and tomatoes. Add the stock with the crushed garlic, chopped mixed herbs and salt and pepper to taste. Cover and cook for 1 hour over a low heat. Then add the diced potato and the peas and continue cooking for a further 15 minutes.

3 During this time, cook the macaroni in a pan of boiling salted water for about 15 minutes or until just tender. Drain and set aside.

4 When the soup is cooked, add the macaroni and serve immediately with grated Parmesan cheese.

Serves 6

Beef and Carrot Soup

1 small onion
450 g (1 lb) carrots
1 medium potato
40 g (1½ oz) (3 tablespoons) butter
2.5 mL (½ teaspoon) salt
freshly ground black pepper
2.5 mL (½ teaspoon) sugar
700 mL (1¼ pints) (3 cups) brown
  stock
15 mL (1 tablespoon) chopped
  parsley
5 mL (1 teaspoon) chopped chervil or
  marjoram

1 Peel and chop onion; peel and dice carrots and potato.

2 Melt butter in a heavy saucepan and add carrots, onion and potato. Add salt, pepper and sugar. Cover pan and cook over a low heat for 15 minutes.

3 Add stock and bring to boil. Lower heat, cover pan and cook a further 15 minutes. Rub soup through a sieve or puree in a blender.

4 Reheat until hot, then serve, sprinkling over the chopped herbs.

Serves 4

Traditional Meatball Soup

1.4 litres (2½ pints) (6 cups) brown
  stock
100 g (¼ lb) (good ½ cup) minced beef
2.5 mL (½ teaspoon) salt
freshly ground black pepper
15 g (3 tablespoons) finely chopped
  parsley
30 mL (2 tablespoons) oil
5 mL (1 teaspoon) paprika
100 g (¼ lb) (½ cup) long grain rice
2 cloves garlic, crushed
50 mL (2 fl oz) (¼ cup) vinegar

1 Put stock into large pan and bring to simmering point. Mix beef with salt, pepper and 10 g/2 tablespoons chopped parsley. Form into small balls about 2.5 cm (1 in) in diameter.

2 Add meatballs to stock and simmer 15 minutes.

3 Heat oil in a small pan, stir in paprika and cook for 2 minutes. Stir into soup.

4 Add rice to soup, cover and simmer 15 minutes or until rice is tender. Stir in remaining parsley, garlic and vinegar. Serve at once. *Serves 6*

Farmhouse Soup

2 carrots
2 turnips
white portion of 2 leeks
2 stalks celery
½ green cabbage
50 g (2 oz) (4 tablespoons) butter
500 g (1 lb) lightly salted bacon, in
  one piece
2 litres (3½ pints) (9 cups) white stock
salt and pepper
150 g (5 oz) (1¼ cups) runner beans
2 potatoes
150 g (5 oz) (1¼ cups) shelled peas
75 g (3 oz) (¾ cup) grated Gruyere
  cheese

1 Peel and wash carrots and turnips. Wash the whites of the leeks and the celery, cut into small cubes. Wash and cut the cabbage into thin strips.

2 Melt butter in a large pan. Add prepared vegetables and soften on low heat for 10 minutes, stirring from time to time.

3 Wash bacon in cold water and put into a saucepan. Cover with cold water, bring to the boil and simmer for 10 minutes on a low heat. Drain and rinse in cold water.

4 Add stock to vegetables, then add bacon, cabbage, salt and pepper. Bring to the boil, reduce heat, cover and simmer very gently for about 1¼ hours.

5 Remove 'strings' from the beans, wash and cut into pieces about 4 cm in length. Peel potatoes, wash and cut into cubes. Cover with water and leave to soak.

6 About 20 minutes before the end of the cooking time, drain potatoes. Add to the soup with peas and green beans and leave to finish cooking.

7 Put grated Gruyere cheese into a bowl, drain the bacon, cut into cubes and put into a heated tureen. Pour on the rest of the soup. Serve with croutons, and Gruyere cheese served separately.

Serves 4

Mulligatawny

500 g (1 lb) chicken fillets
1 large onion
1 medium carrot
1 small green tart apple
30 mL (2 tablespoons) oil
15 mL (1 tablespoon) curry powder
15 g (½ oz) (2 tablespoons) flour
1¼ litres (2½ pints) (6 cups) brown
  stock
200 mL (6 fl oz) (¾ cup) milk
5 mL (1 teaspoon) arrowroot
15 mL (1 tablespoon) cold water
5 mL (1 teaspoon) lemon juice
salt and pepper

1 Cut chicken fillets into 1 cm wide pieces. Slice onion carrot and apple.

2 Heat oil in a large pan, add chicken and cook for 3 minutes. Remove and add sliced vegetables and apple and cook, stirring for about 5 minutes. Stir in curry powder and cook 2 minutes, then blend in flour. Add stock, bring to the boil and return meat to pan. Cover and simmer gently for about 1½ hours.

3 Lift chicken from pan. Rub liquid through a sieve or purée in a blender. Return puree to a clean pan. Stir in milk, reheat but do not boil. Blend arrowroot with cold water, stir into soup with chicken and heat nearly to boiling point till thick. Check seasoning and serve.

Serves 6

Borscht

Borscht

2 carrots
2 leeks
4 onions
2 cloves
750 g (1¼ lb) raw beetroot
1 white cabbage
1 kg (2 lb) beef (chuck, round or
   rump)
1 marrowbone
1 bouquet garni
1 fennel stalk or pinch ground cumin
65 g (2½ oz) (¼ cup) tomato paste
salt and pepper
500 g (1 lb) cooked garlic sausage
5 or 6 Russian or Polish pickled
   cucumbers
300 mL (10 fl oz) (1¼ cups) sour cream

1 Scrape carrots and cut into small rounds. Clean and chop leeks. Peel onions, stud one with cloves and cut the others into very fine slices. Peel beetroot and chop finely. Cut away core and stalks and shred cabbage.

2 Bring a large saucepan, two-thirds filled with water, to the boil. Add meat and marrowbone, return to boil and skim off the scum from the surface as it rises. Add leeks, carrots, onions, bouquet garni, beetroot, cabbage and fennel or cumin.

3 Thin tomato paste with a few tablespoons of hot soup. Pour this back into the pan, season with salt and pepper and bring to the boil. Cover, reduce heat and simmer for 2½ hours. Remove meat and mar-rowbone from pot and chop beef finely.

4 Slice garlic sausage and pickled cucumbers and add with meat to soup. Cover and simmer for about 30 minutes.

5 Lift bouquet garni and the clove-studded onion out of the soup and pour soup into a warmed tureen. Serve cream in a sauce-boat, allowing a generous spoonful per serving.

Serves 4–6

Sausage and Cabbage Soup

450 g (1 lb) cabbage
1 clove garlic
25 g (1 oz) (2 tablespoons) butter or
  margarine
25 g (1 oz) (2 tablespoons) flour
1 litre (2 pints) (5 cups) chicken stock
salt and pepper
6–8 frankfurters

1 Discard stalks and core from cabbage and shred finely. Peel and crush garlic. Cook cabbage and garlic in melted butter for 10 minutes or until soft.

2 Mix in flour and gradually blend in the stock, stirring all the time. Bring to the boil, season with salt and pepper, reduce the heat, cover and simmer 1 hour.

3 Meanwhile slice the frankfurts thinly. When soup is ready skim any fat off the surface, add sliced frankfurts, leave 5 minutes to heat and serve.

Serves 4–6

Scotch Broth

2 onions, chopped
2 carrots, diced
2 stalks celery, trimmed and diced
900 g (2 lb) stewing lamb, with
  bones
1.4 litres (2½ pints) (6 cups) cold
  water
50 g (2 oz) (3 tablespoons) washed
  barley
1 bay leaf
2.5 mL (½ teaspoon) thyme
15 g (3 tablespoons) finely chopped
  parsley
2.5 mL (½ teaspoon) salt
freshly ground black pepper

1 Trim and dice lamb. Put into pan with water, bring to the boil. Reduce heat, cover and simmer 1 hour. Add remaining ingredients and simmer further hour adding more water if necessary.

2 Discard bay leaf. Lift out lamb with a skimmer and separate meat from the bone. Discard bones, cut meat into small pieces and add to the soup. Simmer for 5 minutes.

Serves 6

Dijon Lamb Hotpot

Dijon Lamb Hotpot

30 mL (1 fl oz) (2 tablespoons) oil
6 lamb cutlets
2 sticks celery, sliced
4 carrots, sliced
1 swede, cut in chunks
2 onions, chopped
300 mL (½ pint) (1¼ cups) water
150 mL (¼ pint) (⅔ cup) dry white
  vermouth
pinch marjoram
pinch thyme
salt and pepper
pinch cumin
15 mL (1 tablespoon) vinegar
15 mL (1 tablespoon) honey
1 chicken stock cube
5 mL (1 teaspoon) made Dijon
  mustard

1 Heat oil in frying pan and fry cutlets for about 5 minutes until browned.

2 Preheat oven to 190°C (375°F).

3 Place browned cutlets in an ovenproof dish and cover with vegetables. Pour in water and vermouth, sprinkle in herbs and season with salt and pepper. Stir in cumin, vinegar and honey and crumble in the stock cube.

4 Cover and bake in oven for 1½ hours until meat and vegetables are tender.

5 Stir mustard into stock until well blended with liquid. Serve hot with boiled rice or potatoes.

Serves 6

Tip: If you prefer a casserole-type dish in a thick sauce to a hotpot such as this one which is served in a thin gravy, the liquid can be thickened with cornflour.

Hotpot Soup

2 kg (4 lb) stewing beef, in one piece
1–2 beef bones, chopped into small
  chunks
3 litres (5¼ pints) (13 cups) water
1 bouquet garni
¾ kg (1½ lb) carrots
½ kg (1 lb) turnips
¾ kg (1½ lb) leeks
1 bunch celery
2 large onions
2 cloves garlic
4 cloves
1 large marrowbone, about 10 cm
  (4 in) long
2 slices bread

1 Tie meat with thin string. Place in a large pot with beef bones. Add water except for ¼ cup and bring slowly to the boil, with the lid off.
2 If using fresh herbs for the bouquet garni, tie them together. Peel onions and garlic and stud onion with the cloves.
3 Peel and quarter carrots lengthways; peel and quarter the turnips. Trim and cut away the roots of the leeks, cut in half and wash in several changes of water, till all dirt is removed. Trim the root end of the celery and discard the green leaves; quarter and tie pieces together with the leeks.
4 When the surface of the liquid is covered with scum, take pot off the heat, pour in reserved water and skim at once. Return pot to the heat, cover with a lid and simmer slowly for 1 hour. Add prepared vegetables, bouquet garni, garlic, onions, salt and pepper, and cook slowly for a further 1¾ hours.
5 Wrap the marrowbone in muslin and tie with string to stop marrow from slipping out of the bone. Put wrapped bone in the pot 15 minutes before the end of cooking.
6 When meat is cooked, take out of the pot, remove string, slice and place on a heated serving dish. Drain vegetables, discarding the bouquet garni, and arrange round the meat.
7 Scoop out marrow from marrowbone and spread on hot toast.
8 Serve broth separately with toast, followed by the platter of meat and vegetables.

Serves 6–8

Spring Hotpot

1 kg (2 lb) neck chops
2–3 onions, sliced
550 mL (1 pint) (2½ cups) stock
salt and pepper
450 g (1 lb) potatoes, quartered
100 g (¼ lb) (1 cup) peas, fresh or
  frozen
225 g (½ lb) shredded cabbage
15 mL (1 tablespoon) chopped
  parsley

1 Preheat oven to 190°C (375°F).
2 Place chops in ungreased fry pan and brown on both sides. Add onions, stock and seasoning and bring to the boil. Transfer to an ovenproof casserole and cook in oven for 1 hour.
3 Add potatoes and cook a further 20 minutes.
4 Meanwhile, blanch fresh peas in salted water for 4 minutes and drain.
5 Add peas and cabbage to casserole and cook a further 10 minutes.
6 Check seasoning and serve sprinkled with chopped parsley.

Serves 6

White Stock

1 kg (2 lb) raw knuckle of veal,
  chopped or stewing veal
2.3 litres (4 pints) (10 cups) cold
  water
2.5 mL (½ teaspoon) lemon juice
1 onion, sliced
1 carrot, sliced
1 bouquet garni
5 mL (1 teaspoon) salt
6 peppercorns

1 Put veal into large boiler with the water and lemon juice. Bring to the boil and skim off any scum that rises to the surface.
2 Add sliced vegetables, bouquet garni, salt and peppercorns to veal, bring back to the boil, reduce heat and simmer, with lid on, for about 5 hours.
3 Strain stock and leave to cool. Remove fat from the surface.

*Makes about 1½ litres (2½ pints)
(6¼ cups)*

Brown Stock

1 kg (2 lb) raw meat bones (beef,
  marrowbone or knuckle of veal),
  chopped
½ kg (1 lb) lean stewing beef
2 onions
2 carrots
1 stalk celery
2 litres (3½ pints) (8¾ cups) cold water
1 bouquet garni
5 mL (1 teaspoon) salt
6 peppercorns

1 Wash bones and meat and dry on absorbent paper. Cut meat into cubes.
2 Chop onions, carrots and celery.
3 Put chopped bones, cubes of beef and chopped onion in a roasting pan and bake in a moderate oven 180°C (350°F) until well browned.
4 Strain off any fat in pan and transfer bones, beef and onion to a large boiler. Add water, carrots and celery, bouquet garni and seasonings. Bring to the boil, remove any scum, reduce heat, cover and simmer 5 hours.
5 Strain stock and leave to cool. When cold remove fat.

*Makes about 1½ litres (2½ pints)
(6½ cups).*

Household Stock

1 kg (2 lb) chopped meat bones, raw
  or cooked
1 onion
1 carrot
1 stalk celery, optional
2 litres (3½ pints) (8¾ cups) cold water
1 bouquet garni
5 mL (1 teaspoon) salt
6 peppercorns

1 Wash bones, peel, wash and roughly chop onion and carrot; wash and chop celery.
2 Put bones in a large boiler, add water, bring to the boil and remove any scum that rises to the surface.
3 Add chopped vegetables, bouquet garni and seasonings to pot. Reduce heat and simmer, pan lid on, for about 4 hours.
4 Strain stock and leave to cool. When cold remove fat from the surface.

*Makes about 1½ litres (2½ pints)
(6¼ cups)*

Versatile Veal

Veal is a versatile meat with a greater delicacy of flavour than beef and a much lower fat content than pork or lamb. White ragouts of veal, such as Blanquette de Veau, have long been favoured by gourmets. The Mediterranean veal dishes of Osso Bucco and Veal Marengo are more tangy and robust in flavour and are particularly good served with rice.

Creamy sauces are often used with veal. Potroasting on a bed of vegetables, or braising, are tastier ways of cooking veal than a simple roast. The world-famous Wiener Schnitzel is another popular alternative.

Veal Scaloppine — a delicious dinner party main course

Veal Francesca

1 kg (2 lb) leg of veal
100 g (¼ lb) pork fat
salt and freshly ground black pepper
50 mL (2 fl oz) (¼ cup) oil
450 g (1 lb) shallots (spring onions,
    scallions)
450 g (1 lb) baby carrots
300 mL (½ pint) (1¼ cups) flat light
    beer
150 mL (¼ pint) (⅔ cup) chicken stock
5 mL (1 teaspoon) dried oregano and
    parsley
30 mL (2 tablespoons) honey

1 Preheat oven to 180°C (350°F).
2 Lard the joint of veal with the pork fat, cut into strips. Season lightly with salt and pepper.
3 Heat oil in a pan and fry joint gently on all sides until coloured.
4 Slice shallots and peel carrots, and arrange around veal in an ovenproof dish.
5 Mix beer and stock, and pour half over the meat. Sprinkle over oregano and parsley. Cover and bake for 45 minutes.
6 Heat the rest of the liquid in a small pan with the honey. Remove lid from the oven dish and pour the honeyed stock over the meat. Raise oven to 200°C (400°F). Leave dish uncovered to roast for 20 minutes, basting the joint and vegetables frequently to glaze them. To serve, place the meat on a dish and surround with the vegetables and the cooking juices.

Serves 6–8

Veal Francesca

Veal with Lemon Sauce

Veal with Lemon Sauce

1 kg (2 lb) veal loin, chump end or
*   rolled, boned shoulder*
50 mL (2 fl oz) (¼ cup) oil
2 onions, 2 carrots, 2 sticks celery,
*   diced*
2 lemons
30 mL (½ pint) (1¼ cups) stock
pinch thyme
1 bay leaf
salt and pepper
60 mL (4 tablespoons) sherry
5 g (1 teaspoon) cornflour
50 mL (2 fl oz) (¼ cup) water
pinch caraway seeds

1 Preheat oven to 190°C (375°F).
2 Brown veal in oil in a flameproof casserole, then remove.
3 Put diced onions, carrots and celery in the casserole, and place meat on top.
4 Add the finely chopped rind of one lemon.
5 Pour stock, juice of the 2 lemons, thyme and bay leaf onto the meat and season. Cover and cook in oven for 1½ hours.
6 Remove meat and keep warm.
7 Strain off the liquid and reduce it by fast boiling to 300 mL (½ pint) (1¼ cups). Add sherry and boil 5 minutes.

Mix cornflour and water and thicken the sauce.
8 To serve, carve meat in slices, arrange on a dish with saffron flavoured rice and sprinkle veal with caraway seeds. Serve with sauce.

Serves 8

Shoulder of Veal in Vermouth

1 × 1.5 kg (3 lb) boned shoulder of
    veal
60 mL (4 tablespoons) brandy
salt and pepper
60 mL (4 tablespoons) milk
100 g (¼ lb) (2 cups) fresh
    breadcrumbs
150 g (5 oz) (⅔ cup) cream cheese
100 g (¼ lb) (1 cup) finely chopped
    mushrooms
225 g (½ lb) (1⅓ cups) chopped
    cooked ham
5 g (1 tablespoon) chopped parsley
1 large clove garlic, chopped
2 onions, chopped
1 egg
20 g (¾ oz) (1½ tablespoons) butter
30 mL (2 tablespoons) oil
300 mL (½ pint) (1¼ cups) dry white
    vermouth
150 mL (¼ pint) (⅔ cup) cream

1 Place veal in a dish, spoon over the brandy and season with salt and pepper. Leave to soak, turning once, for 1 hour.
2 Pour milk over the breadcrumbs. Let it soak in, then squeeze bread dry.
3 Put cream cheese, mushrooms, ham, breadcrumbs, parsley, garlic and onions in a bowl. Add egg and season with salt and pepper. Mix thoroughly.
4 Spread this stuffing thinly over the inside of the veal. Roll up and tie securely with kitchen string.
5 Heat butter and oil in a large pan. Add meat and brown on all sides. Add vermouth, cover and cook over a low heat for about 1½ hours.
6 Place meat on a heated serving dish and keep hot.
7 Add cream to pan. Mix quickly with a wooden spoon over a brisk heat. Correct the seasoning, pour the sauce into a sauce-boat and serve with the veal.

Serves 7–8

Veal in Vermouth and Tuna Sauce

1 kg (2 lb) boned rolled leg of veal
25 g (1 oz) (2 tablespoons) butter
15 mL (1 fl oz) (⅛ cup) oil
300 mL (½ pint) (1¼ cups) water

Marinade
500 mL (17½ fl oz) (2 cups) dry
    vermouth
30 mL (1 fl oz) (2 tablespoons) vinegar
1 large onion, sliced
1 large carrot, sliced
2 cloves garlic, peeled and chopped
salt and pepper
pinch basil

Sauce
150 g (5 oz) tuna fish
4 anchovy fillets
3 egg yolks
2 hard-boiled egg yolks
juice 1 lemon
15 mL (1 tablespoon) olive oil
7 mL (½ tablespoon) wine vinegar
salt and pepper
1 pickled cucumber, sliced
25 g (1 oz) (2 tablespoons) capers

1 Mix marinade ingredients and leave veal to marinate for 2 hours. Remove meat and dry with absorbent paper.
2 Put butter and oil in a saucepan and brown meat. Add the marinade and water, bring to the boil and simmer for 1 hour. Allow to cool in the marinade. If convenient, this part may be done the day before.
3 Remove and wipe the meat.
4 Strain marinade and reduce by fast boiling until 300 mL (½ pint) (1¼ cups) remains. Cool.
5 Make the sauce by mixing tuna fish, anchovy fillets, egg yolks, hard-boiled egg yolks, lemon juice, olive oil and vinegar. Add the marinade and blend to a smooth, thick sauce, in a liquidiser if possible. Season with salt and pepper, and add the pickled cucumber.
6 Cut the veal in thin slices, arrange on a dish, and pour on the sauce. Garnish with capers and serve with a rice salad.

Serves 6–8

Veal Vesuvio

15 g (½ oz) (1 tablespoon) butter
15 g (½ oz) (2 tablespoons) flour
150 mL (¼ pint) (⅔ cup) stock
300 mL (½ pint) (1¼ cups) milk
pinch salt, nutmeg, pepper
juice 1 lemon
50 g (2 oz) (4 tablespoons) corn
    kernels
1 kg (2 lb) boned rolled breast of veal
175 g mozzarella cheese, sliced
175 g (6 oz) slices fresh ham
few fresh sage leaves
salt and pepper
50 mL (2 fl oz) (¼ cup) oil
300 mL (½ pint) (1¼ cups) water
few sprigs watercress

1 To make sauce, make a roux and add stock. Boil 10 minutes, add milk, seasoning and lemon juice. Simmer 5 minutes and add corn kernels.
2 Preheat oven to 200°C (400°F).
3 Unroll meat, spread with cheese and ham slices, reserving one for decoration, and sage leaves. Season. Roll meat and tie with string. Season and brush with oil.
4 Roast meat 1 hour then add 300 mL (½ pint) (1¼ cups) water to pan, and cook for ½ hour, basting with the liquid. When cooked, place meat on a dish.
5 Reheat sauce and pour over meat. Decorate with the slice of ham and sprigs of watercress.

Serves 6–8

Veal Vesuvio

42

Veal Oregano

salt and pepper
1.5 kg (3 lb) best end of veal
100 mL (4 fl oz) (½ cup) oil
150 mL (¼ pint) (⅔ cup) dry vermouth
300 mL (½ pint) (1¼ cups) water
2 carrots, chopped
2 onions, chopped
1 stick celery, chopped
150 g (5 oz) (¾ cup) diced bacon
    rashers
50 g (2 oz) (½ cup) flour
50 g (2 oz) (4 tablespoons) tomato
    paste
1 clove garlic, crushed
5 g (1 tablespoon) basil
5 g (1 tablespoon) oregano
bouquet garni
225 g (½ lb) spaghetti
50 g (2 oz) (4 tablespoons) butter
50 g (2 oz) (½ cup) grated Gruyere
    cheese
12 black olives
2 globe artichokes, boiled and
    quartered

1 Preheat oven to 190°C (375°F).
2 Season joint of veal. Brush with
50 mL (2 fl oz) (¼ cup) oil and roast 1½
hours. Baste with vermouth and
water frequently. Remove; keep hot.
3 Heat the rest of the oil in a saucepan and gently fry chopped vegetables and bacon for 8 minutes on a
low heat, covered with a lid.
4 Sprinkle with flour and make a
roux. Stir in the tomato paste. Cook 2
minutes, add garlic and juices from
the roasting pan to make a thin
sauce. Season and add half the herbs,
and bouquet garni and boil for 20
minutes. Strain and keep hot.
5 Boil spaghetti for 10 minutes in
salted water. Drain, toss in butter,
and keep warm.
6 Carve meat between the ribs into
cutlets and arrange on a dish. Surround with spaghetti, sprinkled with
cheese and decorated with 6 black
olives, and quarters of cooked globe
artichokes. Pour a little sauce on the
meat and sprinkle with basil and
oregano. Serve the remainder of the
sauce with the olives.

Serves 6

Stuffed Breast of Veal

2 kg (4 lb) breast of veal (ask the
    butcher to bone the meat and cut a
    deep pocket for stuffing)
550 mL (1 pint) (2½ cups) dry cider
75 mL (2½ fl oz) (5 tablespoons) oil
1 clove garlic, halved
(50 g) (2 oz) (4 tablespoons) butter
2.5 mL (½ teaspoon) cinnamon
15 mL (1 tablespoon) flour
1 parsnip, sliced
1 carrot, sliced
1 leek, sliced
1 stick celery, sliced
15 mL (1 tablespoon) tomato paste
15 mL (1 tablespoon) arrowroot

Stuffing
25 g (1 oz) (2 tablespoons) butter
1 onion, finely chopped
175 g (6 oz) (3 cups) fresh white
    breadcrumbs
100 g (¼ lb) (¾ cup) dried apricots,
    finely chopped
15 mL (1 tablespoon) chopped
    parsley
1 orange
salt and pepper
1 egg, beaten

1 Soak veal in the cider and oil for 2
hours.
2 Prepare the stuffing: melt butter
and fry onion until soft. Stir in
breadcrumbs, apricots, parsley,
finely grated orange rind and 45 mL
(3 tablespoons) orange juice. Season
to taste, and bind together with the
beaten egg, adding little more orange
juice if the mixture is too dry.
3 Preheat oven to 180° (350°F). Wipe
and dry the soaked veal, reserving
the marinade. Fill pocket with stuffing and secure with skewers or
string. Rub meat with the cut side of
the garlic, smother it with the butter
and sprinkle with combined cinnamon and flour. Weigh the stuffed
meat and calculate cooking time,
allowing 30 minutes per 450 g (1 lb).
4 Place veal in a roasting pan and
surround with sliced vegetables and
tomato paste. Bake for the calculated
cooking time, basting the meat from
time to time.
5 Remove skewers or string from the
cooked veal, transfer to a heated
serving dish and keep warm.
6 Place roasting pan and vegetables
over a high heat, add the reserved
marinade and boil for 15 minutes.

Blend arrowroot with a little water
and stir into the boiling liquid. Simmer for 3 minutes, then strain into a
sauce jug to serve.

Serves 6–8

Tip: For a meatier stuffing, replace
some of the breadcrumbs with the
same weight of lean pork sausage
meat, and use an extra egg to bind
the stuffing.

Braised Veal in Mushroom Sauce

1 × 1.25 kg (2½ lb) boned and rolled
    veal joint (leg or shoulder)
75 g (3 oz) (6 tablespoons) butter
2 shallots (spring onions, scallions),
    chopped
2 onions, chopped
1 sprig thyme
1 bay leaf
salt and pepper
400 mL (¾ pint) (1¾ cups) cider
225 g (½ lb) mushrooms, chopped
1 egg yolk
100 mL (4 fl oz) (½ cup) cream
10 g (2 tablespoons) chopped parsley

1 Fry veal gently in 50 g (2 oz) (¼ cup)
of the butter until brown on all sides.
Remove, then fry shallots and onions
until softened.
2 Return veal to the pan and add
thyme, bay leaf, salt and pepper to
taste and the cider. Bring to the boil,
cover and cook over a low heat for
1½ hours.
3 Fry mushrooms in the rest of the
butter for 3–4 minutes.
4 When veal has cooked for 1½
hours, add mushrooms to pan and
cook for 10 minutes.
5 Drain veal and place on a serving
dish. Keep warm. Discard the thyme
and bay leaf.
6 Beat egg yolk with the cream. Beat
into the cooking liquid and cook
gently until thickened. Cover the
meat with this sauce, sprinkle with
parsley and serve hot.

Serves 6

Veal Oregano

Scaloppine alla Zucchini

8 small veal escalopes (scallops), 1 cm (½ in) thick
25 g (1 oz) (4 tablespoons) flour, seasoned with salt and pepper
25 g (1 oz) (2 tablespoons) butter
30 mL (1 fl oz) (2 tablespoons) oil
225 g (½ lb) (2½ cups) sliced button mushrooms
4 zucchini (courgettes), sliced
1.25 mL (¼ teaspoon) dried thyme
150 mL (¼ pint) (⅔ cup) dry cider
30 mL (2 tablespoons) tomato paste
½ chicken stock cube
salt and pepper

1 Toss escalopes (scallops) in the seasoned flour. Shake off excess flour and reserve for the sauce. Heat butter and oil in a frying pan and fry the veal for about 6 minutes until cooked, turning once. Transfer veal to a heated serving dish and keep warm.

2 Add mushrooms to pan, saute for 3 minutes, and arrange over the meat. Fry the zucchini with thyme until tender and arrange on the serving dish.

3 Add reserved flour to pan and cook over a low heat for 2 minutes. Gradually stir in cider and tomato paste, bring to the boil and simmer for 2 minutes. Crumble in the stock cube and stir to dissolve. Season to taste and pour over the meat and mushrooms. Serve immediately.

Serves 4

Veal Escalopes (Scallops) Milanese

1 bunch asparagus
4 veal escalopes (scallops)
50 g (2 oz) (¼ cup) butter
5 mL (1 teaspoon) arrowroot
60 mL (4 tablespoons) white port
45 mL (2 fl oz) (3 tablespoons) cream
sprig tarragon, finely chopped
pinch paprika
salt and pepper

1 Cook asparagus in boiling salted water for 15-20 minutes.

2 Meanwhile, place veal escalopes (scallops) between 2 sheets of dampened greaseproof paper and beat with a mallet or rolling pin until very thin. Heat butter in a frying pan and fry escalopes over a low heat for 5-8 minutes on each side or until cooked through.

3 Mix arrowroot and port. Drain escalopes (scallops) and arrange on a heated serving dish. Keep hot.

4 Pour cream into the frying pan and stir well to mix with pan juices. Add tarragon. Simmer 2 minutes, then add the arrowroot and port. Simmer, stirring, until thickened. Add paprika, salt and pepper to taste.

5 Drain asparagus and arrange round the escalopes (scallops). Pour sauce over the top and serve very hot.

Serves 4

Tip: The asparagus must be very carefully drained to ensure that no extra water is added to the sauce — otherwise it will become diluted.

Veal Scaloppini a la Antonia

50 g (2 oz) (4 tablespoons) butter
700 g (1½ lb) escalopes (scallops) of veal
5 g (1 teaspoon) salt
freshly ground black pepper
2 shallots (spring onions, scallions), thickly sliced
3 tomatoes, skinned, seeded and cut into strips
175 g (6 oz) (1½ cups) thinly sliced mushrooms
150 mL (¼ pint) (⅔ cup) chicken stock
2.5 mL (½ teaspoon) dried oregano
150 mL (¼ pint) (⅔ cup) Bechamel Sauce (see recipe)
pinch nutmeg
5 g (1 tablespoon) chopped parsley

1 Heat butter in a large frying pan and fry escalopes of veal quickly on both sides over a high heat. Remove meat from the pan, season with salt and pepper and keep warm.

2 Add sliced onions to pan and fry gently for 2 minutes then add tomatoes and mushrooms and cook 4-5 minutes. Add stock and oregano, bring to boil and cook 5 minutes.

3 Add Bechamel Sauce and boil again for 8 minutes to reduce liquid by half.

4 Check seasoning and add nutmeg. Return veal to pan and coat with sauce until well heated.

5 Transfer meat and sauce to a warmed serving dish and sprinkle with chopped parsley. Serve with boiled rice and a crisp green salad.

Serves 6

Tip: Instead of using chicken stock, you can add an equal quanitity of white wine. Also, the bechamel sauce can be replaced by the same amount of cream or a mixture of cream and sauce.

Veal Escalopes (Scallops) in Marsala

4 veal escalopes (scallops)
50 g (2 oz) (4 tablespoons) butter
100 mL (4 fl oz) (½ cup) Marsala
200 mL (6 fl oz) (¾ cup) gravy or thickened stock
pinch cayenne pepper

1 Place veal escalopes (scallops) between 2 sheets of dampened greaseproof paper and beat with a mallet or rolling pin until they are 3 mm (⅛ in) thick.

2 Heat the butter in a frying pan and fry escalopes until well browned. Transfer to a warmed serving dish and keep hot.

3 Add Marsala to the fat in the pan and boil for 5 minutes, stirring well. Add the gravy or stock and cayenne, mix well and pour sauce over the veal.

Serves 4

Scaloppine alla Zucchini

5 Transfer escalopes to serving plates. Add mushrooms to the sauce in the pan. Simmer, stirring continually, for 2 minutes and pour the sauce over the escalopes. Garnish escalopes with a little chopped parsley and serve with fried new potatoes, and buttered asparagus and celery.

Serves 4

Veal in Beer and Caper Sauce

4 × 150 g (5 oz) veal escalopes
 (scallops)
50 g (2 oz) (½ cup) flour
salt and pepper
pinch nutmeg
25 g (1 oz) (2 tablespoons) butter
30 mL (1 fl oz) (2 tablespoons) oil
1 onion, chopped
150 mL (¼ pint) (⅔ cup) water
150 mL (¼ pint) (⅔ cup) flat light beer
15 mL (1 tablespoon) vinegar
30 mL (1 fl oz) (2 tablespoons) cream
juice ½ lemon
30 mL (2 tablespoons) capers
2.5 mL (½ teaspoon) chopped parsley

1 Roll escalopes (scallops) in flour seasoned with salt, pepper and nutmeg.
2 Gently fry veal in the butter and oil for 5 minutes on both sides or until cooked. Remove.
3 Drain off half the fat from the pan. Add onion and fry gently for 2 minutes. Add water, beer and vinegar, bring to the boil and cook for 10 minutes. Reduce heat to a gentle simmer. Stir in cream, lemon juice, capers and parsley. Check seasoning and pour over the veal.

Serves 4

Veal Marsala

625 g (1½ lb) cushion of veal (fillet
 part of the thick portion of leg)
25 g (1 oz) (4 tablespoons) flour
piece of blade mace
pinch paprika
pinch basil
pinch oregano
salt and black pepper
30 mL (1 fl oz) (2 tablespoons) oil
50 g (2 oz) (¼ cup) butter
150 mL (¼ pint) (⅔ cup) Marsala
150 mL (¼ pint) (⅔ cup) thickened
 cream
juice ½ lemon
100 g (¼ lb) (1½ cups) button
 mushrooms
10 mL (2 teaspoons) chopped parsley

1 Cut veal into 4 slices, 5 mm (¼ in) thick, and beat each one with a meat mallet, flattening it to the largest possible size. Cut each slice in half.
2 Sieve flour onto a plate. Powder mace, and add to the flour with remaining spices, herbs and seasoning.
3 Pass each escalope in the seasoned flour and shake off any excess. Heat oil and butter in a large frying pan over a table spirit burner. When sizzling hot, add escalopes and fry 1½ minutes on each side, or until golden. Drain off excess butter and oil.
4 Stir Marsala into the pan and boil for 2 minutes. Stir in cream and lemon juice and boil for 1 minute, shaking.

Veal in Beer and Caper Sauce

Vitello Venezia

4 × 100 g (¼ lb) veal escalopes
30 mL (2 tablespoons) flour
100 g (¼ lb) (½ cup) butter
2 cloves garlic, crushed
1 small shallot (spring onion,
    scallion), chopped
150 mL (¼ pint) (⅔ cup) red vermouth
30 mL (2 tablespoons) tomato paste
2 tomatoes, skinned, seeded and
    chopped
salt and pepper
pinch oregano
100 g (¼ lb) (1½ cups) button
    mushrooms, sliced

1 Beat escalopes until flat, and
sprinkle with flour.
2 Heat 50 g (2 oz) (¼ cup) butter in a
frying pan and gently fry veal until
golden-brown. Remove and keep
warm.
3 Fry garlic and shallot for 2–3 minutes, then add vermouth, tomato
paste and chopped tomatoes. Season
with salt and pepper and sprinkle in
the oregano. Bring to the boil, stirring
well, then simmer for about 10 minutes.
4 Heat remaining butter in another
pan and saute mushrooms until
golden.
5 Arrange escalopes in a serving dish
and pour over the sauce. Garnish
with mushrooms. Serve with fresh
broccoli and duchess potatoes.

Serves 4

Wiener Schnitzel

4 veal escalopes (scallops)
40 g (1½ oz) (6 tablespoons) seasoned
    flour
1 egg, beaten
50 g (2 oz) (¾ cup) fine dried
    breadcrumbs
50 g (2 oz) (¼ cup) butter
4 slices lemon

1 Place veal escalopes (scallops)
between 2 sheets of dampened
greaseproof paper and beat with a
mallet or rolling pin until very thin,
3 mm (⅛ in).
2 Coat veal with seasoned flour,
then dip in the beaten egg and
breadcrumbs until thoroughly
coated.
3 Melt butter in a large frying pan.
Add veal and fry over a moderate
heat until golden-brown on both
sides, turning once during cooking.
4 Transfer veal to a warmed serving
dish and serve immediately, garnished with lemon slices. Serve with
new potatoes tossed in parsley and a
green salad.

Serves 4

Roast Veal Steaks Parisienne

1 kg (2 lb) loin of veal, cut in 6 steaks
salt and pepper
100 g (¼ lb) (½ cup) butter
300 mL (½ pint) (1¼ cups) dry white
    wine
800 g (1¾ lb) potatoes, cut into balls
225 g (½ lb) small onions
100 mL (4 fl oz) (½ cup) cream
2 slices cooked ham, diced
225 g (½ lb) cooked mushrooms,
    diced
6 cooked artichoke bottoms
sprig parsley, chopped

1 Preheat oven to 200°C (400°F).
Season veal steaks and spread with
half of the butter. Cook in the oven
for ½ hour, turning once to brown
both sides. While cooking, use the
wine to baste the meat.
2 Meanwhile, fry potato balls and
onions, covered, in the rest of the
butter for 10 minutes. Drain and
keep hot.
3 When meat is cooked, drain the
liquid into a pan and bring to boil.
Add cream and simmer for 5 minutes. Season.
4 Place steaks on an ovenproof dish
and pour a little of the sauce over.
Mix ham and mushrooms and pile
on top of the artichoke bottoms.
Arrange around the meat and heat in
the oven for 12 minutes.
5 Decorate the dish with potato and
onions and sprinkle with parsley.
Serve the rest of the sauce separately.

Serves 6

Veal Steaks with Jerusalem Artichokes

50 mL (2 fl oz) (¼ cup) oil
50 g (2 oz) (4 tablespoons) butter
6 × 225 g (½ lb) veal loin steaks, 1 cm
    (½ in) thick

Sauce
1 onion, chopped
bouquet garni
150 mL (¼ pint) (⅔ cup) dry vermouth
1 stock cube
150 mL (¼ pint) (⅔ cup) water
juice ½ lemon
15 g (½ oz) (1½ tablespoons) cornflour

Garnish
50 g (2 oz) (4 tablespoons) butter
1 kg (2 lb) Jerusalem artichokes, cut
    in halves
1 onion, chopped

1 Heat oil and butter in a pan, add
veal steaks, cover and fry 12–14 minutes over a low heat. Turn steaks
once or twice while cooking. Remove
steaks and keep warm.
2 Make the sauce. Using the fat left
from cooking the meat, fry onion for
5 minutes and then remove surplus
fat. Add bouquet garni and vermouth and boil 8 minutes.
3 Dissolve stock cube in water, add
stock to pan and boil 4 minutes.
Season to taste and add lemon juice.
4 Mix the cornflour with 90 mL
(4 fl oz) (6 tablespoons) water, add to
sauce and boil 1 minute until
thickened. Strain sauce and pour a
little over the veal.
5 For the garnish, heat butter in a
pan and saute Jerusalem artichokes 6
minutes, covered. Add chopped
onion and cook 2 minutes. Drain off
fat, add 100 mL (4 fl oz) (½ cup) of the
sauce and simmer 5 minutes. Season.
6 Serve veal steaks with the garnish
and pour the rest of the sauce into a
sauce boat.

Serves 6

Roast Veal Steaks Parisienne

Veal Cutlets Portuguese

6 × 225 g (½ lb) veal cutlets
salt and pepper
50 g (2 oz) (½ cup) flour
50 mL (2 fl oz) (¼ cup) oil
1 onion, sliced
1 red capsicum (pepper), seeded and
    sliced
2 tomatoes, skinned, seeded and
    chopped
2 cloves garlic, peeled and chopped
pinch rosemary
50 g (2 oz) (½ cup) corn kernels
150 mL (¼ pint) (⅔ cup) dry sherry
150 mL (¼ pint) (⅔ cup) water
1 chicken stock cube
salt and pepper
pinch paprika

1 Sprinkle cutlets with salt and pepper and dredge with flour. Heat oil in a frying pan and fry cutlets for 5 minutes on each side until browned. Transfer cutlets to a shallow ovenproof dish and keep warm.
2 Preheat oven to 190°C (375°F).
3 Fry onion in the same pan for 5 minutes until soft. Add the sliced capsicum and fry a further 2 minutes. Add tomatoes, garlic, rosemary and corn kernels and stir well and sprinkle in the stock cube. Season with salt, pepper and paprika, and boil for 5 minutes.
4 Pour sauce over the veal and braise gently in the oven for 35 minutes, covered with a lid. Serve with plain boiled rice.

Serves 6

Veal Cutlets Provencal

4 tomatoes
salt and pepper
45 mL (3 tablespoons) olive oil
4 × 225 g (½ lb) veal cutlets
50 g (2 oz) (½ cup) flour
100 g (¼ lb) (½ cup) butter
50 g (2 oz) (⅓ cup) green olives,
    stoned and blanched
1 clove garlic, peeled and crushed
1 bunch parsley, chopped

1 Preheat oven to 190°C (375°F).
2 Wash tomatoes and place them in an ovenproof dish. Sprinkle with salt

and pepper, pour in the oil, and place in the oven for about 10 minutes.
3 Tenderise cutlets by beating with a mallet or rolling pin. Season with salt and pepper and dredge with flour.
4 Melt half the butter in a frying pan and fry cutlets for about 5 minutes on each side until browned and cooked.
5 Arrange cutlets in a dish with the olives and baked tomatoes around the edges. Keep warm.
6 Melt the rest of the butter in a pan and fry the garlic and parsley for a minute, stirring constantly. Pour this butter mixture over the cutlets and serve at once.

Serves 4

Veal Cutlets Bonne Femme

4 × 225 g (½ lb) veal cutlets
salt and pepper
50 g (2 oz) (½ cup) flour
100 g (¼ lb) (½ cup) clarified butter or
    butter and oil mixed
225 g (½ lb) (1½ cups) boiled, cold
    potatoes, thinly sliced
100 g (¼ lb) (1 cup) shallots (spring
    onions, scallions)
100 mL (4 fl oz) (½ cup) sherry
150 mL (¼ pint) (⅔ cup) demi-glace
    sauce
5 g (1 tablespoon) chopped parsley

1 Sprinkle the veal cutlets with salt and pepper and dredge with flour.
2 Preheat oven to 200°C (400°F).
3 Heat butter in a frying pan and gently fry cutlets on both sides for a few minutes.
4 Place cutlets on an ovenproof dish in the oven to continue cooking.
5 Fry potatoes in the same pan until golden-brown, remove and keep warm. Then fry onions for 2 minutes. Transfer onions to a saucepan of water and boil until soft.
6 Drain off butter and pour the sherry into pan. Add the demi-glace sauce and bring to the boil, stirring all the time.
7 Arrange cutlets on a serving dish surrounded by fried potatoes and onions. Cover with the sauce and sprinkle with chopped parsley.

Serves 4

Hungarian Cutlets

50 g (2 oz) (½ cup) seasoned flour
50 mL (2 fl oz) (¼ cup) oil
15 mL (1 tablespoon) butter

Cutlets
225 g (½ lb) (1 cup) minced veal
225 g (½ lb) (1 cup) minced pork
100 g (¼ lb) (2 cups) fresh
    breadcrumbs
1 onion, chopped
1 clove garlic, crushed
75 g (3 oz) (¾ cup) diced mushrooms
pinch each mace and nutmeg
salt and pepper
1 egg, beaten
50 mL (2 fl oz) (¼ cup) flat light beer

Sauce
15 mL (1 tablespoon) oil
1 onion, chopped
30 mL (2 tablespoons) flour
150 mL (¼ pint) (⅔ cup) flat light beer
15 mL (1 tablespoon) tomato paste
150 mL (¼ pint) (⅔ cup) stock
sprig rosemary
5 mL (1 teaspoon) brown sugar
salt and pepper

1 Mix together the ingredients for the cutlets. Divide into 6 portions, roll into oval balls and dip in seasoned flour.
2 Heat oil and butter and fry cutlets until cooked and brown. Cover and keep warm.
3 Make the sauce: heat oil and fry onion until tender. Add flour and cook for 2–3 minutes. Add beer, tomato paste, stock, rosemary and sugar. Season with salt and pepper and bring to the boil. Cook gently for 15 minutes and serve with the cutlets with fresh peas and diced beans, turnips and carrots.

Serves 6

Hungarian Veal Paupiettes Step-by-step

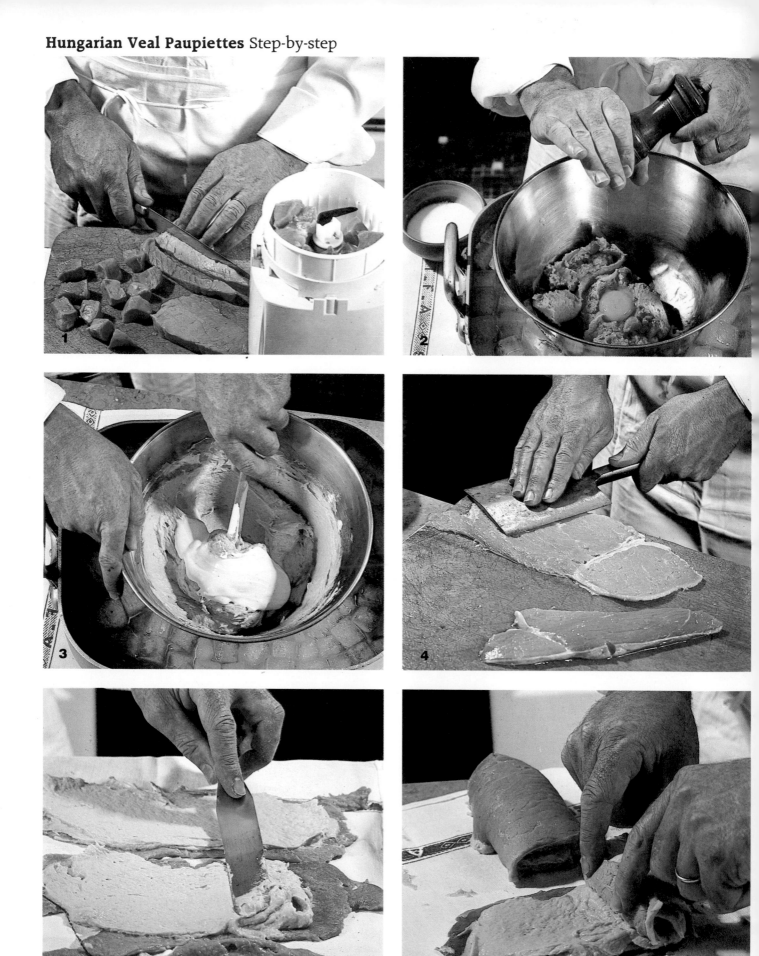

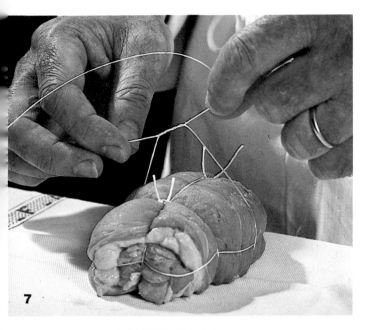

1 Chop the lean pork or veal trimmings to be used for the stuffing and put through a mincer.

2 Place in a bowl and keep cool over ice cubes or chill in a refrigerator when made. Add 1 egg and season with salt and freshly ground pepper.

3 Add the cream gradually and stir to make a smooth firm paste and chill until used.

4 Beat escalopes on wet board until thin.

5 Dry on cloth. Spread stuffing on escalopes.

6 Roll up tightly.

7 Tie up securely with string into neat parcels.

8 Heat a mixture of butter and oil and brown the paupiettes all over, covered with a lid.

9 Add the cream and white wine. Stir carefully, season and add a bouquet garni, bring to the boil and simmer for 1 hour.

10 When the paupiettes are tender, remove from pan. Carefully remove all the string and arrange on a dish. Reduce sauce by fast boiling to 300 mL (½ pint) (1¼ cups). Check the seasoning, pour over the paupiettes and serve hot.

Hungarian Veal Paupiettes

100 g (¼ lb) (½ cup) sausage meat
100 g (¼ lb) (½ cup) ham, minced
1 egg
salt and pepper
6 escalopes (scallops), 100 g (¼ lb)
* each*
50 g (2 oz) (½ cup) flour
50 mL (2 fl oz) (¼ cup) oil
450 g (1 lb) carrots
100 g (¼ lb) bacon rashers
50 g (2 oz) (4 tablespoons) margarine
200 mL (6 fl oz) (¾ cup) white wine
225 g (½ lb) shallots (spring onions,
* scallions)*
300 mL (½ pint) (1¼ cups) stock
5 g (1 tablespoon) chopped parsley

1 Blend sausage meat, minced ham, egg and seasoning to a smooth paste then chill.

2 On a wet board, flatten escalopes (scallops) by beating to make them thin. Spread the filling on each one, then roll up and tie with string, and dip in flour.

3 Heat half the oil in a pan and brown paupiettes for 4 minutes, covered with a lid. Remove to a casserole.

4 Slice carrots. Cut bacon into strips.

5 Heat margarine and rest of the oil and fry bacon for 1 minute, then add carrots. Saute for 3 minutes, then add bacon and carrots to the veal.

6 Add white wine and bring to the boil. Cover dish and simmer for 1 hour.

7 Meanwhile, boil shallots in stock for 2 minutes.

8 Remove paupiettes, discard the string.

9 Reduce the sauce by fast boiling to 300 mL (½ pint) (1¼ cups).

10 Serve the paupiettes surrounded by the bacon, carrots and onions. Pour over the sauce. Sprinkle with parsley.

Serves 6

Paupiettes Surprise

6 × 100 g (¼ lb) veal escalopes
* (scallops)*
6 × 50 g (2 oz) ham slices
6 × 25 g (1 oz) processed cheese
* slices*
30 mL (2 tablespoons) snipped chives
50 g (2 oz) (½ cup) seasoned flour
25 g (1 oz) (2 tablespoons) butter
30 mL (1 fl oz) (2 tablespoons) oil
1 onion, chopped
400 mL (14 fl oz) (1¾ cups) flat light
* beer*
15 mL (1 tablespoon) tomato paste
15 mL (1 tablespoon) vinegar
½ chicken stock cube, powdered
pinch oregano
pinch basil
salt and pepper
few sprigs parsley to decorate

1 Beat escalopes (scallops) with a meat mallet until they are very thin. Place a slice of ham and then cheese on each one and divide chives between them. Fold paupiettes into small bundles and secure with string. Roll in seasoned flour and shake off any excess. Reserve 30 mL (2 tablespoons) of the flour for later.

2 Preheat oven to 190°C (375°F). Heat butter and oil in a pan, brown the paupiettes on all sides for 3 minutes then transfer to a shallow casserole. In the same pan fry the onion until it is transparent. In a bowl, mix 30 mL (1 fl oz) (2 tablespoons) beer with the reserved flour. Add to pan with remaining beer, tomato paste, vinegar, stock cube, herbs and seasoning. Simmer, stirring continually for 2 minutes. Boil 10 minutes, strain and pour the sauce over the paupiettes.

3 Cover and braise paupiettes in the oven for 35 minutes. When they are cooked, remove the string, decorate with parsley and serve.

Serves 6

Veal with Olives

2 large onions, chopped
50 g (2 oz) (¼ cup) butter
100 g (¼ lb) (⅔ cup) calf's liver
100 g (¼ lb) (⅔ cup) bacon
100 g (¼ lb) (1 cup) olives, stoned
100 g (¼ lb) veal trimmings
50 g (2 oz) (1 cup) fresh breadcrumbs
1 egg
salt and pepper
6 veal escalopes (scallops), 175 g (6 oz)
* each*
1 carrot, chopped
15 mL (1 tablespoon) flour
100 mL (4 fl oz) (½ cup) white wine
225 mL (8 fl oz) (1 cup) stock
25 g (1 oz) (2 tablespoons) tomato
* paste*
bouquet garni

1 Lightly brown one chopped onion in 25 g (1 oz) (2 tablespoons) butter and put in a bowl. Brown calf's liver and remove.

2 Mince bacon, one-third of the olives, veal trimmings and liver, and add to onion. Add breadcrumbs and egg.

3 On a wet board, beat escalopes (scallops) till thin. Spread with stuffing, roll up and tie with string.

4 Brown paupiettes in the remainder of the butter, remove and place them in a casserole.

5 Brown the other chopped onion and carrot. Stir in the flour and brown. Add white wine, stock, tomato paste, bouquet garni, salt and pepper to taste.

6 Pour over paupiettes and cook 1 hour. Add the remainder of the olives 10 minutes before the end.

7 Remove paupiettes, discard string and arrange on a dish. Reduce sauce to 300 mL (½ pint) (1¼ cups) and pour over paupiettes.

Serves 6

Veal Marengo

900 g (2 lb) stewing veal (from the
shoulder)
50 mL (2 fl oz) (¼ cup) oil
50 g (2 oz) (4 tablespoons) butter
2 large onions, finely chopped
50 g (2 oz) (½ cup) flour
300 mL (½ pint) (1¼ cups) white wine
4 tomatoes, skinned, seeded and
chopped
2 cloves garlic, crushed
bouquet garni
salt and pepper
450 g (1 lb) shallots (spring onions,
scallions)
15 g (½ oz) (1 tablespoon) butter
15 g (½ oz) (1 tablespoon) sugar
225 g (½ lb) (3 cups) button
mushrooms
4 slices white bread
5 g (1 tablespoon) chopped parsley

1 Cut veal into 3 cm (1¼ in) cubes.
Brown quickly in half the oil and butter, mixed. Add chopped onions and
cook gently with the meat until soft.
Dust with flour and cook until it just
browns.
2 Add white wine and stir to absorb
any juices stuck onto pan. Mix in the
tomatoes, garlic and bouquet garni,
cover with water, and season with
salt and pepper. Bring to the boil,
cover the pan and simmer over low
heat for 1–1¼ hours.
3 Peel shallot bulbs, cutting away
the green leaves, and saute to light
golden in the butter and sugar.
4 Quarter the mushrooms and fry
gently in the other half of the oil and
butter mixture.
5 Cut bread into heart-shaped
croutons, and fry until crisp and
golden-brown in the rest of the oil
and butter.
6 Add shallots and mushrooms to
the meat and simmer 5 minutes.
Chop parsley and dip the pointed
end of each crouton in the meat
sauce and then in the parsley. Serve
in a deep, heated dish, garnished
with the croutons.

Serves 8

Blanquette de Veau

900 g (2 lb) stewing veal, from neck or
shoulder
salt and pepper
2 large carrots
1 large leek
1 stick celery
2 cloves garlic
bouquet garni
1 onion, studded with 2 cloves
100 g (¼ lb) (½ cup) butter
50 g (2 oz) (½ cup) flour
450 g (1 lb) small onions
450 g (1 lb) button mushrooms
juice ½ lemon
2 egg yolks
150 mL (¼ pint) (⅔ cup) thickened
cream
pinch nutmeg

1 Cut veal into 3.5 cm (1½ in) cubes.
Cover with cold water in a saucepan
and bring to the boil. Drain and rinse
in cold water, removing any scum.
Return meat to pan, cover with
water, season with salt and pepper.
Bring to the boil, then simmer.
2 Slice carrots in 4 lengthways, trim
and clean the leek, chop celery and
garlic. Add these vegetables, with the
bouquet garni and the onion studded
with 2 cloves, to the meat. Cover and
simmer gently for 1¼ hours.
3 Make a roux with half of the butter
and the flour. Cook for 2 minutes and
leave to cool.
4 Fry the small onions in half of the
remaining butter. Cook the mushrooms in the other half of the butter,
the lemon juice and 30 mL (2 tablespoons) water, until tender. The
liquor may be added to the stew.
5 Take the meat from the pan and
keep warm. Discard the vegetables
and strain the sauce. Pour some of
the liquid onto the roux and blend to
produce a thin, smooth sauce. Bring
to the boil, adjust seasoning.
6 In another bowl beat together the
egg yolks and cream with a pinch of
nutmeg. Stir in 100 mL (4 fl oz) (½
cup) of the sauce. Pour this liaison
into the stew sauce, stirring briskly
with a whisk to a thick, smooth
sauce.

7 Return meat, mushrooms and
small onions to a pan and pour the
sauce over them through a sieve.
Reheat without bringing to the boil.
Arrange meat and vegetables in a
heated serving dish, pour sauce over
them, and serve hot.

Serves 8

Veal Roulade

6 × 100 g (¼ lb) veal escalopes
(scallops)
salt and pepper
25 g (1 oz) (4 tablespoons) flour
50 mL (2 fl oz) (¼ cup) oil

Stuffing
150 g (5 oz) (1 cup) diced liver
1 onion, chopped
25 g (1 oz) (4 tablespoons) flour
1 egg, beaten
12 asparagus tips

Chaudfroid Sauce
300 mL (½ pint) (1¼ cups) bechamel
sauce
150 mL (¼ pint) (⅔ cup) chicken stock
10 g (2 teaspoons) granulated gelatine

1 Beat each escalope thinly with a
mallet or rolling pin. Season and
dredge with flour.
2 Heat oil in a frying pan and fry
escalopes 5 minutes each side, then
cool.
3 Fry diced liver in the same pan for
4 minutes, add onion and cook 4
minutes. Stir in the flour and cook 1
minute.
4 Mince the stuffing mixture finely
— twice if necessary — and blend
with beaten egg.
5 Spread this liver stuffing over each
escalope, roll up tightly and wrap in
foil. Chill overnight, then unwrap
and place on a rack.
6 Heat the sauce. Heat stock, add
gelatine and simmer for 2 minutes.
Blend half of the jelly stock with
white sauce, put the remainder aside
for glazing and cool.
7 Coat each stuffed veal roll evenly
with the chaudfroid sauce. Leave to
cool and set. Then brush with the
aspic jelly. Decorate each roll with 2
asparagus tips and serve.

Serves 6

Blanquette de Veau Step-by-step

1 Cover veal in pot with water, bring to boil.
2 Drain and rinse in cold water. Return veal to pan, cover with water and season. Bring to the boil.
3 Slice carrots, trim leek, prepare onion, bouquet garni, celery, garlic. Add to meat, simmer 1¼ hours.

4 Make a roux from the butter and flour. Cook 2 minutes and let cool.
5 Fry the small onions in butter.
6 Poach mushrooms in butter, water and lemon juice until soft. Add the liquor to the stew.

10

7 Remove meat from pan and reserve. Discard vegetables. Strain cooking liquor through a sieve.

8 Pour part of the liquor on the roux. Bring to the boil, stirring, and add more liquor if needed to make a smooth thin sauce.

9 Mix cream and egg yolks with some of the sauce. Add to the sauce, beating to thicken.

10 Mix meat, mushrooms and onions. Pour sauce over through sieve. Reheat without boiling.

11 and 12 Place meat in a dish, pour over sauce.

Veal Fricassee

675 g (1½ lb) stewing veal, cut in 3 cm
  (1¼ in) cubes
2 onions, chopped
150 mL (¼ pint) (⅔ cup) white wine
1 bay leaf
pinch thyme
salt and pepper
25 g (1 oz) (¼ cup) flour
25 g (1 oz) (2 tablespoons) butter
30 mL (2 tablespoons) milk
100 g (¼ lb) button mushrooms

1 Preheat oven to 170°C (325°F).
Place veal, onions, wine, herbs and
seasoning to taste in a casserole,
cover and cook for about 1¼ hours or
until the meat is tender. Remove
meat and strain liquid.

2 Make a roux of the flour and butter and cook for 2 minutes. Remove
from heat, add milk to make a
smooth paste, and stir in the cooking
liquid to make up 300 mL (½ pint) (1¼
cups) of smooth sauce.

3 Pour sauce over the veal in the casserole, add mushrooms, and return
to oven for 20 minutes. Serve hot.

Serves 4

Serbian Veal with Yoghurt

2 green capsicums (peppers), seeded
  and diced
30 mL (2 tablespoons) oil
675 g (1½ lb) shoulder veal
2 large onions, quartered
50 g (2 oz) (¼ cup) butter
salt and pepper
225 mL (8 fl oz) (1 cup) white stock
7 g (¼ oz) (1 tablespoon) paprika
4 large tomatoes, peeled, seeded and
  chopped
300 mL (½ pint) (2 cups) yoghurt

1 Fry the diced green capsicums in
the oil for 10–15 minutes over low
heat.

2 Cut meat into 0.5 cm (¼ in) slices
In a saucepan, fry veal and onions in
butter until lightly browned. Season
with salt and pepper, pour in the
stock, add paprika and bring to the
boil. Cover and simmer 20 minutes.

3 Add tomatoes to the capsicums
and cook for 10 minutes over low
heat, stirring constantly.

4 Remove veal and onion from the
saucepan, leaving the liquid, and
place in a warmed serving dish.
Strain the capsicum and tomato,
arrange them around the meat, and
pour any remaining liquid from them
into the meat liquor.

5 Stir yoghurt into the liquor over
heat, and beat for 2 minutes with a
whisk. Pour over veal.

Serves 4

Knuckle of Veal Paysanne

20 shallots (spring onions, scallions)
20 small carrots
salt and pepper
1.5 kg (3 lb) knuckle of veal, cut in
  5 cm (2 in) pieces
25 g (1 oz) (¼ cup) flour
25 g (1 oz) (2 tablespoons) butter
350 mL (12 fl oz) (1½ cups) water
1 chicken stock cube
bouquet garni
20 small new potatoes
450 g (1 lb) (4 cups) green peas

1 Carefully cut shallots into pearl
shapes. Peel and trim the carrots.

2 Season veal and dredge in flour.
Heat butter in a frying pan and
brown the meat in it. Transfer to a
heavy-bottomed stewing pan. Saute
onions and carrots in butter for 1
minute, then add to the meat.

3 Pour on the water, crumble in the
stock cube and bring to the boil.
Reduce heat at once, add the bouquet garni and check seasoning.
Cover and simmer gently for 30 minutes.

4 Peel the new potatoes and add to
pan with the peas. Add more stock, if
necessary, so the vegetables are just
covered. Replace lid on the pan and
simmer again for 45 minutes–1 hour,
until the meat is tender.

Serves 6

Veal Knuckle Riviera with Noodles

600 g (1½ lb) veal knuckle, sawn into
  5 cm (2 in) thick pieces
175 g (6 oz) veal kidney, sliced
50 mL (2 fl oz) (¼ cup) oil
1 large onion, chopped
3 carrots, scraped and sliced
2 stalks celery, sliced
150 mL (¼ pint) (⅔ cup) white wine
150 mL (¼ pint) (⅔ cup) white meat
  stock
1 clove garlic, crushed
225 g (½ lb) (2 cups) noodles
50 g (2 oz) (4 tablespoons) butter
50 g (2 oz) (⅓ cup) grated Parmesan
  cheese
salt and pepper
50 mL (2 fl oz) (¼ cup) cream
large pinch paprika
parsley to garnish

1 Brown the veal knuckle and kidney in oil for 8 minutes, turning
knuckle pieces once. Add vegetables,
cover and cook very gently for 10
minutes.

2 Pour in wine and stock, add garlic
and season to taste. Simmer for 1½–2
hours.

3 Boil noodles in salted water for
8–10 minutes until tender. Drain and
stir in the butter, Parmesan cheese,
and a pinch of salt and pepper.

4 Stir cream and paprika into the
meat mixture. Bring back to boil and
remove from heat.

5 Arrange noodles around the
heated serving dish and fill the
centre with meat and sauce. Garnish
with sprigs of parsley, and serve at
once.

Serves 4

Veal Knuckle Riviera with Noodles

Mediterranean Veal Stew

675 g (1½ lb) shoulder veal, cut into
  3 cm (1¼ in) cubes
3 onions, chopped
45 mL (3 tablespoons) oil
25 g (1 oz) (¼ cup) flour
juice 1 lemon
300 mL (½ pint) (1¼ cups) white stock
2 cloves garlic, peeled and chopped
450 g (1 lb) tomatoes, skinned,
  seeded and chopped
2 green capsicums (peppers), seeded
  and sliced
225 g (½ lb) (2 cups) garden peas
salt and pepper
100 g (¼ lb) (⅔ cup) stoned green
  olives
100 mL (4 fl oz) (½ cup) cream

1 Fry meat and onions in the oil
until lightly browned. Add flour and
stir while cooking for 2 minutes.
2 Stir in the lemon juice, stock, garlic, tomatoes, capsicums, garden peas
and seasoning to taste. Bring to the
boil, cover and simmer gently for 25
minutes.
3 Dip olives into boiling water for 1
minute, drain and chop roughly. Add
to the pan and continue to cook for
15 minutes.
4 Remove the meat and vegetables
and transfer them to a heated serving
dish. Add the cream to the pan and
simmer, stirring constantly, for 5
minutes to thicken. Pour sauce over
meat and serve at once.

Serves 4

Osso Bucco in Beer

1.2 kg (2½ lb) knuckle of veal (sawn
  in 5 cm (2 in) pieces with the bone)
salt and pepper
50 g (2 oz) (½ cup) flour
50 mL (2 fl oz) (¼ cup) oil
2 onions, chopped
2 sticks celery, chopped
6 large tomatoes, peeled, seeded and
  chopped
2 carrots, diced
2 cloves garlic, crushed
bouquet garni
15 mL (1 tablespoon) tomato paste
150 mL (¼ pint) (⅔ cup) chicken stock
300 mL (½ pint) (1¼ cups) flat light
  beer
juice 1 lemon
5 mL (1 teaspoon) chopped parsley

1 Roll the knuckle of veal slices in
seasoned flour and shake off any
excess.
2 Heat oil in a frying pan. Add meat
and fry it gently for 8 minutes, turning frequently to brown it on all
sides. Transfer meat to a shallow
flameproof casserole.
3 Add onions to the pan and stir-fry
for 3 minutes until transparent but
not browned. Spoon onions into the
casserole.
4 Add celery, chopped tomatoes,
chopped carrot, garlic, bouquet garni
and tomato paste. Pour in the stock,
beer and lemon juice and season the
casserole. Cover and simmer for
1½–2 hours.
5 Sprinkle the dish with chopped
parsley. Serve with a bowl of noodles
tossed in butter and Parmesan
cheese, and sprinkled with parsley.

Serves 6

Osso Bucco with Artichoke Hearts

15 g (½ oz) (2 tablespoons) flour
salt and pepper
8 slices knuckle of veal, 2.5 cm (1 in)
  thick
25 g (1 oz) (2 tablespoons) butter
1 large onion, sliced
2 cloves garlic, peeled and crushed
2 carrots, sliced
2 sticks celery, finely chopped
200 mL (6 fl oz) (¾ cup) dry white
  wine
4 large tomatoes, skinned, seeded
  and chopped
15 g (½ oz) (1 tablespoon) tomato
  paste
1 bay leaf
pinch dried rosemary
8 canned artichoke hearts (optional)
grated rind and juice 1 lemon
5 g (1 tablespoon) chopped parsley

1 Season flour with salt and pepper
and dredge the veal in it. Heat butter
in a frying pan, brown the veal,
remove to a heavy-bottomed pan.
2 Lightly fry onion, garlic, carrots
and celery in the oil, then add to
meat.
3 Pour wine over meat and vegetables. Bring to the boil, then lower
heat to simmering. Stir in the tomatoes, tomato paste, bay leaf and
rosemary and season to taste. Cover
and simmer for 1 hour or until meat
is tender.
4 Add the drained artichoke hearts
and the juice and grated rind of the
lemon. Cook for 10 minutes. Immediately before serving, sprinkle on the
chopped parsley. Serve with plain
boiled potatoes, rice or noodles and a
crisp green salad.

Serves 4

Tips: This dish can also be made
using veal knuckles 5 cm (2 in) thick.
Allow 1 per portion and cook for 1½
hours.
The marrow inside the knuckle is
delicious: eat it with the stew.

*Osso Bucco with Artichoke
Hearts*

Cannelloni Crepes

Crepes
200 g (½ lb) (1¼ cups) flour
pinch salt
1 egg, beaten
300 mL (½ pint) (1¼ cups) milk
15 mL (1 tablespoon) butter

Filling
500 g (1 lb) minced veal
1 onion, finely chopped
15 mL (1 tablespoon) finely chopped
   parsley
salt and pepper to taste
1 clove garlic, crushed
15 mL (1 tablespoon) oil
810 g (1¾ lb) can whole peeled
   tomatoes
2.5 mL (1 teaspoon) basil
125 g (¼ lb) mozzarella cheese, grated
50 g (2 oz) (½ cup) Parmesan cheese

1 Sift flour and salt, gradually beat in egg and milk to form batter. Cover and stand 30 minutes. Grease crepe pan with small portion of butter. Drop spoonfuls of mixture onto hot pan. Tilt pan to allow batter to cover base. Cook till mixture sets. Turn. Cook for an extra few seconds. Remove and cool. Layer greaseproof paper between crepes.

2 Combine mince, onion, parsley, salt, pepper, garlic and oil in a large casserole dish. Cover and cook in microwave on high 8–10 minutes. Stir twice during cooking.

3 Add tomatoes and basil. Combine evenly. Cook uncovered on high 5 minutes then reduce to medium and cook a further 5 minutes. Allow to cool slightly.

4 Place 2 tablespoons of meat mixture on centre of each crepe. Roll up. Place, roll side down, in shallow dish. Continue covering base of dish with crepe cannelloni. Top with half the grated mozzarella and Parmesan cheeses.

5 Cook on high 5 minutes then reduce to medium and cook a further 10 minutes. Allow to stand 5 minutes. Serve hot.

Serves 6–8

Veal Mozzarella

500 g (1 lb) veal escalopes
75 g (3 oz) (¾ cup) grated mozzarella
   cheese
15 mL (1 tablespoon) finely chopped
   parsley

Sauce
250 g (½ lb) tomato paste
pinch oregano
2.5 mL (½ teaspoon) basil
pinch garlic salt
2.5 mL (½ teaspoon) sugar
pinch white pepper

1 Combine all sauce ingredients in a medium-sized bowl and cook on high 2 minutes. Reduce power to medium and cook 6 minutes. Set aside.

2 Place veal escalopes in a single layer in baking dish and cook on medium 8–9 minutes. Drain.

3 Spoon sauce over veal. Sprinkle with cheese and parsley and cook on medium 6–7 minutes until cheese melts.

Serves 4

Cannelloni Crepes

Veal Mozzarella

Veal Fillets with Avocado and Hollandaise Sauce

15 mL (1 tablespoon) oil
6 veal fillets
1 large ripe avocado, peeled and
   sliced

Hollandaise Sauce
100 g (4 oz) (½ cup) butter
3 egg yolks
30 mL (2 tablespoons) lemon juice or
   white wine or tarragon vinegar
salt and pepper to taste

1 To prepare sauce, place butter in bowl and melt on high 1 minute. Beat together egg yolks, lemon juice, salt and pepper and stir into the melted butter. Cook on defrost 4 minutes, stirring every 30–45 seconds. Beat sauce while it cools. Sauce will thicken on cooling.
2 Preheat browning dish on high 4 minutes. Add oil and cook veal fillets, 3 at a time, on high 4 minutes, turning once. Repeat for remaining fillets.
3 Serve veal topped with avocado slice and hollandaise sauce.

Serves 6

Veal Scaloppine

8 veal steaks
25 g (1 oz) (¼ cup) seasoned
   breadcrumbs
25 g (1 oz) (⅓ cup) Parmesan cheese
15 mL (1 tablespoon) chopped
   parsley
salt and pepper to taste
5 mL (1 teaspoon) basil
1 egg, beaten
810 g (1¾ lb) can whole peeled
   tomatoes
125 g (¼ lb) mozzarella cheese, grated

1 Pound veal steaks and slice in half. Combine seasoned breadcrumbs, tablespoon Parmesan cheese, parsley, salt, pepper and basil. Dip veal in egg and coat with crumb mixture. Place veal on microwave roasting rack. Cook on medium high uncovered 10–12 minutes turning just once.
2 Chop whole tomatoes. Layer veal steaks, tomato mixture and mozzarella cheese in shallow dish. Sprinkle surface with rest of Parmesan cheese. Cook on medium high 10 minutes. Serve hot with a green salad.

Serves 8–10

Veal Nicoise

500 g (1 lb) veal steaks
1 medium-sized onion, sliced thinly
   in rings
60 mL (4 tablespoons) tomato paste
15 g (1 tablespoon) flour
pinch dried basil
5 mL (1 teaspoon) sugar
10 mL (2 teaspoons) chopped parsley
1 small clove garlic, chopped
pinch salt
pinch freshly ground black pepper
2 large tomatoes, peeled and
   chopped
½ medium-sized green capsicum
   (pepper), thinly sliced
½ medium-sized red capsicum
   (pepper), thinly sliced
30 g (1 oz) (¼ cup) sliced stuffed olives
8 whole black olives
10 mL (2 teaspoons) finely chopped
   parsley

1 Pound veal with meat mallet to tenderise and flatten to 1 cm thickness. Place slices into baking dish and top with onion rings.
2 In a medium-sized bowl blend tomato paste, flour, basil, sugar, parsley, garlic, salt and pepper. Stir in tomatoes and capsicums. Spread veal with vegetable mixture and sprinkle with sliced and whole olives.
3 Cook on high 16–18 minutes until veal is fork tender. Sprinkle lightly with finely chopped parsley to serve.

Serves 4

Veal Scaloppine Step-by-step

1 Coat veal with breadcrumbs, Parmesan cheese and seasonings.

2 Arrange veal in a shallow dish and add tomato mixture and mozzarella cheese.

*Veal Fillets with Avocado
and Hollandaise Sauce*

Hearty Beef

Beef has always enjoyed a sumptuous reputation. A charming tale relates how the 'roast beef of olde England' was knighted by King Henry VIII, and ever after the two hindquarters were called 'Baronne de Boeuf'. Although an interesting tale, the story has no basis in fact.

Feature this meat in Beef Italienne as the highlight of a special dinner — superb fillet steak, flamboyantly garnished. Steak Tartare is another classic dish in which diners garnish raw fillet steak according to their tastes. Hotpot Parisienne served with boiled or fried rice makes a colourful and economical meal.

Marinated Beef

Roasting Beef

There are two methods of roasting beef. The old-fashioned method roasts the meat at a high temperature. This sears the outside of the joint and keeps the meat juices inside. The moisture acts as a heat conductor and so the joint stays moist and juicy long after cooking. Lovers of underdone beef also claim that it has more flavour this way. An alternative is to start the cooking on a high temperature and sear the joint for 20 minutes, then lower the temperature for the remainder of the cooking time.

The second method which is commonly used in America roasts the meat at a low temperature. This way, the meat is cooked throughout and it is difficult to obtain an underdone, juicy, red joint. You will probably find it best to sear your joint first, then lower the temperature.

Basic rules for Roasting

There are some basic rules for roasting and, if you follow them, you should always have good results. They are:

1 Always season the joint lightly with salt and freshly ground pepper.

2 Always handle the meat very gently and never pierce it with a knife or skewer. It is important that the meat juices should stay intact.

3 Always smother your meat with plenty of fat. Use 25 g (1 oz) fat for every 450 g (1 lb) meat. Baste the meat frequently with the fat during cooking.

4 If you can, stand the joint on a rack or grille or trivet above a roasting pan to catch the juices. An alternative is to place the joint on a bed of root vegetables (carrots, celery and onions) or meat bones. The vegetable and meat juices can be used as a base for the gravy.

5 Always use a meat thermometer if you like your meat well-done. It is essential to obtain good results. Insert it into the meat but take care that it does not touch the bone.

6 Always preheat the oven before roasting to 220°C (425°F). Cook the

Rare sliced roasted beef

meat on the middle shelf and sear it at the high temperature. Then if you like your beef underdone, continue cooking it at this temperature. If you prefer well-done beef, lower the temperature to 190°C (375°F).

Serving Roast Beef

The traditional way to serve roast beef is with roast potatoes, Yorkshire puddings and horseradish sauce and mustard. You can make a delicious gravy from the meat juices and vegetable water. Rest the joint for 15 minutes before carving — keep it warm in the bottom of the oven — and garnish with sprigs of watercress.

Suitable Cuts of Meat

Sirloin, wing rib or loin, forerib and middlerib are all suitable for roasting. If these are too expensive, try topside or round which are cheaper and slightly tougher cuts.

Roasting Times

Sirloin, rib and the better cuts of beef should be seared for 20 minutes in a hot oven. Then, if you like your meat underdone, roast it a further 10 minutes for every 450 g (1 lb). For well cooked meat, allow 15–20 minutes per 450 g (1 lb). Topside and the cheaper cuts need 20 minutes also.

Roast Rib of Beef with Potatoes and Celery

2 kg (4 lb) rib of beef
50 g (2 oz) (¼ cup) softened butter
salt and pepper
1½ kg (3 lb) potatoes, peeled
50 g (2 oz) (½ cup) flour
cooking oil
2 heads celery
30 mL (2 tablespoons) butter
300 mL (½ pint) (1¼ cups) stock
watercress to garnish

1 Preheat oven to 180°C (350°F).
2 Rub meat all over with the softened butter. Season to taste and place it in a large roasting bag. Tie bag according to instructions and bake meat in a roasting pan for 1½ hours or until tender.
3 When meat has been in the oven for ½ hour, prepare potatoes. Cut into equal sized pieces and parboil in salted water for 5 minutes. Drain and dry before sprinkling with a little flour. Place in a clean roasting dish with cooking oil and bake for the last hour of the meat's cooking time.
4 Wash and peel celery heads and cut off the tops, leaving 15–20 cm (6–8 in) of heart. Remove outer leaves, then cut hearts in half, or into three if they are large. Sprinkle with seasoning and place in a roasting bag with the butter, cut into knobs. Tie bag according to instructions and place in roasting pan with the meat for the last 45 minutes of the meat's cooking time.
5 When meat and vegetables are ready, reduce heat and leave potatoes in the oven to keep warm. Remove meat and celery from roasting bags, reserving juices. Place meat on a serving dish and celery in a vegetable dish. Keep warm.
   Make the gravy: place reserved juices in the meat's roasting tray. Blend with remaining flour and cook over a gentle heat until it bubbles. Add stock and bring to the boil, stirring constantly. If it is too pale, add a little gravy browning. Serve meat garnished with watercress and surrounded by roast potatoes and celery hearts. Serve gravy separately.

Serves 8–9

Boeuf a la Mode

450 g (1 lb) belly pork fat
salt and pepper
10 g (2 tablespoons) chopped parsley
2 kg (4 lb) braising beef, in one piece
600 mL (1 pint) (2½ cups) red wine
1 bouquet garni
675 g (1½ lb) carrots
1 shallot (spring onion, scallion), sliced
2 large onions, sliced
2 cloves garlic, crushed
6 peppercorns
50 mL (2 fl oz) (¼ cup) brandy
100 mL (4 fl oz) (½ cup) oil
2 calf's feet, cut in half
1 litre (1¾ pints) (4½ cups) beef stock
100 g (¼ lb) (½ cup) butter
10 g (1 teaspoon) sugar
12 shallot (spring onion, scallion) bulbs
25 g (1 oz) (3 tablespoons) cornflour mixed with 150 mL (¼ pint) (⅔ cup) water (optional)

1 Cut pork fat into strips, 1 cm (½ in) thick. Season and sprinkle over parsley. Lard beef at regular intervals with strips.
2 Place meat in an earthenware dish with wine and bouquet garni. Cut half the carrots in slices across and add to dish with shallot, onions, garlic, peppercorns and brandy. Refrigerate for 2 hours, turning from time to time.
3 Preheat oven to 180°C (350°F). Strain meat and vegetables, reserving liquid. Heat oil in an ovenproof casserole, add beef and cook quickly for 10 minutes until browned. Lift out meat and fry strained vegetables and bouquet garni for 5 minutes.
4 Return beef to pan, add calf's feet and pour in reserved liquid and beef stock. Season and bring to the boil. Remove any scum, cover and bake for 2–2½ hours.
5 Heat half the butter in a pan, add the rest of the carrots, the sugar and enough water to cover. Cook until liquid has evaporated. In a separate pan, heat the rest of the butter, add shallot bulbs and enough water to cover and cook 8 minutes.
6 After the meat has been cooking for 1½ hours, remove from oven and transfer beef to another casserole. Dice meat of the calf's feet and discard bones. Add diced meat to the beef with glazed carrots and shallot bulbs. Strain gravy and add about three-quarters to beef. Cover again and return to oven for the rest of the cooking time.
7 Boil the rest of the gravy for 5 minutes to reduce it. Season.
8 Place cooked meat on a serving dish and coat with the reduced gravy. Return to oven for a few minutes to glaze.
9 Surround meat with the vegetables, coat with gravy and serve hot. The gravy can be thickened with cornflour if liked.

Serves 8

Carnival Beef

50 mL (2 fl oz) (¼ cup) oil
450 g (1 lb) piece beef topside
1 onion, chopped
2 tomatoes, skinned, seeded and chopped
15 g (½ oz) (1 tablespoon) tomato paste
900 mL (1½ pints) (3¼ cups) beef stock
1 bay leaf
salt and pepper
5 g (1 teaspoon) chilli powder
150 g (5 oz) (1½ cups) corn kernels
100 g (¼ lb) (¾ cup) prunes, stoned and sliced
2 peaches, peeled, stoned and sliced
1 orange, peeled and sliced

1 Heat oil and brown meat for 10 minutes. Add onion, cover and cook gently for 5 minutes.
2 Stir in tomatoes, tomato paste, beef stock, bay leaf, and season with salt, pepper and chilli powder. Bring to the boil, cover and simmer gently for 1½ hours.
3 Add corn kernels, prunes, peach and orange slices, and cook for another 5 minutes. Serve with rice or boiled potatoes.

Serves 4

1 Collect all ingredients.
2 and 3 Push larding needle through beef, thread strip of fat, draw back through meat.
4 and 5 Add vegetable, garlic, bouquet garni, peppercorns, brandy and wine. Soak 2 hours.
6 Strain, reserving the liquid.
7 Brown the beef and remove.
8 Fry the vegetables and herbs.
9 Return the beef to pan with the calf's feet, reserved liquid and stock.
10 Bring to the boil, remove any scum and place in the oven. Glaze the onions and carrots.
11 After 1½ hours, transfer beef to another casserole. Dice the meat from the calf's feet and add.
12 Add the glazed carrots and onions.
13 Strain over ¾ of the gravy and complete cooking.
14 Reduce rest of gravy; glaze cooked beef.
15 and 16 Serve beef with vegetables.

Fillet of Beef Stuffed with Mushrooms

Fillet of Beef Stuffed with Mushrooms

1 kg (2 lb) beef fillet
550 mL (1 pint) (2½ cups) dry white wine
100 g (¼ lb) (½ cup) butter
1 bay leaf
sprig thyme
1 onion, chopped
225 g (½ lb) button mushrooms
salt and pepper
5 mL (1 teaspoon) chopped parsley

1 Marinate fillet in white wine overnight. Drain fillet, reserving marinade and dry thoroughly.

2 Melt 50 g (2 oz) (¼ cup) butter in a frying pan. Add bay leaf, thyme and chopped onion and saute gently for 5 minutes, or until onion is transparent. Add mushrooms and seasoning. Cover and cook over a low heat for 20 minutes. Add parsley and cook 1 minute before removing from heat.

3 Preheat oven to 200°C (400°F). Using a sharp knife split fillet length-ways and stuff with mushrooms. Reserve any that are left over. Tie fillet with string and place in a roasting tray. Dot with remaining butter and sprinkle with wine from the marinade. Bake meat for 50–60 minutes, basting frequently while it cooks.

4 Transfer meat to a serving dish and surround it with any leftover mushrooms. Serve with new potatoes and a crisp mixed salad.

Serves 6

Rump Steak Royal

1 kg (2 lb) rump steak in 1 piece
5 g (1 teaspoon) crushed peppercorns
45 mL (3 tablespoons) oil
2 cloves garlic, peeled and chopped
50 g (2 oz) (4 tablespoons) peanut butter
150 mL (¼ pint) (⅔ cup) medium vermouth

1 Season steak with peppercorns.

2 Heat oil in a frying pan and shallow fry the steak. Cook for 6 minutes on either side for underdone meat, 12 minutes for medium, 14 minutes for well-done.

3 Remove steak from pan and keep warm on a dish.

4 Mix garlic and peanut butter and put in frying pan. Add vermouth, stir and boil for 4 minutes. Pour over steak.

5 Serve the whole steak and cut into 3 or 4 portions in front of the guests. Serve with a lettuce and orange salad. *Serves 3–4*

Sirloin Steak with Mushrooms

15 mL (1 tablespoon) coarsely ground
   peppercorns
1½ kg (3 lb) sirloin in 1 piece
100 g (¼ lb) (½ cup) butter
salt
500 g (1 lb) button mushrooms,
   washed and trimmed
100 mL (4 fl oz) (½ cup) dry white
   wine
50 mL (2 fl oz) (¼ cup) Madeira or dry
   sherry
gravy browning, optional

1 Preheat oven to 220°C (425°F).

2 Sprinkle pepper on both sides of sirloin and work it into the meat firmly with the palm of the hand.

3 Smother about 25 g (1 oz) (2 tablespoons) butter on the meat to cover on both sides. Put meat on a grid in a roasting pan and place in oven. Roast for about 1 hour, turning the meat once halfway through, then season with salt.

4 Melt 50 g (2 oz) (4 tablespoons) butter into a pan. Add the whole mushrooms and saute over a fairly high heat until lightly browned — about 5 minutes.

5 When meat is done, put it on a serving dish and keep warm.

6 Pour white wine into the roasting pan, place on top of the stove and bring to the boil. Scrape bottom of pan to release any juices stuck to it and let them dissolve. Stir in the Madeira or sherry, and a little gravy browning if liked to darken the sauce.

7 Remove from heat. Pour sauce into a bowl. Add the rest of the butter and whisk. Correct the seasoning.

8 Coat meat with the sauce. Put a few mushrooms on the top of the roast sirloin and serve the rest separately in a vegetable dish.

Serves 8

Boiled Brisket Polish-style

1 kg (2 lb) brisket of beef
3 onions
4 medium carrots
1 small cabbage
salt and pepper
1 bay leaf
peppercorns

Sauce

25 g (1 oz) (2 tablespoons) soft
   margarine
25 g (1 oz) (4 tablespoons) flour
salt and pepper
300 mL (½ pint) (1¼ cups) milk
15 mL (1 tablespoon) dry mustard
10 mL (2 teaspoons) sugar
15 mL (1 tablespoon) vinegar

1 Trim meat of excess fat. Leave onions whole and cut the carrots into quarters lengthways. Cut cabbage into quarters.

2 Place meat in pressure cooker with enough water to just cover, if possible, but don't fill the pan more than half-full when the meat and water have been added. Add seasoning, bay leaf and peppercorns and cook at 6.75 kg (15 lb) pressure for 20 minutes.

3 Reduce pressure with cold water and lift off the weights and cover. Skim liquid and add vegetables. Bring cooker up to pressure again and continue to cook for 5 minutes.

4 Reduce pressure and serve the joint whole or in overlapping slices. Arrange vegetables around the dish and pour over a spoonful of the stock. Keep warm.

5 Make the mustard sauce. Put margarine, flour, seasoning and milk in a saucepan and slowly bring to the boil, whisking continuously. Cook for 2–3 minutes.

6 Blend mustard, sugar and vinegar to a smooth cream and stir into sauce. Serve the sauce separately.

Serves 4

Beef from Burgundy

100 mL (4 fl oz) (½ cup) oil
1 kg (2 lb) silverside, cut into 2.5 cm
   (1 in) cubes
1 carrot, thinly sliced
1 large onion, thinly sliced
25 g (1 oz) (4 tablespoons) flour
500 mL (1 pint) (2½) cups dry red
   wine
salt and pepper
2 cloves garlic, peeled and crushed
1 bouquet garni
100 g (¼ lb) (1 cup) shallots (spring
   onions, scallions)
15 g (½ oz) (1 tablespoon) sugar
50 g (2 oz) (¼ cup) butter
100 g (¼ lb) bacon rashers, cut in
   strips
100 g (¼ lb) (1 cup) mushrooms,
   chopped

1 Heat three-quarters of the oil in a stewpan, put pieces of beef into it and brown over a high heat. Remove meat, pour out remaining oil and add slices of carrot and onion. Brown lightly, then add flour and cook it, stirring constantly with a wooden spoon.

2 Mix in the wine. Bring to the boil and allow at least a third of it to evaporate on a high heat. Return meat to pan and cover with cold water. Add salt, pepper, garlic and bouquet garni. Cover and cook gently for 2½ hours.

3 Put shallots in a pan with sugar, butter and enough water to cover. Cover and cook until the water has evaporated. When a golden caramel mixture remains, roll shallot bulbs in it and put to one side.

4 Heat the rest of the oil in a pan and fry bacon. Drain and reserve. Fry mushrooms in the same oil and reserve.

5 When stew is cooked, sieve sauce, then return it to pan. Add onions, bacon and mushrooms and cook for further 10 minutes.

Serves 6

Beef Italienne

Beef Italienne

675 g (1½ lb) piece fillet steak
4 strips bacon fat
75 mL (3 fl oz) (⅓ cup) oil
1 carrot, 1 onion and 2 celery sticks,
* sliced*

Gravy
150 mL (¼ pint) (⅔ cup) white wine
225 mL (8 fl oz) (1 cup) water
1 stock cube
bouquet garni
5 g (1 teaspoon) cornflour

1 Prepare fillet by removing the tough skin carefully with a knife to avoid damaging the meat. Lay bacon fat along fillet and secure with string, tied at intervals of 2.5 cm (1 in).

2 Preheat oven to 200°C (400°F).

3 Heat oil in a frying pan and brown meat for 8 minutes to seal.

4 Transfer meat to a roasting pan and add carrot, onion and celery.

5 Roast for 40 minutes. Remove from the oven and discard bacon fat, string and vegetables. Place on a serving dish and keep hot.

6 To the juices in the roasting pan, add wine, 150 mL (¼ pint) (⅔ cup) water, stock cube, and bouquet garni and simmer 15 minutes. Thicken with cornflour mixed with the remaining water. Boil for 3 minutes, season and strain.

Serves 6

Tip: As the photograph shows, Beef Italienne may be garnished in several ways.

With small strips of fresh noodle paste deep fried until crisp and golden and arranged in heaps around the dish.

With globe artichokes, boiled in water and lemon juice, after the outside leaves and hairy choke have been removed. The artichokes may be filled with a duxelles of ham, mushrooms, onion and breadcrumbs, sauteed for 5 minutes.

The dish may be decorated with a few button mushrooms, which have been scribed with the point of a knife blade, and then blanched in water with lemon juice or wine.

The garnishes should be prepared before the fillet is cooked.

Apollo Steaks

30 mL (2 tablespoons) oil
4 sirloin or rump steaks

Sauce

1 lamb's kidney, skinned, cored and
   sliced
25 g (1 oz) (2 tablespoons) butter or
   margarine
1 large onion, sliced
2 tomatoes, skinned, seeded and
   chopped
1 green capsicum (pepper), seeded
   and chopped
150 mL (¼ pint) (⅔ cup) red wine
150 mL (¼ pint) (⅔ cup) beef stock
salt and pepper
pinch oregano

1 Fry sauce ingredients, except wine, stock and seasonings, in a saucepan for 5 minutes until tender. Add wine and stock, and season with salt, pepper and oregano. Bring to the boil and simmer for 5 minutes to thicken.

2 Heat oil in a frying pan and fry steaks for 2–8 minutes or according to taste. Pour sauce over them and serve immediately. Serve with buttered new potatoes and a green or mixed salad.

Serves 4

Apollo Steaks

Steak Bordelaise

50 mL (2 fl oz) (¼ cup) oil
4 × 225 g (½ lb) sirloin steaks
1 onion, chopped
50 g (2 oz) (4 tablespoons) butter
300 mL (½ pint) (1¼ cups) red wine
150 mL (¼ pint) (⅔ cup) espagnole
    sauce
salt and pepper
25 g (1 oz) green peppercorns
15 mL (1 tablespoon) brandy

1 Heat oil in a saucepan and fry steaks on both sides until brown. Remove and keep warm.
2 In the same oil, fry onion until soft, then add butter to pan. Toss for a few minutes.
3 Add red wine to pan and boil until the liquid is reduced by half.
4 Add espagnole sauce and season with salt and pepper, then boil the sauce for 15 minutes. Stir in green peppercorns and brandy about 5 minutes before the sauce has finished cooking.
5 Pour sauce over the steaks to serve and garnish with button mushrooms, garden peas and sauted potatoes. Decorate with watercress.

Serves 4

Steak Chasseur

75 g (3 oz) (⅜ cup) butter
4 sirloin steaks, round-cut and each
    weighing about 225 g (½ lb)
sprigs watercress
5 g (1 tablespoon) finely chopped
    parsley and tarragon leaves

Chasseur Sauce
100 g (¼ lb) (1¼ cups) mushrooms,
    wiped and chopped
25 g (1 oz) (¼ cup) shallots (spring
    onions, scallions) or onions, peeled
    and finely chopped
100 mL (4 fl oz) (½ cup) dry white
    wine
300 mL (½ pint) (1¼ cups) Demi-glace
    Sauce (see recipe)
15 mL (1 tablespoon) tomato paste
salt and pepper

1 To make the Chasseur Sauce: heat 25 g (1 oz) (2 tablespoons) butter in a saute pan. Add mushrooms and shallots and soften but do not let them colour. Stir in wine and cook, uncovered, until liquid is reduced by half.
2 Stir in Demi-glace Sauce and tomato paste and simmer sauce for about 5 minutes to mellow flavours. Check seasoning — add salt and pepper as necessary.
3 Heat 50 g (2 oz) (4 tablespoons) butter in a frying pan. When hot, saute steaks for about 5–8 minutes on each side, according to how rare you like your steak. Season with salt and pepper to taste, then take out steaks and arrange on a hot serving platter. Pour sauce over the steaks, garnish with watercress, sprinkle with parsley and tarragon, and serve.

Serves 4

Steak a l'Orange

4 sirloin steaks, 2 cm (¾ in) thick
24 black peppercorns, crushed
rind 1 orange, cut in matchstick strips
15 mL (1 tablespoon) oil
150 mL (¼ pint) (⅔ cup) dry sherry
4 fresh mint leaves
150 mL (¼ pint) (⅔ cup) cream

Marinade
juice 2 oranges
2 cloves garlic, peeled and crushed
5 g (1 teaspoon) fresh root ginger,
    finely chopped
30 mL (2 tablespoons) soy sauce
50 mL (2 fl oz) (¼ cup) oil
30 mL (2 tablespoons) cider vinegar

1 Trim steaks and rub the crushed black peppercorns into them.
2 Thoroughly blend orange juice, garlic, soy sauce, oil, and vinegar to make a marinade. Soak the steaks for 20 minutes and then remove, reserving the marinade.
3 Meanwhile boil orange rind for 8 minutes. Drain and rinse strips in cold water and add to the leftover marinade.
4 Fry steaks in the oil until done to taste. Remove and keep warm. Pour marinade into pan and boil for 4 minutes to reduce. Add sherry and mint leaves and boil for 3 minutes; then stir in cream and boil 3 more minutes. Pour sauce over steaks and serve at once.

Serves 4

Glazed Steaks

6 × 175 g (6 oz) beef steaks
300 mL (½ pint) (1¼ cups) flat light
    beer
bouquet garni
½ chilli, chopped
6 black peppercorns
100 g (¼ lb) (½ cup) softened butter
45 g (3 oz) (6 tablespoons) onion,
    chopped
5 mL (1 teaspoon) chopped parsley
10 mL (2 teaspoons) Worcestershire
    sauce

1 Beat steaks with a meat mallet until doubled in size. Place in earthenware dish and add beer. Tie bouquet garni, chilli and peppercorns in a piece of muslin and add to the steaks. Soak overnight.
2 Lift steaks from marinade and wipe dry. Strain marinade.
3 Mix 75 g (3 oz) (6 tablespoons) butter with onion, parsley and Worcestershire sauce. Spread mixture over the steaks. Heat the rest of the butter in a frying pan and fry the steaks on both sides until cooked to taste. Place steaks on a heated serving dish.
4 Pour fat from pan, reserving the meat juices. Add the strained marinade and boil quickly to reduce to a glaze. Pour glaze over the steaks and serve.

Serves 6

Brandy Steak with Mandarin Rice

175 g (6 oz) (¾ cup) long grain rice
salt and pepper
25 g (1 oz) (2 tablespoons) butter
300 g (11 oz) canned mandarin
  oranges
4 fillet steaks, 150 g (5 oz) each, 4 cm
  (1½ in) thick
4 rashers bacon, blanched
25 g (1 oz) (2 tablespoons) butter
30 mL (2 tablespoons) oil
60 mL (4 tablespoons) brandy
100 mL (4 fl oz) (½ cup) cream

1 Wash rice and cook in boiling salted water for 20 minutes. Drain, and stir in butter. Season and keep warm.

2 Meanwhile, heat the mandarin oranges in their syrup and drain. Keep the juice. Add oranges to rice and keep warm.

3 Season steaks, and tie a rasher of bacon around each. Heat butter and oil in a frying pan, and shallow fry the steaks for 2-3 minutes on each side if you like them rare. Cook for longer if you prefer. If you want the steaks well done, put a lid on.

4 Pour brandy into frying pan and flame steaks. Remove steaks, discard bacon, and put them on a dish and keep warm.

5 Pour cream into frying pan, mix with the meat and juices, and boil for 2 minutes to make a smooth sauce. Remove from the heat, add 1 tablespoon of the mandarin juice and pour over the steaks. Serve at once with the mandarin rice, and a green salad.

Serves 4

Brandy Steak with Mandarin Rice

Steak Diane

675 g (1½ lb) rump or fillet steak
25 g (1 oz) (2 tablespoons) butter
30 mL (1 fl oz) (2 tablespoons) oil
1 onion, chopped
15 mL (1 tablespoon) soy sauce
5 mL (1 teaspoon) Worcestershire
  sauce
salt
freshly ground black pepper
juice 1 lemon
70 mL (2½ fl oz) (⅓ cup) brandy
15 mL (1 tablespoon) chopped
  parsley

1 Cut each piece of steak in half with a sharp kitchen knife. Beat steaks with a meat mallet until they resemble thin escalopes.

2 Melt butter and oil in a frypan. You can do this in the kitchen on top of the cooker or over a spirit burner at the table in front of your guests.

3 Add chopped onion and saute until soft, then remove from pan. Add steaks and fry according to taste.

4 Return onions to the pan and add soy sauce and Worcestershire sauce. Season with salt and freshly ground black pepper.

5 Stir in lemon juice and add brandy. For your piece de resistance, set the brandy alight. Do not let it burn too long or you will lose some of the flavour. Extinguish flames by covering pan with a lid.

6 Sprinkle with chopped parsley and serve immediately with a green salad, asparagus tips or celery.

Serves 4

Steak au Poivre Vert

4 sirloin steaks, 1 cm (½ in) thick
50 mL (2 fl oz) (¼ cup) oil
50 g (2 oz) (4 tablespoons) butter
45 mL (3 tablespoons) brandy
100 mL (4 fl oz) (½ cup) dry sherry or
*   dry Madeira wine*
1 medium onion, chopped
25 g (1 oz) (2 tablespoons) green
*   peppercorns, canned*
30 mL (2 tablespoons) soy sauce
5 mL (1 teaspoon) vinegar
150 mL (¼ pint) (⅔ cup) cream
pinch paprika
5 g (1 tablespoon) chopped fresh
*   parsley*

1 Trim steaks of any excess fat and sinew. Brush with a little oil and season very lightly with salt.

2 Heat the rest of the oil and butter in a frying pan and quickly fry steaks on both sides to sear the flesh, for about 2 minutes. Pour in brandy and set it alight. Almost immediately pour in sherry or Madeira to put out the brandy flames. Remove steaks and keep warm while cooking the sauce.

3 To the mixture in the pan add onion, peppercorns, soy sauce and vinegar. Boil for 4 minutes. Add cream and paprika and boil briskly for another minute.

4 Return steaks to the sauce to reheat for a minute on each side. Serve immediately, garnished with chopped parsley.

Serves 4

Tips: Green peppercorns are the fresh berries of the spice more commonly used in its dried form as black or white ground pepper. They are usually only available in canned form, and have a mild and aromatic flavour.

The given cooking times for the sirloin steak are designed for a rare-cooked steak of 1 cm (½ in) thickness. Thicker steaks should be fried for twice the given length of time, or beaten with a rolling pin or meat mallet to the given thickness. For a medium-cooked steak, fry for 4 minutes. For a well-cooked steak, cover the pan while frying for 4 or 5 minutes.

Steak au Poivre Vert

Sirloin with Peppercorns and Garlic

4 x 350 g (¾ lb) sirloin steaks, 2.5 cm
*   (1 in) thick*
12 black peppercorns
4 cloves garlic, thinly sliced
75 mL (2½ fl oz) (⅓ cup) oil
salt

1 Trim fat from steaks. Crush peppercorns, using a rolling pin, and then sprinkle over both sides of the steaks, pressing well into the meat.

2 Make several slits in the surface of the steaks and insert slices of garlic into the slits. Brush steaks with oil and then cook them under a grill, over a charcoal fire, or in a frying pan. Cook for 2 minutes on both sides for underdone meat, 4 minutes for medium or 8 minutes for well done.

3 Season with salt and serve with French fries and a pat of garlic butter.

Serves 4

Steak Manzanilla

2 rump steaks, about 225 g (½ lb)
    each
30 mL (2 tablespoons) oil
pepper
2 slices Cheddar cheese, ½ cm (⅛ in)
    thick
pinch paprika
4 anchovy fillets
2 stuffed green olives, sliced

1 Brush steaks with oil and season
with plenty of freshly ground black
pepper. Grill steaks under high heat
for 3–4 minutes on each side according to taste.

2 Place a slice of cheese on each
steak, sprinkle with paprika and grill
until cheese is melted and just starting to brown.
3 Place steaks on a warmed serving
dish. Decorate each steak with a
cross of anchovy fillets, and slices of
stuffed olive. Serve immediately.

Serves 2

Steak Manzanilla

Steak Mignonette

4 slices of 150 g (5 oz) fillet steak, cut
    from the thin end
1 medium onion
25 g (1 oz) (2 tablespoons) butter
4 mushrooms
150 mL (¼ pint) (⅔ cup) port
25 g (1 oz) (2 tablespoons) tomato
    paste
pinch thyme
pinch cinnamon
75 mL (2½ fl oz) (⅓ cup) sour cream
salt and pepper
25 mL (1 fl oz) (⅛ cup) oil
8 stuffed olives, sliced

1 Flatten steaks to 12.5 × 5 cm (5 ×
2½ in).
2 Chop onion and fry gently in butter for 4 minutes until tender without
colouring. Chop mushrooms to the
pan and cook for 1 minute. Add port,
tomato paste, thyme and cinnamon.
Boil for 5 minutes. Stir in the cream,
season and put aside. Keep warm.
3 Heat oil in a frying pan. Quickly
cook the steaks for 1 minute on each
side.
4 Put in a dish, pour half of the sauce
over the steaks and sprinkle with
sliced stuffed olives. Serve remainder
of the sauce separately. Serve garnished with braised chicory (endive).

Serves 4

Spiced Sirloin Sandringham

1 kg (2 lb) boned sirloin
salt and pepper
50 mL (2 fl oz) (¼ cup) oil
4 chicory (Belgian endive) leaves
24 asparagus spears, cooked
2 slices red capsicum (pepper)

Glaze
100 g (¼ lb) (⅓ cup) redcurrant jelly
15 mL (1 tablespoon) vinegar
juice 1 orange
5 mL (1 teaspoon) ground ginger
garlic salt
5 mL (1 teaspoon) allspice

1 Preheat oven to 200°C (400°F).
Season meat and rub with oil. Roast
for 45 minutes, then cool.

2 Slice beef and arrange slices in
overlapping layers on a large shallow
dish.

3 Boil ingredients for the glaze 4 minutes, stirring continuously. Brush
cooled slices of meat 3 times with the
glaze and leave to set.

4 Cut each chicory leaf in two and
place 3 asparagus spears in the hollow of each half. Cut red capsicum
into 8 equal strips and place them
over each asparagus basket. Chill and
serve garnished with watercress.

Serves 6–8

Braised Steak Bacchus

4 × 225 g (½ lb) topside steaks
50 mL (2 fl oz) (¼ cup) oil
1 bay leaf
300 mL (½ pint) (1¼ cups) water
1 beef stock cube
salt and pepper
25 g (1 oz) (2 tablespoons) tomato
    paste
15 mL (1 tablespoon) butter
30 mL (2 tablespoons) flour

Marinade
300 mL (½ pint) (1¼ cups) dry red
    wine
1 onion, sliced
1 carrot, sliced
1 stick celery, sliced
1 bay leaf
sprig thyme
1 clove garlic, crushed
6 black peppercorns
5 mL (1 teaspoon) salt
pinch allspice
30 mL (1 fl oz) (2 tablespoons) oil
5 mL (1 teaspoon) honey

Garnish
50 mL (2 fl oz) (¼ cup) oil
150 g (5 oz) shallots (spring onions,
    scallions)
100 mL (4 fl oz) (½ cup) red wine
150 g (5 oz) (2 cups) button
    mushrooms
15 mL (1 tablespoon) chopped
    parsley

1 Mix marinade ingredients and
marinate steaks 3–4 hours.

2 Remove meat and vegetables and
reserve the marinade.

3 Heat oil and saute steaks for about
6 minutes until brown on both sides.
Remove and place in a shallow
ovenproof dish.

4 Preheat oven to 180°C (350°F).

5 Gently fry onion, carrot and celery
from the marinade in the oil until
soft. Place on top of the steaks with
bay leaf and water. Crumble in stock
cube and season with salt and pepper. Stir in reserved wine marinade,
cover and braise in the oven for 1½
hours.

6 Remove steaks and keep warm.
Pour braising liquid into a saucepan
and stir in tomato paste. Boil 5 minutes.

7 Meanwhile, make a roux by melt-
ing the butter in a pan and stirring in
the flour. Cook 2 minutes, then
whisk it, a little at a time, into the
sauce. When sauce thickens, check
seasoning.

8 Meanwhile, prepare the garnish.
Heat oil in a pan and brown shallot
bulbs, cover with red wine and boil
for 5 minutes. Add mushrooms and
boil a further minute.

9 Pour sauce over the steaks, drain
onions and mushrooms and arrange
around sides. Sprinkle with chopped
parsley and serve with triangles of
fried bread and saffron rice.

Serves 4

Beef Ceres

1 kg (2 lb) beef topside
25 g (1 oz) (4 tablespoons) flour
salt and pepper
1 large or 2 medium onions
2 large carrots
2 green capsicums (peppers)
2 cloves garlic
450 g (1 lb) tomatoes
30 mL (1 fl oz) (2 tablespoons) oil
300 mL (½ pint) (1¼ cups) flat light
    beer
300 mL (½ pint) (1¼ cups) meat stock
15 mL (1 tablespoon) malt vinegar
pinch each powdered mace, paprika
    and dried marjoram
15 mL (1 tablespoon) chopped fresh
    parsley
15 mL (1 tablespoon) tomato paste
50 g (2 oz) (½ cup) grated cheese
    (optional)

1 Cut beef into 6 steaks and beat
with a meat mallet to tenderise. Coat
in seasoned flour.

2 Prepare vegetables: slice or
roughly chop onions, slice the carrots, seed and slice capsicum, and
finely chop the garlic. Peel and quarter tomatoes.

3 Fry steaks in oil for a few minutes
on each side to lightly brown.
Arrange in an ovenproof dish. Preheat oven to 180°C (350°F).

4 Fry onions, garlic and carrot in the
rest of the oil for 5 minutes to soften.
Arrange round meat. Arrange capsicum slices and tomatoes over meat.

5 Bring beer (left to stand for ½ hour
to become flat), stock and vinegar to
boil in a pan. Add spices, herbs, and
tomato paste. Simmer 5 minutes.
Pour over meat, cover and bake 1½–2
hours, until meat is tender.

6 For extra flavour, sprinkle cheese
over the dish before cooking; or to
make a golden cheesy crust, sprinkle
on cheese 5 minutes before serving
and melt it under a hot grill. Serve at
once.

Serves 6

Spiced Sirloin Sandringham

Beef Ceres Step-by-step

1 The ingredients: beef topside, beer, tomatoes, onion, garlic, green capsicum, carrots, stock, tomato paste, cheese, flour and seasonings.

2 Cut the beef into 6 steaks and beat them.

3 Coat the steaks in seasoned flour.

4 Slice the onions, carrots and capsicum. Chop the garlic, skin and quarter the tomatoes.

5 Fry the steaks in oil until lightly browned. Arrange them in an ovenproof dish.

6

7

8

9

6 Fry the onion, garlic and carrot for 5 minutes and arrange around the meat. Arrange capsicum slices and the tomatoes over the meat.

7 Mix the beer and the stock with the vinegar and bring to the boil. Season with mace, paprika, marjoram and parsley. Stir in tomato paste and simmer for 5 minutes.

8 Pour over meat until nearly covered. Cover and braise in oven until tender.

9 Sprinkle over cheese 5 minutes before serving and brown under the grill.

Tournedos with Anchovy Butter

Tournedos with Anchovy Butter

6 rashers bacon, blanched
6 tournedos steaks, 150 g (5 oz) each
   4 cm (1½ in) thick
salt and freshly ground pepper
oil for frying steaks
6 green olives
6 anchovy fillets
25 mL (2 tablespoons) tomato sauce

Anchovy Butter
100 g (¼ lb) (½ cup) butter
5 g (1 tablespoon) chopped parsley
juice ½ lemon
4 anchovy fillets, finely chopped

Croutons
6 slices bread
25 g (1 oz) (2 tablespoons) butter
25 mL (1 fl oz) (⅛ cup) oil

1 Prepare anchovy butter by creaming the butter with parsley, lemon juice and anchovy fillets to form a paste. Roll paste into a cylinder, wrap in greaseproof paper, and chill for 1 hour.

2 Make croutons by cutting six bread circles using a plain cutter of 6.5 cm (2½ in). Put the butter and oil in a frying pan and fry bread on both sides until golden. Place croutons on a dish and keep warm.

3 Tie a rasher of bacon round each steak and season. Heat some oil in the frying pan and fry steaks for 4–10 minutes, depending on whether you want the steaks rare, medium or well-done. If preferred, brush the steaks with oil, and grill. Place on the croutons.

4 When ready to serve, cut slices off the roll of anchovy butter and place one on each steak. Place a green olive on each, surrounded by an anchovy fillet, and trickle a little tomato sauce round as decoration. Serve at once with Pommes Allumettes (thin chips) as illustrated.

Serves 6

Beef Olives with Ham

4 thin slices braising steak, 150 g
  (5 oz) each, from leg or shoulder
4 thin slices cooked ham
1 small onion, chopped
1 clove garlic, chopped
few sage leaves, chopped
10 g (2 tablespoons) chopped parsley
salt and pepper
110 g (4½ oz) (8 tablespoons) butter
100 mL (4 fl oz) (½ cup) oil
1 onion, coarsely chopped
1 carrot, coarsely chopped
7 g (1 tablespoon) flour
150 mL (¼ pint) (⅔ cup) red wine
300 mL (½ pint) (1¼ cups) brown stock
10 g (1 tablespoon) capers
150 g (5 oz) (⅔ cup) long grain rice
225 g (½ lb) (2 cups) shallots (spring
  onions, scallions)
225 g (½ lb) (4 cups) button
  mushrooms

1 Preheat oven to 180°C (350°F).

2 Beat steaks until very thin. Place a slice of ham on each steak. Mix together chopped onion, garlic, sage and half the parsley and divide mixture between the steaks. Sprinkle with salt and pepper.

3 Roll up steaks tightly and secure with string or wooden cocktail sticks.

4 Heat 35 g (1¼ oz) (2½ tablespoons) butter and half the oil in a pan, add meat and fry briskly for 5 minutes.

5 Transfer meat to a casserole dish. Add chopped vegetables to the pan, and fry gently, covered, for about 8 minutes or until soft. Sprinkle in flour and cook for 1-2 minutes or until brown. Stir in wine and stock and bring to the boil. Pour contents of the pan over the meat, add capers and season to taste. Cover dish and bake for 1¼ hours.

6 Meanwhile, prepare the garnish. Boil rice in salted water for 18 minutes, drain and blend in 50 g (2 oz) (4 tablespoons) butter and salt and pepper. Heat the rest of the oil and butter in a pan and saute shallot bulbs for 3 minutes until brown. Add mushrooms and cook for 1 minute. Cover the vegetables with water and boil for 6 minutes. Drain.

7 When meat is cooked, arrange rice on a warmed serving dish, place meat on top and garnish with mushrooms, onions and the rest of the parsley.   *Serves 4*

Beef Olives with Ham

Beef Casserole

¼ kg (½ lb) (1 cup) canned chick peas, or half that quantity of dried chick peas
1 kg (2 lb) braising or stewing beef, eg chuck steak
50 mL (2 fl oz) (¼ cup) oil
5 g (1 teaspoon) paprika
4 cloves garlic, peeled and crushed
2 onions, chopped
25 g (1 oz) (2 tablespoons) tomato paste
1½ litres (2½ pints) (6 cups) water
4 medium eggplants (aubergines)
salt and pepper
oil for deep frying

1 If using dried chick peas, soak overnight in water.
2 Cut steak into 4 cm (1½ in) pieces. Heat oil in a large pan, and brown meat and paprika for 5–10 minutes, stirring occasionally.
3 Strain off excess oil. Add the drained chick peas, garlic, onions, tomato paste and water. Bring to the boil, cover and simmer gently for 2–2½ hours.
4 Meanwhile slice eggplants (aubergines), place on a dish or wooden board and sprinkle liberally with salt. Leave 30 minutes, then rinse and dry the slices.
5 Heat oil in a deep fat fryer to 185°C (360°F). Deep fry eggplant slices until golden-brown. Drain on absorbent paper.
6 Add eggplant slices to beef casserole, and season to taste with salt and pepper. Simmer 30 minutes. Serve in a heated serving dish.

Serves 6

Tip: Like many other dishes originating in North Africa and the Middle East, this casserole should contain plenty of richly-flavoured liquid which may be eaten with a spoon, like a soup.
If you are using canned chick peas, add these to the pan with the eggplant (aubergine).

Spanish Braised Beef

50 g (2 oz) (¼ cup) butter
15 mL (1 tablespoon) oil
2 onions, chopped
450 g (1 lb) stewing steak, cubed
25 g (1 oz) (4 tablespoons) flour
300 mL (½ pint) (1¼ cups) stock
30 mL (2 tablespoons) tomato paste
150 mL (¼ pint) (⅔ cup) red wine
salt and pepper
4 zucchini (courgettes), sliced
225 g (½ lb) French beans
2 potatoes, parboiled and cubed

1 Heat butter and oil in a fry-pan at 170°C (325°F) and fry onions until soft and browned. Add stewing steak and brown all over. Stir in flour and cook for 2–3 minutes. Add stock, tomato paste and red wine and bring to the boil, stirring all the time.
2 Season with salt and pepper and reduce the heat to 110°C (225°F). Cover with the lid and simmer gently for about 1 hour. Add the zucchini, French beans and parboiled potatoes and cook for a further 20 minutes until meat and vegetables are tender.

Serves 4

Quick Chicken and Beef Casserole

300 mL (½ pint) (1¼ cups) Bechamel Sauce (see recipe)
50 mL (2 fl oz) (¼ cup) dry sherry
salt and pepper
100 g (¼ lb) (⅔ cup) cooked beef, cut into strips
1 gherkin, sliced
100 g (¼ lb) (⅔ cup) cooked chicken, diced
50 g (2 oz) (⅔ cup) sliced mushrooms
100 g (¼ lb) (⅔ cup) ham, cut into strips
50 g (2 oz) (½ cup) flaked almonds

1 Heat white sauce, stir in sherry and season with salt and pepper.
2 Preheat oven to 180°C (350°F).

3 Place beef and gherkin in the bottom of an ovenproof dish. Pour on half the sauce. Put a layer of chicken, mushrooms and 75 g (3 oz) (½ cup) ham on top. Pour over the remaining white sauce and sprinkle with almonds and ham strips.
4 Place in oven and warm through for 15 minutes.

Serves 4

Austrian Beef Casserole with Horseradish Sauce

1 kg (2 lb) stewing beef
50 mL (2 fl oz) (¼ cup) oil
6 small onions
1½ litres (3 pints) (7½ cups) water
3 beef stock cubes
bouquet garni
6 leeks

Horseradish Sauce
150 mL (¼ pint) (⅔ cup) water
25 mL (1 fl oz) (⅛ cup) white vinegar
150 g (6 oz) horseradish, scraped
150 g (6 oz) cooking apples, peeled and cored
25 g (1 oz) (½ cup) fresh white breadcrumbs
50 mL (2 fl oz) (¼ cup) cream

1 Cut meat into 4 cm (1½ in) cubes.
2 Heat oil in a heavy pan and brown the meat, covered, for 8 minutes. Stir often.
3 Slice onions, add to the meat, and brown for 3 minutes.
4 Cover with water mixed with beef cubes and bouquet garni.
5 Wash leeks, split into 4, tie in a bundle and put with the meat.
6 Bring to the boil, and remove the scum as it rises with a spoon. Simmer 2–2½ hours until meat is tender.
7 Meanwhile, put water and vinegar in a bowl and grate horseradish and apple into it. Soak 1 hour. Drain liquid off, and mix breadcrumbs and cream into the mixture.
8 When meat is cooked, the broth may be strained off and served separately as soup. Remove leeks, discard the string, and place on top of the meat. Serve with sauce.

Serves 6

Austrian Beef Casserole

Beef Stroganoff

1 kg (2 lb) fillet steak
25 g (1 oz) (2 tablespoons) butter
1 large onion, halved and sliced
225 g (½ lb) button mushrooms,
    quartered
salt and pepper
150 mL (¼ pint) (⅔ cup) dry white
    wine
300 mL (½ pint) (1¼ cups) thickened
    cream, whipped
pinch cayenne pepper
juice ½ lemon
15 mL (1 tablespoon) snipped chives

1 Cut beef into slices and flatten
with a meat mallet. Cut slices into
strips.
2 Melt butter in a frying pan and fry
onion gently until soft but not
brown. Increase heat, add strips of
beef and fry briskly for 3 minutes.
3 Quickly stir in mushrooms and fry
for 1 minute.
4 Season to taste, stir in wine, cream
and cayenne and cook for 1 minute
to heat through. Remove from heat
and add lemon juice.
5 Turn onto a heated serving dish,
sprinkle with snipped chives and
serve immediately with freshly
boiled rice.

Serves 6

Tip: The strips of beef in this recipe
are cooked for a very short time and
the finished dish served immediately
to ensure that the beef is rare. You
can cook your Stroganoff at the table
in front of your guests if you have a
suitable table-top burner.

Beef Espana

450 g (1 lb) boiled beef

Sauce
30 mL (1 fl oz) (2 tablespoons) oil
1 medium onion, chopped
15 g (½ oz) (2 tablespoons) flour
25 g (1 oz) (2 tablespoons) tomato
    paste
1 clove garlic, peeled and crushed
300 mL (½ pint) (1¼ cups) water
1 beef stock cube
60 mL (2 fl oz) (¼ cup) medium
    sherry
salt and pepper
12 green olives, stuffed
sprig rosemary

Beef Espana

1 Preheat oven to 200°C (400°F).
2 Slice boiled beef thickly and place
in an ovenproof dish.
3 To make sauce, heat oil in a frying
pan and fry onion lightly for 5 minutes, until tender and slightly brown.
Stir in flour and cook for 1 minute.
Stir in tomato paste and garlic and
pour in water. Crumble in the stock
cube and bring to the boil. Add
sherry and simmer 15 minutes. Pass
sauce through a sieve.
4 Season to taste. Scatter olives over
beef, pour on the sauce and bake 20
minutes. Garnish with a sprig of rosemary and serve hot.

Serves 4

Tip: You can replace the olives with
gherkins or capers.

Prussian Beef Casserole

1 kg (2 lb) stewing beef, cut into
    cubes
50 g (2 oz) (½ cup) seasoned flour
50 g (2 oz) (¼ cup) butter
30 mL (1 fl oz) (2 tablespoons) oil
225 g (½ lb) baby carrots, peeled
225 g (½ lb) shallots (spring onions,
    scallions), peeled
2 cloves garlic, crushed
½ head celery, chopped
300 mL (½ pint) (1¼ cups) beef stock
150 mL (¼ pint) (⅔ cup) red wine
15 mL (1 tablespoon) mixed herbs
5 mL (1 teaspoon) chopped parsley

1 Preheat oven to 180°C (350°F). Roll meat in seasoned flour. Heat butter and oil in a large frying pan, add meat and brown on all sides. Reserve remaining flour. Transfer browned meat to an ovenproof casserole.

2 Add carrots, shallots and garlic to the pan and brown slightly. Transfer to casserole with chopped celery.

3 Add enough of the reserved seasoned flour to the oil in the pan to make a paste, and stir over a gentle heat for 1 minute. Greadually stir in stock, red wine and mixed herbs and cook gently, stirring continually, until the sauce thickens. Check seasoning and pour over the meat in the casserole.

4 Cover and cook casserole in oven for 1–1½ hours or until meat is tender. Garnish with chopped parsley and serve with a dish of new potatoes and a crisp green salad.

Serves 4

Prussian Beef Casserole

Country Beef and Olive Casserole

675 g (1½ lb) stewing beef
30 mL (2 tablespoons) oil
3 carrots, sliced
2 small onions, quartered
1 stick celery, sliced
1 clove garlic, peeled and crushed
25 g (1 oz) (4 tablespoons) flour
300 mL (½ pint) (1¼ cups) water
150 mL (¼ pint) (⅔ cup) sherry
450 g (1 lb) (1¾ cups) canned
   tomatoes
1 beef stock cube
1 bay leaf
few sprigs parsley
salt and pepper
6 stuffed green olives, sliced

1 Cut beef into 4 cm (1½ in) cubes.
2 Preheat oven to 180°C (350°F).
3 Heat oil in a saucepan and fry meat until browned. Remove from pan.
4 Add carrots, onions, celery and garlic to the pan. Fry over a low heat for 5 minutes.

5 Stir in flour and cook gently for a few minutes, then add water, sherry and canned tomatoes. Crumble in the stock cube and stir well. Add bay leaf and parsley and season with salt and pepper.

6 Bring to the boil, stirring until it thickens. Transfer to an ovenproof dish, cover and bake for 2½ hours. Remove bay leaf and parsley. Stir in olives and serve with French beans and boiled potatoes.

Serves 4

Beef Goulash

75 mL (2½ fl oz) (⅓ cup) oil
3 medium onions, thinly sliced
675 g (1½ lb) stewing beef, eg chuck
   steak, cut in 3 cm (1 in) cubes
15 g (½ oz) (1 tablespoon) paprika
good pinch cumin
2 cloves garlic, crushed
salt and pepper
pinch marjoram
3 tomatoes, skinned, seeded and
   chopped
1 green capsicum (pepper), shredded
150 mL (¼ pint) (⅔ cup) red wine
1 litre (1¾ pints) (4½ cups) water
2 beef stock cubes
675 g (1½ lb) potatoes, peeled
25 g (1 oz) (3 tablespoons) cornflour
150 mL (¼ pint) (⅔ cup) sour cream

1 Heat oil in a pan and fry onion for 4 minutes until pale brown. Add meat, reduce heat and cook gently for 8 minutes, stirring from time to time.

2 Add paprika, cumin, garlic, seasoning and marjoram and cook for 1 minute. Add tomatoes and capsicum and simmer 10 minutes. Stir in wine and water and crumble in the stock cubes. Cook gently for 1½ hours.

3 Towards the end of cooking time, boil potatoes in salted water for 18 minutes.

4 When ready to serve, mix the cornflour in 150 mL (¼ pint) (⅔ cup) water, stir into meat and cook 2–3 minutes until thickened.

5 Serve goulash with sour cream and boiled potatoes.

Serves 6

Tip: Shell pasta or rice can be served with this dish in place of boiled potatoes, if preferred.

Beef Goulash Step-by-step

1 Collect all ingredients.
2 Peel the onions and slice finely.
3 Cut the meat into 3 cm (1 in) cubes.
4 Fry onion in oil 4 minutes until pale brown.

5 Add the cubed meat, reduce heat and cook gently for 8 minutes, stirring from time to time.
6 While meat is cooking, deseed capsicum and shred flesh.

7 Add the paprika, cumin, garlic, seasoning and marjoram to the pan and cook for 1 minute.
8 Add tomatoes and capsicum. Cook 10 minutes.
9 Stir in the wine and water and crumble in the beef stock cubes. Cook gently for 1½ hours.
10 Boil the potatoes.
11 Thick goulash, add lemon juice to cream.
12 Serve with sour cream and potatoes.

Carbonnade de Boeuf

1½ kg (3 lb) lean blade of beef
85 mL (3 fl oz) (⅓ cup) oil
3 onions, sliced
3 cloves garlic, crushed
pinch nutmeg
salt and pepper
30 mL (2 tablespoons) flour
300 mL (¼ pint) (1¼ cups) beef stock
400 mL (14 fl oz) (1¾ cups) stout
15 mL (1 tablespoon) malt vinegar
bouquet garni
15 mL (1 tablespoon) sugar

Savoury Crust
1 French stick
100 g (¼ lb) (½ cup) butter
1 clove garlic, crushed
15 mL (1 tablespoon) Dijon mustard

1 Cut beef into 1 cm (½ in) slices, about 7.5 cm (3 in) long and 4 cm (1½ in) wide. Preheat oven to 190°C (375°F).

2 Heat oil in a frying pan and, when it begins to sizzle, add meat. Brown meat on all sides for 3–4 minutes. Remove from pan and drain on absorbent paper.

3 Reduce heat and add onions to pan. Gently fry until golden, but do not allow to burn. Add garlic, nutmeg and seasoning to pan and sprinkle in the flour. Cook for 2 minutes. Pour in stock, stout and vinegar. Stir until sauce comes to the boil.

4 Place meat in an ovenproof casserole. Pour over the sauce and add the bouquet garni. Cover and bake for 2¼ hours.

5 Cut the French stick into 1 cm (½ in) slices. In a bowl blend butter, garlic and mustard. Spread thickly over 1 side of each slice of bread.

6 When Carbonnade is cooked, remove bouquet garni and stir in sugar. Check seasoning. Cover top with the slices of bread, buttered side upwards. Push bread below the surface so that it is well soaked in the gravy. Return casserole to oven and cook uncovered for 30 minutes, so that bread is crisp and golden. Serve straight from the casserole.

Serves 6–8

Ragout de Boeuf a l'Orange

30 mL (2 tablespoons) oil or bacon fat
675 g (1½ lb) stewing steak, cubed
12 shallots (spring onions, scallions)
15 mL (1 tablespoon) flour
100 mL (4 fl oz) (½ cup) red wine
bouquet garni
1 clove garlic, crushed
550 mL (1 pint) (2½ cups) stock
salt and pepper
5 sticks celery, sliced
50 g (2 oz) (⅓ cup) walnuts
25 g (1 oz) (2 tablespoons) butter
30 mL (2 tablespoons) shredded orange rind, blanched

1 Heat oil or fat and fry meat until well browned. Remove and keep warm. In the same pan, cook onions gently until golden-brown. Stir in flour and cook over a low heat for 2–3 minutes.

2 Add wine, bouquet garni, garlic and stock and bring to the boil. Season to taste, stir in the meat and reduce heat. Cover and cook for 1½–2 hours gently, stirring occasionally.

3 Fry celery and walnuts in butter and add to the ragout. Serve at once, garnished with the orange shreds.

Serves 4

Beef Nicoise

1 kg (2 lb) stewing beef
100 g (¼ lb) bacon
50 mL (2 fl oz) (¼ cup) oil
4 onions, sliced
2 cloves garlic, peeled and crushed
bouquet garni
25 g (1 oz) (4 tablespoons) flour
300 mL (½ pint) (1¼ cups) wine
300 mL (½ pint) (1¼ cups) water
1 beef stock cube
25 g (1 oz) (2 tablespoons) tomato paste
6 tomatoes, skinned, seeded and chopped
salt and pepper
6 black olives

1 Cut meat into 2.5 cm (1 in) cubes and bacon into small cubes, 5 mm (¼ in), or, if in rashers, into strips.

2 Heat oil in a thick pan. Brown beef and bacon for 8 minutes, covered. Stir often.

3 Add onion, garlic and bouquet garni, cook for 4 minutes, sprinkle on the flour and cook for 1 minute.

4 Add wine, water, stock cube, tomato paste and chopped tomatoes. Season. Bring to the boil and simmer for 1½–2 hours until meat is tender, or cook in the oven with a lid on at 180°C (350°F) for the same time.

5 When ready to serve, add the olives.

Serves 6

Beef Nicoise

Old English Steak and Kidney Pudding

Suet Pastry
225 g (½ lb) (2 cups) self-raising flour
pinch salt
100 g (¼ lb) (1 cup) beef suet,
  shredded.

Filling
1 large onion
175 g (6 oz) ox kidney
450 g (1 lb) best stewing steak
25 g (1 oz) (2 tablespoons) seasoned
  flour
45 mL (1½ fl oz) (3 tablespoons) beef
  stock

1 To make pastry, sift flour into a mixing bowl with the salt. Mix in suet. Add cold water to form dough.
2 Roll out on a floured board in a circle 25 cm (10 in) in diameter. Cut away one-quarter of the circle and set aside for the lid.
3 Grease a 1 litre (1¾ pint) (4 cup) pudding basin and line it with the dough, allowing a small overlap around the top. Leave to rest in a cool place.
4 Chop onion finely. Remove skin and core from the kidney and slice it. Cut the steak into strips about 12.5 cm (5 in) long. Place a slice of kidney on each and roll up. Dip rolls in seasoned flour and place them in layers in the pudding basin, alternating with layers of chopped onion, until basin is filled. Pour on stock.
5 Roll out the dough reserved for the lid. Dampen edges of the pastry, put on the lid and press edges well together. Grease a large sheet of greaseproof paper and make a pleat in the middle to allow the pudding room to rise. Tie the paper onto the pudding basin with kitchen string and steam in a double saucepan or over a pan of boiling water for 3½ hours. Serve hot.

Serves 6

Tips: To save time, the Steak and Kidney Pudding can be cooked in a pressure cooker. First cook steak, kidney and onion mixture in stock for 15 minutes at high pressure. Then make pastry. Line and fill the pudding basin as described in the recipe. Then follow your manufacturer's instructions pressure.

Hotpot Parisienne

225 g (½ lb) butter or lima beans
675 g (1½ lb) stewing beef, cut into
  2.5 cm (1 in) cubes
50 mL (2 fl oz) (¼ cup) oil
2 onions, chopped
1 clove garlic, crushed
15 g (½ oz) (2 tablespoons) flour
15 g (½ oz) (1 tablespoon) tomato
  paste
300 mL (½ pint) (1¼ cups) water
150 mL (¼ pint) (⅔ cup) white wine
bouquet garni
sprig rosemary
salt and pepper
2 zucchini (courgettes), sliced
4 tomatoes, quartered

1 If using dried beans, soak overnight in water, then bring to boil and simmer until tender. Rinse and drain.
2 Preheat oven to 180°C (350°F). Brown meat in oil for 5 minutes in a saucepan. Add onion and garlic and cook for 2 minutes. Sprinkle in flour and cook for 2 minutes to brown. Stir in tomato paste and pour in water and wine. Season with bouquet garni, rosemary, salt and pepper. Bring to the boil and simmer for 10 minutes.
3 Transfer mixture to an earthenware pot. Add beans, cover, and bake for 1½–2 hours.
4 Remove hotpot from oven, add zucchini and tomatoes, and return to the oven for 15 minutes. Check seasoning, and serve hot.

Serves 6

Pasta Shepherds Pie

30 mL (2 tablespoons) oil
1 onion, peeled and sliced
450 g (1 lb) minced beef
1 clove garlic, crushed
400 g (14 oz) (1½ cups) canned
  tomatoes
15 mL (1 tablespoon) tomato paste
5 mL (1 teaspoon) mixed herbs
salt and pepper
175 g (6 oz) (2 cups) raw macaroni
2 eggs, beaten
300 mL (½ pint) (1¼ cups) sour cream
  or natural yoghurt
75 g (3 oz) (¾ cup) grated cheese

1 Preheat oven to 190°C (375°F).
2 Heat oil in a large pan and fry onion until soft but not golden. Add beef and fry until browned.
3 Add garlic, canned tomatoes and juice, tomato paste, herbs and seasoning. Bring to the boil, and simmer 20 minutes.
4 Meanwhile, cook pasta in boiling salted water for 8–10 minutes, until just tender. Drain.
5 Mix eggs with the sour cream or yoghurt. Add two-thirds of the cheese, and the pasta.
6 Transfer meat mixture to an ovenproof dish and pour pasta mixture over the top. Sprinkle with remaining cheese and bake for 25–30 minutes. Serve hot.

Serves 6

10

11

12

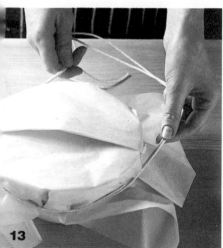

13

14

1 Sift flour into a bowl. Add suet.
2 Add water to form dough.
3 Roll out into a circle, reserving dough for the lid.
4 Grease a pudding basin and line it with dough.
5 Chop steak, onion, kidney.
6 Place the slices of kidney on the strips of beef.
7 Roll them up and dip in seasoned flour.
8 Pour on the stock.

9 Roll out pastry for lid.
10 Seal the edges well.
11 Grease a large sheet of greaseproof paper.
12 Make a pleat in paper.
13 Tie it around the basin.
14 After steaming invert pudding onto serving dish or:
15 Spoon it from pudding basin.

Chilli Con Carne

450 g (1 lb) (1½ cups) dried red
  kidney beans
2 onions
1 clove
1 bouquet garni
salt
450 g (1 lb) tomatoes
1 clove garlic, peeled
45 mL (1½ fl oz) (3 tablespoons) oil
450 g (1 lb) (2 cups) minced beef
5 g (1 teaspoon) paprika
15 g (½ oz) (1 tablespoon) chilli
  powder, or to taste

1 Soak beans in cold water overnight.
2 Drain beans and rinse. Put in a pan
and just cover with cold water. Peel 1
onion and press clove into it. Add to
pan with bouquet garni. Bring to the
boil, then simmer for 1 hour. Add
salt towards the end of the cooking
time.
3 Meanwhile skin, seed and chop
the tomatoes. Slice the remaining
onion. Push a wooden cocktail stick
into the garlic clove.
4 Heat oil in a large pan, add onion
and fry gently until soft. Add minced
beef and fry until evenly browned.
Add garlic.
5 Stir in tomatoes, paprika, chilli
powder and salt to taste.
6 Drain kidney beans and add to
meat mixture. Cover and cook gently
for 1 hour.
7 Remove garlic, adjust seasoning,
and serve hot.

Serves 6

Mexican Hotpot

25 mL (1 fl oz) (⅛ cup) oil
1 large onion, chopped
1 green capsicum (pepper), seeded
  and chopped
1 red capsicum (pepper), seeded and
  chopped
450 g (1 lb) minced beef
pinch paprika
pinch chilli powder
25 g (1 oz) (4 tablespoons) flour
25 g (1 oz) (2 tablespoons) tomato
  paste
400 mL (¾ pint) (2 cups) water
1 beef stock cube
bouquet garni
salt and pepper
225 g (½ lb) (1 cup) canned kidney
  beans, drained

1 Heat oil in a saucepan and fry the
onion until soft. Add the green and
red capsicum and cook for 1 minute.
Add minced beef and brown for 5
minutes, stirring occasionally.
2 Stir in paprika, chilli powder and
flour and cook for 2 minutes. Add
tomato paste and water and crumble
in the stock cube. Bring to the boil,
stirring all the time, then add bouquet garni, lower heat and cook
gently on top of the stove for 30 minutes.
3 Season with salt and pepper to
taste and add drained kidney beans.
Continue cooking for 5 minutes until
kidney beans are heated through,
then serve with plain boiled rice.

Serves 4

Beef in Cider Cream Sauce

350 g (¾ lb) beef topside
15 mL (1 tablespoon) oil
15 mL (1 tablespoon) butter
1 onion, sliced
30 mL (2 tablespoons) flour
150 mL (¼ pint) (⅔ cup) dry cider
15 mL (1 tablespoon) tomato paste
150 mL (¼ pint) (⅔ cup) beef stock
1 bay leaf
pinch dried thyme
salt and pepper
50 mL (2 fl oz) (¼ cup) thickened
  cream
5 mL (1 tablespoon) Dijon mustard
1 teaspoon chopped fresh parsley

1 Preheat oven to 180°C (350°F).
2 Cut meat in thin slices — about
½ cm (¼ in) thick — and then into
strips, about 5 cm (2 in) long. Heat oil
and butter in a frying pan and fry
meat gently for 6 minutes to brown
on both sides.
3 Add sliced onion and cook for 2
minutes to soften. Sprinkle flour into
the pan and cook for 1 minute, stirring. Pour in the cider, tomato paste
and stock, and bring to the boil. Add
bay leaf, thyme and seasoning.
Transfer to an ovenproof casserole,
cover and braise in the oven for 1–1½
hours until meat is tender.
4 Combine cream and mustard.
When meat is cooked, stir cream
mixture into sauce. Sprinkle with
chopped parsley and serve immediately.

Serves 4

Beef in Cider Hotpot

40 g (1½ oz) (3 tablespoons) butter
675 g (1½ lb) beef topside, cut into
  thin slices
1 large onion, sliced
2 large carrots, peeled and sliced
2 turnips, peeled and diced
40 g (1½ oz) (6 tablespoons) flour
450 mL (¾ pint) (2 cups) dry cider, or
  300 mL (½ pint) (1¼ cups) apple
  juice with 150 mL (¼ pint) (⅔ cup)
  water and 15 mL (1 tablespoon)
  vinegar
salt and pepper
1 beef stock cube, crumbled
450 g (1 lb) (3 cups) potatoes, peeled
  and thinly sliced
75 g (3 oz) (¾ cup) grated cheese

1 Preheat oven to 180°C (350°F).
Melt butter and fry beef slices for 5
minutes. Remove. Add onion, carrots
and turnips to pan and fry gently for
10 minutes. Stir in flour for 1 minute.
Remove from heat and pour in cider
or apple juice. Bring to the boil, then
add seasoning and the stock cube.
Cook 5 minutes.
2 Pour into an earthenware pot and
arrange potato slices on top. Cover
and bake for 1½–2 hours. Increase
the oven temperature to 200°C
(400°F). Sprinkle grated cheese on top
and bake for 15–20 minutes
uncovered until cheese is golden-
brown. Serve.

Serves 4

Czardaz Beef with Caraway Rice

30 mL (1 fl oz) (2 tablespoons) oil
1 kg (2 lb) stewing beef, cut into
    2.5 cm (1 in) cubes
3 sticks celery, chopped
1 large onion, sliced
150 mL (¼ pint) (⅔ cup) water
½ beef stock cube
450 g (1 lb) (2⅔ cups) canned
    pineapple cubes, with juice
5 g (1 tablespoon) chopped parsley
good pinch sugar
15 g (½ oz) (1 tablespoon) tomato
    paste
few drops Worcestershire sauce
salt and pepper
350 g (¾ lb) (1½ cups) long grain rice
25 g (1 oz) (2 tablespoons) butter
10 g (2 teaspoons) caraway seeds

1 Preheat oven to 180°C (350°F).
2 Heat oil in a frying pan. Brown meat, remove and place in a casserole. Add celery and onion to the oil and fry for 3 minutes, then add to casserole.
3 Pour water into a pan, bring to the boil and crumble in the stock cube. Drain pineapple and add juice to the stock with parsley, sugar, tomato paste, Worcestershire sauce and salt and pepper to taste. Pour over meat in the casserole, cover and cook for 1½ hours, adding more stock if necessary.
4 Add pineapple 15 minutes before the end of cooking.
5 To cook rice, first place in a sieve and wash thoroughly under cold running water. Remove any discoloured grains. Place in a large pan of boiling, slightly salted water. Boil 12 minutes or until the rice is tender. Drain and return to the pan to dry. Gently stir in the butter and the caraway seeds.

Serves 6

Curried Beef and Golden Rice

225 g (½ lb) (1 cup) long-grain rice
good pinch turmeric
225 g (½ lb) Basic Economy Beef (see
    recipe)
1 carrot, diced
15 g (½ oz) (1 tablespoon) curry
    powder
5 g (1 teaspoon) desiccated coconut
25 g (1 oz) (2 tablespoons) sultanas
1 apple, peeled, cored and diced

1 Boil rice in plenty of salted water to which a good pinch of turmeric has been added. Simmer until tender, rinse and drain. Keep warm.
2 Make the Basic Economy Beef, according to the recipe, but add the diced carrot to onion before frying, and stir in curry powder when browning the meat. Stir in coconut, sultanas and apple.
3 Arrange rice around the edge of a large dish, and pour curry into the middle. Serve hot.

Serves 4

Sweet and Sour Beef

4 beef sausages
30 mL (2 tablespoons) oil
1 onion, chopped
225 g (½ lb) (1⅓ cups) diced, boiled
    beef

Sauce
300 mL (½ pint) (1¼ cups) water
½ cucumber, cut into chunks
2 sticks celery, sliced
1 carrot, cut into thin strips
50 mL (2 fl oz) (¼ cup) soy sauce
1 beef stock cube
1 clove garlic, peeled and chopped
10 g (1 tablespoon) fresh ginger,
    peeled and chopped
25 g (1 oz) (1½ tablespoons) honey
30 mL (2 tablespoons) vinegar
15 g (½ oz) (1½ tablespoons) cornflour

1 Grill or fry sausages. Cool and cut in thick slices.
2 Heat oil and fry onion until soft, then add beef and sausages. Fry for 5 minutes.
3 Bring water to the boil, and cook cucumber, celery and carrot for 5 minutes so that they are still crisp.

4 Add soy sauce and crumble in the stock cube. Add garlic, ginger, honey and vinegar and stir well. Mix the cornflour with a little water and stir into the sauce. Boil for 3 minutes until it thickens, stirring all the time. Stir in sausage, beef and onion mixture and simmer 10 minutes.
5 Arrange on a serving dish, surrounded by boiled rice.

Serves 4

Minced Beef Casserole

150 g (5 oz) (1¼ cups) chopped onion
50 g (2 oz) (4 tablespoons) cooking oil
450 g (1 lb) lean minced beef
25 g (1 oz) (2 tablespoons) tomato
    paste
150 mL (¼ pint) (⅔ cup) beer
300 mL (½ pint) (1¼ cups) water
1 stock cube
15 g (½ oz) (1 tablespoon) sugar
pinch mace
675 g (1½ lb) potatoes
1 egg yolk
40 g (1½ oz) (3 tablespoons) butter
15 g (½ oz) (1½ tablespoons) cornflour
150 mL (¼ pint) (⅔ cup) water
salt and pepper
6 mushrooms

1 Gently fry chopped onion in oil until brown. Add minced beef and cook, stirring, until brown.
2 Add the tomato paste, beer, water, stock cube, sugar and mace, and simmer for 35 minutes.
3 Meanwhile, peel potatoes and boil. Mash and mix with egg yolk and 25 g (1 oz) (2 tablespoons) butter and season.
4 Add cornflour mixed with water to the meat to thicken. Season with salt. Place in a serving dish.
5 Spread a thin layer of the hot mashed potato over the meat.
6 Place the remainder of the mashed potato in a piping bag with a 1 cm (½ in) star tube and pipe a criss-cross pattern. Brown under the grill. Decorate with halved mushrooms, lightly sauteed in 15 g (½ oz) of butter.

Serves 4

Czarda Beef with Caraway Rice

Steam Romanov Step-by-step

1 Cut the fillet into cubes.
2 Brown meat in oil in frying pan.
3 Remove meat from pan.
4 Fry chopped onions, sprinkle on paprika, add tomato

paste and stir. Cook 2 minutes. Add water.
5 Add the cream, stir and boil.
6 Reheat the meat in the sauce. Remove from the heat, add the vodka and season.

Hellenic Casserole

Steak Romanov

450 g (1 lb) fillet (cut from the thin end)
50 mL (2 fl oz) (¼ cup) oil
1 medium onion, or 3 shallots (spring onions, scallions), chopped
7 g (1 tablespoon) paprika
25 g (1 oz) (2 tablespoons) tomato paste
150 mL (¼ pint) (⅔ cup) water
150 mL (¼ pint) (⅔ cup) sour cream
15 mL (1 tablespoon) vodka
salt and pepper

1 Remove skin and fat from the fillet and cut meat into cubes 2 cm (¾ in) thick.

2 Heat oil in a frying pan. Brown meat for 4 minutes, stirring constantly. Remove from pan.

3 In the same pan, fry onions gently for 2 minutes without colouring.

4 Sprinkle on paprika, add the tomato paste and cook for 2 minutes, stirring.

5 Add water and boil for 5 minutes. Add cream to the pan and simmer for 2 minutes.

6 Reheat meat in sauce for 3 minutes. Remove from heat.

7 Just before serving, add vodka and check the seasoning. Serve with boiled rice.

Serves 4

Hellenic Casserole

½ kg (1 lb) eggplants (aubergines), sliced
50 mL (2 fl oz) (¼ cup) oil
2 large onions, thinly sliced
1 clove garlic, crushed
450 g (1 lb) (2 cups) minced beef
25 g (1 oz) (2 tablespoons) tomato paste
salt and pepper
300 mL (½ pint) (1¼ cups) boiling water
1 stock cube
450 g (1 lb) tomatoes, sliced
450 g (1 lb) boiled potatoes, sliced
2 eggs
150 mL (¼ pint) (⅔ cup) cream
50 g (2 oz) (½ cup) grated cheese
25 g (1 oz) (3 tablespoons) grated Parmesan cheese
1 tomato, sliced

1 Sprinkle eggplants with salt and leave for ½ hour. Wash off the bitter juices and dry.

2 Heat oil in a frying pan and cook the slices for ½ minute on each side. Remove from the pan.

3 Preheat oven to 180°C (350°F).

4 Fry onions and garlic until golden-brown. Add minced meat and brown, stirring. Add tomato paste and cook for 2 minutes. Season. Add boiling water mixed with the stock cube. Simmer 10 minutes.

5 Arrange the eggplants, meat and onions, sliced tomatoes and sliced potatoes, in layers in a casserole and bake for 35 minutes.

6 Beat eggs with cream and stir in cheeses. Pour onto casserole and return to oven for 20 minutes until the topping is golden-brown. Garnish with tomato.

Serves 4

Oxtail Matilda

600 mL (1 pint) (2½ cups) tea
225 g (½ lb) (1⅓ cups) prunes
900 g (2 lb) oxtail, jointed
40 g (1½ oz) (6 tablespoons) flour
2 onions, sliced
2 sticks celery, sliced
2 carrots, sliced
600 mL (1 pint) (2½ cups) water
2 beef stock cubes
50 g (2 oz) (4 tablespoons) tomato
   paste
bouquet garni
2 cloves garlic, peeled and crushed
25 g (1 oz) (1 tablespoon) sugar
salt and pepper
6 baby carrots, trimmed
25 g (1 oz) (2 tablespoons) butter
12 shallots (spring onions, scallions)

1 Pour tea into a pan and soak prunes in it for 3 hours. Then bring to the boil and simmer for 15 minutes.
2 Preheat oven to 180°C (350°F).
3 Wash oxtail in cold water and dry. Trim off excess fat and roll in the flour. Place in a frying pan over a very gentle heat for 25 minutes, until the oxtail becomes brown and the fat melts. Remove and place in a casserole. Lightly fry sliced onions, celery and carrots in the fat, then add to the oxtail. Bring water to the boil, crumble in the stock cubes, and pour onto the oxtail. Add tomato paste, bouquet garni, garlic and 10 g (⅓ oz) (1 teaspoon) sugar. Season to taste. Cover, and place in the oven to cook for 3 hours.
4 When oxtail is tender, take it out of the casserole and keep hot. Strain sauce, discard any floating fat and add prune liquor. Replace meat and heat through.
5 Place baby carrots in a pan with enough water to cover. Add butter and remaining sugar, bring to the boil and simmer for 4 minutes. Add shallots and cook 8 minutes. Serve hot, surrounded by prunes, shallots and carrots.

Serves 6

Oxtail Matilda

Winter Stew

675 g (1½ lb) stewing steak
175 g (6 oz) ox kidney
25 g (1 oz) (4 tablespoons) flour
25 g (1 oz) (2 tablespoons) oil
1 large onion, sliced
2 large carrots, sliced
2 small turnips, sliced
450 mL (¾ pint) (2 cups) cider
good pinch ground ginger
1 bouquet garni
salt and pepper

Savoury Dumplings
100 g (¼ lb) (1 cup + 2 tablespoons)
*   self-raising flour*
pinch salt
50 g (2 oz) (¼ cup) sausage meat
50 g (2 oz) (½ cup) shredded beef suet
good pinch mixed herbs
150 mL (¼ pint) (⅔ cup) cider

1 Cut steak into 2.5 cm (1 in) cubes. Skin, core and slice the kidney. Dredge in seasoned flour. Heat oil in a frying pan and fry meats until lightly brown. Add onion and fry for 3 minutes. Transfer to a heavy-bottomed pan. Fry carrot and turnip for 2 minutes, then transfer to the pan. Pour on cider, add ginger and bouquet garni, and season to taste. Cover and simmer for 1½ hours.

2 To make the dumplings, sift the flour and salt into a bowl and mix in sausage meat. Add suet and herbs and mix to soft dough with the cider. Divide into 12 balls and roll in flour.

3 Remove meat with a slotted spoon and pass the sauce through a sieve. Replace the meat, add the dumplings, and simmer for a further ½ hour.

Serves 6

Hungarian Meatballs Casserole

450 g (1 lb) (2 cups) minced beef
25 g (1 oz) (½ cup) fresh breadcrumbs
1 egg
salt and pepper
5 g (1 tablespoon) chopped parsley
50 g (2 oz) (½ cup) flour
50 mL (2 fl oz) (¼ cup) oil
3 large onions, sliced
25 g (1 oz) (2 tablespoons) paprika
50 g (2 oz) (4 tablespoons) tomato
*   paste*
15 g (½ oz) (2 tablespoons) flour
1 stock cube
300 mL (½ pint) (1¼ cups) boiling
*   water*
pinch caraway seeds (optional)
450 g (1 lb) potatoes, sliced
watercress

1 Mix minced meat, breadcrumbs, egg, salt and pepper, and parsley in a bowl. Make 12 meatballs and dust with flour.

2 Preheat oven to 190°C (375°F).

3 Heat most of the oil in a frying pan, brown meatballs and place in a casserole.

4 To make the sauce, brown onions in the rest of the oil. Add paprika and tomato paste and cook 2 minutes. Sprinkle on flour. Stir; cook for 1 minute.

5 Add the stock cube mixed with boiling water. Season and add caraway seeds.

6 Pour sauce over meatballs. Arrange slices of potato round the dish and bake for 45 minutes. Serve garnished with watercress.

Serves 4

Daube of Beef with Red Wine

225 g (½ lb) belly of pork
225 g (½ lb) white belly pork fat
*   (optional)*
50 mL (2 fl oz) (1¼ cup) brandy or port
5 g (1 tablespoon) chopped parsley
2 kg (4 lb) topside of beef
3 large carrots, chopped
3 large onions, chopped
3 large tomatoes, chopped
3 cloves garlic, crushed

8 mushrooms
225 g (½ lb) pork rind (optional)
½ bottle red wine
100 mL (4 fl oz) (½ cup) oil
salt
12 peppercorns, crushed
pinch allspice
300 mL (½ pint) (¼ cups) water
bouquet garni
7 g (1 tablespoon) cornflour (optional)

1 Cut the lean belly of pork into strips and blanch by plunging in boiling water for 1 minute. Cool

2 Cut the white belly pork fat (if used) into strips 5 cm × 5 mm (2 × ¼ in), sprinkle with a few drops of brandy and a pinch of parsley. Chill ½ hour.

3 Cut meat into 4 cm (1½ in) cubes. If using the pork fat, take a larding needle, and thread each piece with a strip of fat.

4 Place belly of pork and meat in a bowl with carrots, onions, tomatoes, garlic, mushrooms and pork rind (if used).

5 Pour on wine, brandy and half of the oil. Add salt, peppercorns and allspice and marinate for 2 hours. Remove meat and dry on absorbent paper.

6 Preheat oven to 180°C (350°F).

7 Put the remainder of the oil in a thick pan, add meat and belly of pork and brown 5 minutes. Add vegetables and brown 3 minutes. Add marinade, water, and bouquet garni and bring to the boil. Cover and bake for 2½ hours, or until the meat is tender.

8 When cooked, remove fat from the surface carefully with a ladle. Remove bouquet garni and pork rind (if used).

9 If you wish, thicken daube with cornflour mixed with 100 mL (4 fl oz) (½ cup) water and cook for 2 minutes, stirring gently.

10 Place meat on a serving dish, pour over the sauce and sprinkle with the remainder of the chopped parsley. Serve with new potatoes.

Serves 8

Daube of Beef with Red Wine Step-by-step

1 Collect the ingredients.
2 Cut the belly of pork and white belly pork fat into strips. Put the belly pork fat in a dish, sprinkle with brandy and chopped parsley and chill.

3 Cube meat. Thread each with a strip of fat.
4 Place ingredients in a bowl: add mushrooms.
5 Pour over the red wine, oil and brandy. Season and marinate for 2½ hours. Remove the meat and belly of pork

and dry. Put some oil in the casserole and brown the meat.
6 Add vegetables: brown. Add marinade and water.
7 Bring to boil and bake 2½ hours at 180°C (350°F).
8 When meat is tender, remove fat with ladle, and

remove bouquet garni and pork rind.
9 Place the meat on a serving dish and pour the sauce over. Sprinkle with the parsley.

Meatballs with Zucchini (Courgettes)

Meatballs with Zucchini (Courgettes)

50 g (2 oz) (⅓ cup) chick peas, cooked or canned and drained
450 g (1 lb) (2 cups) lean minced beef
1 clove garlic, peeled and crushed
50 g (2 oz) (1 cup) fresh breadcrumbs
50 g (2 oz) (⅓ cup) hazelnuts, finely chopped
1 egg, beaten
1 small green chilli pepper, finely chopped
5 g (1 tablespoon) chopped parsley
pinch cumin
salt and pepper
15 g (½ oz) (2 tablespoons) flour
60 mL (2 fl oz) (¼ cup) oil

Sauce
30 mL (2 tablespoons) oil
1 onion, chopped
1 clove garlic, peeled and crushed
4 zucchini (courgettes), sliced
4 tomatoes, skinned, seeded and chopped

150 g (5 oz) (1¼ cups) peas, fresh or frozen
300 mL (½ pint) (1¼ cups) water
1 chicken stock cube
5 g (1 tablespoon) mixed mint and parsley, chopped

1 Preheat oven to 200°C (400°F).
2 Mash chick peas with a fork. Place in a mixing bowl, and add beef, garlic, breadcrumbs, hazelnuts, beaten egg and chilli pepper. Blend well and add parsley, cumin, salt and pepper. Shape into slightly flattened balls and dust with flour.
3 Heat oil in a frying pan and fry meatballs for 6–8 minutes. Drain and keep hot.
4 To make sauce, pour away oil in which meatballs were cooked and wipe pan clean. Heat 30 mL (2 tablespoons) oil and gently fry the onion for 4 minutes, until soft but not brown. Add the garlic, zucchini, tomatoes and peas. Pour on the water and crumble in the stock cube. Bring to the boil, add parsley and mint and

season to taste. Transfer to a casserole, add meatballs, and bake for 20 minutes.

Serves 4

Tips: Try using equal quantities of minced pork and beef for a good texture as well as a delicious flavour.

For economy, replace 150 g (5 oz) (good ½ cup) minced beef with 65 g (2½ oz) texturised vegetable protein.

Meatballs can be braised in the oven or deep fried and any kind of cereal binder can be used such as matzo meal, oats, cooked rice or rusk.

South Seas Meatballs

450 g (1 lb) (2 cups) lean minced beef
1 egg, beaten
pinch each salt and pepper
15 mL (1 tablespoon) oil
3 small shallots (spring onions,
    scallions), chopped
15 g (2 tablespoons) flour
450 g (1 lb) pineapple chunks
15 mL (1 tablespoon) soy sauce
5 mL (1 teaspoon) wine vinegar
½ green capsicum (pepper), finely
    chopped
25 g (1 oz) (¼ cup) almonds, blanched

1 In a large bowl blend beef, beaten egg, salt and pepper. Make into 4 flattened balls, brush with oil and grill for 10 minutes, turning once. Keep warm.

2 Heat oil in a frying pan. Add shallots and fry gently for 3 minutes. Take out. Stir in flour and cook the roux for 3 minutes more. Pour in juice from the canned pineapple, and bring to the boil, stirring. Add soy sauces and vinegar. Season to taste.

3 Add shallots, pineapple chunks, green capsicum and almonds. Place meatballs in pan and heat through, spooning the sauce over.

Serves 4

Marengo Meatballs

Marengo Meatballs

1 large slice white bread
30 mL (2 tablespoons) milk
675 g (1½ lb) (3 cups) lean minced
    beef
1 egg yolk
1 onion, finely chopped
pinch salt and pepper
15 g (½ oz) (1 tablespoon) flour
50 g (2 oz) (4 tablespoons) butter
75 mL (3 fl oz) (⅓ cup) dry white wine
4 large tomatoes, skinned, seeded
    and chopped
pinch sugar
350 g (¾ lb) (1½ cups) long grain rice
30 mL (2 tablespoons) cream
5 g (1 tablespoon) chopped parsley

1 Soak the bread in the milk for 5 minutes. Squeeze out, remove excess liquid and crumble.

2 In a mixing bowl, combine beef, egg yolk, onion, salt and pepper and breadcrumbs. Divide into 6 and roll into flattened balls. Dust with flour.

3 Heat the butter in a frying pan and fry the meatballs for 10 minutes, turning them once. Pour on the wine, then add the tomatoes and a pinch of sugar. Bring to the boil, then reduce the heat and simmer for 25 minutes.

4 Meanwhile, place the rice in a pan of slightly salted water. Bring to the boil and cook for 15 minutes or until the rice is just tender. Drain. Heat cream in a small pan and pour over the rice. Arrange in the centre of a serving dish, garnished with the parsley and surrounded by the meatballs and sauce.

Serves 6

Mushroom and Beef Gnocchi

300 mL (½ pint) (1¼ cups) milk
1 clove garlic, crushed
50 g (2 oz) (½ cup) grated cheese
50 g (2 oz) (⅓ cup) semolina
salt and pepper
2 egg yolks
30 mL (2 tablespoons) oil
1 small onion, chopped
100 g (¼ lb) (1 cup) chopped
  mushrooms
100 g (¼ lb) (½ cup) minced beef
50 g (2 oz) (½ cup) seasoned flour
oil for deep frying

Garnish
30 mL (2 tablespoons) oil
10 large mushroom caps
10 small tomatoes
50 g (2 oz) (4 tablespoons) butter
10 slices toasted French bread
few sprigs parsley
1 lemon, sliced

1 Place milk, garlic and cheese in a pan and bring to the boil. Stir in semolina and cook 4 minutes. Season with salt and pepper and stir in the egg yolks when cool.

2 Heat oil in a saute pan and fry onion, mushrooms and beef until cooked (about 5 minutes). Allow to cool.

3 Mix meat and semolina mixtures and shape into balls. Roll in seasoned flour.

4 Heat oil and deep fry the meatballs for 2 minutes. Drain and keep warm.

5 Heat oil and fry mushroom caps. Grill tomatoes. Butter the rounds of French bread.

6 Place a mushroom cap on top of each slice of bread and a meatball in the middle. Surround gnocchi with tomatoes and garnish with parsley and lemon slices.

Serves 5

Salonika Cutlets

225 g (½ lb) (1 cup) minced beef
225 g (½ lb) (1½ cups) cooked rice
1 egg, beaten
1 onion, chopped
salt and pepper
grated lemon rind
50 g (2 oz) (⅓ cup) sultanas
50 g (2 oz) (½ cup) seasoned flour
50 mL (2 fl oz) (¼ cup) oil

1 Mix beef, rice, egg, onion, salt and pepper, grated lemon rind and sultanas together and form into four triangular 'cutlets', 1 cm (½ in) thick.

2 Dredge with seasoned flour.

3 Heat oil in a frying pan and fry for 8 minutes on each side until golden.

4 Serve with boiled rice and a tomato sauce. Fried marrow fritters would go well with this dish.

Serves 4

Mushroom and Beef Gnocchi

110

Mushroom Burgers

25 g (1 oz) (2 tablespoons) butter
30 mL (2 tablespoons) oil
2 onions, finely chopped
225 g (½ lb) (2 cups) finely chopped
    mushrooms
good pinch mixed herbs
1 clove garlic, peeled and crushed
675 g (1½ lb) (3 cups) lean minced
    beef
pinch salt and pepper
15 g (½ oz) (2 tablespoons) flour
4 mushroom caps
fresh herbs to garnish

1 Heat butter and 15 mL (1 table-spoon) oil in a frying pan. Gently fry onions and mushrooms for 5 minutes. Add mixed herbs and crushed garlic clove and cook for a further minute. Allow to cool.

2 In a bowl, combine beef with onion and mushroom mixture. Season. Divide into balls, then flatten slightly. Dust with flour.

3 Heat the rest of the oil in the pan and fry mushroom burgers slowly for 4–6 minutes each side. Remove to a serving plate and keep warm.

4 Fry mushroom caps in the fat remaining in the pan until tender. Drain and place on the serving dish. Garnish with fresh herbs and serve hot.

Serves 4

Tip: To make a quick, tasty sauce, take the burgers out of the pan when they are cooked and add 100 mL (4 fl oz) (½ cup) sherry, wine or fruit juice to the pan. Boil rapidly until the sauce is reduced by half and pour it over the burgers.

Giant Pasta Burger

Giant Pasta Burger

450 g (1 lb) (2 cups) minced beef
1 onion, grated
salt and pepper
2 g (1 teaspoon) mixed chopped
    herbs
1 egg
100 g (¼ lb) spaghetti
60 mL (4 tablespoons) tomato sauce
25 g (1 oz) (2 tablespoons) butter
75 g (3 oz) (¾ cup) grated cheese

1 Mix minced beef with onion, seasoning, herbs and an egg and form into a large, flat, hamburger shape. Refrigerate for 30 minutes.

2 Meanwhile, cook spaghetti in boiling salted water until tender, then drain and mix with tomato sauce.

3 Heat butter in a large frying pan and fry burger gently until browned on the underside. Turn burger over and cook until brown on the other side and cooked through.

4 Top burger with spaghetti and tomato sauce and sprinkle cheese over the top. Cover pan and cook for a few minutes more until cheese has melted and spaghetti is hot. Cut into wedges and serve.

Serves 4–6

Beefsteak a la Lindstrom

Beef and Pork Dumplings in Tomato Sauce

1 medium onion, peeled and coarsely chopped
1 medium carrot, peeled and coarsely chopped
2 sticks celery, peeled and coarsely chopped
2 cloves garlic
75 mL (2½ fl oz) (⅓ cup) oil
450 g (1 lb) (2 cups) lean minced beef (from shin or skirt)
250 g (9 oz) (1 cup) pork sausage meat
1 egg, beaten
100 g (¼ lb) (2 cups) fresh white breadcrumbs
salt and black pepper
pinch oregano
pinch each paprika, ground ginger and mace
5 g (1 tablespoon) freshly chopped parsley
225 g (½ lb) spaghetti
400 mL (¾ pint) (1¾ cups) tomato sauce

1 Pass vegetables twice through a mincer or work in a blender. Heat oil in a saucepan and saute the vegetables, with the lid on, for 5 minutes to concentrate the flavour.

2 Remove mixture from heat. Mix thoroughly in a large bowl with minced beef and sausage meat. Bind mixture with egg and breadcrumbs. Season with salt, pepper, oregano, paprika, ginger, mace and chopped parsley.

3 Preheat oven to 180°C (350°F).

4 Divide mixture and roll into small balls, about 25 g (1 oz) in size, on a work surface sprinkled with flour.

5 Grease a roasting pan and place dumplings on it at regular intervals. Bake 30 minutes.

6 Meanwhile cook spaghetti in a large pan of boiling water for 10–12 minutes or until just tender. Drain and turn into a hot serving dish; dot with a knob of butter.

7 Remove dumplings when cooked and place on the spaghetti. The tomato sauce can either be poured over the dumplings or served separately, together with grated Parmesan, Gruyere or Cheddar cheese.

Serves 6

Beefsteak a la Lindstrom

450 g (1 lb) (2 cups) lean minced beef
1 onion, finely chopped
4 sprigs parsley, chopped
15 g (1 tablespoon) capers
1 cooked beetroot, chopped
1 hard-boiled egg
1 egg, beaten
good pinch salt
pinch white pepper
pinch sugar
50 g (2 oz) (¾ cup) dried breadcrumbs
45 mL (3 tablespoons) oil

1 In a large mixing bowl, combine minced beef, onion, chopped parsley, capers and chopped beetroot. Mash hard-boiled egg with a fork and add. Mix well and knead.

2 Blend beaten egg into mixture with a spoon and season with salt, pepper and sugar

3 Divide mixture into 4 balls, then flatten slightly. Place breadcrumbs on a plate. Coat hamburgers evenly with them.

4 Heat oil in a frying pan and fry hamburgers for 5 minutes each side. Serve hot.

Serves 4

Beef Fritters with Spaghetti Creole Sauce

50 g (2 oz) (½ cup) flour
2 eggs, beaten
50 g (2 oz) cornflakes, crushed
15 g (½ oz) chopped almonds
oil for deep frying
225 g (½ lb) spaghetti
50 g (2 oz) (4 tablespoons) butter
50 g (2 oz) (½ cup) grated cheese

Fritters

225 g (½ lb) (1 cup) minced beef
100 g (¼ lb) (½ cup) minced pork
100 g (¼ lb) (1 cup) chopped
    mushrooms
100 g (¼ lb) (½ cup) chopped onion
1 egg
50 g (2 oz) (1 cup) fresh breadcrumbs
5 g (1 tablespoon) chopped parsley
1 clove garlic, chopped
salt and pepper
pinch paprika

Sauce

25 mL (1 fl oz) (⅛ cup) oil
1 small onion, chopped
25 g (1 oz) (3 tablespoons) diced
    bacon
25 g (1 oz) (2 tablespoons) flour
1 dried chilli
75 g (3 oz) (6 tablespoons) tomato
    paste
500 mL (1 pint) (2½ cups) water
1 beef stock cube, crumbled
bouquet garni
2 mint leaves

1 Combine ingredients for fritters and divide into 8 balls. Roll in flour, dip in beaten egg and roll in cornflakes and almonds. Heat oil to 190°C (375°F) and fry fritters for 4 minutes.

2 Cook spaghetti in boiling salted water for 10–12 minutes then drain, season and add butter and cheese. Mix well and keep warm.

3 Next make the sauce. Heat oil in a pan and fry onion and bacon for 5 minutes. Add flour and cook for 1 minute.

4 Add remaining ingredients, bring to the boil and simmer 15 minutes.

5 Season sauce and strain. Blend half the sauce with the cooked spaghetti.

6 Arrange fritters in a circle on a plate and pour the spaghetti in its sauce into the centre. Serve the rest of the sauce separately.

Serves 4

Cannelloni with Olives

6 tubes cannelloni
15 mL (1 tablespoon) oil
1 onion, chopped
225 g (½ lb) (1 cup) minced beef
15 g (½ oz) (1 tablespoon) tomato
    paste
2 g (1 teaspoon) basil
7 g (1 teaspoon) sugar
8 stuffed olives
salt and pepper
1 tomato, thinly sliced

Sauce

300 mL (½ pint) (1½ cups) white sauce
2.5 mL (½ teaspoon) made mustard
salt and pepper
100 g (¼ lb) (1 cup) grated cheese

1 Blanch cannelloni in a pan of salted boiling water for 5 minutes. Drain and place under running cold water until cool.

2 Heat oven to 190°C (375°F).

3 Heat the oil in a frying pan and fry onion until soft. Add minced beef and cook until brown. Stir in the tomato paste, basil and sugar.

4 Chop 6 olives and add to the beef mixture and season with salt and pepper.

5 Using a piping bag or spoon, fill cannelloni tubes with mixture. Place in a shallow ovenproof dish.

6 Heat white sauce and flavour with mustard, salt and pepper. Stir in most of the cheese, reserving a little for the top.

7 Pour sauce over cannelloni and sprinkle with remaining cheese. Bake for 20 minutes.

8 Decorate the top with the remaining sliced olives and tomato and serve hot.

Serves 3–6

Tip: This dish can be served as an appetiser, in which case allow 1 cannelloni tube per person. If serving as a main course, allow 2 per person.

Corn Tamale

50 g (2 oz) (⅓ cup) cornmeal
75 g (3 oz) (¾ cup) flour
2 eggs, beaten
300 mL (½ pint) (1¼ cups) milk and
    water
salt and pepper
25 mL (1 fl oz) (⅛ cup) oil
300 mL (½ pint) (1¼ cups) tomato
    sauce
pinch cayenne pepper
50 g (2 oz) (½ cup) grated cheese

Filling

50 mL (2 fl oz) (¼ cup) oil
1 medium onion, chopped
1 green chilli, sliced
225 g (½ lb) (1 cup) minced beef
25 g (1 oz) (2 tablespoons) flour
15 g (½ oz) (1 tablespoon) tomato
    paste
150 mL (¼ pint) (⅔ cup) water with 1
    chicken stock cube added
1 egg, beaten

1 Preheat oven to 200°C (400°F). Blend cornmeal and flour and stir in eggs. Blend in milk and water with a pinch of salt. Leave batter to rest for 15 minutes.

2 Oil a small pan and then use batter to make 8 or 9 crepes. Spread crepes on kitchen paper to cool.

3 Make filling: heat oil in a pan and cook the onion until soft. Add chilli and beef, cover and simmer for 5 minutes. Stir in the flour and tomato paste, cook 3 minutes, then stir in chicken stock. Cook 15 minutes. Season and cool, then use egg to bind the mixture.

4 Spread the mixture over each crepe and roll them up. Place side by side on a greased ovenproof dish.

5 Heat tomato sauce, add cayenne pepper, and pour sauce over the crepes. Sprinkle with cheese and bake for 20 minutes.

Serves 4

Oat and Beef Rolls

Oat and Beef Rolls

25 mL (1 fl oz) (2 tablespoons) oil
1 clove garlic, chopped (optional)
2 onions
350 g (¾ lb) (1½ cups) minced beef
150 g (5 oz) (1¼ cups) chopped
*   walnuts*
75 g (3 oz) (⅔ cup) oats
salt and pepper
pinch mace
100 mL (4 fl oz) (½ cup) sherry
6 rolls
sprig watercress

1 Heat oil in frying pan and fry garlic, if used and onions for 2 minutes.

2 Add beef and brown for 5 minutes. Add walnuts and oats. Stir and cook for 2 minutes. Season with salt, pepper and mace. Add sherry and simmer for 20 minutes.

3 Preheat oven to 220°C (425°F).

4 Cut the top off the rolls and scoop out the soft crumb inside. Fill with oat and beef mixture. Put in the oven for 5 minutes and serve piping hot.

Serves 6

Macaroni and Chicken Liver Ring

225 g (½ lb) macaroni
2 eggs, beaten
50 g (2 oz) (4 tablespoons) butter
25 g (1 oz) (3 tablespoons) grated
*   Parmesan cheese*
4 chicken livers, halved
15 g (½ oz) (2 tablespoons) flour
30 mL (2 tablespoons) oil
225 g (½ lb) (1 cup) minced beef
100 g (¼ lb) (1¼ cups) sliced
*   mushrooms*
100 mL (4 fl oz) (½ cup) red wine
4 tomatoes, skinned, seeded and
*   chopped*
15 g (½ oz) (3 teaspoons) tomato paste
salt and pepper
5 g (1 tablespoon) chopped parsley

1 Cook macaroni in boiling salted water for 15 minutes. Drain thoroughly, and blend in a bowl with beaten eggs, butter and cheese.

2 Preheat oven to 190°C (375°F).

3 Press macaroni mixture into a buttered 1.75 litre (3 pint) buttered ring mould. Stand mould in a pan of hot water and bake for 20 minutes.

4 Meanwhile, coat chicken liver with flour. Heat oil in a frying pan and fry beef until brown, then add chicken livers and mushrooms and fry for 5 minutes.

5 Stir in wine and cook until mixture thickens, then add tomatoes and tomato paste and seasoning. Cook gently for 15 minutes.

6 Turn macaroni mould out onto a warm serving dish and fill centre with the meat filling. Sprinkle with chopped parsley and serve.

Serves 4

Steak Tartare

Steak Tartare is the name given to a delicious, unusual and highly digestible dish of raw steak. You should use fillet steak — preferably the thin, tail end — but you can use sirloin or rib, both of which are very tender. Make sure the meat is absolutely fresh: locally killed beef is best. Allow 150 g (5 oz) (good ½ cup) meat for a generous portion per person, and make sure it is passed through a mincer twice.

600 g (1¼ lb) (2½ cups) minced fillet steak
salt and freshly ground black pepper
100 g (¼ lb) (½ cup) shallots (spring onions, scallions), finely chopped
10 g (2 tablespoons) chopped parsley
8 anchovy fillets, chopped
15 g (1 tablespoon) capers
15 g (1 tablespoon) gherkins, chopped
4 teaspoons made mustard
150 mL (¼ pint) (⅔ cup) vinaigrette sauce
150 mL (¼ pint) (⅔ cup) mayonnaise
4 eggs

1 Season minced steak with salt and freshly ground black pepper. Divide into 4 portions and shape each into a ball. Place each in the centre of a dinner plate, flatten slightly and make a small cavity in the centre.

2 Either surround each portion with, or serve separately, the shallots, parsley, anchovy fillets, capers, mustard and gherkins. Serve a bowl each of vinaigrette sauce and mayonnaise.

3 Carefully break each egg and separate the white from the yolk. Leave the yolk in half the shell and place in the centre of each steak.

4 Allow your guests to help themselves to the various garnishes and sauces.

Serves 4

Tip: Serve Tartare with a crisp salad. Try lettuce and chicory (Belgian endive), or potato or orange and watercress or Waldorf Salad, which combines celery, crisp eating apples and walnuts.

Steak Tartare

115

Chinese Fondue

Chinese Fondue

100 g (¼ lb) (1 cup) peas
100 g (¼ lb) (1 cup) corn kernels
225 g (½ lb) (1 cup) bamboo shoots
50 g (2 oz) (½ cup) shallots (spring onions, scallions), chopped
450 g (1 lb) (6 cups) boiled long-grain rice
450 g (1 lb) fillet or sirloin steak, cut into thin strips
350 g (¾ lb) chicken breasts, skinned and cut into strips
4 egg yolks

Fondue Stock
1 litre (1¾ pints) (4 cups) water
50 mL (2 fl oz) (¼ cup) soy sauce
150 mL (¼ pint) (⅔ cup) dry sherry
25 g (1 oz) (2 tablespoons) fresh ginger, chopped
1 stick celery, thinly sliced
1 carrot, thinly sliced
1 leek, thinly sliced
1 beef stock cube

1 Prepare fondue stock. Place ingredients in a large pan, boil 5 minutes, reduce heat and simmer 30 minutes. Strain, place in a large casserole dish and keep warm.

2 Meanwhile, prepare side-dishes. Cook peas and warm through corn kernels and bamboo shoots. Keep warm.

3 Fill a fondue pan with water and bring to the boil at the table.

4 Arrange garnishes (peas, corn kernels, bamboo shoots, shallots and rice) around the fondue. Place steak and chicken on a plate. The guests cook the meat themselves, dipping it into the boiling water for 5–8 minutes on long-handled forks.

5 Place an egg yolk in each guest's bowl — the stock can be added to this, as desired. *Serves 4*

116

Sukiyaki

225 g (½ lb) (1 cup) rice
salt
225 g (½ lb) (3 cups) finely shredded
   white cabbage
1 large leek, cleaned and sliced
   diagonally
225 g (½ lb) canned water chestnuts
2 large carrots, thinly sliced
100 g (¼ lb) radishes, sliced
4 unbroken egg yolks
450 g (1 lb) fillet beef, cut in 3 mm
   (⅛ in) slices, about 5 cm (2 in) long

Stock
600 mL (1 pint) 2½ cups) water
2 beef stock cubes
50 mL (2 fl oz) (¼ cup) soy sauce
150 mL (¼ pint) (⅔ cup) dry sherry

1 Boil rice in salted water until just
tender. Rinse and drain. Prepare
vegetables and arrange in a wide
dish.

2 At the table, serve each diner with
a bowl of rice and a side dish containing an unbroken egg yolk. Bring
water to the boil in the fondue pot.
Crumble in the stock cubes and stir
to dissolve. Pour in soy sauce and
sherry, bring back to the boil and
keep just under boiling point.

3 Place pieces of each vegetable in
the stock, and a piece of meat for
each diner in the middle. Diners may
remove the meat when it is cooked
to their individual taste — a couple of
minutes should be enough. Serve the
vegetables, also cooked to taste, on
the rice, and dip the pieces of meat in
the egg yolk before eating. Replenish
the stock with vegetables and meat
as required.

Serves 4

Sukiyaki

Meat Cider Sauce for Pasta

1 onion, finely chopped
1 clove garlic, crushed
15 mL (1 tablespoon) oil
15 mL (1 tablespoon) butter
225 g (½ lb) (1 cup) minced beef and
   pork
30 mL (2 tablespoons) flour
300 mL (½ pint) (1¼ cups) dry cider
150 mL (¼ pint) (⅔ cup) meat stock
15 mL (1 tablespoon) tomato paste
15 mL (1 tablespoon) chopped
   parsley and oregano
salt and pepper
15 mL (1 tablespoon) cornflour

1 Gently fry onion and garlic in oil
and butter for 3 minutes to soften.
Add meat and fry, stirring constantly, for 5–8 minutes until meat is
browned. Strain off any excess fat
that has melted out of the meat.

2 Stir in flour and cook for 1 minute.
Add cider, stock, and tomato paste,
and bring to the boil. Add herbs, salt
and pepper. Simmer over low heat
for 30–40 minutes, stirring from time
to time.

3 Thicken at the end if necessary
with the cornflour dissolved in a
little water. Serve as a sauce with
spaghetti or macaroni.

Serves 4

Basic Economy Beef

1 large onion, chopped
25 g (1 oz) (2 tablespoons) margarine
450 g (1 lb) (2 cups) minced beef
25 g (1 oz) (4 tablespoons) flour
25 g (1 oz) (2 tablespoons) tomato
   paste
300 mL (½ pint) (1¼ cups) water
1 beef stock cube
salt, pepper
pinch mace

1 Fry onion gently in fat until soft.
Stir in beef and flour and cook until
browned. Add tomato paste and
cook for 2 minutes.

2 Pour in the water, in which the
stock cube has been dissolved, and
season with salt, pepper and a pinch
of mace. Simmer ½ hour, stirring
from time to time.

Makes 675 g (1½ lb)
Serves 4

MICROWAVE Beef

Beef Bourguignonne

1 kg (2 lb) sirloin steak, cut into thin strips
4 slices bacon, cut into 2 cm pieces
75 g (3 oz) (⅓ cup) flour
250 g (½ lb) mushrooms, sliced
4 medium-sized onions, cut into sixths
1 medium carrot, sliced
1 clove garlic, finely chopped
225 mL (8 fl oz) (1 cup) dry red wine
100 mL (4 fl oz) (½ cup) beef consomme or stock
15 mL (1 tablespoon) chopped parsley
5 mL (1 teaspoon) salt
2.5 mL (½ teaspoon) thyme
pinch pepper
2 bay leaves

1 Place bacon in 3 litre casserole. Cover and cook on high 3 minutes. Drain, leaving 1 tablespoon of dripping. Stir in beef strips, sprinkle with flour and toss to coat evenly.

2 Mix in remaining ingredients. Cover and cook on high 5 minutes. Stir. Cook on medium 40 minutes or until fork tender, stirring during cooking to thicken sauce evenly. Let stand 10 minutes before serving. Serve with buttered noodles or rice.

Serves 6–8

Note: For long slow cooking, microwave on low 60–75 minutes.

Beef Roulades with Brazil Nut Stuffing

500 g (1 lb) rump steak, thinly slices
1 small onion, finely chopped
60 g (2 oz) (½ cup) celery, thinly sliced
30 g (1 oz) (2 tablespoons) butter
100 mL (4 fl oz) (⅓ cup) beef consomme or stock
60 g (2 oz) (½ cup) chopped Brazil nuts
100 g (4 oz) (1 cup) prepared stuffing mix
20 g (¾ oz) (1½ tablespoons) seasoned flour
15 mL (1 tablespoon) peanut oil
125 mL (¼ pint) (⅔ cup) beef consomme or stock
125 mL (¼ pint) (⅔ cup) red wine
15 mL (3 teaspoons) arrowroot
15-30 mL (1-2 tablespoons) cold water
30 g (1 oz) (¼ cup) Brazil nuts

1 Cut steak into 10 cm squares. Pound lightly with meat mallet. Combine onions, celery and butter in a medium-sized bowl. Cook on high 3–4 minutes. Add ⅓ cup stock and cook on high 1 minute. Stir in ½ cup Brazil nuts and stuffing. Allow to cool.

2 Spread filling over meat slices, roll up and tie with string. Coat rolls evenly with seasoned flour. Heat browning dish on high 6 minutes. Add oil and heat 1 minute. Cook roulades 6 minutes, turning during cooking. Add 125 mL stock and wine and cook on medium 12 minutes.

3 Remove string from rolls and transfer to serving plate. Blend arrowroot with water, stir into pan liquids and cook on high 3 minutes or until boiling. Strain sauce and pour over roulades. Garnish with sliced Brazil nuts to serve.

Serves 4–6

Stroganoff

1 quantity of basic beef mix, thawed
125 g (¼ lb) mushrooms, chopped
100 mL (4 fl oz) (½ cup) beef consomme
25 g (1½ tablespoons) seasoned flour
2.5 mL (1 teaspoon) Worcestershire sauce
200 mL (6 fl oz) (⅔ cup) sour cream

1 In a 2 litre casserole combine beef mixture, mushrooms, consomme, flour and sauce. Blend well and cook on high 6 minutes, stirring twice during cooking.

2 Blend in sour cream and reheat on high 1–2 minutes. Serve with rice or pasta.

Serves 4–6

Marinated Beef

1.5-2 kg (3½-4 lb) whole fillet beef
15 mL (1 tablespoon) wholegrain mustard
15 mL (1 tablespoon) oil
juice and rind 1 lemon
15 mL (1 tablespoon) honey
2.5 mL (½ teaspoon) soy sauce

1 Combine mustard, oil, lemon juice and rind, honey and soy sauce. Coat fillet with mixture.

2 Cook fillet on roasting rack on medium high 30–35 minutes. Turn once about halfway through cooking.

3 Stand covered with foil 15 minutes. Slice beef thinly to serve.

Serves 8–10

Marinated Beef

Roasted Ribs with Sweet Sour Sauce

Roasted Ribs with Sweet Sour Sauce

1–1.5 kg (2–3 lb) beef ribs, cut in 5 cm lengths
1 medium-sized onion, thinly sliced.
2.5 mL (1 teaspoon) basil
225 mL (8 fl oz) (1 cup) sweet sour sauce or barbecue sauce
15 mL (1 tablespoon) lemon juice, strained

Sweet Sour Sauce
25 g (1 oz) (¼ cup) brown sugar
30 g (1 tablespoon) cornflour
100 mL (4 fl oz) (½ cup) pineapple juice
50 mL (2 fl oz) (¼ cup) vinegar
30 mL (2 tablespoons) soy sauce

1 Arrange ribs in roasting dish in a single layer for even cooking. Top with onion rings and basil and cook on high 5 minutes. Reduce power to medium and cook for 15 minutes.

2 Rearrange and turn ribs over. Cook on medium 15–20 minutes. Drain off liquid.

3 To make the sauce combine sugar and cornflour in a jug. Blend in remaining sauce ingredients and cook on high 3 minutes or until thickened, stirring every minute.

4 Pour sauce over ribs and cook for a further 6 minutes.

Serves 4–6

Fillet of Beef with Oyster Sauce

6 fillet steaks
15 g (1 tablespoon) butter
1 clove garlic, crushed

Oyster Sauce
15 mL (1 tablespoon) oil
15 g (1 tablespoon) cornflour
15 mL (1 tablespoon) parsley,
   chopped
salt and pepper
dash Worcestershire sauce
225 mL (8 fl oz) (1 cup) dry white
   wine
dash medium-sweet sherry
24 oysters

1 Preheat browning dish on high 7
minutes. Add butter and garlic. Cook
1 minute more then sear steaks.
Cook steaks, 3 at a time, on high for 9
minutes, turning once.

2 Combine all ingredients for sauce
and cook on high 3–5 minutes. Stir
vigorously then add oysters.

3 Arrange steaks on a microwave-
safe dish, reheat on high 30–60
seconds and serve with sauce.

Serves 6

Savoury Beef Roll

750 g (1½ lb) lean minced beef
2 eggs
25 g (1 oz) (¼ cup) dry breadcrumbs
15 mL (1 tablespoon) barbecue sauce
2.5 mL (1 teaspoon) beef seasoning
75 g (3 oz) (¾ cup) chopped green
   capsicum (pepper)
75 g (3 oz) (¾ cup) chopped red
   capsicum (pepper)
1 onion, chopped
100 g (4 oz) (1 cup) grated cheese

1 Combine mince, egg, breadcrumbs, sauce and seasoning. On a
sheet of plastic wrap pat out to a rectangle 2 cm thick.

2 Cook capsicum and onion on high
2 minutes. Cool. Place onto meat
leaving 2.5 cm border on all sides.
Roll up and press edges together to
seal. Place in baking dish seam side
down.

3 Cook on high 5 minutes, then on
medium 25–30 minutes. During the
last 10 minutes of cooking time
sprinkle with grated cheese.

Serves 4–6

Filet Mignon

4 × 180 g (⅓ lb) filet mignon
15 g (1 tablespoon) butter

1 Preheat browning grill on high 9
minutes. Butter one side of each
mignon and place buttered side
down on preheated grill. Cook on
high 3 minutes. Brush tops with butter
and turn mignons over. Cook on high
3 minutes for rare. Serve with mushroom sauce.

Serves 2

Mushroom Sauce
125 g (¼ lb) mushrooms
15 g (1 tablespoon) butter
15 g (1 tablespoon) flour
300 mL (½ pint) (1¼ cups) canned
   beef consomme
1 egg yolk
30 mL (2 tablespoons) cream
pinch salt
pinch pepper

1 Place butter in jug and heat on
high 1 minute. Add mushrooms and
cook 1 minute. Blend in flour. Cook a
further minute on high. Stir in consomme and cook on high 3–4 minutes, stirring after 2 minutes.

2 Combine egg and cream in bowl.
Add 2 tablespoons of sauce and
blend well. Fold into remaining
sauce. Season. Pour over mignons or
other grilled meat.

Makes 300 mL

T-bone Steak

2 T-bone steaks, 2 cm thick

1 Preheat browning grill on high 9
minutes. Butter grill and cook steaks
on high 3 minutes on first side, 2 minutes on second side for rare. Serve
with herb butter.

Serves 2

Basic Beef Mix

1.25 kg (2½ lb) lean minced beef
2 onions, sliced
2 cloves garlic, chopped
30 mL (2 tablespoons) peanut oil
15 mL (1 tablespoon) chilli sauce
25 mL (1½ tablespoons) onion soup
   mix
25 mL (1½ tablespoons) Gravox
   powder

1 Combine onion, garlic and oil in 2
litre casserole. Cook on high 3 minutes. Crumble in mince and cook on
high 7–8 minutes. Stir in remaining
ingredients and cook on high 6 minutes, stirring twice during cooking.
Cool.

2 The mixture can now be placed in
a plastic container and frozen until
ready to use for savoury mince
dishes such as lasagna or Bolognese
sauce, or for stuffing vegetables.

Serves 8–12

Presenting Pork and Ham

Pork has a distinctive flavour which is quite different from other meats. As well as providing us with tasty joints and chops, the pig also furnishes bacon, ham and many types of sausage. Pork is traditionally served with apple or gooseberry sauce but there are many variations. It is a favourite meat in oriental dishes and is often served with ginger, soy sauce or pineapple.

Pork Portuguese served with rice is a delicious way of serving pork in white wine with tomatoes, celery and peppers. Or try Sausage Kebabs Romana, a meaty mixture of liver marinated in wine and Worcestershire Sauce, cooked with sausages.

Roast Pork

Crown Roast of Pork Step-by-step

1 Remove the chine bones from the two pork joints.
2 Cut 4 cm (1½ in) of fat from ends of the bones.
3 Trim away the sinew from between the bones.
4 Bend two joints round to form crown shape. Tie.
5 Place the crown in a roasting pan and brush all over with

the melted butter.
6 Wrap aluminium foil round ends of bones.
7 Heat the rest of the butter in a frying pan, add the onion and celery and fry until soft.
8 Add the sausage meat and cook until the fat runs out of

the meat.

9 Drain the excess fat from pan.

10 Add the breadcrumbs, rosemary, parsley, seasoning and stock and mix well.

11 Place stuffing in centre of crown and cover with a circle of aluminium foil to prevent drying. Roast in oven, allowing 30 minutes per 450 g (1 lb).

12 Remove from the oven, discard the pieces of foil and place a cutlet frill on the end of each bone.

13 Garnish joint with peas and roast potatoes.

Crown Roast of Pork

2 loins of pork, each containing
    8 chops, chined
50 g (2 oz) (4 tablespoons) melted
    butter
1 onion, finely chopped
2 sticks celery, finely chopped
225 g (½ lb) (1 cup) pork sausage meat
100 g (¼ lb) (2 cups) fresh
    breadcrumbs
5 mL (1 teaspoon) rosemary
30 mL (2 tablespoons) finely chopped
    parsley
2.5 mL (½ teaspoon) thyme
salt and pepper
50 mL (2 fl oz) (¼ cup) chicken stock

1 Remove chine bone from the loins.
Cut 4 cm (1½ in) of the fat away from
the ends of the bones. Trim away
sinew from between bones.

2 Bend the 2 loins round to form the
crown and secure with string. Place
crown in a roasting pan and brush
the outside with half the melted butter. Wrap pieces of aluminium foil
round the ends of the bones to prevent them burning.

3 Preheat oven to 180°C (350°F). Prepare the stuffing: heat remaining butter in a frying pan, add onion and celery and fry until they are soft.

4 Add sausage meat and cook until
all the fat has run out of the meat.
Drain excess fat from the pan.

5 Stir in breadcrumbs, rosemary,
parsley, thyme, seasoning and stock
and mix.

6 Place stuffing in the centre of the
crown and cover stuffing with a circle
of foil.

7 Roast crown in the oven, allowing
30 minutes per 450 g (1 lb).

8 Before serving, remove the pieces
of foil and place a cutlet frill on the
end of each bone. Serve the crown
roast garnished with peas and roast
potatoes.

Serves 8

Braised Leg of Pork

1.5 kg (3 lb) joint of pork, from the
    thick part (cushion) of the leg
300 mL (½ pint) (1¼ cups) dry white
    wine
70 mL (2½ fl oz) (⅓ cup) brandy
2 shallots (spring onions, scallions),
    sliced
1 clove garlic, crushed
2 carrots, sliced
1 bay leaf
sprig thyme
sprig parsley
salt and pepper
25 g (1 oz) (2 tablespoons) fat
25 g (1 oz) (½ cup) brown
    breadcrumbs
50 mL (2 fl oz) (¼ cup) water
5 mL (1 teaspoon) cornflour

1 Preheat oven to 230°C (450°F).
Trim pork all round. Remove rind
and some of the fat.

2 Place in a large bowl and cover
with wine, brandy, shallots, garlic,
carrots, bay leaf, thyme and parsley.
Cover and allow meat to marinate
for 6 hours, turning from time to
time.

3 Wipe it, season to taste with salt
and pepper and place in a roasting
pan. Add the fat and sear meat in the
oven for 30 minutes. Strain off any
excess fat.

4 Reduce the heat to 180°C (350°F).
Add vegetables and herbs and baste
meat with the marinating liquor
from time to time, until it is cooked.
The cooking time will depend on the
weight of the leg. Allow at least 30
minutes per 450 g (1 lb). When
cooked, sprinkle meat with the
brown breadcrumbs.

5 Strain juices into a saucepan.
Season, add water and boil for 5 minutes. If necessary, thicken with cornflour mixed with a little water. Serve
sauce in a gravyboat with the meat.

Serves 8–10

Glazed Loin of Pork with Stuffed Pears

1.5 kg (3 lb) boned and rolled loin of
    pork
45 mL (3 tablespoons) cream cheese
30 mL (2 tablespoons) sweet pickle
40 g (1½ oz) (½ cup) chopped walnuts
6 canned pear halves, drained
6 gherkins, cut into fans

Marinade
30 mL (2 tablespoons) each clear
    honey, vinegar and oil
60 mL (4 tablespoons) orange juice
15 mL (1 tablespoon) soy sauce
5 mL (1 teaspoon) paprika
salt and pepper

1 Weigh meat and calculate cooking
time, allowing 20 minutes per 450 g
(1 lb) and 20 minutes over.

2 Combine marinade ingredients
and place in a shallow dish with the
pork. Marinate for several hours,
turning frequently.

3 Preheat oven to 200°C (400°F).
Remove pork from marinade and
place in a roasting pan. Bake for the
calculated cooking time, reducing the
oven temperature after 15 minutes to
190°C (375°F) and basting with the
marinade for the last 30 minutes.
Cool meat on a rack. Remove string.

4 Blend cream cheese, pickle and
walnuts and divide between pear
halves. Garnish the cold meat with
the stuffed pears and gherkins.

Serves 6

*Glazed Loin of Pork with Stuffed
Pears*

Pork with Rosemary

Loin of Pork with Cheese Glazing

1.2 kg (2½ lb) loin of pork, boned and derinded
salt and pepper
350 g (¾ lb) Gruyere cheese, diced
150 g (5 oz) (2½ cups) fresh breadcrumbs
15 mL (1 tablespoon) kirsch
15 mL (1 tablespoon) oil
225 mL (8 fl oz) (1 cup) beef stock
1 onion, quartered
2 sticks celery, diced
300 mL (½ pint) (1¼ cups) dry white wine
5 mL (1 teaspoon) cornflour
50 g (2 oz) (½ cup) grated Cheddar cheese
5 mL (1 teaspoon) chopped celery leaves

1 Preheat oven to 190°C (375°F)
2 Make a slit along the pork and season the inside. Prepare the stuffing: combine the Gruyere, breadcrumbs and kirsch and place in the centre of the meat. Roll up pork and secure with string. Brush the outside with oil and place on a rack in a roasting pan. Bake for 1¼ hours, basting occasionally with the beef stock.
3 Twenty minutes before the end of the cooking time, add onion and celery and return pan to the oven for 10 minutes.
4 Add the wine and return pan for 10 minutes.
5 When the cooking time is complete, drain gravy into a saucepan, remove surplus fat and thicken with cornflour mixed with a little water. Season the gravy.
6 Remove string from the meat, sprinkle with grated Cheddar and return to oven for a few minutes to melt the cheese. Serve with gravy, and sprinkle with celery leaves.

Serves 6–8

Pork with Rosemary

1 kg (2 lb) lean boned shoulder or loin of pork
salt and pepper
150 g (5 oz) (⅝ cup) butter
1 carrot, sliced
1 large onion, chopped
1 stick celery, diced
350 g (¾ lb) mushrooms
300 mL (½ pint) (1¼ cups) water
150 mL (¼ pint) (⅔ cup) dry white wine
2 sprigs rosemary
1 clove garlic, crushed

1 Preheat oven to 190°C (375°F). Season meat.
2 Melt half the butter in a flameproof casserole. Add the meat and brown on all sides. Remove casserole from heat.
3 In a separate pan heat remaining butter. Add carrot and saute for 5 minutes. Add onion and celery and saute for 5 minutes. Add mushrooms, cover and cook on a low heat for 2 minutes.

4 Pour contents of pan into casserole. Add water, wine, one rosemary sprig and garlic. Check seasoning. Cover and bake for 1½ hours or until the meat is well cooked.

5 Serve garnished with the second sprig of rosemary.

Serves 6

Pork with Pineapple

75 g (3 oz) (6 tablespoons) butter
70 mL (2½ fl oz) (⅓ cup) oil
1 kg (2 lb) best end of pork
salt and pepper
150 mL (¼ pint) (⅔ cup) water
1 small pineapple, cut into chunks, or 225 g (½ lb) canned pineapple pieces, drained

Gravy
15 mL (1 tablespoon) flour
70 mL (2½ fl oz) (⅓ cup) water
30 mL (1 fl oz) (2 tablespoons) Worcestershire sauce
70 mL (2½ fl oz) (⅓ cup) pineapple juice
15 mL (1 tablespoon) cornflour

1 Preheat oven to 190°C (375°F). Melt butter in a saucepan and combine with the oil.

2 Remove back spine bone from joint and all the rind from the pork. Season meat with salt and pepper and brush all over with half the butter and oil mixture. Place pork on a rack in a roasting pan and roast in the oven for 1½ hours or until meat is well cooked. Baste from time to time with the water.

3 Meanwhile heat remaining butter and oil in a pan and fry pineapple pieces for 3 minutes on both sides or until golden. Remove from pan and keep warm.

4 When meat is cooked, prepare the gravy. Remove most of the fat from the meat juice. Add flour and stir over a low heat for 3–4 minutes until browned. Add water, Worcestershire sauce, and pineapple juice. Bring to the boil and simmer for 5 minutes, stirring all the time. Thicken with cornflour mixed with a little water. Check seasoning.

5 Place meat on a heated serving tray, surround it with the pineapple pieces and, just before serving, pour over gravy.

Serves 8

Boned Blade of Pork with Apricot and Walnut Stuffing

2 kg (4 lb) blade or shoulder of pork, boned
1 onion, finely chopped
15 g (½ oz) (1 tablespoon) butter
50 g (2 oz) (⅜ cup) dried apricots, soaked in water overnight and finely chopped
12 walnut halves, finely chopped
50 g (2 oz) (1 cup) fresh white breadcrumbs
15 mL (1 tablespoon) chopped parsley
salt and pepper
1 egg
15 mL (1 tablespoon) oil
5 mL (1 teaspoon) salt

1 Preheat oven to 230°C (450°F). Score rind of the pork with a very sharp knife.

2 Fry onion gently in the butter until lightly golden.

3 Mix together apricots, walnuts, onion, breadcrumbs, parsley and salt and pepper to taste. Mix in egg.

4 Place stuffing on the inner side of the meat. Roll up meat and tie tightly with string. Place in a greased roasting pan, brush with oil and rub salt into the skin.

5 Roast for 30 minutes or until the surface has crackled. Turn oven to 190°C (375°F) and roast for a further hour.

Serves 6

Pork with Pineapple

129

8

9

10

1 Score pork rind with sharp knife.
2 Peel and finely chop the onion.
3 Fry onion in butter until soft and golden.
4 Finely chop apricots and walnuts. Mix with onion, breadcrumbs and parsley. Season.
5 Bind with the egg and mix well.

6 Place the stuffing on the inner side of the meat and press it down well.
7 Roll the meat up and tie it tightly with string.
8 Brush the skin all over with the oil.
9 Salt skin well to ensure a crisp crackling.
10 Serve the stuffed pork with boiled, sliced leeks.

Pork with Prune and Almond Stuffing

1 kg (2 lb) boned fillet of pork, rind and some fat removed
salt and pepper
100 g (¼ lb) (½ cup) long grain rice

Stuffing
100 g (¼ lb) (¾ cup) stoned prunes, cooked
50 g (2 oz) (½ cup) flaked almonds
100 g (¼ lb) (2 cups) fresh breadcrumbs
1 egg
pinch allspice

Gravy
300 mL (½ pint) (1¼ cups) stock
½ beef stock cube
5 mL (1 teaspoon) cornflour
100 mL (4 fl oz) (½ cup) port or dry sherry (optional)

1 Preheat oven to 190°C (375°F).
2 Spread meat flat and season the inside. Combine the stuffing ingredients and place along the centre of the meat. Roll up and secure with string. Season the outside of the meat and roast in oven for 1¼ hours, basting from time to time with a little water.
3 Meanwhile, cook rice in boiling salted water until tender. Drain and keep warm.
4 Place stock in a pan, crumble in the stock cube and bring to the boil. Add cornflour mixed with a little water and cook for a few minutes more. Season gravy and add the port or sherry, if used.
5 Place rice on a serving dish and lay roast pork on top. Serve with gravy and apple sauce.

Serves 6

Tip: You can substitute other nuts such as chopped walnuts for the almonds in the stuffing.

Stuffed Pork with Eggplants (Aubergines)

1.2 kg (2½ lb) boneless loin of pork, rind and some fat removed
salt and pepper
450 g (1 lb) onions, chopped
1 clove garlic, crushed
30 mL (1 fl oz) (2 tablespoons) oil
8 tomatoes, skinned, seeded and chopped
5 mL (1 teaspoon) chilli powder
50 g (2 oz) (⅓ cup) seedless raisins
175 g (6 oz) cooked rice
1 egg, beaten
150 mL (¼ pint) (⅔ cup) dry white wine
150 mL (¼ pint) (⅔ cup) stock
2 eggplants (aubergines), peeled and sliced
25 g (1 oz) (¼ cup) flour
oil for deep frying

1 Preheat oven to 190°C (375°F). Cut pork almost in half lengthways and season.
2 Fry onions and garlic in oil until soft. Add tomatoes and chilli powder and simmer for 5 minutes. Add raisins.
3 Blend half the tomato mixture with rice and egg and place stuffing on pork. Fold over the meat and tie at intervals. Place in a roasting pan and cook in the oven for 1 hour.
4 Pour out the fat which has collected in the roasting pan. Mix remaining tomato mixture with wine and stock and add to pan. Return to oven for 30 minutes or until meat is cooked. Baste occasionally, adding more wine to the sauce if it becomes too thick.
5 Meanwhile, soak the eggplants in salted water for 15 minutes, then drain and dry. Coat in flour and deep fry until golden. Keep warm.
6 Remove string from joint and place the meat in a serving dish. Pour sauce round it and add the eggplant slices.

Serves 6–8

Pork Orloff

50 g (2 oz) (4 tablespoons) margarine
few bacon rinds
1.5 kg (3 lb) loin of pork in 1 piece
1 onion
1 carrot, sliced
1 bay leaf
bouquet garni
salt and pepper
45 mL (3 tablespoons) grated Parmesan cheese
25 g (1 oz) (2 tablespoons) butter, cut in pieces

Puree
50 g (2 oz) (4 tablespoons) margarine
15 mL (1 tablespoon) oil
4 onions, chopped
450 g (1 lb) mushroom caps, diced
150 mL (¼ pint) (⅔ cup) thick white sauce
150 mL (¼ pint) (⅔ cup) thickened cream
pinch grated nutmeg
45 mL (3 tablespoons) grated Parmesan cheese

1 Heat margarine in a pan, add bacon rinds and pork and cook until browned. Add onion, sliced carrot, bay leaf, bouquet garni and seasoning and then cover with water. Cover and cook slowly for 1¾ hours.
2 Meanwhile, make the puree. Heat margarine and oil in a pan and gently fry chopped onion for 10 minutes, without browning. Add diced mushrooms and cook for 1 minute.
3 Strain off fat and add white sauce and cream. Mix well and season with salt, pepper and nutmeg. Stir in cheese and cook for 3 minutes. Cool.
4 Preheat oven to 230°C (450°F). Lift pork from pan and carve into thick slices. Spread each slice with puree and replace slices to resemble the original joint.
5 Cover with remaining puree and sprinkle with grated Parmesan cheese and the pieces of butter. Return to oven for 5–10 minutes to brown.

Serves 6–8

Pork with Prune and Almond Stuffing

Flemish Pork with Red Cabbage

1 kg (2¼ lb) best end of pork, or loin
salt and pepper
good pinch allspice
600 mL (2¼ fl oz) (4 tablespoons) oil
1 small red cabbage, shredded
1 onion, chopped
1 clove garlic, finely chopped
100 mL (4 fl oz) (½ cup) vinegar
2 apples, peeled, cored and thinly
    sliced
15 mL (1 tablespoon) sugar
5 mL (1 teaspoon) chopped parsley
½ beef stock cube dissolved in
    300 mL (½ pint) (1¼ cups) water
15 mL (1 tablespoon) tomato paste
10 mL (2 teaspoons) cornflour, mixed
    with water

1 Preheat oven to 190°C (375°F). Remove rind from pork and season with salt, pepper and allspice. Brush with oil and place on a rack in a roasting pan. Roast in oven for 1¼ hours, basting frequently with 225 mL (8 fl oz) (1 cup) water.

2 Place cabbage in an earthenware bowl with onion, garlic, vinegar and 550 mL (1 pint) (2½ cups) water. Leave to stand for 15 minutes.

3 Add apples to cabbage with sugar and seasoning. Transfer to a stainless steel pan, bring to the boil and simmer for 20 minutes.

4 Transfer pork to a serving dish. Surround with cabbage in its liquid and sprinkle with parsley.

5 Pour off fat from the roasting pan, retaining meat juices. Add stock and tomato paste, bring to the boil and simmer 5 minutes. Add cornflour to the pan and simmer 1 minute, stirring. Season and strain into a sauce boat or jug to serve.

Serves 6

Tips: If you are not a lover of red cabbage, don't ignore this recipe. You can substitute white Savoy cabbage and omit the vinegar. However, if you do use red cabbage and want to make this dish extra special, use red wine instead of water.

Pickled Pork with Saffron Rice

1.5 kg (3 lb) pork loin, boned
15 mL (1 tablespoon) saltpetre
450 g (1 lb) sea salt
5 mL (1 teaspoon) powdered ginger
salt and pepper
4 cloves
450 g (1 lb) (2 cups) long grain rice
1.25 mL (¼ teaspoon) powdered
    saffron
50 g (2 oz) (4 tablespoons) butter

1 Buy pork loin the day before the dish is to be served. Rub saltpetre over it. Put a layer of sea salt in an earthenware bowl. Lay in the meat and cover with the rest of the salt. Leave for 24 hours in a cool place.

2 Remove pork from salt, wash thoroughly in cold water and dry it.

3 Preheat oven to 190°C (375°F). Spread out a cloth and put the meat onto it, fat side down. Sprinkle with ginger and pepper to taste. Roll up, seasoned side inside, tying it tightly with string.

4 Using the point of a very sharp knife, cut fat in criss-cross lines forming a diamond pattern. Stud meat with 4 cloves; season with pepper.

5 Pour 100 mL (4 fl oz) (½ cup) of warm water into a roasting pan containing a rack. Place meat on the rack and roast in the oven for about 1¼ hours or until cooked through.

6 Put rice into a pan with 1.2 litres (2 pints) (5 cups) cold water, the saffron and salt to taste. Cover and cook for 20 minutes, until rice is tender and the water absorbed. Add butter, season with pepper and fluff up with a fork.

7 Arrange sliced pork on the rice to serve.

Serves 8

Tip: You can use ordinary table or cooking salt for curing the pork instead of sea salt.

Pork Chops Provencal

30 mL (2 tablespoons) olive oil
15 mL (1 tablespoon) vinegar
salt and pepper
15 mL (1 tablespoon) mixed fresh
    chopped sage, parsley, thyme
4 pork chops
100 g (¼ lb) sliced bacon
1 large onion, thinly sliced
25 g (1 oz) (2 tablespoons) butter
450 g (1 lb) canned tomatoes
15 mL (1 tablespoon) tomato paste
2.5 mL (½ teaspoon) sugar
5 mL (1 teaspoon) Worcestershire
    sauce
10 mL (2 teaspoons) cornflour
    (optional)

1 Prepare marinade by mixing together oil, vinegar, salt and pepper, and herbs. Place spare rib chops in a shallow dish. Cover with marinade and leave for 3 hours or overnight, turning occasionally.

2 To make the sauce: remove bacon rind and chop the slices. Fry bacon and onion in the butter for 5 minutes over low heat, until onion is soft.

3 Add tomatoes, tomato paste, sugar and Worcestershire sauce. Bring quickly to the boil and simmer for 5–10 minutes, stirring frequently.

4 Meanwhile, preheat oven to 180°C (350°F). Drain pork chops from the marinade. Place chops in an ovenproof dish and pour the sauce over them. Bake for about 40 minutes. Serve at once with savoury rice.

Serves 4

1 Twelve hours before dish is required, prepare the marinade. Mix two pinches each of salt, pepper and paprika and sprinkle over the pork chops.

2 Place the chops in a plastic bag and top each one with a bay leaf. Insert a sprig of thyme.

3 Pour in half of the wine and the rum, holding the opening of the bag upright so that the liquid does not seep out.

4 Seal bag tightly. Leave the chops to marinate overnight.

5 Pour other half of wine over prunes. Soak 1 hour. Then place in saucepan, bring to boil and simmer 15 minutes.

6 Melt the oil and butter in a pan and coat the pork chops in flour. Saute the chops a few minutes on each side to brown them.

7 Pour the strained marinade over the chops. Cover pan and simmer gently 20 minutes.

8 Transfer the chops to a heated serving dish.

9 Simmering the pan juices over low heat, stir in the cream with a wooden spoon until well blended. Cook, stirring for 5 minutes.

10 Strain the prunes and add them to the sauce. Taste, and add more salt and pepper if required. Stir and simmer for a few more minutes.

11 To serve, arrange the prunes in the middle of the dish on top of the pork chops and strain the sauce over the whole dish.

Uncle Tom Pork Chops

2 good pinches each salt, pepper,
    paprika
4 pork chops
4 bay leaves
sprig thyme
300 mL (½ pint) (1¼ cups) muscadet
    or other dry white wine
50 mL (2 fl oz) (¼ cup) rum
350 g (¾ lb) (2 cups) prunes
30 mL (1 fl oz) (2 tablespoons) oil
25 g (1 oz) (2 tablespoons) butter
25 g (1 oz) (¼ cup) flour
50 mL (2 fl oz) (¼ cup) cream

1 Prepare marinade by mixing salt,
pepper and paprika and sprinkling it
over both sides of the pork chops.
Place chops in a dish or plastic bag,
top each one with a bay leaf, and add
a sprig of thyme, half the wine and
rum. Leave to marinate for 12 hours
or overnight.

2 Soak prunes in the rest of the wine
for an hour, then put them in a saucepan and bring to the boil. Simmer 15
minutes and drain from the liquid.

3 Remove pork chops from the marinade, and pat dry with a kitchen
towel. Strain and reserve the marinade. Heat oil and butter in a frying
pan. Coat chops in flour and fry for a
few minutes on each side until just
browned.

4 Pour marinade over chops, cover
pan and leave to simmer over low
heat for 20 minutes.

5 Remove chops to a serving dish
and keep warm. Stir cream into pan
juices, and cook for 5 minutes at a
gentle simmer. Add prunes and stir
for a few more minutes.

6 Strain prunes from sauce with a
perforated spoon and arrange in the
middle of the serving dish on the
chops. Strain sauce over the whole
dish and serve very hot.

Serves 4

Pork Chops with Cider Cream Sauce

Pork Chops with Cider Cream Sauce

4 pork chops
15 g (½ oz) (2 tablespoons) flour
salt and pepper
50 g (2 oz) (4 tablespoons) butter
1 large onion, chopped
175 g (6 oz) (1½ cups) sliced
    mushrooms
300 mL (½ pint) (1¼ cups) dry cider
50 mL (2 fl oz) (¼ cup) thickened
    cream
15 mL (1 tablespoon) chopped
    parsley

1 Coat pork chops in half the flour
seasoned with salt and pepper. Melt
butter in a large frying pan and fry
pork chops slowly until cooked
through. Remove chops from pan
and keep warm.

2 Add onion to the meat cooking
juices and fry gently for 3 minutes.

3 Stir in mushrooms and cook for
another 3 minutes.

4 Stir in the rest of the flour and cook
for 1 minute. Take pan off heat and
stir in cider to make a smooth sauce.
Return pan to heat and stir 1 minute.

5 Over a low heat, stir in cream and
season with salt and pepper. Heat to
just below boiling point. Pour sauce
over the pork chops, garnish with
chopped parsley, and serve at once.

Serves 4

Pork in Cider

100 mL (4 fl oz) (½ cup) oil
2 carrots, diced
2 onions, diced
1 clove garlic, crushed
2 shallots (spring onions, scallions), chopped
1 stick celery, thinly sliced
50 g (2 oz) (½ cup) flour
3 tomatoes, skinned, seeded and chopped
300 mL (½ pint) (1¼ cups) dry cider
bouquet garni
225 g (½ lb) (1 cup) canned, creamed corn kernels
salt and pepper
6 × 225 g (½ lb) pork chops
15 mL (1 tablespoon) chopped parsley

1 Heat half the oil in a saucepan and gently fry carrots, onions, garlic, shallots and celery until tender.
2 Sprinkle in half the flour, stir and cook for 1 minute. Add tomatoes and cider and bring to the boil. Add bouquet garni and corn kernels and season with salt and pepper. Simmer for 15–20 minutes.
3 Coat chops in remaining seasoned flour and heat the rest of the oil in a pan. Shallow fry the pork for about 10 minutes until browned.
4 Preheat oven to 180°C (350°F).
5 Remove chops from pan and arrange in an ovenproof dish. Cover with sauce and check seasoning. Bake in covered ovenproof dish for 20 minutes.
6 Sprinkle with parsley and serve with boiled new potatoes.

Serves 6

Tip: If you have no cider, you can always use apple juice or white wine or a mixture of both. Fresh sliced apples will increase the fruity flavour. Fresh corn on the cob or canned corn kernels will give the casserole a more crunchy texture.

Pilsener Pork Chops

4 pork chops
15 mL (1 tablespoon) oil
15 mL (1 tablespoon) butter
1 onion, sliced
50 g (2 oz) (⅔ cup) sliced button mushrooms
salt and pepper
pinch dried sage and marjoram
300 mL (½ pint) (1¼ cups) flat pilsener or light beer
5 mL (1 teaspoon) cornflour

1 Fry pork chops gently in oil and butter until just browned on each side. Remove from pan and arrange in an ovenproof dish.
2 Preheat oven to 180°C (350°F).
3 Fry onion for 2 minutes to soften. Add mushrooms fry 2 minutes.
4 Arrange onions and mushrooms over pork chops. Season with salt and pepper and the herbs. Pour on the beer. Cover lightly with foil and bake for about 40 minutes until chops are tender, basting from time to time.
5 Drain liquid from the dish and thicken it if necessary with cornflour dissolved in a little water. Pour liquid over chops and serve.

Serves 4

Italian-style Pork Chops

25 g (1 oz) (2 tablespoons) butter
15 mL (1 tablespoon) oil
450 g (1 lb) onions, thinly sliced
4 pork chops or steaks
a little gravy browning
100 mL (4 fl oz) (½ cup) Marsala (or port)
salt and pepper

Veloute Sauce
30 g (3 tablespoons) flour
15 g (½ oz) (1 tablespoon) butter
300 mL (½ pint) (1¼ cups) chicken stock
squeeze lemon juice
15 mL (1 tablespoon) cream

1 Heat butter and oil in fry pan at 180°C (350°F) and fry onions until golden. Remove and keep warm.
2 Fry chops until well-browned on both sides (about 15–20 minutes).

Remove from pan and keep warm.
3 Meanwhile, while the chops are cooking, make the veloute sauce. Make a roux with the flour and butter. Cook for 3 minutes, then add stock and bring to the boil, stirring until it is thick and smooth. Simmer gently and stir in lemon juice and cream.
4 Add veloute sauce, gravy browning and Marsala to pan juices and boil up, stirring well, until thick and smooth and reduced by one-third.
5 Return onions and chops to the pan. Heat through in the sauce, season and serve with new potatoes and green vegetables.

Serves 4

Pork with Rice and Capsicums (Peppers)

6 pork chops
50 g (2 oz) (½ cup) seasoned flour
50 mL (2 fl oz) (¼ cup) oil
1 onion, chopped
1 green capsicum (pepper), seeded and cut in strips
1 red capsicum (pepper), seeded and cut in strips
1 clove garlic, crushed
100 mL (4 fl oz) (½ cup) water
salt and pepper
175 g (6 oz) (¾ cup) long grain rice
50 g (2 oz) (4 tablespoons) butter

1 Coat pork chops in seasoned flour. Heat oil in a frying pan and cook them for about 10 minutes until browned on both sides.
2 Remove chops and keep warm. Saute onion, green and red capsicums and garlic until soft. Then return chops to the pan and add water and seasoning. Bring to the boil, then simmer, covered, for 20 minutes.
3 Meanwhile, cook rice in boiling salted water until tender. Drain and place in a buttered mould. Press down firmly and turn out onto a serving dish.
4 Surround moulded rice with chops, capsicums and onion and serve immediately.

Serves 6

Pork Chops with Brussels Sprouts

Pork Chops with Brussels Sprouts

75 g (3 oz) (6 tablespoons) butter
1 large onion, chopped
225 g (½ lb) (1 cup) long grain rice
550 mL (1 pint) (2½ cups) water
5 mL (1 teaspoon) salt
450 g (1 lb) Brussels sprouts
salt and pepper
4 pork chops, about 150 g (6 oz) each
5 mL (1 teaspoon) chopped parsley

1 Melt 25 g (1 oz) (2 tablespoons) butter in a saucepan. Add chopped onion; fry lightly without browning.

2 Add rice, stir well and cook for 1 minute. Stir in water and salt. Bring to the boil and stir once. Lower heat, cover and simmer for 15 minutes until rice is tender and the liquid absorbed.

3 Cook Brussels sprouts in boiling salted water for about 8 minutes until cooked but still firm. Drain. Melt 25 g (1 oz) (2 tablespoons) butter in a pan, add the drained Brussels sprouts, cover and cook very lightly for 10 minutes, shaking pan from time to time.

4 Melt remaining butter in a frying pan. Season pork chops with salt and pepper and fry over a medium heat for about 10 minutes on each side. Remove chops to a warmed serving dish. Add 30 mL (1 fl oz) (2 tablespoons) water to the juices in the pan, and bring to the boil, stirring.

5 Arrange rice and Brussels sprouts around chops and pour over the sauce. Sprinkle with chopped parsley and serve.

Serves 4

Fruity Pork Chops

4 × 175 g (6 oz) pork chops
salt and pepper
50 mL (2 fl oz) (¼ cup) oil
pinch oregano
½ red capsicum (pepper), cut in strips
100 g (¼ lb) (½ cup) long grain rice
225 g (½ lb) green grapes, halved

1 Sprinkle pork chops with salt and freshly ground black pepper.

2 Heat the oil in a frying pan and gently fry chops until brown on both sides. Sprinkle in the oregano.

3 Add the strips of red capsicum and fry until soft.

4 Meanwhile, cook rice in boiling salted water until tender, but still firm.

5 Add halved grapes to the pork and capsicum and heat through.

6 Arrange rice on a heated serving dish and pile chops in the centre. Spoon capsicum and grapes over the top and serve.

Serves 4

Crisp Pork Chops with Peaches

4 pork chops, 225 g (½ lb) each
15 mL (1 tablespoon) flour, seasoned
  with good pinch each salt, pepper
  and dry mustard
1 egg, lightly beaten
40 g (1½ oz) (¾ cup) fresh
  breadcrumbs
50 mL (2 fl oz) (¼ cup) oil
4 canned peach halves in syrup
5 mL (1 teaspoon) cornflour
5 mL (1 teaspoon) made mustard
5 mL (1 teaspoon) vinegar
½ beef stock cube, dissolved in
  150 mL (¼ pint) (⅔ cup) boiling
  water
pepper to taste

1 Coat pork chops with seasoned flour. Dip into beaten egg and then into breadcrumbs, pressing them firmly to the meat with a knife.
2 Heat oil in a frying pan and fry chops over a low heat for 7 or 8 minutes on each side.
3 Meanwhile drain the peach halves, reserving the syrup. Mix together cornflour, made mustard, vinegar and 30 mL (1 fl oz) (2 tablespoons) peach syrup in a small bowl. Bring stock to the boil, stir in the cornflour mixture and simmer 2 minutes, stirring.
4 Season to taste with pepper, add peaches and simmer 5 minutes.
5 Arrange pork chops on a warmed serving dish with the peaches and pour sauce over. Garnish with parsley.

Serves 4

Pork Chops a l'Orange

4 thick pork chops
1 onion, finely chopped
50 g (2 oz) (4 tablespoons) butter
60 mL (2¼ fl oz) (4 tablespoons) oil
50 g (2 oz) (1 cup) fresh breadcrumbs
salt and pepper
good pinch dried sage
grated rind and juice 1 orange
30 mL (2 tablespoons) flour
300 mL (½ pint) (1¼ cups) chicken
  stock

1 Cut a pocket in each pork chop by making a slit in the same direction as the bone, cutting from the fat side through to the bone.
2 Gently fry chopped onion in half of the butter and oil for 5 minutes until softened but not browned.
3 Stir in breadcrumbs, salt and pepper to taste, sage, and the grated orange rind, so that the mixture absorbs the cooking fats and forms a thick paste. If necessary, remove from heat and use milk to bind.
4 Preheat oven to 170°C (325°F). Stuff a quarter of the breadcrumb mixture into each chop, securing if necessary with a cocktail stick. Arrange chops in an ovenproof dish.
5 Heat the rest of the butter and oil in pan, scraping up any residue. Fry flour for 3 minutes. Remove from heat, stir in stock and orange juice and bring to the boil, stirring.
6 Pour sauce over the chops, cover, and cook in the oven for 15 minutes or until cooked.

Serves 4

Pork Chops with Rhubarb

450 g (1 lb) rhubarb
50 g (2 oz) (4 tablespoons) butter
4 large pork chops
15 g (½ oz) (2 tablespoons) flour
salt and pepper
15 mL (1 tablespoon) honey
pinch cinnamon
15 mL (1 tablespoon) chopped
  parsley

1 Thoroughly clean rhubarb and cut into chunks. Boil for 5 minutes and drain.
2 Melt butter in a large frying pan. Dip pork chops in flour seasoned with salt and pepper, and fry them gently in the butter until cooked through, turning once. Transfer to a serving dish and keep warm.
3 Add rhubarb to meat juices in the pan, and stir in the honey and a pinch of cinnamon. Cook gently, stirring frequently, until rhubarb is tender. Serve pork and rhubarb together, each pork chop garnished with a little chopped parsley.

Serves 4

Tip: According to the sweetness of the rhubarb and your own taste, sweeten the rhubarb with more honey or sharpen it with a little lemon juice.

Pork Chops with Pine Kernels

1.5 kg (3 lb) fresh spinach
90 mL (6 tablespoons) oil
salt and pepper
175 g (6 oz) (1 cup) seedless raisins
75 g (3 oz) (¾ cup) pine kernels
2 cloves garlic, crushed
6 pork chops
6 small sprigs parsley

1 Wash spinach thoroughly and strip leaves from stalks. Heat half of the oil in a pan, add spinach leaves and cook over a gentle heat for 15 minutes. Add seasoning, raisins, pine kernels and crushed garlic and cook for 15 minutes.
2 Meanwhile, remove excess fat from pork chops. Heat remaining oil in a frying pan and fry pork chops for 10–15 minutes on each side, until cooked through and golden-brown.
3 Transfer cooked chops to a heated serving dish and arrange spinach and pine kernel mixture along one side. Garnish each chop with a sprig of parsley. Serve with new potatoes.

Serves 6

Pork Chops with Pine Kernels

Pojarski Cutlets

225 g (½ lb) (1⅓ cups) minced pork
50 g (2 oz) (1 cup) fresh breadcrumbs
50 g (2 oz) (⅓ cup) chopped pineapple
2 eggs
salt and pepper
pinch ginger
100 g (¼ lb) (1 cup + 2 tablespoons)
　　flour
100 g (¼ lb) (2 cups) mixed
　　breadcrumbs, crushed bran and
　　cornmeal
125 mL (5 fl oz) (⅝ cup) oil
25 g (1 oz) (2 tablespoons) butter
350 g (¾ lb) (4 cups) cooked rice
100 g (¼ lb) (1 cup) cooked peas
100 g (¼ lb) (1 cup) cooked
　　mushrooms

Garnish
3 pineapple rings
3 glace cherries

1 Mix pork, breadcrumbs and pineapple with 1 egg, seasoning and the
ginger.
2 Divide into 6 pieces and shape
each into a triangular shape, 5 mm
(¼ in) thick.
3 Dip in seasoned flour, and the
other egg, beaten, and in the mixed
breadcrumbs, bran and cornmeal.
4 Shallow fry in 100 mL (4 fl oz) (½
cup) oil for 8 minutes, turning, until
cooked through and golden-brown.
Keep warm.
5 In a separate pan, heat butter and
the rest of the oil and add rice, peas
and mushrooms and season with salt
and pepper. Heat through quickly,
shaking the pan to prevent the rice
from sticking.
6 Place on a serving dish, arrange
cutlets on top, garnish with pineapple rings and put a glace cherry in
the middle of each.

Serves 6

Pojarski Cutlets

Barbecued Pork Chops

50 mL (2 fl oz) (¼ cup) oil
6 pork chops
50 g (2 oz) (4 tablespoons) butter
1 small onion, chopped
100 mL (4 fl oz) (½ cup) water
25 g (1 oz) (2 tablespoons) brown
　　sugar
2.5 mL (½ teaspoon) made mustard
15 mL (1 tablespoon) vinegar
15 g (½ oz) (1 tablespoon) tomato
　　paste
salt and pepper
2 tomatoes, skinned, seeded and
　　chopped
5 mL (1 teaspoon) Worcestershire
　　sauce
70 mL (2½ fl oz) (⅓ cup) tomato sauce
pinch paprika

1 Heat oil and fry pork chops until
well browned on both sides.
2 Meanwhile, make the barbecue
sauce. Melt butter in a saucepan and
fry onion until soft. Add water and
stir in brown sugar, mustard, seasoning and vinegar. Bring to the boil,
then simmer for 5 minutes.
3 Add all the remaining ingredients,
stir well and simmer for 15 minutes.
4 Serve pork chops with the barbecue sauce on a bed of plain boiled
rice.

Serves 6

Pork Vindaye

*450 g (1 lb) spare rib chops or blade of
    pork*
2 onions
2 cloves garlic
1 red capsicum (pepper)
30 mL (1 fl oz) (2 tablespoons) oil
10 mL (2 teaspoons) vinegar
15 mL (1 tablespoon) curry powder
10 mL (2 teaspoons) powdered ginger
salt
225 mL (8 fl oz) (1 cup) water

1 Cut meat into large chunks or, if
using spare rib chops, remove excess
fat and cut in half.

2 Finely chop onions and garlic.
Seed red capsicum and chop. Mix
these together with the oil and vinegar and pound to a paste with a
pestle and mortar.

3 Stir in curry powder, ginger and a
good pinch of salt. Coat the pieces of
meat with this mixture and place in a
large saucepan. Pour in the water,
cover, and simmer 2 hours. Serve
with golden rice — boiled with a
pinch of turmeric for colour.

Serves 4

Pork Spare Ribs

*3 kg (6 lb) pork spare ribs, cut into
    separate ribs*
salt
85 mL (3 fl oz) (⅓ cup) clear honey
45 mL (3 tablespoons) soy sauce
15 mL (1 tablespoon) lemon juice
*2.5 mL (½ teaspoon) chopped fresh
    ginger*

1 Preheat oven to 190°C (375°F).
Place ribs in a roasting dish. Sprinkle
with salt and bake for 45 minutes,
pouring off the fat as it collects.

2 Meanwhile, gently heat honey in a
small saucepan. Stir in soy sauce,
lemon juice and ginger. Remove from
heat.

3 After 45 minutes, lower oven temperature to 170°C (325°F). Pour the
honey sauce over ribs and cook for 30
minutes, turning ribs occasionally.

Serves 6

Spareribs Tahiti

900 g (2 lb) pork spareribs
100 mL (4 fl oz) (½ cup) vinegar
300 mL (½ pint) (1¼ cups) water
200 mL (6 fl oz) (¾ cup) tomato sauce
175 g (6 oz) (¾ cup) brown sugar
7.5 mL (1½ teaspoons) soy sauce
25 g (1 oz) (3 tablespoons) cornflour
60 mL (2¼ fl oz) (4 tablespoons) water

1 Preheat oven to 170°C (325°F). Divide meat into individual ribs. Pour
vinegar and water over them in a
roasting pan and bake for 1 hour.
Skim off any fat from the liquid,
strain liquid and reserve.

2 Stir tomato sauce, brown sugar
and soy sauce into cooking liquid.
Mix cornflour with 60 mL (2¼ fl oz)
(4 tablespoons) water and add to the
liquid. Stir over heat to thicken.

3 Pour sauce over spareribs and
return to oven and bake for 30 minutes or until browned. Serve immediately with rice.

Serves 4

Pacific Pork

675 g (1½ lb) pork tenderloin
25 g (1 oz) (¼ cup) flour
25 g (1 oz) (2 tablespoons) oil
*225 mL (8 fl oz) (1 cup) pineapple
    juice*
*100 g (¼ lb) (½ cup) crushed canned
    pineapple*
*2.5 mL (½ teaspoon) each: salt,
    pepper, powdered ginger, allspice*
15 g (½ oz) (1½ tablespoons) cornflour
30 mL (1 fl oz) (2 tablespoons) water

1 Preheat oven to 180°C (350°F). Cut
tenderloin into 6 pieces, and coat
with flour.

2 Heat the oil in a frying pan and
brown pork lightly. Transfer pork to
an ovenproof dish. Combine pineapple juice and fruit, salt, pepper, ginger and allspice. Pour mixture over
the meat and bake uncovered for 45
minutes or until meat is tender.

3 Remove meat to a serving dish and
keep warm. Pour the rest of the cooking liquid into the pan and thicken
with the mixture of cornflour and
water. Pour sauce over the meat and
serve.

Serves 6

Loin of Pork Spanish-style

*450 g (1 lb) haricot beans, soaked
    overnight*
2 cloves garlic, crushed
1 bay leaf
50 mL (2 fl oz) (¼ cup) olive oil
2 onions, sliced
1 kg (2 lb) boned loin of pork, cubed
*225 g (½ lb) chorizo (spicy Spanish
    sausage), cut in 2 cm (¾ in) slices*
*225 g (½ lb) smoked bacon, cut in
    small strips*
*3 tomatoes, skinned, seeded and
    chopped*
15 mL (1 tablespoon) paprika
pinch saffron
*1 litre (1¾ pints) (4½ cups) boiling
    water*
salt and pepper
*350 g (¾ lb) runner beans, trimmed
    and cut in 3 cm (1¼ in) lengths*
small round cabbage, quartered
6 eggs

1 Drain haricot beans, rinse and
place in a pan. Cover with fresh cold
water and add 1 clove of garlic and
the bay leaf. Bring to the boil, reduce
heat and simmer 1 hour.

2 Heat oil in a pan and add the
onion, pork, chorizo, bacon, the
remaining garlic and tomatoes. Add
paprika and saffron and cook gently
for 7 or 8 minutes, stirring constantly.

3 Pour in boiling water, season with
salt and pepper and cook over a low
heat for 45 minutes.

4 When the haricot beans have
cooked for 1 hour, drain and add
them to the pork and simmer for a
further 30 minutes.

5 Add runner beans and cabbage
and cook for 20 minutes.

6 Meanwhile, cook eggs in boiling
water for 10 minutes, cover with cold
water and then remove the shells.

7 Transfer pork mixture to a heated
serving dish and garnish with the
hard-boiled eggs. Serve very hot.

Serves 6

Pork Portuguese

900 g (2 lb) lean pork, cut into cubes
25 g (1 oz) (4 tablespoons) flour
salt and pepper
50 mL (2 fl oz) (¼ cup) oil
2 large onions, chopped
3 sticks celery, coarsely diced
1 green capsicum (pepper), seeded
    and cut into squares
2 large tomatoes, skinned, seeded
    and chopped
300 mL (½ pint) (1¼ cups) water
300 mL (½ pint) (1¼ cups) dry white
    wine
25 g (1 oz) (2 tablespoons) tomato
    paste
1 clove garlic, crushed
bouquet garni

1 Preheat oven to 180°C (350°F). Roll pork in the flour seasoned with salt and pepper. Shake off any excess.
2 Heat oil in a pan, add meat, cover and brown for 10 minutes. Transfer to a casserole.
3 In the same pan gently brown chopped onions. Add celery, capsicum and tomatoes and cook on a moderate heat for 5 minutes. Transfer vegetables to casserole.
4 Stir in water, wine and tomato paste. Add garlic and bouquet garni and season to taste.
5 Cover and braise in oven for 1¼ hours or until the meat is tender.
6 Serve with a bowl of piping hot savoury rice.

Serves 6

Pork Goulash with Sour Cream

675 g (1½ lb) pork fillet, cubed
salt and pepper
25 g (1 oz) (4 tablespoons) paprika
25 g (1 oz) (2 tablespoons) butter
1 large onion, chopped
25 g (1 oz) (¼ cup) flour
150 mL (¼ pint) (⅔ cup) chicken stock
100 g (¼ lb) (1¼ cups) mushrooms
8 tomatoes, chopped
150 mL (¼ pint) (⅔ cup) sour cream

1 Toss pork in the seasoning and half the paprika.
2 Brown meat in butter in a casserole, and remove.
3 Fry onion for 5 minutes and remove from dish.
4 Add flour and remaining paprika and fry for 3 minutes.
5 Add stock, stir; bring to boil.
6 Return pork and onion to casserole, add mushrooms and tomatoes, cover and simmer for 45 minutes.
7 Add the sour cream.   *Serves 4*

Pork Portuguese

Pork Piedmontese

50 mL (2 fl oz) (¼ cup) oil
675 g (1½ lb) lean pork, cut into cubes
15 g (½ oz) (2 tablespoons) flour
15 g (½ oz) (1 tablespoon) tomato
    paste
300 mL (½ pint) (1¼ cups) water
150 mL (¼ pint) (⅔ cup) dry white
    wine
85 mL (3 fl oz) (⅓ cup) cream
juice 1 lemon
pinch oregano
salt and pepper
3 medium zucchini (courgettes)

Stuffing
100 g (¼ lb) calf's liver
salt and pepper
15 g (½ oz) (2 tablespoons) flour
30 mL (1 fl oz) (2 tablespoons) oil
1 onion, chopped
50 g (2 oz) bacon, finely sliced
50 g (2 oz) mushrooms, finely sliced
15 mL (1 tablespoon) Parmesan
    cheese
50 mL (2 fl oz) (¼ cup) dry white wine
85 mL (3 fl oz) (⅓ cup) thickened
    cream

1 Preheat oven to 180°C (350°F). Heat oil in a pan. Add meat and brown for 12 minutes. Sprinkle in the flour and stir. Cook for 1 minute, then add the tomato paste, water and wine. Bring to the boil and simmer 15 minutes. Stir in the cream, lemon juice and oregano. Season and transfer to a casserole. Bake in preheated oven for 1 hour or until meat is tender.

2 Meanwhile cut the zucchini in half lengthways. Cook for 5 minutes in boiling salted water. Drain and keep warm.

3 If necessary remove the membrane from the liver. Cut into small cubes and roll in seasoned flour.

4 In a separate pan, heat oil. Add onion and saute until soft. Add bacon, liver, mushrooms and Parmesan cheese and cook for 5 minutes on a moderate heat. Pour in wine and cream. Stir and simmer for a further 5 minutes. Check seasoning.

5 With a spoon scoop out the seeds from the zucchini halves. Place on a warm serving dish and spoon the stuffing mixture into the cavities. Surround with the hot pork casserole and serve.

Serves 6

Tips: You can use this tasty stuffing for other vegetables besides zucchini. Try using it in eggplants (aubergines) or even red and green capsicums (peppers). To give it an even richer, more distinctive flavour, substitute fortified wine such as sherry or port for the white wine.

Pork Alentago

675 g (1½ lb) lean pork tenderloin,
    boned
200 mL (6 fl oz) (¾ cup) dry white
    wine
2 cloves garlic, crushed
2 bay leaves
5 mL (1 teaspoon) paprika
salt and pepper
2 slices bacon, diced
4 slices white bread
1 clove garlic, halved
30 mL (1 fl oz) (2 tablespoons) oil
275 g (10 oz) canned mussels or
    clams, drained

1 Cut pork into 2.5 cm (1 in) cubes.

2 Combine wine, garlic, bay leaves and paprika in a bowl. Season with salt and pepper and add pork. Cover tightly with plastic or foil and refrigerate for 24 hours.

3 Fry bacon in a heavy frying pan until the fat runs out.

4 Drain pork cubes, dry thoroughly and brown in the bacon fat. Cover and cook over a very low heat for 30 minutes.

5 Strain the marinade and add the liquid to the pan. Simmer uncovered for 20 minutes.

6 Meanwhile, remove crusts from the bread and rub with the garlic clove. Heat oil in a pan and saute bread until brown. Place bread slices in a shallow casserole and keep warm.

7 Add mussels or clams to the pork and marinade and heat through. Pour pork and shellfish over the bread and serve.

Serves 4

Potato and Sauerkraut Casserole

1 kg (2 lb) canned sauerkraut
100 g (¼ lb) canned goose fat, chicken
    fat or butter
6 black peppercorns
1 clove garlic, crushed
6 juniper berries or 30 mL
    (2 tablespoons) gin
4 carrots
2 onions, studded with 4 cloves
1 bouquet garni
2 bay leaves
salt and pepper
300 mL (½ pint) (1¼ cups) dry white
    wine
600 mL (1 pint) (2½ cups) water
450 g (1 lb) piece unsmoked ham or
    bacon
1 knuckle ham, 675 g (1½ lb)
900 g (2 lb) peeled potatoes
6 frankfurts

1 Preheat oven to 200°C (400°F). Wash sauerkraut and drain, pressing well to remove moisture.

2 Place dried sauerkraut in a dish. Warm fat in a pan and mix with sauerkraut.

3 Tie peppercorns, garlic and juniper berries in a small piece of muslin. Transfer half of sauerkraut to an ovenproof dish and add the muslin bag, carrots, onions, bouquet garni, bay leaves and seasoning. Cover with the rest of the sauerkraut. Pour in gin, if used, and wine and water. Cover with foil; bake 20 minutes.

4 Remove foil and add meat. Bring to boil, cover and simmer 1¼ hours.

5 Lift out meat and add potatoes. Cover and cook for 20 minutes or until they are cooked and the liquid has almost evaporated. Meanwhile, keep meat warm in the oven.

6 Add frankfurts to a pan of boiling water and simmer for 8 minutes until warmed through. Drain.

7 Discard the muslin bag, carrots, bouquet garni and onions. Place sauerkraut on a serving dish. Cut meat into neat slices and arrange them round the pile of sauerkraut with the frankfurts and potatoes.

Serves 6

Mexican Turkey and Pork Ragout

Mexican Turkey and Pork Ragout

700 g (1½ lb) turkey escalopes
700 g (1½ lb) pork fillet (tenderloin)
2 shallots (spring onions, scallions)
3 sprigs parsley
100 g (¼ lb) (½ cup) butter
2.5 mL (½ teaspoon) paprika
2.5 mL (½ teaspoon) coriander seeds
2.5 mL (½ teaspoon) caraway seeds
salt and pepper
500 mL (1 pint) (2½ cups) water
3 medium onions
4 cloves
3 cloves garlic
6 tomatoes
10 g (½ oz) (2 squares) cooking
  chocolate

1 Cut turkey and pork into small dice. Peel and chop shallots. Chop parsley finely.

2 Melt half the butter in a large frying pan, add shallots and parsley and fry until lightly coloured.

3 Add a quarter of the turkey and pork, fry until golden-brown then remove from pan with a slotted spoon and place in a flameproof casserole.

4 Fry remaining meat in batches, adding more butter when necessary. Add each batch to the casserole.

5 Sprinkle meats with the paprika, coriander, caraway and salt and pepper to taste. Pour in the water.

6 Peel onions and stud one of them with the cloves. Peel and crush garlic. Add to casserole; cook on low heat.

7 Preheat oven to 190°C (375°F).

8 Skin tomatoes, chop the flesh and remove the seeds.

9 Add tomatoes and chocolate to the casserole, increase heat and cook for 5 minutes until chocolate has melted.

10 Cover casserole, transfer to oven and cook for 1 hour or until the meat is tender.

11 Serve hot straight from the casserole with freshly boiled rice.

Serves 6

Ravioli

450 g (1 lb) noodle paste
15 mL (1 tablespoon) oil
100 g (¼ lb) (½ cup) finely chopped
  onion
225 g (½ lb) (1 cup) minced pork, veal,
  beef or chicken
100 g (¼ lb) (¼ cup) cooked spinach
salt and pepper
pinch ground nutmeg
1 egg, beaten

1 Divide paste into 2 equal portions. Roll each into a rectangle, 3 mm (⅛ in) thick. Leave to rest in a cool place.

2 Heat oil in a frying pan. Gently fry onion until soft but not coloured. Remove and lightly fry meat. Drain and place in a bowl with onion and spinach, from which all water has been squeezed. Season with salt, pepper and nutmeg. Mince finely and bind with beaten egg.

3 Either spoon the filling, or pipe it, in little walnut-sized heaps at 4 cm (1½ in) intervals along one half of the paste. Brush with water between the fillings and cover with the second layer of paste. Mark the paste over the fillings with a pastry cutter turned upside down. Then, using a ruler and a serrated pastry wheel or ravioli cutter, cut ravioli into squares. Line a baking tray with greaseproof paper and sprinkle with uncooked semolina. Place squares on it and leave to dry for 1 hour.

4 Bring a large pan of water to the boil. Add ravioli and boil for 8 minutes. Refresh in cold water and drain.

5 Preheat oven to 190°C (375°F). Place ravioli in a buttered casserole and cover with tomato sauce. Sprinkle with grated cheese and bake for 20 minutes.

Makes 16

Pork and Bamboo Shoots

Pork and Bamboo Shoots

45 mL (2 fl oz) (3 tablespoons) oil
1 onion, chopped
1 clove garlic, crushed
450 g (1 lb) pork tenderloin, thinly
  sliced
225 g (½ lb) bamboo shoots, thinly
  sliced
5 mL (1 teaspoon) cornflour
2.5 mL (½ teaspoon) powdered
  ginger
5 mL (1 teaspoon) soy sauce
2.5 mL (½ teaspoon) anchovy essence
150 mL (¼ pint) (⅔ cup) pineapple
  juice
pepper

1 Heat oil in a frying pan and fry onion and garlic until soft but not brown. Add pork and stir-fry until browned.

2 Add bamboo shoots to pan, cover and cook gently for 10 minutes.

3 Mix cornflour, ginger, soy sauce and anchovy essence with enough pineapple juice to make a smooth paste. Add to pan with the remaining juice and simmer gently, uncovered, for 15 minutes.

4 Season with pepper and serve with boiled rice and kumquat pickle.

Serves 4

Chinese Pork Butterflies

1 clove garlic
8 shallots (spring onions, scallions)
350 g (¾ lb) pork fillet
8 mushrooms
100 g (¼ lb) bamboo shoots
225 g (½ lb) pasta butterfly shapes
50 mL (2 fl oz) (¼ cup) oil
5 g (1 tablespoon) ginger root,
  chopped
30 mL (2 tablespoons) soy sauce
5 g (1 teaspoon) sugar
5 g (1 teaspoon) salt
30 mL (2 tablespoons) sherry
100 mL (4 fl oz) (½ cup) chicken stock
5 g (1 teaspoon) cornflour
50 mL (2 fl oz) (¼ cup) water
100 g (¼ lb) cucumber, cut into strips

1 Finely chop or crush garlic. Slice the shallots, pork, mushrooms and bamboo shoots into small strips. Keep each in a separate bowl.

2 Cook butterfly shapes in boiling salted water for 5 minutes. Drain and run cold water over them. Keep in cold water until needed.

3 In a wok (Chinese conical pan) or frying pan, heat the oil. Add ingredients in the following order and stir-fry for the times given: garlic and ginger for ½ minute; shallots for ½ minute; pork for 2 minutes; mushrooms and bamboo shoots for ½ minute.

4 Add butterfly shapes, lower heat, cover and cook for 3–5 minutes to ensure that the pork is cooked through.

5 Meanwhile, mix soy sauce, sugar, salt, sherry and chicken stock. Pour into the wok or pan, and stir to heat through. When bubbling, mix the cornflour with the water and add to the sauce. Cook for 2 minutes, stirring.

6 Serve on a dish, garnished with strips of cucumber.

Serves 4

Pork Canton

675 g (1½ lb) lean minced pork
50 g (2 oz) (½ cup) chopped onions
salt and pepper
1.25 mL (¼ teaspoon) fresh root
  ginger, chopped
1 egg, beaten
30 mL (1 fl oz) (2 tablespoons) oil

Sauce

50 g (2 oz) (½ cup) chopped onion
2 sticks celery, diced
30 mL (2 tablespoons) cornflour
1.25 mL (¼ teaspoon) fresh root
  ginger, chopped
25 g (1 oz) (2 tablespoons) sugar
15 mL (1 tablespoon) soy sauce
225 mL (8 fl oz) (1 cup) chicken stock
100 mL (4 fl oz) (½ cup) peach juice
50 mL (2 fl oz) (¼ cup) vinegar
225 g (½ lb) canned peaches, drained
  and diced

1 Combine pork, onion, salt, pepper and ginger in a bowl. Bind with beaten egg.

2 Roll mince mixture into balls which are approximately 4 cm (1½ in) in diameter.

3 Heat oil in a frying pan and cook meatballs for about 10 minutes or until done. Remove meat from pan and drain well.

4 Prepare sauce. Drain all but 15 mL (1 tablespoon) of fat from the pan. Saute onion and celery in the fat until onion is transparent.

5 Combine remaining ingredients, except peaches, and pour into pan. Stir thoroughly and cook until sauce is thick and clear.

6 Finally add meatballs and diced peaches. Cover and simmer gently for 10 minutes to allow sauce flavour to impregnate meat. Serve with hot rice or noodles.

Serves 6

Sweet 'n' Sour Pork

450 g (1 lb) pork tenderloin, cubed
30 mL (1 fl oz) (2 tablespoons) sherry
15 mL (1 tablespoon) soy sauce
1.25 mL (¼ teaspoon) sugar
5 mm (¼ in) piece fresh root ginger,
  grated
salt and pepper
4 celery sticks, sliced
1 red capsicum (pepper), seeded and
  diced
8 shallots (spring onions, scallions),
  cut into 5 cm (2 in) pieces
¼ English cucumber, cut into wedges
45 mL (2 fl oz) (3 tablespoons) oil
225 g (½ lb) canned pineapple chunks
  with juice
50 g (2 oz) (6 tablespoons) cornflour
50 mL (2 fl oz) (¼ cup) vinegar
100 mL (4 fl oz) (½ cup) sweet white
  wine
15 mL (1 tablespoon) brown sugar
oil for deep frying

1 Mix pork with sherry, soy sauce, sugar and ginger. Add pepper to taste and mix well. Marinate for 30 minutes.

2 Fry vegetables in oil until soft but not brown. Drain pineapple reserving juice and add chunks to pan. Stir-fry for 2 minutes.

3 Mix 30 mL (2 tablespoons) of the cornflour with the vinegar, and stir into the pan with pineapple juice, wine and sugar. Season and simmer for 2 minutes, stirring.

4 Heat oil for deep frying. Remove pork from marinade and add marinade to sauce.

5 Coat pork in remaining cornflour and fry in hot oil. Drain well.

6 Serve pork on a bed of fried noodles with sauce poured over.

Serves 4

3 Heat 15 mL (1 tablespoon) oil in a pan, add tomatoes, garlic, wine, thyme, basil, paprika and salt to taste and simmer gently for 25 minutes. Pass it through a sieve or liquidise, and return to pan.

4 Remove rind from bacon rashers, and roll up tightly. Cut the 2 reserved tomatoes into quarters. Put the capsicum and shallot bulbs into boiling, salted water and boil for 3 minutes. Drain and rinse in cold water.

5 Thread pork, bacon, tomato, capsicum, bulbs and bay leaves onto 4 long skewers.

6 Put rice into a pan with 450 mL (¾ pint) (1¾ cups) cold salted water. Bring to the boil, cover and cook very gently for about 20 minutes.

7 Cook kebabs under a very hot grill for about 10 minutes, until the meat is cooked through. Turn kebabs frequently and brush with the marinade and remaining oil.

8 Arrange a little cooked rice on a heated serving dish. Lay kebabs on top and moisten with some of the reheated tomato sauce. Serve remaining rice and sauce separately.

Serves 4

Herby Kebabs

Herby Kebabs

225 g (½ lb) pork tenderloin
2 onions, peeled and sliced
2 fresh sage leaves, chopped, or
 2.5 mL (½ teaspoon) dried
60 mL (2 fl oz) (4 tablespoons) brandy
60 mL (2 fl oz) (4 tablespoons) oil
salt and pepper
800 g (1¾ lb) tomatoes
2 cloves garlic, crushed
30 mL (1 fl oz) (2 tablespoons) dry
 white wine
2.5 mL (½ teaspoon) dried thyme
1.25 mL (¼ teaspoon) dried basil

5 mL (1 teaspoon) paprika
225 g (½ lb) bacon rashers
½ green capsicum (pepper), cut into
 2.5 cm (1 in) cubes
8 shallot (spring onion, scallion) bulbs
8 small fresh bay leaves
175 g (6 oz) (¾ cup) long grain rice

1 Cut pork into 2.5 cm (1 in) cubes and place in a dish with onions, sage, brandy and 30 mL (1 fl oz) (2 tablespoons) of the oil. Season and marinate for 12 hours.

2 Make sauce, reserving 2 small tomatoes for the kebabs. Skin and seed tomatoes and chop the flesh.

Brochettes de Porc au Romarin

675 g (1½ lb) lean pork from the
 shoulder or loin
15 mL (1 tablespoon) fresh rosemary,
 chopped
salt and pepper
50 mL (2 fl oz) (¼ cup) olive oil
few sprigs fresh rosemary

1 Cut pork into 2.5 cm (1 in) cubes and thread on 4 skewers. Blend rosemary, seasoning and oil. Marinate brochettes in the oil overnight.

2 Remove from marinade and grill, turning occasionally, for 10–15 minutes or until tender. Baste occasionally with a little oil from the marinade.

3 Arrange on a dish and decorate with a few rosemary sprigs.

Serves 4

Brochettes de Porc au Romarin

Sate

450 g (1 lb) pork fillet
50 mL (2 fl oz) (¼ cup) soy sauce
50 mL (2 fl oz) (¼ cup) sherry
1 clove garlic, crushed
1 thin slice fresh root ginger, finely
   chopped
5 mL (1 teaspoon) curry powder
30 mL (1 fl oz) (2 tablespoons) oil
100 g (¼ lb) (⅔ cup) fresh peanuts,
   finely chopped
5 mL (1 teaspoon) honey
few drops chilli sauce
5 mL (1 teaspoon) tomato sauce
5 mL (1 teaspoon) lemon juice
50 g (2 oz) (¼ cup) peanut butter
5 mL (1 teaspoon) cornflour

1 Cut pork into 3 cm (1¼ in) cubes.
Mix together soy sauce, sherry, garlic, ginger, curry powder and oil, and
marinate the pork pieces in this for 3
hours, stirring from time to time.
2 Strain meat from marinade and
thread the pieces on to kebab
skewers. Grill kebabs, turning frequently, until browned on all sides.
3 Meanwhile, pour marinade into a
saucepan and add the rest of the
ingredients except the cornflour.
Heat gently, stirring to blend them
into a smooth sauce. Thicken if
required with cornflour mixed with a
little water.
4 Take cooked pork from the kebab
skewers. Arrange meat around a
heated serving dish, and pour the
peanut sauce into the middle. Use
cocktail sticks to dip the meat pieces
into the sauce. Serve with rice.

Serves 4

Indonesian Rice

100 g (¼ lb) (½ cup) long grain rice
pinch turmeric
30 mL (1 fl oz) (2 tablespoons) oil
50 g (2 oz) (⅓ cup) fresh peanuts,
   skinned
5 mL (1 teaspoon) cumin seeds
25 mL (1½ tablespoons) desiccated
   coconut
salt and pepper

1 Boil rice in salted water with a
pinch of turmeric. Rinse and drain.
2 Heat oil in a frying pan. Add rice
and stir-fry for 3 minutes. Add the
other ingredients, stir well and fry for
3 minutes.

Serves 4

Pork Paupiettes Braised in Beer

450 g (1 lb) lean loin of pork
salt and pepper
25 g (1 oz) (2 tablespoons) fat
100 g (¼ lb) carrots
450 g (1 lb) small onions
25 g (1 oz) (4 tablespoons) flour
15 mL (1 tablespoon) tomato paste
400 mL (14 fl oz) (1¾ cups) brown
   stock
300 mL (½ pint) (1¼ cups) light beer
bouquet garni

Stuffing

30 mL (2 tablespoons) chopped onion
15 mL (1 tablespoon) oil
50 g (2 oz) (1 cup) white breadcrumbs
5 mL (1 teaspoon) chopped parsley
pinch thyme
½ egg to bind
25 g (1 oz) chopped apricots
25 g (1 oz) chopped walnuts
10 mL (2 teaspoons) butter

1 Cut meat across the grain into 4
thin slices and pound them. Trim to
approximately 12.5 × 10 cm (5 ×
4 in) and chop trimmings into small
pieces. Season the meat slices.
2 Prepare the stuffing. Saute onion
in oil until soft. Combine onion with
other ingredients and mix in the
chopped pork trimmings. Spread a
quarter of the stuffing down the
centre of each meat slice. Roll up and
secure with string.
3 Heat fat in a pan. Add paupiettes
and lightly brown all over. Add carrots and onions and continue cooking until meat is golden all over.
Remove from heat.
4 Drain off fat and pour 25 g (1 oz) (2
tablespoons) into a clean pan. Add
flour and stir on a low heat until you
have a brown roux. Mix in tomato
paste and allow to cool. Boil stock
and add to pan with the beer. Bring
sauce to the boil, remove any scum,
season and pour over meat.
5 Add bouquet garni, cover and
allow to simmer on a low heat for
1–1½ hours.
6 Remove string and place
paupiettes on a warm serving dish.
Surround with vegetables and pour
over the sauce.

Serves 4

Italian Stuffed Squid

1 kg (2 lb) squid, frozen and thawed
   or fresh
5 mL (1 teaspoon) chopped parsley

Stuffing

450 g (1 lb) pork sausage meat
2 eggs, beaten
1 clove garlic, crushed
15 mL (1 tablespoon) chopped
   parsley
salt and pepper

Sauce

30 mL (1 fl oz) (2 tablespoons) oil
1 onion, chopped
1 clove garlic, crushed
450 g (1 lb) tomatoes, skinned,
   seeded and chopped
15 mL (1 tablespoon) tomato paste
150 mL (¼ pint) (⅔ cup) water
½ chicken stock cube

1 Prepare the squid. Wash them in
cold water and remove tentacles, ink
sac and membranes. You should be
left with just the hoods.
2 Make the stuffing by mixing
together all ingredients.
3 Place stuffing inside the squid, and
arrange in a shallow ovenproof dish.
4 Preheat oven to 180°C (350°F).
5 Heat oil for the sauce in a pan and
saute onion and garlic until soft. Add
tomatoes, tomato paste, water and
stock cube. Boil 2–3 minutes; then
season.
6 Pour sauce over the stuffed squid
and braise in the oven, covered, for
1¼–1½ hours.
7 Cut into slices, sprinkle with
chopped parsley and serve.

Serves 6

Ham Stuffed Chicken

2 kg (4 lb) chicken
50 g (2 oz) bacon fat
30 mL (2 tablespoons) olive oil

Stuffing
125 g (good ¼ lb) bacon, slightly
   salted
1 onion
2 shallots (spring onions, scallions)
small bunch parsley
125 g (good ¼ lb) lean veal
2 cloves garlic
pinch allspice
1.25 mL (¼ teaspoon) dried thyme
pinch ground bay leaf
100 g (¼ lb) (1 cup) dry white
   breadcrumbs
15 mL (3 tablespoons) milk
1 egg
salt and pepper
2–4 slices cooked ham

Garnish
1 kg (2 lb) green capsicums (peppers)
1 kg (2 lb) tomatoes
2 onions
2 cloves garlic
few sprigs parsley

1 Wash, drain and wipe the chicken. Wipe the giblets and reserve.

2 Make the stuffing. Dice the bacon. Heat some water in a saucepan and as soon as it is boiling, put in bacon pieces and blanch for about 5 minutes. Drain, cool in cold water, and dry.

3 Peel onion and cut in quarters. Peel shallots. Wash and dry parsley.

4 Work in a blender or through a mincer the following stuffing ingredients: bacon, lean veal, chicken liver, onion, shallots and parsley.

5 Peel and finely chop cloves of garlic. Add to the rest of the stuffing ingredients, together with the allspice, thyme and bay leaf.

6 Rub dry breadcrumbs through a sieve. Moisten with milk then squeeze out any excess liquid.

7 Add the whole egg to breadcrumbs and mix well. Fold into stuffing ingredients. Season with salt and pepper to taste and mix well to obtain an even consistency.

8 Wrap stuffing in slices of ham and slide them into the chicken. Sew up the opening with a trussing needle and thread.

9 Cut bacon fat into small pieces.

Heat oil in a large flameproof casserole. Add diced bacon fat and melt over a low heat. Put chicken into casserole and brown over a moderate heat, so that it is sealed on all sides. Cover pan and leave the chicken to cook for about 45 minutes.

10 Meanwhile, prepare the garnish. Wash and dry capsicums. Cut in half, remove membranes and take out seeds. Cut into strips. Skin tomatoes by placing in a bowl of boiling water, let stand for 1 minute, then drain and skin; take out seeds and dice the pulp. Peel onions and cut them into quarters. Peel and crush garlic. Wash, dry and chop parsley.

11 When the chicken has cooked for about 45 minutes, add onions, green capsicums and garlic. Season with salt and pepper to taste and fry for 15 minutes.

12 Mix in tomatoes and chopped parsley. Cover and finish the cooking (about 15 minutes).

Serves 6–8

Ham Stuffed Chicken

Ham and Leek Mornay

4 young leeks
4 large slices ham
25 g (1 oz) (2 tablespoons) butter
300 mL (½ pint) (1¼ cups) Bechamel
   Sauce (see recipe)
100 g (¼ lb) (1 cup) grated Cheddar
   cheese
salt and pepper

1 Preheat oven to 190°C (375°F). Trim and remove outer leaves of the leeks. Cut off the green part and cook them for 15 minutes in boiling salted water.

2 Roll a slice of ham around each leek. Grease a shallow ovenproof casserole dish with half the butter, and place the leeks inside. Add 75 g (3 oz) (¾ cup) of the cheese to the Bechamel Sauce and season it.

3 Pour cheese sauce over the leeks. Sprinkle with remaining cheese and dot with the rest of the butter.

4 Bake for 15 minutes and serve.

Serves 4

Cinnamon Ham with Apricots

2 kg (4 lb) cooked ham, derinded
225 g (½ lb) canned apricot halves, drained

Glaze
5 mL (1 teaspoon) made mustard
50 g (2 oz) (4 tablespoons) softened butter
50 g (2 oz) (3 tablespoons) honey
pinch powdered cinnamon
pinch powdered ginger
30 mL (1 fl oz) (2 tablespoons) brandy

1 Preheat oven to 190°C (375°F). Combine mustard with softened butter, honey, cinnamon, ginger and brandy. Place ham in a roasting pan, spread glazing mixture over the surface of the meat and place in the oven for 5–8 minutes to caramelise the glaze.

2 Remove ham from the oven and decorate with the drained apricot halves. Serve cold with a salad of lettuce, celery and apple mixed with a yoghurt dressing.

Serves 8

Tip: A cooked ham can be glazed in a number of ways and is therefore a very versatile dish to prepare. The basic glaze can be varied to include the ingredients you have or the flavours you prefer. In this recipe, for instance, try using a different spirit and change the fruit used for decoration — try peaches, oranges or pawpaws.

Ham Steaks and Watercress Cream

2 large or 3 small bunches watercress
salt and pepper
50 g (2 oz) (4 tablespoons) butter
4 ham steaks
150 mL (¼ pint) (⅝ cup) cream

1 Blanch watercress in a pan of salted, boiling water for 5 minutes. Drain and rinse well.

2 Melt butter in a frying pan and fry steaks until just browned. Remove from pan and keep warm.

3 Add cress to pan and fry over a very low heat, stirring frequently, for 15 minutes. Remove from heat, add salt and pepper and stir in cream. Serve steaks on a bed of the watercress cream.

Serves 4

Ham Steaks and Watercress Cream

Ham Steak Charcutiere

30 mL (1 fl oz) (2 tablespoons) oil
1 large onion, chopped
15 mL (1 tablespoon) flour
15 mL (1 tablespoon) tomato paste
300 mL (½ pint) (1¼ cups) stock
salt and pepper
sprig thyme
15 mL (1 tablespoon) capers
1 gherkin cut in matchstick strips
1 small cooked beetroot, cut in matchstick strips
5 mL (1 teaspoon) vinegar
5 mL (1 teaspoon) honey
4 thick ham steaks

1 Heat oil and fry onion until soft. Stir in flour and cook for 2–3 minutes. Add tomato paste and stock. Season lightly and add thyme. Bring to the boil and simmer briskly for 15–20 minutes to make a sauce.

2 Strain sauce, season to taste and stir in capers, gherkin, beetroot, vinegar and honey. Cook 5 minutes.

3 Heat ham steaks under the grill and arrange on a serving dish. Pour sauce over them and serve.

Serves 4

Ham Steaks with Pears

25 g (1 oz) (2 tablespoons) butter
5 mL (1 teaspoon) honey
grated rind 1 orange
pinch cinnamon
4 ham steaks
2 pears

1 Cream together butter, honey, orange rind and cinnamon.
2 Preheat oven to 200°C (400°F).
3 Arrange steaks in a greased ovenproof dish. Spread the butter mixture over the top of them. Bake 12 minutes.
4 Remove from oven. Peel pears, cut in half and remove cores. Place a half pear on top of each ham steak, and serve.

Serves 4

Tips: A teaspoon of mild mustard may be added to the glaze for tang. Peaches, apricots, or fresh pineapple slices may be substituted for the pear halves.
If the ham is very salty or dry, poach steaks in meat stock for 10 minutes before cooking. Soaking the steaks in cold water for an hour before cooking will also remove excess salt.

Canadian Ham Steaks

175 g (6 oz) (¾ cup) brown sugar
30 mL (2 tablespoons) flour
10 mL (2 teaspoons) mustard powder
50 mL (2 fl oz) (¼ cup) vinegar
150 mL (¼ pint) (⅔ cup) apple juice
3 apples
6 thick ham steaks
40 g (1½ oz) (2 tablespoons) cranberry jelly

1 Mix together brown sugar, flour and mustard. Stir in the vinegar and apple juice to make a smooth sauce.
2 Peel and core apples and slice.
3 Preheat oven to 170°C (325°F). Place steaks in a greased ovenproof dish. Cover with slices of apple and pour sauce over them.
4 Cover and bake for ½ hour. Remove the lid and bake for another ½ hour, basting from time to time. Serve each steak with the sauce and topped with a teaspoon of the cranberry jelly.

Serves 6

Ham and Apple Casserole

50 g (2 oz) (4 tablespoons) butter
2 onions, sliced
2 apples, peeled, cored and sliced
4 ham steaks
25 g (1 oz) (4 tablespoons) flour
300 mL (½ pint) (1¼ cups) dry cider
150 mL (¼ pint) (⅔ cup) chicken stock
salt and pepper
pinch powdered clove
2.5 mL (½ teaspoon) mustard powder
225 g (½ lb) (2 cups) canned corn kernels, drained
75 g (3 oz) (½ cup) raisins
100 g (¼ lb) mushrooms, washed and sliced

1 Preheat oven to 190°C (375°F). Melt butter in a pan. Fry onions and apples until soft. Add ham slices and brown on both sides. Transfer the ham to a flameproof casserole.
2 Add flour to the pan and stir over a low heat for 2 minutes. Add cider and stock and bring to the boil, stirring all the time.
3 Simmer and add the seasoning, mustard, corn kernels, raisins and mushrooms. Cook for 1 minute and pour into the casserole dish. Cover and cook in the oven for 45 minutes or until well cooked.

Serves 4

Italian Turkey Roll-Ups

4 turkey breasts
flour for dusting
4 slices lean ham
50 g (2 oz) (½ cup) each grated Cheddar cheese, grated Parmesan cheese, mixed together
3 tomatoes
50 g (2 oz) shelled walnuts
oil for frying
chopped parsley for decoration

1 Using a heavy rolling pin or steak bat, beat out the turkey breasts until very thin and doubled in size.
2 Dust each of the escalopes with flour, then place a slice of ham on each and trim edges to fit the turkey. Sprinkle with a little of the mixed cheeses and roll up.
3 Skin and finely chop tomatoes; finely chop walnuts.
4 Heat oil in a saute pan and fry each escalope until golden brown on the outside and cooked inside.
5 Place escalopes on a flameproof serving dish or grill tray and sprinkle with remaining cheese, then with chopped tomato and walnuts. Grill for a few minutes until the cheese melts. Garnish with chopped parsley and serve.

Serves 4

Ham with Chablis

7 mL (1½ teaspoons) butter
4 × 5 mm (¼ in) thick slices of cooked ham
200 mL (6 fl oz) (¾ cup) Chablis or other dry white wine
350 g (¾ lb) (3¾ cups) trimmed and finely sliced mushrooms
1 clove garlic, chopped
2 shallots (spring onions, scallions)
salt and pepper
250 mL (8 fl oz) (1 cup) sour cream

1 Preheat oven to 200°C (400°F).
2 Butter an ovenproof dish and place slices of ham in it. Pour in 60 mL (2 fl oz) (¼ cup) of the Chablis, cover and bake for 10 minutes.
3 Place mushrooms, garlic and shallots in a saute pan, pour over the rest of the wine and season. Bring quickly to the boil, then simmer 10 minutes.
4 Add sour cream, boil 5 minutes.
5 Remove ham from oven and add cooking juices to the mushrooms. Boil sauce again for 5 minutes.
6 Place the slices of ham in a deep serving dish, pour over the sauce and serve hot.

Serves 4

Ham with Chablis

Ham Florentine

Ham with Wine and Tomato

50 g (2 oz) (4 tablespoons) butter
6 large slices cooked ham
6 shallots (spring onions, scallions)
   chopped
70 mL (2½ fl oz) (⅓ cup) dry white
   wine
4 tomatoes, skinned, seeded and
   chopped
10 mL (2 teaspoons) tomato paste
salt and pepper
150 mL (¼ pint) (⅔ cup) thickened
   cream
1 sprig parsley

1 Preheat oven to 190°C (375°F). Grease a small baking dish with a little butter. Roll ham slices into cylinders and place them side by side in the dish. Dot ham with 15 mL (1 tablespoon) butter and place in oven for 15 minutes or until heated.
2 Meanwhile, gently heat the remaining butter in a frying pan and saute shallots for 3 minutes.
3 Add wine and boil for 2 minutes before adding tomatoes and tomato paste. Season. Allow sauce to boil for 5 more minutes while gradually stirring in the cream. Check seasoning.
4 Pour sauce over the ham, and garnish with parsley.

Serves 6

Ham Florentine

25 mL (1 fl oz) (2 tablespoons) oil
50 g (2 oz) (4 tablespoons) butter
1 carrot, diced
1 onion, chopped
50 g (2 oz) bacon, derinded and cubed
30 mL (2 tablespoons) flour
300 mL (½ pint) (1¼ cups) chicken
   stock
100 mL (4 fl oz) (½ cup) Madeira
salt and pepper
pinch thyme
1 bay leaf
2 kg (4 lb) spinach, cooked and
   chopped
100 mL (4 fl oz) (½ cup) thickened
   cream
6 thick slices cooked ham

1 Heat oil with half the butter and fry carrot, onion and bacon until slightly browned. Sprinkle in flour and cook for 2 minutes more, stirring. Mix in stock and Madeira, season and add thyme and bay leaf. Cover and cook for 25 minutes.
2 Preheat oven to 200°C (400°F). Mix spinach with the cream and seasoning. Divide spinach between the slices of ham and roll up. Place in an ovenproof dish greased with the rest of the butter.

3 Strain sauce and pour half over the rolls. Place in the oven for 10 minutes, then serve with the sauce.

Serves 6

Ham Provencal

1 onion, finely chopped
1 clove garlic, crushed
50 mL (2 fl oz) (¼ cup) oil
225 g (½ lb) tomatoes, peeled, seeded
   and chopped
10 mL (2 teaspoons) tomato paste
150 mL (¼ pint) (⅔ cup) white wine
salt and black pepper
4 slices of ham, about 50–75 g (2–3 oz)
   each

1 Fry onion and garlic gently in oil until soft.
2 Stir in tomatoes and tomato paste. Add white wine and season with salt and freshly ground black pepper. Cook gently for 5 minutes.
3 Roll up the ham slices and place in the pan, spooning some of the tomato sauce over them. Simmer for 5 minutes. Serve immediately with boiled noodles or rice.

Serves 4

Ham with Wine and Tomato

Ham and Fennel Rolls

Ham Slices au Gratin

Ham and Fennel Rolls

2 medium fennel bulbs
50 mL (2 fl oz) (¼ cup) oil
100 g (¼ lb) bacon, sliced
1 large onion, finely chopped
15 mL (1 tablespoon) flour
450 g (1 lb) tomatoes, peeled, seeded
    and chopped
100 mL (4 fl oz) (½ cup) white wine
300 mL (½ pint) (1¼ cups) stock
1 clove garlic, crushed
bouquet garni
salt and pepper
75 g (3 oz) (¾ cup) grated Gruyere
    cheese
4 large slices ham

1 Clean fennel and cut each bulb in quarters. Boil in salted water for 8 minutes, drain and refresh in cold water.

2 Heat half the oil in a frying pan and fry fennel until golden, turning the pieces frequently. Cover pan and cook over low heat until tender. Remove from pan and keep warm.

3 Add the rest of the oil to the pan and fry bacon and onion until just browned. Stir in flour and cook until just coloured.

4 Stir in tomatoes and cook for 1 minute. Add wine and stock, garlic and bouquet garni, and season. Simmer for 20 minutes.

5 Preheat oven to 200°C (400°F). Pass sauce through a strainer. Mix half the sauce with the fennel and stir in the grated cheese; cook gently for 5 minutes.

6 Grease an ovenproof dish. On the slices of ham place ¼ of the fennel mixture. Roll ham slices round the fennel and arrange rolls in the dish. Pour over the rest of the sauce and sprinkle with the remainder of the grated cheese. Bake 10 minutes until golden. Serve hot.

Serves 4

Ham Slices au Gratin

12 thin slices raw ham
100 g (¼ lb) (1 cup) grated cheese
25 g (1 oz) (2 tablespoons) butter
freshly ground black pepper

1 On each of the ham slices place a little grated cheese. Roll the slices up, enclosing the cheese.

2 Arrange ham rolls on a buttered ovenproof dish. Sprinkle the remainder with cheese over the top and dust liberally with freshly ground black pepper.

3 Grill ham until cheese is soft and just starting to brown. Serve at once with baked potatoes.

Serves 6

Tip: The ham rolls may be filled with cooked spinach, celery hearts or asparagus tips. To add moisture sprinkle with sherry or vermouth while cooking.

Ham Cordon Bleu

50 g (2 oz) (¾ cup) chopped button
    mushrooms
15 mL (1 tablespoon) butter
salt and pepper
15 mL (1 tablespoon) chopped fresh
    parsley and chives
8 slices ham, 5 mm (¼ in) thick
4 slices cheese, the same size as ham
    slices
30 mL (2 tablespoons) flour
1 large egg, beaten
50 g (2 oz) (¾ cup) breadcrumbs
50 mL (2 fl oz) (¼ cup) oil

1 Fry mushrooms gently in butter with a little salt and pepper and chopped herbs, for 5 minutes. Divide mushrooms into 4 and spread each part over the middle of a ham slice.

2 Cover the 4 ham and mushroom slices with a slice of cheese to cover the mushrooms. Place the slices under the grill until cheese is melted and soft.

3 While cheese is still hot place a plain ham slice on top of each one to form a sandwich, stuck together by the melted cheese.

4 Dust each sandwich with seasoned flour and coat with beaten egg and breadcrumbs. Fry in oil until the outside is crisp and golden-brown.

Serves 4

Ham Mousse

30 mL (2 tablespoons) powdered
    gelatine
30 mL (1 fl oz) (2 tablespoons)
    medium sherry
70 mL (2½ fl oz) (⅓ cup) stock
225 g (½ lb) (1 cup) minced cooked
    ham
150 mL (¼ pint) (⅔ cup) white sauce
salt and pepper
pinch grated nutmeg
pinch paprika
150 mL (¼ pint) (⅔ cup) thickened
    cream
15 mL (1 tablespoon) oil

1 Place gelatine in a bowl, pour over the sherry and soak for a few minutes to soften the gelatine.

2 Bring stock to the boil and pour it over the gelatine. Stir until dissolved.

3 Stir ham and white sauce into the gelatine and stock mixture and season with salt and pepper. Add a pinch of grated nutmeg and paprika.

4 Transfer mixture to a pan and bring to the boil. simmer for 5 minutes, then cool.

5 Once the ham mixture is cold, whip the cream until it is stiff and fold it in.

6 Oil a 900 mL (1½ pint) (3¾ cup) mould and place the ham mixture in it. Refrigerate for at least 2 hours to chill it thoroughly.

7 Turn mousse onto a flat plate and serve with a salad of lettuce and avocado, garnished with orange and grapefruit segments.

Serves 4

Cabbage and Bacon Hotpot

1 kg (2 lb) corn beef
450 g (1 lb) lean, salted belly pork
1.5 litres (2½ pints) (6 cups) water
1 kg (2 lb) cabbage, washed and
*   quartered*
4 celery sticks, halved
4 leeks, cleaned and halved
3 onions, peeled and studded with
*   cloves*
4 carrots, peeled and quartered
4 small turnips, quartered
1 bouquet garni
3 cloves garlic, peeled and crushed
salt and pepper
2 beef stock cubes
450 g (1 lb) beef sausages

1 Soak corn beef and belly pork in water overnight and drain.

2 Cover meat with water and bring to the boil, then simmer for 1½ hours, removing the surface scum.

3 Add cabbage, celery, leeks, onions, carrots, turnips, bouquet garni and garlic. Season and crumble in the stock cubes. Bring to the boil, then simmer for 20 minutes until tender.

4 Meanwhile, grill beef sausages for 20 minutes and keep warm.

5 Add cabbage to hotpot and cook for 15 minutes. Strain off liquid and place vegetables on a serving dish.

6 Remove cooked meat and cut into thick slices. Arrange meat and sausages on top of the vegetables and serve.

Serves 8

Bacon and Cheese Cornets

6 crepes
4 eggs
few drops Worcestershire sauce
pinch salt
pinch pepper
30 mL (1 fl oz) (2 tablespoons) milk
50 g (2 oz) (½ cup) grated cheese
100 g (¼ lb) (½ cup) butter
6 rashers lean bacon, chopped
75 g (3 oz) sliced button mushrooms,
*   cooked gently in butter*
sprig parsley

1 Beat eggs with Worcestershire sauce, seasoning and milk. Add grated cheese.

2 Melt 25 g (1 oz) (2 tablespoons) butter in a pan. Add chopped bacon and cook gently for a few minutes.

3 Stir in beaten egg mixture; cook until it forms soft, creamy flakes. Stir in cooked mushrooms and an extra 25 g (1 oz) (2 tablespoons) butter. Fold each crepe in half, then in half again, to form 'fan' shapes.

4 Fill one cavity in each crepe with the egg mixture. Warm the rest of the butter in a pan. Put crepes on a serving dish and pour over hot butter. Garnish with parsley.

Serves 6

Bacon and Cheese Cornets

Cabbage and Bacon Hotpot

Pork Sausages

50 g (2 oz) (1 cup) fresh breadcrumbs
50 mL (2 fl oz) (¼ cup) milk
450 g (1 lb) lean pork, minced
100 g (¼ lb) pork fat, minced
salt and pepper
pinch mace
pinch nutmeg
pinch ground coriander
1 egg, beaten
pinch mace
pinch black pepper
pinch paprika

1 Combine pork and beef with the other ingredients.
2 Finely mince mixture, and fill sausage skins.
3 Hang prepared sausages overnight in the refrigerator.

Makes 10–12 sausages

English Sausages

450 g (1 lb) lean pork, finely minced
100 g (¾ lb) beef suet, finely minced
grated rind ½ lemon
pinch thyme
pinh marjoram
2.5 mL (½ teaspoon) chopped sage
pinch nutmeg
salt and pepper
½ beaten egg

1 Blend pork, suet, lemon rind, herbs, nutmeg, salt and pepper.
2 Bind with beaten egg and fill sausage skins.

Makes 10–12 sausages

Tip: A novel alternative to the sausage skins is to cook the sausage meat in crepes. Prepare a batter and make 12 very thin crepes. Mould the meat mixture into 12 narrow sausage shapes and wrap each one in a crepe. Chill for 1 hour. When ready to cook, brush with oil and bake for 15 minutes at 200°C (400°F).

Brandy and Garlic Sausages

450 g (1 lb) lean pork
100 g (¼ lb) lean beef, minced
50 mL (2 fl oz) (¼ cup) brandy
50 g (2 oz) (1 cup) fresh breadcrumbs
15 mL (1 tablespoon) chopped
   parsley
2 cloves garlic, crushed
1 egg, beaten
5 mL (1 teaspoon) salt

1 Soak breadcrumbs in milk for 30 minutes. Drain and squeeze out any excess moisture.
2 Blend pork, fat, breadcrumbs and seasoning. Blend in the beaten egg and mince finely.
3 Stuff mixture into sausage skins.

Makes 10–12 sausages

Sausage Kebabs Romana

225 g (½ lb) pig's liver
15 mL (1 tablespoon) Worcestershire
   sauce
150 mL (¼ pint) (⅔ cup) Marsala
15 mL (1 tablespoon) oil
1 clove garlic, finely chopped
1.25 mL (¼ teaspoon) oregano
pinch each salt and pepper
350 g (¾ lb) pork chipolata sausages

1 Skin the pig's liver and cut into 8 pieces.
2 Mix the Worcestershire sauce, Marsala, oil, garlic, oregano and seasoning. Add liver and marinate for 20 minutes.
3 Thread 3 sausages and 2 cubes of liver on each of 4 long skewers.
4 Place skewers in a grill pan and brush liberally with the marinade. Grill for 8 minutes, turning and brushing frequently with the marinade.
5 Serve kebabs with sauteed potatoes, garnished with parsley.

Serves 4

Spanish Omelette with Spiced Sausage

3 onions
2 capsicums (peppers)
450 g (1 lb) tomatoes
2 cloves garlic
100 mL (4 fl oz) (1 cup) oil
1 bouquet garni
salt and pepper
200 g (7 oz) chorizo (Spanish sausage)
150 mL (¼ pint) (⅔ cup) white stock
8 eggs

1 Peel onions. Mince 1 and shred the other two. Wash and dry capsicums and cut them in halves. Remove seeds and cut in thin strips. Skin and chop tomatoes, discarding seeds. Peel and crush garlic.
2 To make the tomato puree: heat 25 mL (1 fl oz) of the oil in a small saute pan. Add minced onion. Cook until golden-brown, then add tomatoes, bouquet garni, and half the crushed garlic. Cover and cook for 15 minutes over a low heat.
3 In the meantime, cut the chorizo or other sliced sausage into thin slices.
4 Heat 50 mL (2 fl oz) oil in a frying pan. Add chorizo, cook gently, then drain and keep warm.
5 Cook shredded onions in the same oil until they are golden-brown. Add capsicums and cook until soft. Season with salt and pepper.
6 When capsicums begin to brown, add the rest of the garlic. Cook for 5 minutes then remove from heat and keep hot with the chorizo.
7 Pour tomato puree through a fine strainer. Return to a low heat and thin with stock. Adjust seasoning and leave to cook over the low heat.
8 Break eggs into a mixing bowl. Season with salt and pepper. Beat gently with a fork until frothy.
9 Heat the rest of the oil in a frying pan. When hot, pour in the beaten eggs and mix, scraping the bottom of the pan with a fork. Before the eggs start to set add onions, capsicums and chorizo, stirring all the time.
10 When omelette is cooked, place on a warmed serving dish. Serve hot with the tomato sauce in a sauceboat.

Serves 4

Sausage and Vegetable Casserole

Somerset Sausage Casserole

50 g (2 oz) (4 tablespoons) butter
450 g (1 lb) pork sausages
1 onion, sliced
2 apples, peeled, cored and sliced
150 mL (¼ pint) (⅔ cup) cider
½ chicken stock cube
bouquet garni
pinch each allspice and cinnamon
salt and pepper
15 g (½ oz) (1 tablespoon) tomato
    paste
10 mL (2 teaspoons) cornflour
50 mL (2 fl oz) (¼ cup) water

1 Preheat oven to 200°C (400°F).
2 Heat butter in a flameproof casserole dish. Fry sausages, onion and apples until sausages are browned, and onion and apples are soft.
3 Add cider and crumble in the stock cube. Bring to the boil, then add bouquet garni, spices, seasoning and tomato paste.

4 Cover and bake for about 35 minutes.
5 Mix cornflour with the water and stir into casserole on top of the stove, over heat, until liquid thickens. Serve with baked jacket potatoes topped with chives and sour cream. Fried slices of pumpkin and garden peas go well this dish.

Serves 4

Sausage and Vegetable Casserole

100 g (¼ lb) (⅓ cup) red kidney beans,
    soaked overnight
¼ small green cabbage, shredded
2 potatoes, peeled and sliced
2 carrots, peeled and chopped
1 large leek, sliced
2 onions, peeled and sliced
2 beef stock cubes dissolved in
    900 mL (1½ pints) (4 cups) boiling
    water
salt and pepper
450 g (1 lb) pork chipolata sausages

1 Put kidney beans into a large saucepan with cabbage, potatoes, carrots, leek, onions, stock and seasoning. Bring to the boil, reduce the heat and simmer for 1 hour.
2 Twist each sausage into 3, to give chains of 3 small sausages. Add to casserole and simmer for 15 minutes, or until sausages are cooked.
3 Serve with crusty bread.   *Serves 4*

Spicy Mexican Rice with Sausages

50 g (2 oz) (4 tablespoons) butter
225 g (½ lb) frankfurt sausages
225 g (½ lb) pork chipolata sausages
1 large onion, chopped
½ red capsicum (pepper), seeded and
    finely chopped
½ green capsicum (pepper), seeded
    and finely chopped
175 g (6 oz) (¾ cup) long grain rice
chilli powder to taste
1 chicken stock cube, dissolved in
    450 mL (¾ pint) (2 cups) boiling
    water
15 mL (1 tablespoon) tomato paste
100 g (¼ lb) (½ cup) canned
    sweetcorn, drained
salt and black pepper
2 tomatoes
5 mL (1 teaspoon) snipped chives

1 Melt butter in a large frying pan. Fry frankfurts and chipolata sausages over a medium heat for 4 or 5 minutes, shaking pan to prevent sticking. Remove sausages from pan with a slotted spoon and cut into chunky pieces.
2 Add onion and capsicum to pan and fry until onions are golden.
3 Add rice and chilli powder and fry over a gentle heat for 2 to 3 minutes, stirring.
4 Stir in stock, tomato paste, sweetcorn, sausage pieces and seasoning. Bring to the boil, stir well, cover and simmer gently for 15 minutes, until rice is tender and the liquid absorbed.
5 Cut tomatoes into wedges and add to pan for the last 5 minutes of cooking.
6 Sprinkle with snipped chives and serve.

Serves 4

Tip: To vary this dish, try replacing the chilli powder with fresh chillies, which should be seeded and chopped and added with the onion.

Devilled Pork Sausages

450 g (1 lb) pork sausages
30 mL (1 fl oz) (2 tablespoons) oil
1 onion, chopped
15 g (½ oz) (2 tablespoons) flour
225 g (½ lb) (1 cup) canned tomatoes
100 g (¼ lb) (½ cup) canned corn
    kernels
1.25 mL (¼ teaspoon) sugar
dash Worcestershire sauce
5 mL (1 teaspoon) made mustard
salt and pepper

1 Brown sausages in hot oil and remove from pan.
2 Fry onion lightly. Stir in flour and cook for 1 minute.
3 Add tomatoes and bring to the boil, stirring. Add remaining ingredients with the sausages, cover and simmer for 30 minutes.

Serves 4

Spicy Mexican Rice with Sausages

Farmhouse Sausages

225 g (½ lb) (1⅓ cups) red lentils
salt and pepper
25 g (1 oz) (2 tablespoons) butter
30 mL (1 fl oz) (2 tablespoons) oil
450 g (1 lb) thick pork sausages
2 rashers bacon, diced
2 onions, chopped
5 mL (1 teaspoon) dried thyme
30 mL (2 tablespoons) flour
300 mL (½ pint) (1¼ cups) dry cider
100 g (¼ lb) (1¼ cups) sliced button
    mushrooms

1 Wash lentils and put them in a pan with 550 mL (1 pint) (2½ cups) cold water and seasoning. Bring to the boil and simmer gently for 30 minutes until soft.
2 Heat butter and oil in a frying pan and fry sausages gently until golden-brown and cooked through. Remove from pan.
3 Add bacon and onions to pan and fry until onions are lightly golden. Drain any excess liquid from the cooked lentils and add lentils to bacon and onions with thyme. Cook for 5 minutes. Add flour and cook for 3 minutes.
4 Add cider, mushrooms and sausages and cook gently for 10–15 minutes. Serve hot, with creamed potatoes.

Serves 4

Savoury Sausage Roly Poly

1 medium cooking (green) apple
225 g (½ lb) sausage meat
1 onion, chopped
30 mL (2 tablespoons) chopped
    parsley
225 g (½ lb) (2 cups) plain flour
2.5 mL (½ teaspoon) salt
10 mL (2 teaspoons) baking powder
100 g (¼ lb) (1 cup) shredded suet
cold water

For Serving
1 beaten egg

1 Preheat oven to 200°C (400°F). Peel, core and chop apple. Place in a bowl with sausage meat, onion and parsley and mix well.

2 Sieve flour with salt and baking powder into a clean bowl and mix well. Lightly knead in shredded suet, adding just enough water to make a soft but not sticky dough. Roll out dough on a floured board to a rectangle, 23 cm (9 in) wide and 5 mm (¼ in) thick.
3 Spread sausage mixture over the dough leaving a 2.5 cm (1 in) border all round. Dampen border lightly and rolll up the dough like a Swiss roll. Seal ends and join line. Place the roly poly in a lined and greased 1 kg (2 lb) loaf tin. Brush with the beaten egg. Make a few slits in the top of the roly poly to allow any steam to escape and bake for 40–50 minutes. Serve with carrots, beans and a bowl of hot onion gravy.

Serves 4

Toad in the Hole

450 g (1 lb) pork sausages
2 eggs, beaten
pinch salt
150 mL (¼ pint) (⅔ cup) water
150 mL (¼ pint) (⅔ cup) milk
100 g (¼ lb) (⅔ cup + 2 tablespoons)
    flour
25 g (1 oz) (2 tablespoons) fat

1 Preheat oven to 220°C (425°F).
2 Place sausages under a hot grill for about 5 minutes until beginning to brown.
3 Meanwhile make the batter for the Yorkshire Pudding. Place beaten eggs in a bowl with a pinch of salt. Add the water and milk, a little at a time, beating continuously.
4 Sieve flour into another bowl and beat in the batter liquid until mixture is smooth.
5 Place fat in a small roasting pan in the oven.
6 When fat is hot, pour in half the batter and bake for 20 minutes. Then lay sausages on top and cover with remaining batter.
7 Bake 20 minutes until batter is set, well risen and golden-brown. Serve at once.

Serves 4

Tip: Another way to make Toad in the Hole is to place sausages in pan and pour all the batter over the top and cook until risen, crisp, and golden-brown. You can substitute beef for pork sausages in this dish.

Zampone and Spinach

225 g (½ lb) (1⅓ cups) dried lentils
1 onion, studded with 2 cloves
450 g (1 lb) zampone or mortadella
    sausage
1 kg (2 lb) spinach
50 g (2 oz) (4 tablespoons) butter
salt and pepper

1 Soak lentils in water overnight. Drain and place in a saucepan of water. Boil for 10 minutes. Remove scum from surface and, when liquid is clear, add onion and cook gently for 45 minutes until tender.
2 Twenty minutes before the lentils are cooked, place zampone with them in the same pan, and heat.
3 Wash spinach leaves, then boil in salted water for 5 minutes. Drain and squeeze out surplus water. Mix in butter, season, and arrange on a dish.
4 Slice zampone and place on the same dish as the spinach. Serve cooked lentils separately.

Serves 6

Salami Hotpot

2 × 225 g (½ lb) French or other mild
    salami sausages
225 g (½ lb) piece smoked belly of
    bacon
3 medium onions
3 cloves
bouquet garni
2 bay leaves
900 mL (1½ pints) (3¾ cups) water
1.5 kg (3 lb) small potatoes
300 mL (½ pint) (1¼ cups) dry white
    wine
salt and pepper

1 Place the 2 whole salamis in a pan with the bacon, onions studded with the cloves, bouquet garni, bay leaves and water.
2 Bring to the boil and simmer for 40 minutes. Skim.
3 Add peeled potatoes, wine and seasoning to the pan and simmer for 30 minutes, or until potatoes are cooked.
4 Cut salami into chunks to serve.

Serves 6

Salami Hotpot

MICROWAVE Pork and Ham

Roast Pork

2.5 kg (5 lb) leg or loin of pork in one piece
45 mL (3 tablespoons) oil
5 mL (1 teaspoon) salt
5 mL (1 teaspoon) five spice powder
juice of half a lemon

1 Score rind of pork. Brush with oil. Rub salt and five spice powder into the skin and allow to stand for 15 minutes. Pour lemon juice over.

2 Place on roasting rack in casserole dish and cook 40–45 minutes. (It is not necessary to turn pork over during cooking.) Wrap in foil and allow to stand 20 minutes before carving.

3 During last 4 minutes of cooking, place slices of apple and pineapple around pork. Glaze slices with apricot jam.

Serves 6

Roast Pork Ribs

750 g (1.5 lb) pork spareribs
Marinade
1 medium onion, chopped
30 mL (2 tablespoons) dark soy sauce
45 mL (3 tablespoons) honey
30 mL (2 tablespoons) lemon juice
1 clove garlic, crushed
pinch salt
pinch pepper
2.5 mL (½ teaspoon) curry powder
pinch chilli powder
2.5 mL (½ teaspoon) ground ginger
50 mL (2 fl oz) (¼ cup) oil

1 Remove rind and excess fat from ribs. Prick with a skewer and place into marinade for 2 hours.

2 Place ribs onto a roasting rack and cook 20 minutes, turning after 10 minutes. Spare ribs may also be cooked in an oven bag.

Serves 4

Pickled Pork with Caper Sauce

2.5 kg (5 lb) lean pickled pork
15 g (1 tablespoon) brown sugar
1 cinnamon stick
5 mL (1 teaspoon) peppercorns
6 whole cloves
3 bay leaves
1 onion, chopped
1 stalk celery, cut in 2 cm lengths
225 mL (8 fl oz) (1 cup) water
100 mL (4 fl oz) (½ cup) pineapple or orange juice

1 Place pork in a 2–3 litre casserole dish. Add remaining ingredients, cover and cook on high 10 minutes. Reduce power to medium and cook for 45 minutes.

2 Turn pork over and cover. Cook on medium 60–90 minutes or until pork is tender. Let stand 10–20 minutes, covered, before carving. Serve with caper sauce.

Serves 8–10

Caper Sauce
15 mL (1 tablespoon) capers
10 mL (2 teaspoons) chopped parsley
15 g (1 tablespoon) butter
15 g (1 tablespoon) flour
pinch salt
pinch pepper
250 mL (⅓ pint) (1⅛ cups) milk

1 Place butter into medium-sized bowl. Cook on high 45 seconds until melted. Stir in flour, salt, pepper and add milk. Cook on high 3 minutes or until boiling, stirring after each minute. Fold in capers and parsley.

Makes 2–3 cups

Pork Fillets with Prune and Almond Stuffing

4 x 400 g (¾ lb) pork fillets
16 prunes
4 anchovy fillets
16 toasted almonds
15 g (1 tablespoon) butter
15 g (1 tablespoon) flour
225 mL (8 fl oz) (1 cup) beef consomme
pinch salt
pinch pepper
90 mL (6 tablespoons) red wine
8 pickling onions, peeled

1 Cut each fillet lengthwise two-thirds through and open out. Remove seeds from each prune. Cut each anchovy into quarters. Stuff one almond and a piece of anchovy into each prune and reshape.

2 Place 4 stuffed prunes into each cut fillet and tie each fillet with white string to enclose prunes. Preheat browning casserole on high for 8 minutes. Add butter and fillets and cook on high 4 minutes, turning every minute. Remove from casserole.

3 Blend flour into pan drippings and cook on high 1 minute. Blend in consomme, salt, pepper and red wine. Cook on high 4 minutes. Add fillets and pickling onions and mask with sauce. Cover and cook on high 3 minutes, then reduce to medium. Cook 18 minutes, turning 4 times during cooking.

Serves 4

Roast Pork

Savoury Lasagne

8 sheets short lasagne
2 cups boiling water
2.5 mL (½ teaspoon) salt
810 g can whole peeled tomatoes,
  chopped
2.5 mL (½ teaspoon) basil
250 g (½ lb) peperoni sausage, sliced
1 onion, finely chopped
1 clove garlic, crushed
freshly ground black pepper
250 g (½ lb) ricotta cheese
2 eggs, beaten
100 mL (4 fl oz) (½ cup) cream
250 g mozzarella cheese, grated
30 g (1 oz) (¼ cup) Parmesan cheese

1 Place 4 sheets short lasagne in a shallow dish, add boiling water and salt. Cover with plastic wrap and cook on high 4 minutes. Carefully lift out pasta and allow to drain. Cook remaining lasagne on high 4 minutes and drain.

2 Mix together tomatoes, basil, peperoni sausage, onion, garlic and black pepper and set aside. Combine ricotta cheese, eggs and cream in a glass jug. Cook on high 3 minutes, stirring twice.

3 Starting with lasagne sheets, arrange lasagne, tomato and sausage mixture and ricotta sauce in layers in a greased shallow dish. Sprinkle ricotta layer with grated mozzarella and Parmesan cheeses. Top with ricotta mix and Parmesan cheese.

4 Cook on medium high 10 minutes, then reduce power and cook on medium 10 minutes. Stand 5 minutes uncovered. Serve hot.

Serves 8–10

Pork and Mushroom Stroganoff

500 g (1 lb) pork fillet, sliced thinly
1 medium onion, peeled and sliced
2.5 mL (½ teaspoon) basil
45 mL (3 tablespoons) oil
125 g (¼ lb) button mushrooms
30 mL (2 tablespoons) cornflour
salt and pepper to taste
225 mL (8 fl oz) (1 cup) chicken stock
300 mL (½ pint) (1¼ cups) sour cream
15 g (1 tablespoon) chopped parsley

1 Place pork, onion, basil and 1 tablespoon oil in a shallow dish. Cover and cook on medium high 10 minutes stirring once. Add mushrooms and cook a further 5 minutes on medium. Set aside.

2 Combine rest of oil, cornflour, salt, pepper and stock in glass jug. Cook on high 3–5 minutes. Stir vigorously when cooked. Fold through pork mixture. Cover and cook on medium 5 minutes. Add sour cream and parsley. Stir through evenly. Cook uncovered on high 5 minutes. Serve hot with rice or noodles.

Serves 6–8

Chinese Ravioli

250 g (½ lb) pork mince
125 g (¼ lb) raw prawn meat, minced
4 dried mushrooms, soaked in warm
  water for 20 minutes and finely
  chopped
1 shallot (spring onion, scallion),
  finely chopped
15 mL (1 tablespoon) soy sauce
2.5 mL (½ teaspoon) salt
2.5 mL (½ teaspoon) sesame oil
1 beaten egg yolk
30 dim sim pastry skins
1 egg white
1.5 litres (7 pints) (6–8 cups) boiling
  water
50 mL (2 fl oz) (¼ cup) oil

1 Combine pork and prawn meat, mushrooms and shallots together in a small bowl. Mix in the soy sauce, salt and sesame oil and stir in the beaten egg yolk so that the mixture resembles a thick paste.

2 Place 1 teaspoon of filling into centre of each pastry skin. Brush edges with egg white. Fold over pastry to form a triangle or fold opposite corners together. Press edges to seal.

3 **Steamed method** Pour boiling water into a large casserole. Add half the triangles and cook on medium 10 minutes. Drain and repeat with remaining triangles.

4 **Fried Method** Preheat browning dish on high 5 minutes. Add oil and cook in batches of 6 on high for 4–6 minutes turning once while each batch is cooking.

5 Serve with ready-made chilli sauce

Makes 30

Sweet and Sour Pork Casserole

750 g (1½ lb) pork, cut into 2 cm
  pieces
30 g (2 tablespoons) seasoned
  cornflour
45 mL (3 tablespoons) soy sauce
30 g (1 oz) (¼ cup) brown sugar
50 mL (2 fl oz) (¼ cup) vinegar
pinch ground ginger
1 × 440 g can pineapple pieces in
  juice
1 onion, chopped
½ red capsicum (pepper), chopped
1 stalk celery, chopped
1 clove garlic, finely chopped

1 Toss pork in seasoned cornflour. Put into a 2 litre casserole dish. Add remaining ingredients except capsicum. Cover and cook on high 5 minutes. Reduce power to medium and cook for 20 minutes, stirring twice during cooking.

2 Add capsicum, adjust seasonings and thickening if necessary and continue cooking on medium 10 minutes. Serve with rice or fried noodles.

Serves 6

Sweet and Sour Pork Casserole

Succulent Lamb

Lamb is tender, tasty and easily digested. It is a reliable meat as most cuts can be cooked by dry and moist cooking methods. Don't overdo seasoning as lamb has a delicate flavour which may become disguised. Herbs should only be used to complement.

Algerian Lamb Casserole flavoured with wine and cumin brings a taste of North Africa to your table. Spicy Lamb Curry is served surrounded by sambals, chutneys, coconut and boiled rice. Lamb Cutlets Hotpot has all the country goodness of fresh vegetables and cider and will delight your family.

Roasted Rosemary Leg of Lamb

Carving Lamb

Carving may look easy but it is more skilful than it appears. It is very important that you have a really sharp carving knife, with a 25 cm (10 in) blade. Always sharpen the knife before carving with a traditional steel or an electric knife sharpener. You may have an electric carving knife — these are really good and enable you to carve meat very thinly and thus it will go further.

Always use a carving fork with a thumb guard and, if possible, place the joint of meat on a spiked carving dish so that it does not slip. Allow the meat to stand for 15 minutes before carving it. Carve thin, consistent slices in order to obtain the best flavour. When possible, cut the lamb against the grain. This will give you more tender slices.

When a joint is carved well it looks more attractive and the meat goes further. Each joint needs different carving and there are no hard and fast rules. It depends on the position of the bones and the way in which the meat and fat are distributed. You will probably find that it is much easier to carve if you are standing up. Always use a long, even sawing action and keep the blade at the same angle. Do not press down on the meat too much or you will squeeze out the juices. Serve the carved meat on very warm plates.

Leg of Lamb: Carve the leg with the round side uppermost, inserting the fork near the knuckle. Make the first cut down to the bone diagonally. Cut out a thick wedge-shaped slice, then carve slices from either side of the cut. Turn the joint over and carve in long slices parallel to the leg bone.

Shoulder of Lamb: Carve the shoulder downwards towards the knuckle end. Turn over and carve downwards in long slices.

Loin of Lamb: Ask your butcher to cut through the sections of the backbone, then it can be divided into chops.

Best End of Neck of Lamb: Your butcher will chine this joint for you (saw along the backbone to release the meat from the bone). Remove the chined bone from the cooked meat and carve between the ribs.

Carving Shoulder of Lamb Step-by-step

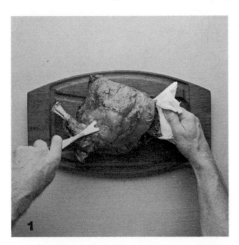
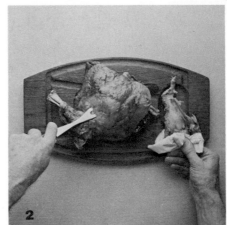
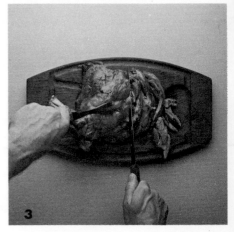

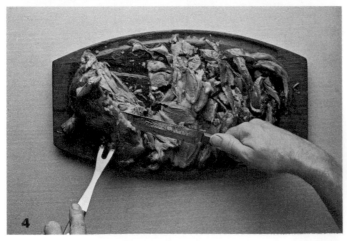
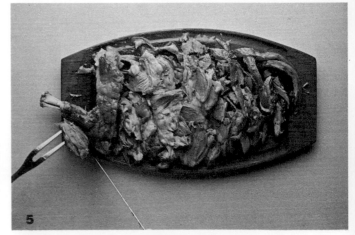

1 With left hand, insert carving fork in shoulder. Grip the exposed bone.
2 Twist blade bone until free and then pull out.

3 Carve down diagonally from one end to other.
4 Turn and slice parallel until you reach end bone.
5 The finished carved joint.

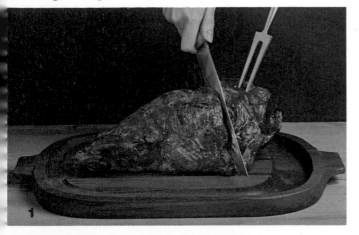

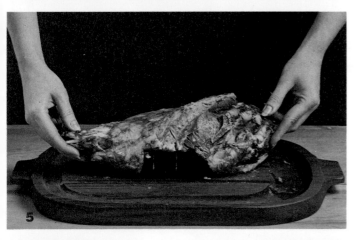

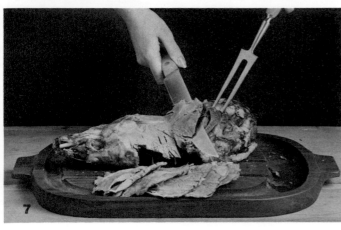

1 Spear the leg of lamb with a carving fork in your left hand. Taking the carving knife in your right hand, cut down through the middle of the joint.

2 Carve in wedges, drawing the knife diagonally down through the joint, then cut across the bottom of the wedges horizontally.

3 Using both the fork and knife, lift out the carved middle wedges and arrange on a serving dish or individual plates.

4 Carve diagonally down through the botton of the lamb under the bone.

5 Lift the leg of lamb off the spikes and turn it over. Replace it on the spikes.

6 Carve diagonally down through the joint.

7 Slice toward the bone until lamb has been carved.

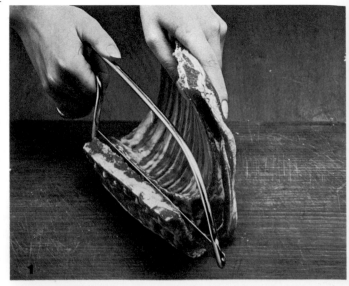

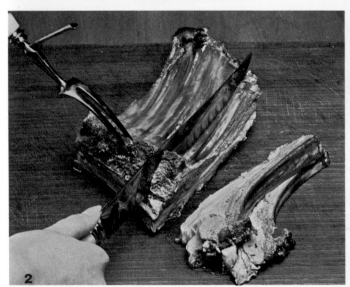

1 Before cooking the loin, cut through the chine bone. Remove the central bone.
2 When joint is cooked, carve into neat slices.
3 The carved joint.

1 Chine joint by sawing along the backbone.
2 When the meat is cooked, carve downwards between the rib bones to form cutlets.
3 The carved best end.

Crown Roast of Lamb

2 best ends of lamb, chined
10 mL (2 teaspoons) butter
1 cooking (green) apple, peeled, cored
  and chopped
225 g (½ lb) pork sausage meat
30 mL (2 tablespoons) fresh
  breadcrumbs
15 mL (1 tablespoon) chopped
  parsley
15 mL (1 tablespoon) finely chopped
  mint or 2.4 mL (½ teaspoon) mixed
  herbs
glace cherries

1 Preheat oven to 180°C (350°F). Trim skin and fat from the ends of the rib bones so that 2.5 cm (1 in) of the bone protrudes. Place the two joints back to back with the bones curving upwards and outwards. Secure with kitchen thread.
2 Heat butter in a pan and saute apple. Add sausage meat, cook 2–3 minutes, then stir in rest of the ingredients.
3 Place stuffing in the cavity of the crown. Cover tips of the bones with foil and roast for 30 minutes per 450 g (1 lb) plus 30 minutes.
4 Decorate bone ends with cutlet frills and serve with roast potatoes.

Serves 6–8

Glazes for Lamb

You can make your joint of roast lamb more exciting by glazing it with one of these glazes for the last half hour of cooking. Just mix together:
1 Brown sugar and mustard.
2 Peanut butter and crushed peanuts.
3 Apple juice, brown sugar, mixed spice and cider vinegar.
4 Honey, soy sauce, vinegar, pineapple juice and garlic.
5 Honey and mustard.
Or just brush the joint with redcurrant, mint or lime jelly.

Roast Lamb with Lemon Sauce

1.5 kg (3 lb) leg of lamb
2 clove garlic, sliced
salt and pepper
50 mL (2 fl oz) (¼ cup) oil
50 g (2 oz) (4 tablespoons) butter
2 carrots, sliced
2 sticks celery, sliced
1 onion, chopped
2 lemons
275 mL (9 fl oz) (1⅛ cup) water
100 g (¼ lb) (½ cup) sugar
15 mL (1 tablespoon) vinegar
7 mL (½ tablespoon) cornflour

1 When buying the leg of lamb, ask the butcher to cut out the aitchbone (pelvic bone) and to trim the knuckle.
2 Preheat oven to 200°C (400°F).
3 Make cuts in the flesh and insert slices of garlic. Season leg, smother with oil and butter and place in a roasting tin on a bed of carrots, celery, onion, 1 sliced lemon and the aitchbone.
4 Roast 1¼ hours (allowing 20 minutes per 450 g (1 lb) and 20 minutes over) basting from time to time. When cooked, rest meat for 15 minutes, then remove and place on a clean dish and keep warm.
5 Make the gravy. During roasting time, cut the other lemon into segments, and simmer 8 minutes in 225 mL (8 fl oz) (1 cup) water with sugar and vinegar.
6 When joint has been removed, put roasting tin on top of the stove over a gentle heat for 2 minutes to allow sediment to settle. Carefully pour off fat, leaving sediment and juices. Cook 3 minutes until brown, then add 300 mL (½ pint) (1¼ cups) lemon liquid (add water if necessary to make up the amount). Stir and scrape tin to loosen the browned sediment, and cook 8 minutes. Thicken with the cornflour mixed with 45 mL (3 tablespoons) water. Cook 5 minutes to clear. Strain.
7 To serve, decorate leg of lamb with a frill round the bone, and pour a little sauce over it. Arrange lemon segments on top. Serve the rest of the sauce separately. Serve with boiled rice, sprinkled with chopped parsley.

Serves 6

Glazed Lamb with Sherry Sauce

1.75 kg (3½ lb) boned leg of lamb
150 g (5 oz) bacon, chopped or
  minced
50 g (2 oz) (1 cup) fresh breadcrumbs
1 egg, beaten
salt and pepper
pinch dried thyme and rosemary
300 mL (½ pint) (1¼ cups) dry sherry
300 mL (½ pint) (1¼ cups) water
3 carrots, cleaned and chopped
2 sticks celery, chopped
few sprigs each fresh parsley and
  tarragon
1 clove garlic, crushed
30 mL (2 tablespoons) oil
50 g (2 oz) (4 tablespoons) butter
150 mL (¼ pint) (⅔ cup) sour cream
15 mL (1 tablespoon) made mustard
1 egg yolk
5 mL (1 teaspoon) chopped fresh
  parsley

1 Ask the butcher to bone the leg of lamb for you. Mix bacon, breadcrumbs, egg, seasoning and herbs to a paste and use to stuff the leg. Tie meat into shape with fine string and marinate it for 5 hours or overnight in the sherry, water, vegetables, fresh herbs and garlic, turning it from time to time to soak all sides.
2 Preheat oven to 200°C (400°F). Drain joint from marinade and dry it. Brush with oil and butter, season with a pinch of salt and pepper, and roast for 35 minutes.
3 Meanwhile drain vegetables from the marinade, reserving both. Place vegetables under the joint and continue to roast for 15 minutes.
4 Reduce oven temperature to 180°C (350°F). Pour marinade around the joint, cover and cook for 1 hour.
5 Mix sour cream, mustard, egg yolk and parsley. Remove meat from the oven and pour vegetables and cooking liquid into a pan. Turn the oven up to 220°C (425°F). Spread the sour cream mixture over the joint and return to the oven for 10 minutes until it is golden-brown.
6 Meanwhile boil marinade to reduce it to a thicker consistency. Strain vegetables out and pour sauce into a sauce-boat. Serve the meat on a heated dish with the sauce.

Serves 8

Spring Lamb in Mushroom Sauce

Spring Lamb in Mushroom Sauce

*2 kg (4 lb) shoulder of spring lamb,
    boned*
salt and pepper
pinch thyme
*450 g (1 lb) (5 cups) button
    mushrooms*
150 g (5 oz) (⅔ cup) butter
2 large onions, chopped
15 g (½ oz) (2 tablespoons) flour
*30 mL (2 tablespoons) thickened
    cream*
50 g (2 oz) (1 cup) fresh breadcrumbs
30 mL (2 tablespoons) oil
*225 g (½ lb) (2 cups) shallot (spring
    onion, scallion) bulbs*
bouquet garni
150 mL (¼ pint) (⅔ cup) stock

1 Cover working surface with a cloth and lay meat out on it, skin downwards. Open up meat and season inside with salt, pepper and thyme. Roll shoulder and put aside while preparing the stuffing.

2 Wash, dry and chop half of the button mushrooms. Melt 25 g (1 oz) (2 tablespoons) butter in a saucepan and fry onions and mushrooms over a low heat until soft.

3 Remove onions and mushrooms from the pan and puree in a blender.

4 Return puree to pan and add flour. Cook 1 minute over a low heat, stirring all the time. Gradually, stir in cream, then breadcrumbs. Correct seasoning.

5 Preheat oven to 200°C (400°F).

6 Unroll the shoulder of lamb, spread with the onion and mushroom mixture, then roll up again and tie with string.

7 Place lamb on a roasting tray and smother it with oil and 75 g (3 oz) (6 tablespoons) butter. Season well and place in oven. After 35 minutes, reduce temperature to 180°C (350°F). Roast for 1½ hours.

8 Heat remaining butter in a pan and fry the rest of the mushrooms and shallot bulbs until golden-brown. Add bouquet garni, season and pour in stock. Cover and cook over a low heat 15 minutes.

9 When lamb is cooked, carve it and serve on a heated serving dish, surrounded by the mushroom and shallot garnish.

10 If you like, you can make a gravy with the meat juices and the stock and pour it over the meat. *Serves 6*

Lamb Venison-style

2 kg (4 lb) leg of lamb
100 g (¼ lb) bacon, chopped
2 onions, sliced
3 cloves garlic, crushed
1 large carrot, sliced
1 stick celery, chopped
bouquet garni
150 mL (¼ pint) (⅔ cup) red wine
   vinegar
50 mL (4 fl oz) (½ cup) oil
500 mL (1 pint) (2½ cups) red wine
salt and pepper
3 whole cloves
5 mL (1 teaspoon) roughly crushed
   juniper berries
15 g (½ oz) (1 tablespoon) brown
   sugar
1 kg (2 lb) potatoes
225 g (½ lb) meat bones, broken by
   the butcher
75 g (3 oz) (¾ cup) flour
500 mL (1 pint) (2½ cups) meat stock
few sprigs watercress to garnish

1 Place joint in a deep dish or pot. Prepare and add bacon, vegetables, bouquet garni, vinegar, half the oil, red wine, seasoning, cloves, juniper berries and brown sugar, mixed well together. Leave to marinate for 5 hours or overnight, turning meat so that all sides are soaked.

2 Peel potatoes and parboil them in salted water for 5 minutes. Strain and dry. Preheat oven to 200°C (400°F). Remove meat from marinade and drain it of liquid. Strain vegetables from marinade, keeping both. Place lamb on a rack in a roasting pan, arrange potatoes around it, brush with half remaining oil and season. Roast for 20 minutes per 450 g (1 lb) and an extra 20 minutes, basting from time to time and turning the potatoes.

3 Meanwhile heat the rest of the oil, and brown the vegetables from the marinade and the broken bones in it. Add flour and stir until lightly browned. Add stock and remaining marinade, bring to the boil and simmer for 1 hour to reduce until it is thickened.

4 Remove meat from roasting pan and set on a heated serving dish. Arrange roast potatoes around the joint, and garnish with watercress. Drain excess fat from roasting pan and mix meat juices with sauce. Strain sauce into a sauce-boat and serve it with the meat

Serves 6–8

Tip: The meat may be given extra tenderness and a stronger flavour by cutting the bacon into thin strips and, with a larding needle inserting it at regular intervals over the surface of the meat before marinating it with the other ingredients.

Lamb Venison-style

Persian Lamb with Apricots

1¼ kg (2½ lb) loin of lamb, boned
30 mL (1 fl oz) (2 tablespoons) oil
25 g (1 oz) (2 tablespoons) butter
1 kg (2 lb) potatoes, peeled
pinch turmeric
9 anchovy fillets
9 canned apricot halves

Marinade
50 mL (2 fl oz) (¼ cup) juice from
    canned apricots
15 mL (1 tablespoon) vinegar
juice 1 lemon
15 mL (1 tablespoon) soy sauce
150 mL (¼ pint) (⅔ cup) dry sherry
15 mL (1 tablespoon) oil
pinch allspice
salt and pepper

1 Soak loin of lamb in marinade ingredients for at least 2 hours, basting it and turning it from time to time so that it absorbs the marinade.
2 Preheat oven to 200°C (400°F). Remove loin from marinade and dry lightly with a kitchen towel.
3 Brush lamb with the oil and butter and season with a little salt and pepper. Roast for 45 minutes.
4 Parboil potatoes in salted water with a pinch of turmeric, which will give them a light yellow colour. Then drain and arrange around the loin of lamb to roast with it for the last ½ hour. Baste meat and potatoes occasionally.
5 Meanwhile pour marinade into a pan, bring to the boil, and simmer 10 minutes to reduce it. Pour sauce into a sauce-boat and keep it warm.
6 When meat is cooked, raise the oven temperature to 220°C (425°F). Take meat and potatoes from oven, drain potatoes and arrange around sides of a heated serving dish.
7 Roll up anchovy fillets and pierce each one with a cocktail stick. Arrange canned apricot halves over the fat side of the meat, pinning each one in place with a cocktail stick and anchovy roll.
8 Pour a little of the marinade sauce over the joint and return to oven for 5 minutes to glaze.
9 Set joint in the middle of the serving dish with potatoes. Serve with a green vegetable such as garden peas or French beans.   *Serves 4*

Tips: Fresh apricots, peaches, nectarines, plums or pears may be used in place of apricots. For extra luxury soak the fruit in 30 mL (1 fl oz) (2 tablespoons) brandy before using, and glaze the joint with a little honey. Serve without the marinade sauce.

Normandy Lamb

1 clove garlic
2 kg (4 lb) leg of lamb
salt and pepper
5 mL (1 teaspoon) thyme
75 g (3 oz) (6 tablespoons) butter
225 mL (8 fl oz) (1 cup) cider
5 mL (1 teaspoon) flour
50 mL (2 fl oz) (¼ cup) Calvados,
    (apple brandy) or brandy
150 mL (5 fl oz) (⅔ cup) cream

1 Preheat oven to 200°C (400°F).
2 Insert clove of garlic, peeled, into knuckle end of leg of lamb with the point of a knife. Salt and pepper the meat generously and sprinkle with thyme. Rub in well so that the flavours sink into the meat.
3 Heat butter, reserving 5 mL (1 teaspoon) in a casserole. Add lamb and brown for 8 minutes. Cover and cook, allowing 20 minutes per 450 g (1 lb) and 20 minutes over, basting with half the cider from time to time.
4 Blend 5 mL (1 teaspoon) flour with 5 mL (1 teaspoon) butter for a 'beurre manie' to thicken gravy later on.
5 When lamb is cooked, pour on the Calvados (apple brandy) or brandy and flame. Then place meat on a serving dish and keep warm.
6 Pour remainder of the cider into pan. Boil 2 minutes, scraping casserole to loosen the browned sediment.
7 Add cream and stir for 1 minute, then add the 'beurre manie' and cook gently until it thickens.
8 Serve sauce separately with the lamb.

Serves 6–8

Lamb Espagnola

2 kg (4 lb) leg or shoulder of lamb
2 cloves garlic, crushed
5 mL (1 teaspoon) mixed dried herbs
few sprigs fresh rosemary
60 mL (4 tablespoons) sherry
60 mL (4 tablespoons) water
12 small onions or shallots (spring
    onions, scallions), peeled
6 stuffed green olives, sliced

1 Place lamb in a roasting pan. Spread crushed garlic and dried herbs evenly over the surface and arrange rosemary sprigs on top and underneath. Pour sherry over meat and leave to stand for 3 hours.
2 Preheat oven to 190°C (375°F). Add water to the roasting pan and arrange the peeled, whole onions around the joint. Roast in oven for 20 minutes per 450 g (1 lb) and 20 minutes more, basting from time to time.
3 Set lamb on a heated serving dish and arrange onions around it. Stir sliced olives into cooking juices and pour liquid over the joint.

Serves 6–8

Festive Leg

225 g (½ lb) canned pineapple rings
    with juice
2 kg (4 lb) leg of lamb
salt and pepper
glacé cherries for decoration

1 Preheat oven to 200°C (400°F).
2 Remove juice from the can of pineapple rings.
3 Put lamb in a roasting tin and pour pineapple juice over. Season with salt and pepper.
4 Roast in oven, allowing 20 minutes per 450 g (1 lb) and 20 minutes over, basting occasionally with the juice.
5 When cooked place on a dish and garnish with halved pineapple rings with a cherry between each. Serve with roast potatoes.

Serves 6–8

Leg of Lamb with Spinach

Leg of Lamb with Spinach

2 kg (4 lb) leg of lamb
2 cloves garlic
25 g (1 oz) (2 tablespoons) butter,
   melted
30 mL (2 tablespoons) oil
5 mL (1 tablespoon) each chopped
   fresh thyme and rosemary

Marinade
bouquet garni
1 clove garlic
salt and pepper
5 mL (1 teaspoon) mustard powder
225 mL (8 fl oz) (1 cup) dry white
   wine
45 mL (3 tablespoons) olive oil
15 mL (1 tablespoon) red wine
   vinegar

Garnish
2 kg (4 lb) fresh spinach
40 g (1½ oz) (3 tablespoons) butter
15 mL (1 tablespoon) oil
2 anchovy fillets, finely chopped

1 Mix marinade ingredients well in a bowl large enough to hold the leg of lamb. Put meat in marinade and leave for at least 3 hours (or overnight), turning it so that all sides of the joint absorb the liquid.

2 Preheat oven to 200°C (400°F). Drain meat and keep remaining marinade. Peel garlic, cut into slivers, and insert into small knife cuts regularly spaced over the meat surface. Place meat in a roasting pan, brush with melted butter and oil, and sprinkle with thyme, rosemary and a pinch of salt and pepper. Roast for about 20 minutes per 450 g (1 lb) and an extra 20 minutes basting occasionally.

3 Meanwhile, wash spinach thoroughly and remove any thick stems and wilted leaves. Place in a pan with a little salt, cover, and cook gently for 5 minutes. Drain and squeeze out all excess moisture from the leaves. Chop roughly.

4 Heat butter and oil in the same pan, mix in chopped anchovy fillets, and stir in spinach. Cook for 1 minute until heated through, stirring constantly.

5 Remove lamb from oven and leave to stand 10–15 minutes. Drain excess fat from cooking juices and then stir marinade into the meat juice over heat. Bring to the boil and strain into a sauce-boat. Place lamb on a large heated serving dish, surround it with spinach, and serve with gravy.

Serves 6–8

Leg of Lamb Minorca

1.75 kg (3½ lb) leg of lamb
2 cloves garlic
salt and pepper
2 sprigs fresh rosemary
2 onions, chopped
3 carrots, quartered
30 mL (2 tablespoons) oil
75 g (3 oz) (6 tablespoons) butter
300 mL (½ pint) (1¼ cups) rose wine
25 g (1 oz) (2 tablespoons) tomato
   paste
100 g (¼ lb) (1 cup) sliced button
   mushrooms
12 stuffed green olives
15 g (½ oz) (1½ tablespoons) cornflour
45 mL (3 tablespoons) water
12 small tomatoes

1 Remove the aitchbone (pelvic bone) or ask the butcher to do it for you, and keep it. Cut garlic into slivers and insert into slits on surface of the meat. Season with salt and pepper, and rosemary sprigs.

2 Preheat oven to 190°C (375°F). Place onions and carrots in a roasting pan with the bone. Brush joint with oil and 50 g (2 oz) (4 tablespoons) butter and set it on the vegetables. Roast 45 minutes.

3 Add wine and tomato paste, cover and continue to cook for 45 minutes.

4 Remove meat from roasting pan and keep warm. Take the bone and carrots from the liquid. Boil liquid to reduce it.

5 Fry mushrooms in the rest of butter for 5 minutes. Add to sauce with green olives. Thicken sauce with cornflour dissolved in water.

6 Grill tomatoes for 5 minutes. Arrange them around the joint on a serving dish. Impale 2 tomatoes on a kebab skewer with a few stuffed olives and stick it into the meat to decorate. Pour sauce over joint and serve.

Serves 6–8

Britannia Saddle of Lamb

1¼ kg (2½ lb) saddle of lamb
100 mL (4 fl oz) (½ cup) brandy
5 mL (1 teaspoon) allspice
75 g (3 oz) (6 tablespoons) butter
225 g (½ lb) (1 cup) minced lean pork
100 g (¼ lb) (½ cup) minced liver
150 g (5 oz) (2½ cups) fresh white
   breadcrumbs
2 eggs, beaten
20 g (4 tablespoons) chopped parsley
10 g (2 tablespoons) chopped fresh
   mint
2 mL (1 teaspoon) rosemary
salt and pepper
350 g (¾ lb) pieces belly of pork fat
100 g (¼ lb) ox tongue, cut in strips

1 When buying the saddle of lamb, ask the butcher to bone it completely, leaving enough flap to wrap under the saddle and enclose the stuffing.

2 Remove underfillets and marinate them with a little of the brandy and allspice for ½ hour. Saute them in 25 g (1 oz) (2 tablespoons) butter for 5 minutes.

3 Make the stuffing by mixing minced lean pork and liver with breadcrumbs, eggs, chopped parsley, mint, rosemary and brandy. Season with salt and pepper.

4 Preheat oven to 200°C (400°F).

5 Spread the pieces of belly of pork fat on a board and place a layer of stuffing on top, then arrange a few strips of ox tongue and the underfillets and continue until all is used. Wrap in the belly of pork fat to make a sausage shape, the same length as the saddle and about 7.5 cm (3 in) in diameter.

6 Turn saddle upside down on the board, and place filling inside. Cover with the two flaps of the saddle. Season and tie firmly with string at 2.5 ccm (1 in) intervals.

7 Place saddle in a roasting tin and smother with the rest of the butter and roast for 30 minutes, then reduce the heat to 180°C (350°F) for 1¼ hours (allowing 30 minutes to 450 g (1 lb) and 30 minutes over).

8 Remove saddle, discard string, and keep warm. Make gravy from the juices in the pan. Serve with mint jelly and redcurrant sauce.

Serves 4

Springtime Saddle of Lamb

1.25 kg (2½ lb) saddle of lamb
salt and pepper
75 g (3 oz) (6 tablespoons) butter
225 g (½ lb) French beans
12 asparagus spears
225 g (½ lb) small carrots
5 mL (1 teaspoon) sugar
3 small onions, peeled
225 g (½ lb) (2 cups) peas
450 g (1 lb) new potatoes
sprig mint
15 mL (1 tablespoon) chopped
   parsley
1 head celery
6 tomatoes

1 Preheat oven to 200°C (400°F).

2 Place saddle in a roasting pan. Season with salt and pepper and smother it with 50 g (2 oz) (4 tablespoons) butter. Roast ½ hour, then reduce heat to 180°C (350°F) for 40 minutes, basting from time to time.

3 Meanwhile, head and tail the French beans. Scrape asparagus and tie in bundles.

4 Put carrots in a saucepan with sugar and onions, and cover with water. Boil 15 minutes. Add peas and cook 8 minutes until water has almost evaporated. Then add remaining butter.

5 Boil new potatoes with mint, until cooked, and drain. Mix with carrots and peas, season with salt and pepper and sprinkle with parsley. Keep warm.

6 Boil asparagus in salted water for 15 minutes, drain, remove string, and keep warm.

7 Boil celery in salted water for 15 minutes, drain and keep warm.

8 Drop tomatoes in boiling water for 2 minutes, then skin and warm in the oven.

9 When ready to serve, arrange saddle on a large dish and surround with asparagus, celery, tomatoes, new potatoes, carrots, onions, peas and French beans. Sprinkle with chopped parsley.

Serves 4

Leg of Lamb Minorca

Soubise Saddle of Lamb

1.25 kg (2½ lb) saddle of lamb
salt and pepper
50 g (2 oz) (4 tablespoons) butter
225 g (½ lb) (1 cup) onion puree
500 mL (1 pint) (2½ cups) thick white
    sauce
2 egg yolks
75 mL (5 tablespoons) white wine
15 g (½ oz) (1½ tablespoons) grated
    Parmesan cheese
slices of truffle for decoration
    (optional)

1 Preheat oven to 200°C (400°F).
2 Place saddle in a roasting tin.
Season and spread with butter. Roast
½ hour, then reduce heat to 180°C
(350°F) for 40 minutes (allowing 20
minutes for every 450 g (1 lb) and 20
minutes over).
3 Mix puree of onions with white
sauce and egg yolks, and season.
4 Remove loins by making a deep
cut along the backbone and slipping
knife underneath. Carve into thick
slices.
5 Increase oven temperature to
220°C (425°F).
6 Spread slices of meat with half the
sauce, sandwich together to the original shape and place on bones.
7 Dilute remainder of the sauce with
white wine and pour over saddle.
Sprinkle with Parmesan cheese.
Brown in oven for 8 minutes until
golden-brown. This can be decorated
with slices of truffle (optional).

Serves 4

Waipura

1.25 kg (2½ lb) saddle of lamb, boned
    and skinned
7 mL (½ tablespoon) chopped parsley
1 clove garlic, crushed
salt and pepper
one 350 g (¾ lb) pork fillet
50 g (2 oz) (4 tablespoons) butter

1 Ask the butcher to bone and skin
the saddle of lamb.
2 Preheat oven to 200°C (400°F).
3 Sprinkle meat with parsley, garlic,
salt and pepper, and use the pork
fillet to fill the cavity left by the

removal of the backbone. Roll up and
tie with string.
4 Place in a roasting tin, and smother
with butter. Roast ½ hour, then
reduce heat to 180°C (350°F) for 1¼
hours (allowing 30 minutes to 450 g
(1 lb) and 20 minutes over).
5 When cooked, rest 15 minutes.
Make gravy from pan juices. Serve
with roast potatoes and a green
salad.

Serves 6

Shoulder of Lamb with Apricot and Pawpaw Sauce

1 kg (2 lb) shoulder of lamb
salt and pepper
50 g (2 oz) (4 tablespoons) butter
5 mL (1 teaspoon) allspice
50 g (2 oz) (2 tablespoons) honey
1 pawpaw
225 g (½ lb) (1 cup) canned apricots
few sprigs parsley for decoration

1 Preheat oven to 200°C (400°F).
2 Season lamb with salt and pepper,
cover with butter, and place in a
roasting tin.
3 Roast meat for ½ hour, then reduce
temperature to 180°C (350°F) for ½
hour.
4 Mix spice with honey and baste
meat with this during the roasting.
5 Scoop out the pawpaw into balls
with a melon baller. Add canned
apricots and pawpaw to the pan ¼
hour before the end of roasting.
6 When cooked, remove the meat
and place on a dish. Surround meat
with the apricots and pawpaw.
7 Use some of the canned juice to
loosen the browned sediment in the
tin. Boil, season, strain and serve separately as a sauce.
8 Garnish dish with sprigs of
parsley, and serve with new potatoes
and peas.

Serves 4

Cranberry Shoulder of Lamb

1 × 2 kg (4 lb) shoulder of lamb
1 clove garlic, sliced
50 mL (2 fl oz) (¼ cup) oil
5 mL (1 teaspoon) powdered ginger
5 mL (1 teaspoon) dry mustard
5 mL (1 teaspoon) brown sugar
225 g (½ lb) (¾ cup) cranberry sauce
175 g (6 oz) (½ cup) cherry jam
30 mL (2 tablespoons) port wine
300 mL (½ pint) (1¼ cups) water
15 g (½ oz) (2 tablespoons) cornflour

1 Preheat oven to 200°C (400°F).
2 Cut 2 or 3 slits in the lamb and
insert a sliver of garlic in each. Brush
lamb with oil.
3 Mix ginger, mustard and sugar and
sprinkle over lamb.
4 Place lamb, fat side up, on a rack in
a shallow roasting pan. Place on the
middle shelf in oven.
5 After ½ hour, reduce temperature
to 180°C (350°F) and roast for 1¼–1½
hours.
6 Meanwhile, mix cranberry sauce
and cherry jam and heat in a saucepan. When it melts, stir in port.
7 When meat has been roasting for 1
hour, pour sauce over lamb and continue to baste from time to time.
8 When meat is cooked, remove
from pan and place on a warm serving dish. Skim excess fat from meat
juices in pan and add most of the
water to them. Mix the rest of the
water with the cornflour and add to
pan. Bring to the boil, stirring well
until the sauce thickens. Season with
salt and pepper and pour over lamb.
Serve with Brussels sprouts, French
beans and boiled new potatoes.

Serves 6

Shoulder of Lamb with Apricot and Pawpaw Sauce

Boiled Shoulder of Lamb with Turnips

Boiled Shoulder of Lamb with Turnips

1 onion
4 cloves
5 carrots, diced
225 g (½ lb) swede, diced
4 medium leeks, chopped
1 stick celery, chopped
2½ litres (4½ pints) (10¼ cups) water
bouquet garni
salt and pepper
2 kg (4 lb) shoulder of lamb, boned, rolled and tied
900 g (2 lb) small turnips, peeled
50 g (2 oz) (¼ cup) butter
100 mL (4 fl oz) (½ cup) cream

1 Stud onion with cloves.
2 Put all the vegetables except the turnips in a large pan, add water, bouquet garni, salt and pepper. Bring to the boil and simmer ½ hour. Add meat and simmer, allowing 20 minutes per 450 g (1 lb) and 20 minutes over.
3 Tie peeled turnips in a piece of muslin and put in pan for the last ½ hour.
4 When the turnips are tender, remove from pan and drain. Put them in a liquidiser and blend to a puree, then place in a saucepan with butter and cream and stir until heated through. Season with salt and pepper.
5 Remove meat and keep warm. Make a sauce from the liquid in the casserole. The fat should be removed, and the liquid boiled with the addition of a little water if necessary. Season and strain.
6 When ready to serve, put the lamb on a dish, and serve the puree of turnips and sauce separately.

Serves 6

Beswick Lamb

1½ (3 lb) loin of lamb, boned
25 g (1 oz) (2 tablespoons) butter
30 mL (1 fl oz) (2 tablespoons) oil
450 g (1 lb) garden peas
1 sprig mint
6 shallot (spring onion, scallion)
  bulbs
50 mL (2 fl oz) (¼ cup) sherry
juice 1 orange

Stuffing
2 slices bacon, chopped
2 lamb's kidneys, skinned, cored and
  chopped
50 g (2 oz) (4 tablespoons) butter
1 onion, finely chopped
100 g (¼ lb) (1 cup) chopped
  mushrooms
salt and pepper
5 mL (1 teaspoon) tomato paste
50 g (2 oz) (1 cup) fresh breadcrumbs

1 To make the stuffing, fry chopped bacon and kidney in the butter for 3 minutes. Stir in the onion and cook 3 minutes. Add mushrooms and fry 2 minutes. Season, stir in tomato paste and breadcrumbs, and stir to bind all ingredients together to a loose mixture, adding a little melted butter if necessary. Allow stuffing to cool.

2 Preheat oven to 200°C (400°F). Spread stuffing on the inside of the loin of lamb, roll up meat and tie with fine string. Place in a roasting pan, brush with butter and oil and season. Roast for 1–1½ hours.

3 Boil peas in salted water with a sprig of mint and the shallot bulbs until tender. Drain and pile peas on a heated serving dish.

4 When meat is cooked, carve into slices and arrange on bed of garden peas.

5 Strain off excess fat from cooking juices. Pour sherry and orange juice into roasting pan and boil for 3 minutes. Season to taste. Pour sauce into a sauce-boat and serve with meat, peas, and some redcurrant or cranberry jelly.

Serves 8

Beswick Lamb

Breast of Lamb with Apple and Onion Stuffing

1½ kg (3 lb) breast of lamb, boned
30 mL (2 tablespoons) oil
25 g (1 oz) (2 tablespoons) butter
salt and pepper
300 mL (½ pint) (1¼ cups) chicken
  stock
15 g (½ oz) (1½ tablespoons) cornflour

Stuffing
100 g (¼ lb) (½ cup) long grain rice
2 onions, finely chopped
2 large apples, peeled, cored and
  diced
25 g (1 oz) (2 tablespoons) butter
pinch allspice

1 Cook rice in salted water, rinse and drain. Fry onion and apple in butter until softened. Mix rice, onion and apple together and season with salt and pepper and a pinch of allspice.

2 Preheat oven to 200°C (400°F). Spread stuffing on the lamb, roll and tie. Brush with oil and butter, season and roast for 20 minutes.

3 Reduce oven heat to 180°C (350°F). Pour stock into pan and cover, cook for 1 hour. Remove meat from pan and thicken gravy with cornflour diluted with a little water. Serve it with the meat.

Serves 6

*Breast of Lamb with Fruit and
Nut Stuffing*

Breast of Lamb with Fruit and Nut Stuffing

1½ kg (3 lb) breast of lamb, boned
salt and pepper
30 mL (2 tablespoons) oil
25 g (1 oz) (2 tablespoons) butter
300 mL (½ pint) (1¼ cups) chicken
*   stock*
25 g (1 oz) (2 tablespoons) flour
25 g (1 oz) (2 tablespoons) butter

Stuffing
100 g (¼ lb) (2 cups) fresh white
*   breadcrumbs*
75 mL (2½ fl oz) (⅓ cup) milk
225 g (½ lb) (1 cup) sausage meat
1 egg, beaten
100 g (¼ lb) (¾ cup) dates, stoned and
*   finely chopped*
100 g (¼ lb) (1 cup) shelled chopped
*   walnuts*
5 mL (1 tablespoon) chopped fresh
*   parsley*
grated rind 1 orange

1 Preheat oven to 200°C (400°F). To
make the stuffing: soak breadcrumbs
in milk. Mix them into the rest of the
stuffing ingredients and seasoning, to
form a thick smooth paste.

2 Trim any excess fat or skin from
the meat. Cut a pocket in between
the outer skin and inner membrane
of the breast. Spread stuffing evenly
inside the pocket of meat. Season
meat with salt and pepper, roll it up
and tie neatly with string.

3 Brush joint with oil and butter and
roast for 20 minutes. Then reduce the
oven heat to 180°C (350°F), and add
chicken stock to the roasting pan and
cover. Cook for 1 hour.

4 Remove meat from pan and keep
it warm. Strain off any excess fat
from the cooking liquid. Thicken
with a roux of flour and butter and
season to taste. Pour gravy into a
sauce-boat and serve with meat.
Serve with seasonal vegetables such
as cauliflower.

Serves 6

Stuffed Breast of Lamb with Caper Sauce

1.5 kg (3 lb) breast of lamb, boned
salt and pepper
225 g (½ lb) (1 cup) sausage meat
4 hard-boiled eggs, shelled
30 mL (2 tablespoons) oil
25 g (1 oz) (2 tablespoons) butter
600 mL (1 pint) (2½ cups) chicken
*   stock*
bouquet garni

Sauce
25 g (1 oz) (2 tablespoons) butter
25 g (1 oz) (4 tablespoons) flour
150 mL (¼ pint) (⅔ cup) cream
30 mL (2 tablespoons) chopped
*   capers*
5 mL (1 teaspoon) chopped fresh
*   parsley*

1 Trim meat of excess fat or skin,
and season well on both sides.

2 Season sausage meat and spread
evenly on the inside surface of the
lamb breast. Preheat the oven to
200°C (400°F).

3 Arrange hard-boiled eggs across
the width of the meat. Roll breast up
around the row of eggs and tie it
neatly in shape with fine string.

4 Brush joint with the oil and butter
and roast 20 minutes. Reduce the
oven heat to 180°C (350°F). Pour
stock into roasting pan, add bouquet
garni, cover and cook for 1 hour.

5 Remove meat from pan and keep
warm. Discard bouquet garni. Strain
off excess fat from cooking liquid and
thicken with a roux of the butter and
flour. Stir in cream, capers and
parsley. Pour sauce into a sauce-boat
and serve with meat. Serve with
vegetables such as carrots and French
beans

Serves 6

Norfolk Parcel

1 kg (2 lb) boned breast of lamb, cut
in 4 equal pieces
30 mL (2 tablespoons) oil
25 g (1 oz) (2 tablespoons) butter

Stuffing
2 large onions, chopped
25 g (1 oz) (2 tablespoons) butter
150 mL (¼ pint) (⅔ cup) chicken stock
225 g (½ lb) (1 cup) sausage meat
100 g (¼ lb) (2 cups) fresh
*   breadcrumbs*
salt and pepper
15 mL (1 tablespoon) fresh sage,
*   finely chopped*
15 mL (1 tablespoon) chutney

1 Trim excess fat from meat, and beat lightly with a rolling pin or meat mallet. Preheat oven to 200°C (400°F).

2 To make stuffing, fry onion gently in butter until soft but not browned. Add stock and boil for 5 minutes, until the liquid is well reduced. Remove from heat and stir in sausage meat, breadcrumbs, a pinch of salt and pepper, sage and chutney. Blend well to make a thick paste.

3 Divide stuffing into 3 and spread it over the pieces of meat. Place pieces of meat on top of each other to make a sandwich, and tie together neatly with fine string. Season with salt and pepper and brush oil and butter over the top and sides.

4 Roast meat parcel in oven for 20 minutes. Then turn oven temperature down to 180°C (350°F) for 1½–2 hours, basting meat frequently. Place meat on a heated serving dish. Strain fat from cooking juices and pour the rest over the meat. Serve.

Serves 6

Norfolk Parcel

Shoulder of Lamb with Chestnut Stuffing

salt and pepper
2 kg (4 lb) boned shoulder of lamb
30 mL (2 tablespoons) oil
50 g (2 oz) (4 tablespoons) butter
150 mL (¼ pint) (⅔ cup) stock

Chestnut Stuffing
225 g (½ lb) (1 cup) sausage meat
225 g (½ lb) (1 cup) canned chestnuts,
*   drained and chopped*
1 egg, beaten
25 g (1 oz) (¼ cup) flour
15 mL (1 tablespoon) sherry

1 Preheat oven to 200°C (400°F). Blend stuffing ingredients.

2 Season lamb and spread stuffing evenly over the inside. Roll and tie. Brush with oil and butter and roast, basting frequently, for 1¾ hours. After 20 minutes reduce oven heat to 180°C (350°F).

3 Remove meat from pan and drain excess fat. Add chicken stock, season, and boil for 5 minutes to thicken. Serve gravy with meat.

Serves 8

Shoulder of Lamb with Apricot Stuffing

2 kg (4 lb) shoulder of lamb, boned
salt and pepper
30 mL (2 tablespoons) oil
50 g (2 oz) (4 tablespoons) butter
150 mL (¼ pint) (⅔ cup) chicken stock
60 mL (4 tablespoons) syrup from
* canned apricots*
15 mL (1 tablespoon) wine vinegar
15 g (½ oz) (1½ tablespoons) cornflour
12 canned apricot halves

Apricot Stuffing
100 g (¼ lb) (¾ cup) dried apricots
100 g (¼ lb) (½ cup) pork sausage
* meat*
100 g (¼ lb) (½ cup) beef sausage meat
50 g (2 oz) (1 cup) fresh white
* breadcrumbs*
1 egg, beaten

1 Soak dried apricots for several hours or overnight in water. When soft, drain and chop finely.

2 Preheat oven to 200°C (400°F). Blend ingredients for stuffing to make a thick smooth paste.

3 Spread boned shoulder of lamb open, season, and cover inside evenly with stuffing. Roll up and tie into shape with fine string. Place in a roasting pan and brush with oil and butter.

4 Roast meat for 20 minutes, then lower oven heat for 180°C (350°F). Cook for 1½ hours, basting frequently.

5 Remove meat from roasting pan and drain off excess fat. Add stock, syrup and vinegar, season and boil for several minutes to evaporate. Thicken with cornflour dissolved in a little water.

6 Place stuffed lamb on a serving dish or carving board and surround it with canned apricot halves. Serve each portion with an apricot half and the sauce poured over.

Serves 8

Andorran Shoulder of Lamb

2 kg (4 lb) shoulder of lamb, bones
* and fat removed*
25 g (1 oz) (2 tablespoons) butter
30 mL (1 fl oz) (2 tablespoons) oil
225 mL (8 fl oz) (1 cup) stock
225 mL (8 fl oz) (1 cup) dry white
* wine*
100 mL (4 fl oz) (½ cup) anisette

Stuffing
225 g (½ lb) sausage meat
1 egg, beaten
15 mL (1 tablespoon) brandy
* (optional)*
100 g (¼ lb) (1 cup) chopped
* mushrooms*
2 sprigs thyme, finely chopped
sprig rosemary, finely chopped
15 mL (1 tablespoon) chopped
* parsley*
1 shallot (spring onion, scallion),
* chopped*
1 clove garlic, peeled and chopped
salt and pepper
25 g (1 oz) (2 tablespoons) butter
15 mL (1 tablespoon) oil

Tomato Sauce
45 mL (3 tablespoons) oil
1 onion, chopped
700 g (1½ lb) tomatoes, skinned and
* chopped*
1 clove garlic, peeled
1 chilli, seeded and chopped
1 sugar lump
1 sprig thyme

1 To make the stuffing, mix all the ingredients, except the butter and oil, together in a bowl.

2 Heat butter and oil in a pan, add stuffing and cook for 7–8 minutes until golden-brown.

3 Spread lamb flat on the work surface. Spread stuffing over the meat, taking it to within 3 cm (1¼ in) of the edge. Roll up meat and secure with kitchen string.

4 Heat butter and oil in a heavy-bottomed pan and fry meat until golden-brown all over. Pour in stock and white wine, cover and leave to cook over a low heat for 2¼ hours.

5 Meanwhile, prepare the tomato sauce. Heat oil in a pan, add the onion, tomatoes, garlic, chilli, sugar and thyme and season with salt and pepper. Cook over a high heat until golden-brown, then reduce heat, cover and cook over a low heat for 40 minutes.

6 Pour sauce through a fine conical strainer, cover and return to a low heat. If the sauce becomes too thick, add a few spoonfuls of the cooking liquor from the meat.

7 When meat is cooked, transfer to a heated serving dish and pour sauce into a sauce-boat.

8 Just before serving, warm anisette, sprinkle over the meat and set it alight. Serve with rice, noodles or French beans.

Serves 6–8

Andorran Shoulder of Lamb

Stuffed Leg of Lamb

25 g (1 oz) (2 tablespoons) currants
75 g (3 oz) (6 tablespoons) butter
1 onion, chopped
4 apples, peeled, cored and diced
175 g (6 oz) (¾ cup) long grain rice
salt and pepper
2 kg (4 lb) leg of lamb, boned
100 mL (4 fl oz) (½ cup) oil
100 mL (4 fl oz) (½ cup) stock
juice 1 lemon

1 Preheat oven to 200°C (400°F).
2 Soak currants in water.
3 Heat butter in a frying pan. Fry onion gently, add apples and cook until all the liquid evaporates.
4 Boil rice for 10 minutes.
5 Mix onion and apples with drained currants and the rice. Season with salt and pepper. Stuff leg with the mixture and sew up opening. Season and brush with oil.
6 Roast 2¼ hours in all, 35 minutes at 200°C (400°F) and for 1 hour 40 minutes with the temperature reduced to 180°C (350°F).
7 When leg is cooked, remove from pan and put on a serving dish. Make a gravy with the juices in the pan and the stock and flavour with lemon juice.

Serves 6–8

Braised Stuffed Lamb

1.2 kg (2½ lb) best end, boned
50 mL (2 fl oz) (¼ cup) oil
25 g (1 oz) (2 tablespoons) butter
450 g (1 lb) small onions
350 g (¾ lb) carrots, quartered
1 beef stock cube
300 mL (½ pint) (1¼ cups) water
15 g (½ oz) (1½ tablespoons) cornflour
Stuffing
25 g (1 oz) (2 tablespoons) butter or
  margarine
75 g (3 oz) (6 tablespoons) chopped
  onion
350 g (¾ lb) sausage meat
5 mL (1 teaspoon) chopped parsley
pinch mixed herbs
pinch thyme
salt and pepper
1 egg

1 Preheat oven to 200°C (400°F).
2 Prepare the stuffing: heat the fat in a pan, add chopped onion and cook for 5 minutes. Mix in the sausage meat, herbs and seasoning and blend well. Cover and cook for 5 minutes. Remove from heat and blend in egg to make a smooth paste.
3 Spread stuffing over the meat, roll up and secure with a kitchen thread. Brush with a little oil and brown for 20 minutes.
4 Reduce the heat to 180°C (350°F) and cook for one hour, brushing with more oil if necessary.
5 Meanwhile, heat butter in a pan and saute small onions until brown (about 4 minutes). Cover onions with water and boil for 8 minutes until tender. Drain and keep hot.
6 Boil carrots in salted water for about 20 minutes until tender. Drain and keep hot.
7 Twenty minutes before the meat has finished cooking, dissolve the beef stock cube in the water and pour it over the meat. Return meat to the oven for the rest of the cooking time.

8 When meat is cooked, lift it from the roasting pan, transfer to a serving dish and keep hot while preparing the gravy.
9 Place roasting tin with the cooking juices on top of the stove and boil for 5 minutes. Season, strain and thicken with the cornflour dissolved in 90 mL (6 tablespoons) of water.
10 Surround meat with carrots and onions, pour over a little of the gravy and serve the rest in a sauce-boat.

Serves 6

Braised Lamb in Wine

4 cloves garlic
2 kg (4 lb) leg of lamb
100 mL (4 fl oz) (½ cup) oil
2 onions, chopped
2 carrots, diced
100 mL (4 fl oz) (½ cup) white wine
1 litre (1¾ pints) (4½ cups) stock
bouquet garni
salt and pepper

1 Preheat oven to 200°C (400°F).
2 Cut each clove of garlic into four and insert each into a gash cut in the leg of lamb.
3 Heat oil in a frying pan and brown lamb on all sides for 8 minutes. Remove and place in a casserole.
4 Brown onions and carrots and add to lamb.
5 Pour white wine and stock into casserole. Add bouquet garni, salt and plenty of pepper and bring to the boil. Cover and braise in the oven for 2 hours.
6 When meat is cooked, remove from casserole and keep warm. Strain liquid from casserole into a saucepan. Remove fat and boil until only 300 mL (½ pint) (1¼ cups) remains.
7 The lamb may be served sliced, with a little sauce poured over it, or whole to be carved at table.

Serves 6–8

Guard of Honour

Guard of Honour

2 best ends of lamb, chined
salt and pepper
few parsley sprigs

1 Preheat oven to 180°C (350°F).

2 Trim skin and fat from the ends of the rib bones so that about 7.5 cm (3 in) of bone protrudes. Stand joints together in a roasting pan with bone ends criss-crossing. Secure with kitchen thread.

3 Sprinkle with salt and pepper, cover the ends of the bones with foil, and bake for about 1½ hours.

4 Decorate with parsley sprigs and serve with creamed potato and peas.

Serves 6–8

Pot Roast Lamb

salt and pepper
2 kg (4 lb) leg of lamb, boned, rolled
* and tied*
2 cloves garlic
50 g (2 oz) (4 tablespoons) butter
30 mL (2 tablespoons) oil
3 carrots, sliced
3 onions, sliced
3 leeks, sliced
450 mL (16 fl oz) (2 cups) beef stock
450 g (1 lb) (2 cups) cooked flageolet
* or lima beans*
350 mL (12 fl oz) (1½ cups) water
7 mL (½ tablespoon) cornflour

1 Season leg of lamb and insert slices of garlic into cuts in the flesh.

2 Heat 25 g (1 oz) (2 tablespoons) but-ter and oil in a casserole, and brown lamb all over for 8 minutes. Remove. Brown carrots, onions and leeks in the same fat for 5 minutes. Pour off fat. Return lamb to casserole. Add stock, bring to the boil, and simmer for 2 hours.

3 Reheat beans in the rest of the but-ter and season with salt and pepper. Keep warm.

4 When meat is cooked, remove from casserole and keep warm. Pour off fat, add 300 mL (½ pint) (1¼ cups) water and boil 5 minutes. Thicken with cornflour mixed with the rest of the water. Boil 5 minutes, strain and season.

5 To serve, slice meat and arrange on a dish, surrounded by beans. Serve sauce separately.

Serves 8

Pot Roast Lamb

Grilled Lamb Chops

4 large lamb chops
black pepper
garlic salt (optional)
50 g (2 oz) (¼ cup) butter
15 mL (1 tablespoon) finely chopped
  fresh parsley
finely grated zest 1 lemon
5 mL (1 teaspoon) lemon juice
pinch cayenne pepper

1 Preheat grill to moderate.
2 Season lamb chops lightly with freshly ground black pepper, and a dusting of garlic salt, if wished. Lightly oil grill plates and arrange meat on them. Cook for 8–10 minutes, according to taste.
3 Meanwhile, blend butter, parsley, lemon zest and juice, and cayenne pepper. When the chops are cooked, arrange on a bed of rice, and melt lemon and herb butter over them. Serve immediately.

Serves 4

Canterbury Chops

8 lamb chops
15 g (½ oz) (1 tablespoon) melted
  butter
salt and pepper
4 canned pear halves with their
  syrup
a little mint jelly

1 Brush chops with butter, season and grill until tender.
2 Meanwhile, warm pears in a little of the syrup and drain. Decorate each with a spoonful of mint jelly, arrange round chops and serve.

Serves 4

Chops Royale

4 double chops
25 mL (1 fl oz) (2 tablespoons) oil
salt and pepper
pinch mace
4 large onions
100 g (¼ lb) (1 cup) flour
100 mL (4 fl oz) (½ cup) milk
oil for deep frying
4 mushrooms
4 tomatoes
bunch watercress

1 Brush chops with oil, season with salt and pepper and a pinch of mace, and grill for 12–15 minutes, turning once.
2 Meanwhile, cut onions into rings, dip in flour, then milk, then flour again, and deep-fry for ½ minute. Drain on absorbent paper.
3 Brush mushrooms with oil and grill for 2 minutes. Make two cross cuts on the top of each tomato, brush with oil and grill for 2–3 minutes until the skin blisters.
4 When ready to serve, garnish chops with mushrooms, tomatoes, onion and watercress.

Serves 4

Chops Royale

Chops with Barbecue Sauce

1 onion, chopped
1 stick celery, chopped
1 clove garlic, crushed
25 g (1 oz) (2 tablespoons) butter
5 mL (1 teaspoon) dry mustard
5 mL (1 teaspoon) demerara (caster)
    sugar
2.5 mL (½ teaspoon) Tabasco
300 mL (½ pint) (1¼ cups) tomato
    juice
5 mL (1 teaspoon) Worcestershire
    sauce
juice ½ lemon
5 mL (1 teaspoon) vinegar
1 bay leaf
4 double chops, grilled

1 Fry onion, celery and garlic in butter for 5 minutes. Add remaining ingredients, except the chops and simmer for 15 minutes. Remove bay leaf.

2 Serve chops on a dish and the sauce separately.

Serves 4

Lamb Louise

8 lamb loin chops
30 mL (2 tablespoons) oil
3 medium onions, chopped
30 mL (2 tablespoons) flour
300 mL (½ pint) (1¼ cups) apple juice
30 mL (2 tablespoons) soy sauce
5 mL (1 teaspoon) sugar
15 mL (1 tablespoon) chopped mint
2 red apples
25 g (1 oz) (2 tablespoons) butter
15 mL (1 tablespoon) chopped fresh
    parsley

1 Brown chops lightly on both sides in oil. Drain, remove from pan, and keep warm. Add onions to pan and cook until lightly browned.

2 Stir in flour and cook for 1 minute. Add apple juice and bring to the boil.

3 Lower heat to a simmer; add soy sauce, sugar and mint. Return chops to pan, cover and simmer for 30 minutes.

4 To serve: core and slice apples and cook gently in butter for 5–10 minutes. Mix sliced apples into chop sauce.

Serves 4

Lamb Chops Orleans

8 lamb chops
salt and pepper
60 g (2½ oz) (5 tablespoons) butter
4 thin slices dry bread
30 mL (1 fl oz) (2 tablespoons) oil
4 shallots (spring onions, scallions),
    chopped

Sauce
40 g (1½ oz) (3 tablespoons) butter
1 small carrot, finely diced
1 onion, chopped
25 g (1 oz) (¼ cup) flour
400 mL (14 fl oz) (1¾ cups) stock
4 chicken livers
30 mL (1 fl oz) (2 tablespoons)
    thickened cream
30 mL (1 fl oz) (2 tablespoons)
    Calvados or brandy

1 To make the sauce, melt butter in a saute pan and fry carrot and onion until brown. Sprinkle with flour and cook, stirring, until brown. Stir in stock and cook for 10 minutes.

2 Meanwhile, liquidise the chicken livers and mix them with the cream and Calvados or brandy. Beat well.

3 Strain the stock mixture and put on one side.

4 Rub lamb chops on both sides with the salt and pepper. Melt 40 g (1½ oz) (3 tablespoons) butter in a frying pan, add chops and cook until browned on both sides and tender.

5 Meanwhile, cut crusts off the bread and cut each slice into 2 triangles. Heat the rest of the butter with the oil in another pan and fry the bread triangles until golden-brown. Drain.

6 Drain chops and arrange on a heated serving dish. Keep hot.

7 Add shallots to the butter left from cooking the chops and cook 1 minute. Add the strained stock mixture, stirring well. Reduce heat so the sauce does not boil and stir in the chicken liver mixture. Beat until heated through, then pour over the chops.

8 Arrange bread triangles around the edge of the dish and serve very hot.

Serves 4

Lamb Cutlets Barcelona

6 lamb cutlets
25 g (1 oz) (¼ cup) flour
pinch dry mustard
6 peppercorns, crushed
pinch dried mint and sage
pinch garlic salt
pinch ground ginger
2 eggs, beaten
100 g (¼ lb) (1½ cups) dried white
    breadcrumbs
oil for deep frying
5 mL (1 teaspoon) arrowroot
75 mL (2½ fl oz) (⅓ cup) water
6 slices cucumber

Barbecue Tomato Sauce
225 g (½ lb) (¾ cup) tomato pulp
15 g (½ oz) (1 tablespoon) tomato
    paste
5 mL (1 teaspoon) sugar
5 mL (1 teaspoon) vinegar
pinch allspice
pinch paprika and cayenne
pinch salt

1 Trim cutlets and scrape the rib bone clean. Beat cutlets to widen the area of the meat. Mix flour with mustard, peppercorns, herbs, garlic salt and ginger.

2 Pass each cutlet in seasoned flour, then in beaten egg and finally in breadcrumbs.

3 Heat oil to 190°C (350°F) and fry cutlets for 6 minutes until tender and golden-brown.

4 Meanwhile, make the sauce. Boil the ingredients together for 5 minutes and then thicken with the arrowroot mixed with the water. Cook 2 minutes.

5 Drain cutlets, arrange on a serving dish and decorate with cucumber slices. Serve the tomato barbecue sauce as a dip in the centre.

Serves 6

Lamb Cutlets Hungarian-style

6 lamb cutlets
50 mL (2 fl oz) (¼ cup) oil
225 g (½ lb) (4 cups) button
*   mushrooms*
bunch watercress

Paprika Sauce
1 onion, chopped
5 mL (1 teaspoon) flour
5 mL (1 teaspoon) paprika
15 g (½ oz) (1 tablespoon) tomato
*   paste*
300 mL (½ pint) (1¼ cups) white wine
½ chicken stock cube
salt and pepper

1 Trim cutlets and fry in oil for about 10 minutes until tender. Remove from pan, place on a serving dish and keep warm.

2 Add mushrooms to the pan and saute for 2 minutes. Add to cutlets and keep warm.

3 Prepare the sauce. To the same oil used for the meat and mushrooms, add onion and fry until soft, about 4 minutes. Sprinkle in flour and paprika and cook for 1 minute more. Stir in tomato paste and wine, crumble in the stock cube and season to taste. Boil 8 minutes.

4 Strain sauce over cutlets and mushrooms and garnish with watercress. Serve with boiled potatoes or rice.

Serves 3

Lamb Cutlets Reform

4 double cutlets
175 g (6 oz) (3 cups) fresh
*   breadcrumbs*
30 mL (2 tablespoons) chopped ham
10 mL (2 teaspoons) chopped parsley
salt and pepper
pinch clove
175 g (6 oz) (1½ cups) seasoned flour
2 eggs, beaten
100 g (¼ lb) (½ cup) butter

Reform Sauce
25 g (1 oz) carrot, finely chopped
25 g (1 oz) onion, finely chopped
25 g (1 oz) celery, finely chopped
½ bay leaf
sprig thyme
15 g (½ oz) (1 tablespoon) margarine
15 mL (1 tablespoon) lemon juice
6 peppercorns, crushed
300 mL (½ pint) (1¼ cups) brown
*   sauce*
15 mL (1 tablespoon) port
15 mL (1 tablespoon) redcurrant jelly

Garnish
½ small cooked beetroot
hard-boiled white of ½ egg
1 gherkin
1 mushroom
15 g (½ oz) ham
15 g (½ oz) tongue

1 When you buy the double cutlets ask the butcher to remove one of the bones from each.

2 To make the Reform Sauce: gently fry carrot, onion, celery, bay leaf and thyme in the margarine in a pan for 3 minutes. Drain off fat. Add lemon juice and crushed peppercorns, and cook until the liquid has evaporated by two-thirds.

3 Add brown sauce, and simmer ½ hour. Remove any scum from the surface.

4 Add port and redcurrant jelly. Bring to the boil and strain through a fine sieve. Keep warm.

5 Prepare garnish by cutting the ingredients into matchsticks.

6 Put breadcrumbs, ham, parsley, seasoning and pinch of clove in a basin and mix well.

7 Flatten each cutlet slightly, and dip each in the seasoned flour, and in beaten egg.

8 Press breadcrumb mixture well into both sides of the cutlets. If you like, add a professional touch by making criss-cross lines on each side with the blade of a knife.

9 Heat butter in a pan and saute the cutlets for 4–5 minutes on each side.

10 Just before serving, add garnish to the sauce and reheat. Serve separately, with cutlets placed on a dish.

Serves 4

Worcestershire Cutlets

4 double cutlets
20 asparagus spears
30 mL (2 tablespoons) oil
2 strips red capsicum (pepper)

Sauce
150 mL (¼ pint) (⅔ cup) tomato sauce
150 mL (¼ pint) (⅔ cup) brown sauce
10 mL (2 teaspoons) Worcestershire
*   sauce*
30 mL (2 tablespoons) pineapple juice
salt and pepper

1 When you buy the cutlets, ask the butcher to remove one bone. Scrape tip of the remaining bone clean.

2 Scrape asparagus and boil 15 minutes. Drain and keep warm.

3 To make the sauce, heat tomato and brown sauces. Add Worcestershire sauce and pineapple juice. Check seasoning. Keep warm.

4 Season cutlets, brush with oil and grill or saute for 4–5 minutes on each side.

5 Place cutlets on a serving dish, with a paper frill on each bone tip, and garnish with asparagus decorated with strips of capsicum. Serve sauce separately.

Serves 4

Worcestershire Cutlets

Chump Chops Catalania Step-by-step

1 The ingredients: lamb chump chops, potatoes, tomatoes, zucchini, onion, garlic, parsley, white wine, milk and cheese.
2 Dredge chops with flour and shallow fry until browned.

Place them in a shallow ovenproof dish.
3 Blanch zucchini and cover chops.
4 Fry the onions until soft, then add the chopped tomatoes, garlic, water, wine, stock cube and seasoning. Sim-

5

7

6

8

mer for 5 minutes.
5 Pour tomato mixture over zucchini.
6 Cover with a layer of thinly sliced potatoes.
7 Make a basic roux sauce and then a white sauce by add-

ing milk. Stir in a little cheese and then pour the sauce over the layer of potatoes.
8 Sprinkle with the remaining cheese, then bake for about 45 minutes.

Chump Chops Catalania

6 lamb chump chops
25 g (1 oz) (¼ cup) seasoned flour
50 mL (2 fl oz) (¼ cup) oil
3 onions, sliced
4 tomatoes, skinned, seeded and
   chopped
1 clove garlic, crushed
150 mL (¼ pint) (⅔ cup) white wine
150 mL (¼ pint) (⅔ cup) water
1 chicken stock cube
salt and pepper
bouquet garni
4 zucchini (courgettes), sliced
450 g (1 lb) potatoes
150 mL (¼ pint) (⅔ cup) white sauce
75 g (3 oz) (¾ cup) grated Cheddar

1 Dredge lamb chops in seasoned flour. Heat oil in a frying pan and fry lamb chops until well-browned on both sides. Remove from pan and arrange in the bottom of a shallow ovenproof dish.

2 Preheat oven to 180°C (350°F).

3 In the same oil, fry onions until soft, then add chopped tomatoes and garlic. Pour in wine and water and crumble in the stock cube. Season with salt and pepper and add bouquet garni. Simmer for about 5 minutes.

4 Meanwhile, blanch the zucchini in boiling water for 3–4 minutes and arrange over the lamb chops in the dish.

5 Pour tomato and wine mixture over the top.

6 Blanch potatoes in boiling water for 4 minutes. Cut in thin slices and arrange them, overlapping, across the top of the dish.

7 Heat white sauce and stir in 50 g (2 oz) (½ cup) grated cheese. Blend and pour sauce over the potatoes. Sprinkle with remaining grated cheese.

8 Bake for 45 minutes.

Serves 6

Braised Lamb in Beer

50 mL (2 fl oz) (¼ cup) oil
6 middle cutlets or chump chops
450 g (1 lb) (4 cups) sliced onions
225 g (½ lb) sliced carrots
225 g (½ lb) (1¾ cups) sliced parsnips
150 mL (¼ pint) (⅔ cup) water
300 mL (½ pint) (1¼ cups) flat light
   beer
20 mL (2 tablespoons) vinegar
25 g (1 oz) (2 tablespoons) sugar
15 g (½ oz) (1 tablespoon) tomato
   paste
bouquet garni
pinch ground mace
salt and pepper

Topping
100 g (¼ lb) (½ cup) butter
5 mL (1 teaspoon) French mustard
1 egg yolk
pinch sugar
stick French bread

1 Preheat oven to 180°C (350°F). Heat oil in a pan and brown meat for 5 minutes on each side. Remove and place in a casserole.

2 In the same pan fry onions until slightly browned. Arrange on top of the meat. Add carrots and parsnips.

3 Pour in water, beer and vinegar to cover the meat and vegetables, adding more beer if necessary.

4 Add sugar, tomato paste, bouquet garni, mace and seasoning.

5 Cover and bake for 1 hour.

6 Meanwhile prepare the topping. Cream the butter in a bowl. Add mustard, egg yolk and sugar and blend until you have a paste of a smooth consistency. Cut French bread into slices 2.5 cm (1 in) thick and spread each slice generously with the paste.

7 When vegetables in the casserole are tender, remove from the oven.

8 Place the bread, buttered side upwards, on top of the casserole so it is completely covered. Increase the oven temperature to 190°C (375°F) and cook the casserole uncovered and on the top shelf for a further ½ hour.

Serves 6

Minced Lamb Cutlets with Asparagus

225 g (½ lb) (1 cup) minced raw lamb
   from the shoulder
225 g (½ lb) (1 cup) sausage meat
50 g (2 oz) (1 cup) fresh breadcrumbs
1 egg
1 small onion, chopped
25 g (1 oz) (2 tablespoons) raisins
15 mL (1 tablespoon) fresh parsley
15 mL (1 tablespoon) corn kernels
1 red capsicum (pepper), ¼ cut in
   strips, ¾ chopped
50 g (2 oz) (½ cup) seasoned flour
75 mL (3 fl oz) (⅓ cup) oil
12 asparagus spears

Sauce
1 onion, chopped
1 bacon rasher, diced
1 clove garlic
15 mL (1 tablespoon) flour
30 mL (2 tablespoons) tomato paste
150 mL (¼ pint) (⅔ cup) white wine
300 mL (½ pint) (1¼ cups) stock
1 bay leaf

1 Combine lamb, sausage meat and breadcrumbs with egg, onion, raisins, parsley, corn kernels and ½ the chopped red capsicum. Divide into 6 portions and shape each into a "cutlet" shape. Dip in seasoned flour and brown in 50 mL (2 fl oz) (¼ cup) oil for 6 minutes. Then place in a casserole.

2 To make the sauce, heat 25 mL (1 fl oz) (2 tablespoons) oil and fry onion, bacon, garlic and half of the diced red capsicum for 5 minutes. Sprinkle on the flour, add tomato paste, white wine and stock. Season and add bay leaf. Simmer 5 minutes.

3 Preheat oven to 190°C (375°F).

4 Pour sauce over cutlets and braise in oven for 30 minutes.

5 Meanwhile, scrape asparagus, tie, and boil for 15 minutes.

6 When ready to serve, arrange cutlets in a dish, pour sauce over and garnish with asparagus and strips of red capsicum.

Serves 4

Minced Lamb Cutlets with Asparagus

Lamb and Rice Casserole

30 mL (2 tablespoons) oil
50 g (2 oz) (4 tablespoons) butter
2 onions, chopped
2 large carrots, chopped
1 stick celery, chopped
2 leeks, cleaned and sliced
6 lamb chops
*25 g (1 oz) (4 tablespoons) seasoned
    flour*
sprig thyme
1 bay leaf
salt and pepper
pinch nutmeg
550 mL (1 pint) (2½ cups) water
1 chicken stock cube
350 g (¾ lb) (1½ cups) rice
100 g (¼ lb) (1 cup) peas

1 Heat oil and butter in a flameproof casserole dish. Gently fry onions, carrots, celery and leeks until tender, stirring from time to time.

2 Preheat oven to 190°C (375°F).

3 Dredge lamb chops in seasoned flour. Remove fried vegetables from casserole and keep warm. Shallow-fry lamb chops until well-browned on both sides. Return vegetables to casserole, add thyme, bay leaf, salt and pepper and nutmeg.

4 Pour in water and crumble in the stock cube. Bring to the boil on top of the stove, then bake for 30 minutes.

5 Remove and stir in rice. Bring to the boil on top of the stove, add peas and cover. Bake for 20 minutes until rice is tender. If necessary, you can add extra stock during cooking if the rice absorbs too much liquid.

Serves 6

Eggplant (Aubergine) and Beef Casserole

2 large eggplants (aubergines)
salt and pepper
15 mL (1 tablespoon) oil
1 kg (2 lb) middle cutlets lamb
25 g (1 oz) (4 tablespoons) flour
15 mL (1 tablespoon) curry powder
2 onions, sliced
4 carrots, chopped
2 sticks celery, chopped
100 g (¼ lb) (1⅓ cups) haricot beans
*900 mL (1½ pints) (3½ cups) beef
    stock*
1 chilli, ground
*15 g (½ oz) (1 tablespoon) tomato
    paste*

Lamb and Rice Casserole

1 Cut eggplants into slices 1.5 cm (½ in) thick. Sprinkle each slice with salt and leave for 30 minutes. Rinse and drain.

2 Preheat oven to 180°C (350°F). Heat oil in a pan. Roll lamb in flour seasoned with curry powder. Shake off any excess. Place meat in the pan, cover and brown for 4 minutes on each side. Transfer meat to casserole.

3 In the same pan gently fry onions, carrots and celery for 5 minutes and add to casserole.

4 Boil haricot beans for 10 minutes in salted water. Remove scum from surface, drain and add to casserole with the eggplant.

5 Pour over stock and add chilli and tomato paste.

6 Cover and bake for 1–1½ hours or until meat and beans are tender.

Serves 4

Eggplant (Aubergine) and Bean Casserole

Mutton and Sausage Casserole

4 mutton cutlets
25 g (1 oz) (4 tablespoons) flour
30 mL (1 fl oz) (2 tablespoons) oil
450 g (1 lb) shallots (spring onions, scallions)
4 pork or beef chipolata sausages
300 mL (½ pint) (1¼ cups) water
1 chicken stock cube
25 g (1 oz) (2 tablespoons) tomato paste
salt and pepper
pinch cumin
pinch paprika
bouquet garni
4 slices garlic sausage
50 g (2 oz) (1 cup) fresh breadcrumbs

1 Dredge mutton cutlet in flour.

2 Heat oil in a frying pan and shallow-fry cutlets until browned on both sides. Cover and cook gently for 8 minutes.

3 Preheat oven to 190°C (375°F).

4 Remove cutlets from pan and arrange in a shallow ovenproof dish. Add onions to pan and quickly brown, then place in dish on top of cutlets

5 Meanwhile, grill the chipolata sausages until brown and cooked. Place on top of onions.

6 Pour water into a saucepan and crumble in the stock cube. Bring to the boil and add tomato paste, salt and pepper, cumin, paprika and the bouquet garni.

7 Boil stock for about 5 minutes, then pour over meat, onions and sausages. Add garlic sausage to the dish and sprinkle top with breadcrumbs.

8 Bake casserole 20–25 minutes. Serve very hot with boiled rice, beans or couscous.

Serves 4

Mutton Ragout with Chicory (Belgian Endive)

25 mL (1 fl oz) (2 tablespoons) oil
6 large mutton cutlets
1 large onion, sliced
6 heads of chicory (Belgian endive)
300 mL (½ pint) (1¼ cups) water
salt and pepper
juice 1 lemon

1 Preheat oven to 190°C (375°F).

2 Heat oil and shallow fry cutlets for 8 minutes to brown all over. Place in casserole dish.

3 In the same pan, fry onion for 3 minutes and add to cutlets.

4 Clean chicory (Belgian endive) and arrange around cutlets. Pour on water, and season with salt and pepper. Squeeze lemon juice over the chicory (Belgian endive). Cover and bake 1 hour. Serve very hot.

Serves 6

Mutton and Sausage Casserole

Armenian Mutton Platter

6 large mutton chump chops
15 mL (1 tablespoon) flour
5 mL (1 teaspoon) curry powder
pinch cumin
pinch paprika
75 mL (2½ fl oz) (⅓ cup) oil
4 large onions
6 cardamon pods
50 g (2 oz) (⅓ cup) seedless raisins
50 g (2 oz) (⅓ cup) dried apricots,
    soaked with liquid
25 g (1 oz) (2 tablespoons) tomato
    paste
15 mL (1 tablespoon) vinegar
5 mL (1 teaspoon) honey
bouquet garni
salt and pepper
pinch cayenne
350 g (12 oz) (1½ cups) long grain rice
5 mL (1 teaspoon) turmeric
1 pomegranate (optional)

1 Trim off any fat from the chops.
2 Rub chops with the combined flour, curry powder, cumin and paprika.
3 Heat 50 mL (2 fl oz) (¼ cup) oil in a frying pan and brown chops for 8 minutes. Transfer to a flameproof dish.
4 Fry onions for 1 minute, and add to meat. Add cardamon, raisins and apricots. Dilute tomato paste with the liquid from the soaked apricots and make up, if necessary, to 300 mL (½ pint) (1¼ cups) with water.
5 Add vinegar, honey and bouquet garni. Season and add to meat.
6 Cover and simmer for 40 minutes until 200 mL (6 fl oz) (¾ cup) of liquid remains.
7 Meanwhile, boil rice for 20 minutes and drain.
8 Heat the rest of the oil and stir-fry rice for 3 minutes. Add turmeric and cook for 1 minute. Season with salt and pepper.
9 To serve, press rice firmly in a 25 cm (10 in) dish and then turn out on a serving dish. Arrange meat and vegetables on the rice. Garnish with pomegranate seeds.

Serves 6

Algerian Lamb Casserole

50 mL (2 fl oz) (¼ cup) oil
1 kg (2 lb) lamb chops
450 g (1 lb) onions, sliced
450 g (1 lb) potatoes, peeled and
    thinly sliced
500 mL (1 pint) (2½ cups water)
150 mL (¼ pint) (⅔ cup) white wine
bouquet garni
pinch cumin
salt and pepper
1 bay leaf

1 Preheat oven to 180°C (350°F).
2 Heat oil in a flameproof dish and brown lamb chops on both sides. Add onions and fry until soft.
3 Cover with sliced potatoes, water and white wine.
Add bouquet garni, cumin and salt and pepper. Stir in bay leaf and cover with a lid.
4 Bake for 1¼–1½ hours until lamb is tender and potatoes are cooked. Check seasoning and serve with cooked fennel, celery, carrots or pumpkin.

Serves 4–6

Lamb Chops Hotpot

50 mL (2 fl oz) (¼ cup) oil
12 middle or neck chops
3 medium onions, sliced
6 carrot, sliced
550 mL (1 pint) (2½ cups) dry cider
30 mL (1 fl oz) (2 tablespoons) cider
    vinegar
300 mL (½ pint) (1¼ cups) water
25 g (1 oz) (2 tablespoons) tomato
    paste
bouquet garni
1 clove garlic, crushed
sprig mint
salt and pepper
1 chicken stock cube
450 g (1 lb) new potatoes

1 Preheat oven to 180°C (350°F).
2 Heat oil in a pan and cook chops for about 5 minutes until browned on both sides. Transfer chops to an ovenproof casserole.

3 Add onions to the pan and cook for 2 minutes. Add carrots and cook 2 minutes. Stir in cider, vinegar, water, tomato paste, bouquet garni, garlic, mint and seasoning and crumble in the stock cube. Mix thoroughly and transfer the mixture to casserole. Bake for about 1½ hours.
4 Add potatoes and cook 30 minutes. Serve.

Serves 6

Lancashire Hotpot

675 g (1½ lb) middle neck of lamb, cut
    in chops
15 mL (1 tablespoon) seasoned flour
25 mL (1 fl oz) (2 tablespoons) oil
4 medium onions, sliced
2 lamb's kidneys, skinned, cored and
    sliced
225 g (½ lb) (2 cups) sliced
    mushrooms
1 parsnip, sliced
675 g (1½ lb) potatoes, sliced
550 mL (1 pint) (2½ cups) stock

1 Preheat oven to 180°C (350°F).
2 Trim any excess fat from chops and coat in seasoned flour.
3 Heat oil in pan, add lamb and cook a few minutes until browned on both sides.
4 Arrange lamb, onions, kidneys, mushrooms, parsnip and potatoes in layers in a large casserole, finishing with a layer of potatoes. Pour in stock and cover.
5 Bake in preheated oven for 2 hours. Remove lid and cook a further ½ hour to brown potatoes.

Serves 4

Lamb and Pasta Stew

salt and pepper
2 zucchini (courgettes), cut in chunks
50 mL (2 fl oz) (¼ cup) oil
4 chump chops
1 onion, chopped
25 g (1 oz) (¼ cup) flour
25 g (1 oz) (2 tablespoons) tomato
   paste
30 mL (½ pint) (1¼ cups) stock
juice 2 oranges
15 mL (1 tablespoon) thin strips of
   orange peel
225 g (½ lb) pasta wheels
15 mL (1 tablespoon) chopped fresh
   mint
few mint leaves

1 Sprinkle salt on the zucchini and leave for ½ hour. Wash off bitter juice and dry.

2 Preheat oven to 180°C (350°F).

3 Heat oil and brown chops. Remove from pan and place in an ovenproof dish.

4 In the same pan, fry onion for 3 minutes; stir in the flour and cook 1 minute. Add tomato paste and cook 1 minute. Stir in stock and orange juice and boil 15 minutes. Season with salt and pepper and strain over chops.

5 Meanwhile, blanch strips of orange peel in boiling water for 6 minutes. Drain and add to meat.

6 Put meat in the oven to cook for 1 hour.

7 During this time, boil the pasta for 8 minutes. Drain and add to stew with zucchini 15 minutes before the end of the cooking time.

8 When ready to serve, check seasoning, sprinkle with chopped mint and garnish with a few whole leaves for decoration.

Serves 4

Devon Lamb Stew

8 lamb chops, 100 g (¼ lb) each
50 g (2 oz) (4 tablespoons) butter
675 g (1½ lb) small potatoes
225 g (½ lb) mushrooms, roughly
   sliced
225 g (½ lb) small onions, peeled
150 mL (¼ pint) (⅔ cup) chicken stock
300 mL (½ pint) (1¼ cups) dry white
   wine
150 mL (¼ pint) (⅔ cup) thickened
   cream
salt and pepper
1 bay leaf
pinch thyme
5 mL (1 teaspoon) chopped parsley

1 Trim fat from the chops. Heat butter in a large frying pan and gently fry chops on both sides for 2 minutes. Transfer meat to a plate.

2 Cut potatoes in half and add with mushrooms and onions to pan. Fry vegetables gently for 5 minutes, stirring, and add to meat.

3 Drain fat from the pan and add stock, wine and cream. Bring to the boil, reduce heat and simmer, stirring continually, for 10 minutes.

4 Return lamb chops and vegetables to pan. Add bay leaf and thyme. Cover and simmer for 1 hour or until meat and potatoes are tender. Remove bay leaf, sprinkle with chopped parsley and serve immediately.

Serves 4

Tip: To enrich the wine flavour of this dish, try stirring in 30 mL (1 fl oz) (2 tablespoons) of white port or medium sherry to the sauce, 5 minutes before the meat and vegetables are cooked.

Spicy Lamb Curry

50 mL (2 fl oz) (¼ cup) oil
1 kg (2 lb) middle neck lamb chops
1 large onion, chopped
1 apple, peeled, cored and sliced
500 mL (1 pint) (2½ cups) water
50 g (2 oz) (⅔ cup) desiccated coconut
10 mL (2 teaspoons) curry powder
pinch cumin
pinch paprika
25 g (1 oz) (4 tablespoons) flour
50 g (2 oz) (4 tablespoons) tomato
   paste
150 mL (¼ pint) (⅔ cup) pineapple
   juice
1 bay leaf
50 g (2 oz) (3 tablespoons) mango
   chutney
salt and pepper
75 g (3 oz) (½ cup) almonds

Garnish
2 bananas, sliced
100 g (¼ lb) (1¼ cups) desiccated
   coconut
100 g (¼ lb) (½ cup) pineapple chunks
100 g (¼ lb) (⅓ cup) mango chutney
100 g (¼ lb) (⅓ cup) peach chutney

1 Heat oil in a heavy saucepan and fry lamb chops for 8 minutes until browned. Remove.

2 Fry onion and apple until soft.

3 Meanwhile, bring water to the boil and soak coconut for 3–4 minutes.

4 Add curry powder, cumin, paprika, flour and tomato paste to the pan. Cook for 3 minutes. Return chops to pan.

5 Add strained coconut water, pineapple juice and bay leaf and bring to the boil, stirring all the time. Add mango chutney and seasoning and simmer for 1½ hours.

6 Sprinkle with almonds and serve with boiled rice, bananas, coconut, pineapple, mango and peach chutney arranged around the curry in small bowls.

Serves 4–6

Carbonnade of Lamb

4 slices lamb cut from the top of the
leg across the bone, 1 cm (½ in)
thick
15 g (½ oz) (2 tablespoons) seasoned
flour
50 mL (2 fl oz) (¼ cup) oil
225 g (½ lb) (2½ cups) sliced onions
1 clove garlic, crushed
1 green capsicum (pepper), seeded
and sliced
450 g (1 lb) tomatoes, skinned and
sliced
2 carrots, sliced
salt and pepper
bouquet garni
300 mL (½ pint) (1¼ cups) dry white
wine
5 mL (1 teaspoon) chopped parsley

1 Preheat oven to 190°C (375°F).
Coat lamb slices with seasoned flour.
Heat oil in a pan, add lamb slices,
cover, and fry gently each side for 4
minutes. Transfer meat to a casserole
dish.

2 In the same pan gently fry onions
for 4 minutes or until they are tender.

3 Add garlic, green capsicum, tomatoes and carrots. Cover and cook on
a low heat for 1 minute.

4 Add seasoning, bouquet garni and
gradually pour in the wine, stirring
all the time. Boil for 5 minutes.

5 Pour contents of pan over meat.
Cover casserole with a lid and bake
for ¾–1 hour. When cooked, there
should be no more than 15–30 mL
(1–2 tablespoons) of liquid left in the
casserole. It is a good idea to check
the casserole while cooking to ensure
that it does not dry out. Add extra
wine if necessary.

6 Before serving, check seasoning.
Serve garnished with chopped
parsley.

Serves 4

Lamb and Chicken Galantine

225 g (½ lb) cooked chicken
100 g (¼ lb) cooked lamb shoulder
100 g (¼ lb) (½ cup) sausage meat
50 g (2 oz) (¼ cup) diced bacon
100 g (¼ lb) (½ cup) lamb's liver
2 cloves garlic, chopped
50 g (2 oz) (1 cup) fresh breadcrumbs
1 onion, finely chopped
2 eggs, beaten
15 mL (1 tablespoon) brandy
45 mL (3 tablespoons) ruby port wine
salt and pepper
2.5 mL (½ teaspoon) mace
15 g (½ oz) (1 tablespoon) butter or
margarine
1 bay leaf
25 g (1 oz) (2 tablespoons) butter

1 Chop chicken meat except for a
few thin slices of breast meat. Chop
lamb shoulder. Pass chopped
chicken, lamb, sausage meat, diced
bacon and liver through a mincer.

2 Blend minced meats with garlic,
breadcrumbs and onion, and bind
together with ½ the beaten egg.
Blend in brandy and port, season
well and add mace. Mix thoroughly
to form a thick smooth paste.

3 Preheat oven to 180°C (350°F).
Grease an earthenware pate dish or
deep casserole with butter or margarine and press a layer of meat mixture
into the dish. Lay slices of the
chicken breast on it, cover with
another layer of meat and then of
chicken slices, and top with a final
layer of meat mixture. Brush with
beaten egg and place a bay leaf in the
centre.

4 Cover dish with foil and place in a
tray containing about 2 cm (1 in) hot
water in the oven. Bake 1½ hours,
remove the foil for the last ½ hour to
allow a crust to form.

5 The meat is cooked when it starts
to come away from the sides of the
dish. Remove from the oven and
place a weighted dish on top of the
meat while it cools.

6 When meat is cold, melt butter
gently in a pan and clarify by skimming off any froth. Pour clarified butter over the galantine and let cool.
Chill dish overnight. Serve the galantine in slices with hot toast and a
green salad, as an hors d'oeuvre.

Serves 6–8

Creamy Lamb Supper

50 g (2 oz) (¼ cup) margarine
4 eggs
150 mL (¼ pint) (⅔ cup) milk or cream
salt and pepper
225 g (½ lb) (1⅓ cups) cooked diced
lamb
150 mL (¼ pint) (⅔ cup) stock or gravy
100 g (¼ lb) (1½ cups) mushrooms

1 Preheat oven to 190°C (375°F).

2 Grease a casserole dish with half
the margarine.

3 Whisk eggs with milk or cream
and season with salt and pepper.

4 Mix lamb with stock or gravy and
put in dish.

5 Heat the rest of the margarine in a
frying pan and gently fry the whole
mushrooms for 4 minutes. Place on
top of lamb.

6 Cover with egg mixture and bake
for 1 hour.

Serves 4

Lamb in Sour Cream

25 g (1 oz) (4 tablespoons) flour
2.5 mL (½ teasoon) thyme
salt and pepper
900 g (2 lb) loin of lamb, cubed
45 g (1½ oz) (3 tablespoons) butter
1 large onion, sliced in rings
300 mL (½ pint) (1¼ cups) stock
150 mL (¼ pint) (⅔ cup) sour cream
225 g (½ lb) mushrooms

1 Mix flour and thyme and season.
Roll cubes of lamb in the mixture.

2 Heat butter in a frying pan and
brown meat for 8 minutes. Add the
onion and cook for 2 minutes.

3 Add stock and simmer, covered,
for 40 minutes until meat is tender.
Add sour cream and mushrooms and
heat gently for 5 minutes.

4 Serve with noodles tossed in butter.

Serves 6

Tips: To add extra zip to this dish,
add a little grated horseradish.

If sour cream is not available, use the
same quantity of cream and, after
heating gently for 5 minutes, add the
juice of 1 lemon, stir quickly and
serve.

Mutton Ragout with Tomatoes

50 mL (2 fl oz) (¼ cup) oil
900 g (2 lb) cubed lean mutton
1 large onion, chopped
2 cloves garlic, chopped
25 g (1 oz) (2 tablespoons) tomato paste
6 tomatoes, skinned, seeded and chopped
575 mL (1 pint) (2½ cups) chicken stock
15 mL (1 tablespoon) vinegar
bouquet garni
pinch marjoram
salt and pepper
450 g (1 lb) potatoes, peeled and quartered

1 Heat oil and shallow fry meat for 10 minutes, covered.
2 Add onion and garlic and cook for 3 minutes. Then stir in tomato paste and cook 2 minutes. Add chopped tomatoes, chicken stock, vinegar, bouquet garni, and pinch of marjoram. Season and simmer for 1 hour.
3 Add potatoes and cook for ½ hour, covered. Check seasoning.

Serves 6

Lamb and Cabbage Casserole

1½ kg (3 lb) boneless shoulder of lamb
30 mL (1 fl oz) (2 tablespoons) oil
1 kg (2 lb) cabbage
10 mL (2 tablespoons) salt
450 mL (¾ pint) (1¾ cups) hot beef stock
1 bay leaf
a little freshly chopped parsley

1 Cut lamb into cubes. Heat oil in a flameproof casserole, add lamb and fry briskly until browned on all sides. Remove from pan and pour off oil.
2 Wash and trim cabbage, separating the leaves. Put lamb and cabbage in alternate layers in the casserole, sprinkling each layer with salt.
3 Pour in stock, add bay leaf and bring to the boil. Reduce heat, cover and cook gently for 1½ hours or until lamb is tender, adding a little more water if the meat becomes dry during cooking.
4 Remove bay leaf, taste and adjust seasoning. Sprinkle with parsley and serve hot.

Serves 6

Lamb Blanquette

1 kg (2 lb) lamb from the shoulder cut into 2.5 cm (1 in) cubes
2 onions
2 cloves
½ head celery, diced
1 bay leaf
pinch fresh thyme
salt and pepper
150 mL (¼ pint) (⅔ cup) dry white wine
25 g (1 oz) (2 tablespoons) butter
25 g (1 oz) (4 tablespoons) flour
juice ½ lemon
2 cloves garlic, crushed
pinch cayenne pepper
2 egg yolks
75 mL (2½ fl oz) (⅓ cup) cream
5 mL (1 teaspoon) chopped parsley

1 Place lamb in a large saucepan. Stud each onion with a clove and add to meat with celery, bay leaf, thyme, salt and pepper. Pour in wine and enough water to cover. Cover and cook on a low heat for 1½ hours.
2 Strain, reserving 550 mL (1 pint) (2½ cups) of the stock. Remove onions and place celery and meat in a casserole dish.
3 Melt butter and stir in flour. Simmer on a low heat and continue to stir until a smooth paste is formed. Bring the reserved stock to the boil and gradually add to the roux sauce, stirring all the time. Check seasoning. Stir in lemon juice, crushed garlic and cayenne pepper.
4 Beat egg yolks and cream together in a bowl. Add 150 mL (¼ pint) (⅔ cup) of the sauce to mixture and blend well.
5 Gradually pour mixture into sauce, stirring all the time. Simmer 5 minutes.
6 Add sauce to meat and reheat. Sprinkle with chopped parsley and serve.

Serves 4

Casserole of Lamb Basquaise

1 kg (2 lb) shoulder of lamb
50 mL (2 fl oz) (¼ cup) oil
3 large onions, quartered
1 green capsicum (pepper), seeded and cut in strips
150 g (5 oz) (⅔ cup) diced raw bacon
4 large mushrooms, sliced
2 cloves garlic, crushed
150 mL (¼ pint) (⅔ cup) dry white wine
300 mL (½ pint) (1¼ cups) water
1 chicken stock cube
bouquet garni
sprig tarragon
4 large tomatoes, skinned, seeded and chopped
salt and pepper
25 g (1 oz) (3 tablespoons) cornflour

1 Cut lamb into 1 cm (½ in) cubes.
2 Preheat oven to 190°C (374°F).
3 Heat oil in a saucepan and fry onions and capsicum until soft. Add lamb and bacon, cover and cook for 3 minutes. Then add sliced mushrooms and garlic.
4 Pour wine and water into pan and crumble in the stock cube. Add bouquet garni, tarragon and chopped tomatoes and season with salt and pepper.
5 Transfer to a flameproof casserole dish, cover and bake for 1¼ hours. The meat should be tender and the liquid reduced.
6 Mix the cornflour with a little of the liquid from the casserole and stir into dish. Bring to the boil on top of the stove stirring all the time, until the sauce thickens. Serve casserole with boiled rice or roast potatoes.

Serves 6

Tip: For a different flavour, try substituting red wine, dry sherry or vermouth for white wine in this casserole. The addition of basil or oregano will give it a taste of the Mediterranean.

215

Shoulder of Lamb Bordeaux

*700 g (1½ lb) boneless shoulder of
    lamb*
100 g (4 oz) (½ cup) butter
45 mL (3 tablespoons) oil
salt and pepper
450 g (1 lb) small potatoes, peeled
*700 g (1½ lb) (7½ cups) sliced
    mushrooms*
3 cloves garlic, crushed
1 small bunch parsley, chopped

1 Cut meat into medium-sized pieces. Then heat 40 g (1½ oz) (3 tablespoons) butter and 15 mL (1 tablespoon) oil in a frying pan. When fat is very hot add meat and brown.
2 When meat is golden-brown reduce heat. Season with salt and pepper and leave to finish cooking.
3 Heat 25 g (1 oz) (2 tablespoons) remaining butter and 15 mL (1 tablespoon) oil in a heavy bottomed pan and quickly brown potatoes, then reduce heat. Cover pan and leave them to finish cooking.
4 Heat the rest of the oil and butter and saute mushrooms. Season with salt and pepper.
5 When mushrooms and potatoes are cooked, add to meat with garlic and chopped parsley. Warm for a few minutes over a high heat.
6 Arrange lamb and mushrooms on a warm serving dish with potatoes around the edge. Serve immediately.

Serves 4

Lamb Ratatouille

50 mL (2 fl oz) (¼ cup) oil
1 onion, chopped
*225 g (½ lb) (1⅓ cups) diced, cooked
    lamb*
1 clove garlic, crushed
2 zucchini (courgettes), sliced
2 sticks celery, sliced
*4 tomatoes, skinned, seeded and
    chopped*
5 mL (1 teaspoon) tomato paste
juice ½ lemon
pinch each cumin and curry powder
salt and pepper
pinch each chopped chervil and mint

1 Heat oil in a saucepan and saute onion until soft. Add meat and cook for 3 minutes.
2 Add garlic, zucchini, celery and tomatoes. Simmer 5 minutes.
3 Add remaining ingredients and simmer 15 minutes. Serve cold, sprinkled with chopped herbs.

Serves 6

Lamb Bordelaise

150 g (5 oz) mushroom caps
450 g (1 lb) potatoes
100 mL (4 fl oz) (½ cup) oil
*675 g (1½ lb) lean lamb from the
    shoulder, cut into 2.5 cm (1 in)
    cubes*
salt and pepper
1 onion, chopped
bouquet garni
4 cloves garlic, chopped
300 mL (½ pint) (1¼ cups) beef stock
*150 mL (¼ pint) (⅔ cup) dry white
    wine*
oil for deep frying
*15 mL (1 tablespoon) chopped
    parsley*

1 Thoroughly wash mushroom caps. Drain, dry and cut into quarters.
2 Peel, wash and cut potatoes into balls, 2.5 cm (1 in) in diameter, with a potato or melon baller.
3 Heat oil in a pan and add meat. Cover and cook for 12 minutes or until browned. Season. Add onion and bouquet garni. Stir and cook for 5 minutes.
4 Add mushrooms and garlic and cook 2 minutes. Remove excess fat from pan.
5 Add stock and wine. Stir and cook on a low heat for 40 minutes or until tender.
6 About 10 minutes before the lamb is ready to serve, heat the deep fat fryer to 190°C (375°F) and deep fry the potato balls for 4 minutes or until cooked and golden-brown. Drain and keep warm.
7 Pour lamb into a shallow meat dish. Serve garnished with chopped parsley and surrounded by potato balls.

Serves 4

Lamb Bourgignonne

*900 g (2 lb) lean shoulder of lamb, cut
    in 2.5 cm (1 in) cubes*
50 mL (2 fl oz) (¼ cup) oil
3 rashers bacon, diced
2 onions, chopped
*25 g (1 oz) (2 tablespoons) tomato
    paste*
*5 mL (1 teaspoon) molasses or dark
    treacle*
150 g (5 oz) (⅔ cup) long grain rice
50 g (2 oz) (4 tablespoons) butter
6 mushrooms, sliced
salt and pepper
pinch allspice

Marinade
300 mL (½ pint) (1¼ cups) red wine
150 mL (¼ pint) (⅔ cup) water
1 bay leaf
2 cloves garlic, crushed
bouquet garni
30 mL (1 fl oz) (2 tablespoons) vinegar

1 Mix ingredients for marinade. Place lamb in a bowl, pour over the marinade and soak for 3 hours.
2 Lift meat from marinade and dry it. Heat oil in a pan and cook lamb and bacon for about 6 minutes until browned. Add onions and cook 3 minutes.
3 Add marinade, tomato paste and molasses or treacle and bring to the boil. Reduce heat and simmer for 1½ hours.
4 Meanwhile, cook rice in boiling salted water, drain and mix with half of the butter.
5 Saute mushrooms in the rest of the butter for 2 minutes.
6 When the stew has finished cooking, discard bay leaf and bouquet garni. Add mushrooms, check the seasoning and add a pinch of allspice. Arrange boiled rice on a serving dish and pour the lamb bourgignonne over it.

Serves 6

Lamb Bourgignonne

Lamb Navarin with New Potatoes

550 g (1¼ lb) stewing lamb
salt and pepper
25 g (1 oz) (2 tablespoons) butter or
  margarine
100 g (¼ lb) (1 cup) diced carrots
100 g (¼ lb) (½ cup) diced onion
25 g (1 oz) (4 tablespoons) flour
15 g (½ oz) (1 tablespoon) tomato
  paste
1 clove garlic
900 mL (1½ pints) (3¾ cups) beef
  stock
1 bouquet garni
450 g (1 lb) new potatoes
5 g (1 tablespoon) chopped parsley

1 Preheat oven to 180°C (350°F).
Trim meat into even-sized pieces and
season.

2 Heat fat in an ovenproof casserole,
add meat and fry for 5 minutes. Add
chopped carrot and onion and cook
for a further 3 minutes.

3 Drain off extra fat, add flour and
mix. Cook for 5 minutes until
browned.

4 Add tomato paste and garlic and
stir in stock and seasoning. Add bouquet garni, bring to the boil, skim,
and cover. Cook in oven for 1½
hours.

5 Meanwhile, parboil new potatoes
in salted water for 10 minutes.

6 After 1½ hours, remove casserole
from oven and add potatoes. Return

to oven and cook for ½ hour or until
meat and potatoes are tender.

7 Arrange meat and vegetables on a
warmed serving dish, correct seasoning of liquid and pour over. Sprinkle
with chopped parsley.

Serves 4

*Lamb Navarin with New
Potatoes*

Spiced Lamb Lasagne

Spiced Lamb Lasagne

1 onion, finely chopped
30 mL (2 tablespoons) oil
450 g (1 lb) (2 cups) minced lamb, raw
  or cooked
7 g (1 tablespoon) chilli powder
1 green capsicum (pepper) seeded
  and chopped
15 g (½ oz) (1 tablespoon) tomato
  paste
salt and pepper
450 mL (¾ pint) (1⅔ cups) meat stock
50 g (2 oz) (⅓ cup) raisins
175 g (6 oz) lasagne sheets
150 mL (¼ pint) (1 cup) plain yoghurt
1 egg
15 g (½ oz) (1 tablespoon) chopped
  walnuts
1 small red capsicum (pepper),
  seeded and cut in rings

1 Fry onion in oil for 3 minutes until softened. Add minced lamb and stir to brown. Add ⅔ chilli powder and cook 1 minute. Add green capsicum, tomato paste, seasoning, stock and raisins. Bring to the boil, cover and simmer for 15 minutes if using cooked lamb, or 40 minutes if using raw lamb.

2 Boil lasagne sheets in salted water for about 5 minutes or until just tender. Wash lasagne briskly under cold running water to remove starch and separate sheets. Drain and dry sheets on a clean cloth or paper towel.

3 Preheat oven to 190°C (375°F). Spoon a layer of meat sauce into the bottom of an ovenproof dish. Cover with a layer of lasagne. Repeat until sauce and lasagne are all used, finishing with a layer of sauce on top.

4 Beat together yoghurt, egg, and chopped walnuts, adding the rest of the chilli powder. Pour yoghurt mixture over the top of the dish. Arrange rings of red capsicum over the yoghurt. Return to oven and cook 20 minutes. Serve immediately with a crisp green salad.

Serves 6

Tip: Extra flavour may be given to lasagne dishes by brushing the pasta layers with butter while making up the dish.

Roman-style Shoulder of Lamb

Roman-style Shoulder of Lamb

6 small globe artichokes
50 g (2 oz) (4 tablespoons) butter
1.25 kg (2½ lb) shoulder of lamb,
  cubed
100 mL (4 fl oz) (½ cup) dry white
  wine
100 mL (4 fl oz) (½ cup) stock
salt and pepper
100 g (¼ lb) (1 cup) flour
60 mL (4 tablespoons) oil
4 eggs
50 g (2 oz) (⅓ cup) grated Parmesan
  cheese
15 mL (1 tablespoon) chopped
  parsley

1 Cut artichoke stalks level with the bases. Remove any tough, discoloured leaves and cut off the leaves' tips.

2 Place artichokes in a pan of salted boiling water and cook 10 minutes. Drain, remove the choke and cut each artichoke into 8 pieces.

3 Melt butter in a pan and fry lamb until all the liquid has evaporated and begun to caramelise.

4 Preheat oven to 180°C (350°F).

5 Add stock and season with salt and pepper. Stir well and transfer to an ovenproof dish.

6 Cover and bake for 35 minutes.

7 Meanwhile, coat artichoke pieces with the flour and fry in oil until well browned.

8 Break eggs into a bowl, and beat with Parmesan and parsley.

9 Remove meat dish from oven, arrange pieces of artichoke around the sides and pour beaten egg mixture over the top.

10 Reduce oven heat to 150°C (300°F), and return the dish to the oven for 10 minutes. Leave it uncovered then remove and serve immediately.

Serves 6

Tip: This dish is typically Italian and goes well with a fresh green salad. If you cannot buy fresh artichokes, you can use canned artichoke bottoms. Fill with chopped mushrooms or mixed vegetables in a cheese sauce, then sprinkle with Parmesan cheese.

Yugoslavian Casserole

2 onions, thinly sliced
2 capsicum (peppers), seeded and
    sliced
150 mL (¼ pint) (⅔ cup) oil
4 tomatoes, skinned, seeded and
    chopped
salt and pepper
100 g (¼ lb) (½ cup) long grain rice
800 g (1¾ lb) lamb shoulder, cubed
300 mL (½ pint) (1¼ cups) hot water
5 mL (1 teaspoon) paprika

1 Gently fry onions and capsicum in
45 mL (3 tablespoons) oil for 10 minutes. Add the tomatoes, cook 2 minutes and season. Place half the mixture in a flameproof casserole.
2 Preheat oven to 180°C (350°F).
Heat 45 mL (3 tablespoons) oil in the
pan and fry rice for 2 minutes. Add
rice to casserole and cover with the
rest of the tomatoes.
3 Brown meat in the rest of the oil,
season and add to the casserole. Add
water, cover and bring to the boil.
Bake for 1½ hours.
4 Sprinkle with paprika and serve.

Serves 5

Casserole of Lamb Polish-style

675 g (1½ lb) stewing lamb, cut into
    cubes
75 mL (3 fl oz) (⅓ cup) oil
2 onions, chopped
5 mL (1 teaspoon) paprika
pinch caraway seeds
25 g (1 oz) (¼ cup) flour
25 g (1 oz) (2 tablespoons) tomato
    paste
600 mL (1 pint) (2½ cups) water
1 bay leaf
salt and fresh milled black pepper
675 g (1½ lb) new potatoes
4 tomatoes, skinned, halved and
    seeded
150 mL (¼ pint) (⅔ cup) sour cream or
    yoghurt

1 Preheat oven to 190°C (375°F).
2 Remove any fat from meat. Heat
oil in a heavy casserole and add
meat. Cover and cook for 8 minutes,
stirring from time to time, until the
meat is evenly browned. Add

chopped onions and cook for 2 minutes.
3 Sprinkle in paprika, caraway seeds
and flour and add tomato paste. Stir
and cook for 1 minute. Pour in water
and add the bay leaf. Bring to the
boil, season and place in oven for
¾–1 hour.
4 Meanwhile, boil potatoes in salted
water for about 20 minutes or until
tender.
5 Five minutes before the casserole
has finished cooking, remove from
oven and add the drained potatoes.
Decorate with halved tomatoes and
return to oven for the rest of the
cooking time.
6 Serve casserole with the sour
cream or yoghurt poured over the
top or served separately.

Serves 6

Lamb and Prawns Spanish-style

50 mL (2 fl oz) (¼ cup) oil
1 kg (2 lb) boned middle lamb cutlets,
    cut in small, thin slices
1 large onion, sliced
12 stuffed olives, sliced
2 cloves garlic, chopped
300 mL (½ pint) (1¼ cups) water
150 mL (¼ pint) (⅔ cup) medium
    sherry
1 bay leaf
pinch saffron
100 g (¼ lb) (½ cup) long grain rice
225 g (½ lb) tomatoes, skinned,
    seeded and chopped
1 small red capsicum (pepper),
    seeded and chopped
175 g (6 oz) (1¼ cups) peeled prawns
175 g (6 oz) (1½ cups) sliced
    mushrooms
salt and pepper
15 mL (1 tablespoon) chopped
    parsley.

1 In a large saute pan, heat oil and
cook lamb for 8 minutes, covered.
2 Add onion, cook for 1 minute,
then add olives, garlic, water, sherry,
bay leaf and saffron, and bring gently
to the boil. Reduce heat and simmer
for ½ hour.
3 Add rice, tomatoes and capsicum
and simmer for 20 minutes.

4 Add prawns and mushrooms,
season and cook for 4 minutes.
Sprinkle with chopped parsley and
serve.

Serves 6

Lamb Portuguese

1.2 kg (2¼ lb) lamb from the leg, loin
    or shoulder, cut into 2.5 cm (1 in)
    cubes
25 g (1 oz) (4 tablespoons) flour
salt and pepper
50 mL (2 fl oz) (¼ cup) oil
225 g (½ lb) (1 cup) chopped onion
50 g (2 oz) (4 tablespoons) tomato
    paste
900 mL (1½ pints) (3¾ cups) water
225 mL (8 fl oz) (1 cup) red wine
45 mL (1½ fl oz) (3 tablespoons)
    vinegar
bouquet garni
pinch fresh rosemary
1 clove garlic, chopped
225 g (½ lb) (1¼ cups) haricot beans,
    soaked overnight

1 Roll lamb in flour seasoned with
salt and pepper. Shake to remove
any excess.
2 Heat oil in a heavy-based casserole
dish and lightly brown meat. Add
onion and stir over a moderate heat
for 5 minutes.
3 Add tomato paste, water, wine
and vinegar. Stir. Add bouquet garni
and season with salt, pepper, rosemary and garlic. Cover and stew over
a low heat for 1 hour.
4 While stew is cooking, boil the
soaked haricot beans in salted water
for 10 minutes. Remove scum from
the surface, reduce heat and simmer
for a further 40 minutes.
5 Drain beans and add to casserole.
Check seasoning. Cook for ½ hour or
until meat and beans are tender.

Serves 6

Tips: Dishes described as 'Portuguese' are strongly flavoured with
tomato. You may either increase or
decrease the amount of tomato paste
used according to taste. Ideally, fresh
tomatoes should be used. In this
recipe, you may substitute 450 g (1 lb)
of skinned, seeded and chopped
tomatoes for the tomato paste.

Lamb Azinna

5 mL (1 teaspoon) Indian tea leaves
225 g (½ lb) (1½ cups) dried peaches
1 kg (2 lb) shoulder of lamb
50 g (2 oz) (½ cup) flour
5 mL (1 teaspoon) curry powder
50 mL (2 fl oz) (¼ cup) oil
1 large onion, chopped
225 g (½ lb) carrots, peeled and sliced
    or diced
2 zucchini (courgettes), sliced
3 large sticks celery, cut in chunks
150 mL (¼ pint) (⅔ cup) orange juice
juice 1 lemon
100 g (¼ lb) canned red capsicum
    (peppers)
2 tomatoes, peeled and chopped
15 mL (1 tablespoon) tomato paste
500 mL (1 pint) (2½ cups) chicken
    stock
salt and pepper
2 mint leaves, finely chopped

1 Infuse tea for 5 minutes in 900 mL
(1½ pints) (3¾ cups) boiling water.
Strain out tea leaves and pour tea
over dried peaches in a bowl. Leave 2
hours to soak.

2 Meanwhile, bone shoulder of
lamb. Remove excess fat and cut
meat into 2 cm (¾ in) cubes. Mix
flour and curry powder and dust
meat.

3 Set the slow cooker to HIGH or follow the manufacturer's instructions.
Heat oil in a large saucepan and fry
meat for about 3 minutes, until
browned. Strain meat from the pan
and place in slow cooker.

4 Fry onion and carrot in oil for 5
minutes to soften. Strain and place in
cooker. Drain excess oil from saucepan and place peaches and tea, and
the rest of the ingredients in it, mixing with a wooden spoon. Bring to
the boil.

5 Remove saucepan from heat and
transfer contents to the slow cooker.
Cover and cook for 30 minutes.
Change setting to LOW and cook for
6–7 hours. Serve with boiled rice or
baked potatoes.

Serves 6–8

Moroccan Mutton Tajine

900 g (2 lb) shoulder of mutton
25 g (1 oz) (4 tablespoons) flour
50 mL (2 fl oz) (¼ cup) oil
1 large onion, chopped
2 sticks celery, chopped
1 clove garlic
25 g (1 oz) (2 tablespoons) tomato
    paste
good pinch cumin
1 green chilli, sliced
5 mL (1 teaspoon) turmeric
salt and pepper
1.2 litres (2 pints) (5 cups) weak tea
3 lemons, green and unripe if
    possible or 4 limes
5 mL (1 teaspoon) honey
1 bay leaf
sprig fresh mint
225 g (½ lb) macaroni

1 Preheat oven to 190°C (375°F).

2 Cut mutton into pieces, removing
as much fat as possible. Remove all
bones, except from the middle cutlets.

3 Dip meat in flour.

4 Heat oil in a frying pan and brown
meat for 10 minutes, covered.

5 Add onion and celery and fry 2
minutes. Add garlic and fry ½ minute. Add tomato paste and cook ½
minute. Add cumin, chilli, turmeric,
salt and pepper.

6 Pour on tea and stir. Bring to the
boil and add the grated rind of the
lemons. Cover casserole and bake 1¼
hours.

7 Add the juice of the lemons and
honey, bay leaf and sprig of mint.
Cook for ½ hour. Remove any fat
from surface.

8 Boil macaroni in salted water for
10 minutes. Drain and add to ragout
10 minutes before the end of cooking.

9 The ragout may be served at once,
or may be reheated the next day.

Serves 4

Peachy Baghdad Lamb

1.5 kg (3 lb) shoulder of lamb
5 mL (1 teaspoon) ground cinnamon
5 mL (1 teaspoon) ground cloves
30 mL (2 tablespoons) soft brown
    sugar
1 medium onion, chopped
30 mL (2 tablespoons) lemon juice
5 mL (1 teaspoon) white pepper
10 mL (2 teaspoons) cornflour
15 mL (1 tablespoon) water
2.5 mL (½ teaspoon) salt
225 g (½ lb) canned peach slices
150 mL (¼ pint) (⅔ cup) yoghurt

1 Bone shoulder and cut meat into
1.25 cm (½ in) cubes. Place meat in a
shallow dish.

2 Mix together cinnamon, cloves
and sugar. Sprinkle mixture over
meat and stir well. Sprinkle with
chopped onion, lemon juice and pepper and cover with a paper towel.
Cook at medium for 5 minutes and
rest 5 minutes. Repeat 3 times, stirring well after each rest period.

3 Mix cornflour to a cream with the
water. Drain liquid from lamb and
blend it into cornflour with the salt.
Pour over lamb and mix well. Cook
at medium uncovered for 1½ minutes.

4 Gently stir in the drained peach
slices and cook at medium,
uncovered, for 1½ minutes. Serve
accompanied by yoghurt, plain
boiled rice and a lettuce salad.

Serves 4

Oriental Lamb with Cardamon

675 g (1½ lb) stewing lamb, cubed
100 g (¼ lb) (1 cup) seasoned flour
50 mL (2 fl oz) (¼ cup) oil
1 medium onion, chopped
10 mL (2 teaspoons) curry powder
15 mL (1 tablespoon) chopped root
   ginger
pinch cumin
8 black peppercorns, crushed
25 g (1 oz) (2 tablespoons) tomato
   paste
550 mL (1 pint) (2½ cups) water
5 mL (1 teaspoon) treacle
1 bay leaf
50 g (2 oz) (⅔ cup) desiccated coconut
15 mL (1 tablespoon) cardamon
   seeds
2 tomatoes, skinned and quartered

1 Roll meat in seasoned flour.

2 Heat oil in a pan and brown meat for 8 minutes, covered with a lid. Lift out meat and keep warm.

3 In the same pan, fry onion for 4 minutes. Add curry powder, root ginger, cumin and crushed peppercorns. Cook 2 minutes. Stir in tomato paste and add water, treacle, bay leaf and desiccated coconut. Bring to the boil and add cardamon seeds.

4 Return meat to pan and cover. Reduce heat and simmer 1½ hours until meat is tender.

5 When ready to serve, decorate with quartered tomatoes. Serve with plain boiled rice and a plate of freshly fried pappadums. *Serves 6*

Lamb Biriani

675 g (1½ lb) diced lean lamb
1.2 litres (2 pints) (5 cups) water
sprig coriander or parsley
3 chillies, red and green
50 mL (2 fl oz) (¼ cup) oil
50 g (2 fl oz) (4 tablespoons) butter
4 onions
450 g (1 lb) patna rice
5 mL (1 teaspoon) turmeric
15 mL (1 tablespoon) coriander seeds
pinch cumin
2 cloves garlic, crushed
salt and pepper
8 crushed cardamons
100 g (¼ lb) (⅔ cup) seedless raisins
4 canned lychees
sprig watercress

1 Scald lamb in boiling water for 5 minutes. Drain and place in a saucepan with the fresh water, the coriander or parsley, and the chillies. Simmer for 1½ hours. Remove meat, keep the stock.

2 Heat half the oil and butter and fry 2 chopped onions for 5 minutes. Add rice and cook for 1 minute. Add half the turmeric, coriander, cumin, and garlic. Fry 1 minute. Add stock and season. Cover and simmer for 20 minutes.

3 Heat remaining oil and butter and brown meat. Sprinkle with the rest of the spices and raisins and brown for 3 minutes.

4 Preheat oven to 190°C (375°F).

5 Slice remaining onions and fry separately until golden.

6 Mix meat and rice in a dish and cover with onions. Reheat in oven for 15 minutes. Garnish with lychees and watercress.

Serves 4

Lamb and Nut Korma

50 g (2 oz) cashew nuts
3 dried chillies
2.5 mL (½ teaspoon) cinnamon
pinch powdered cardamon
5 mL (1 teaspoon) ginger
pinch cloves
2 cloves garlic, crushed
10 mL (2 teaspoons) coriander
5 mL (1 teaspoon) cumin
150 mL (¼ pint) (⅔ cup) water
2 onions, chopped
50 g (2 oz) (4 tablespoons) butter
150 mL (¼ pint) (⅔ cup) yoghurt
675 g (1½ lbs) lean lamb, cubed
grated rind ½ lemon
10 mL (2 teaspoons) lemon juice
2.5 mL (½ teaspoon) turmeric

1 Grind nuts and chillies in a liquidiser; add water if needed.

2 Mix cinnamon, cardamon, ginger, cloves, garlic, coriander and cumin. Add nuts and chillies, and mix with water to a paste.

3 Fry onion gently for 5 minutes in butter. Add the paste and yoghurt and fry until the oil separates.

4 Add lamb, lemon rind and juice, and turmeric. Cover and simmer for 1 hour.

Serves 4

South Sea Lamb

675 g (1½ lb) stewing lamb, cubed
30 mL (2 tablespoons) paprika
40 g (1½ oz) (3 tablespoons) butter
100 g (¼ lb) (1½ cups) mushrooms
1 large cooking (green) apple
450 g (1 lb) (2 cups) canned pineapple
   chunks, with juice
550 mL (1 pint) (2½ cups) stock
salt and pepper
20 mL (1½ tablespoons) cornflour

1 Roll cubes of stewing lamb in paprika and fry in a saucepan in butter for 10 minutes, covered.

2 Slice mushrooms. Peel, core and thinly slice apple. Fry mushrooms in the same pan. Add apple and drained pineapple chunks. Cook until mushrooms and apple are soft.

3 Add pineapple juice and stock. Bring to the boil, reduce heat and stew gently for 1½ hours until lamb is tender.

4 Season to taste and thicken with cornflour mixed with 75 mL (3 fl oz) (⅓ cup) water. Serve with plain boiled rice.

Serves 4

Oriental Lamb with Cardamon

Lamb Stew with Celery and Pepper

1 kg (2 lb) lean stewing lamb, cut into
   2.5 cm (1 in) cubes
50 mL (2 fl oz) (¼ cup) oil
2 onions, chopped
1 red capsicum (pepper), diced
1 stick celery, diced
15 g (½ oz) (1 tablespoon) tomato
   paste
75 mL (2½ fl oz) (⅓ cup) medium
   sherry
salt and pepper
pinch ground mace
600 mL (1 pint) (2½ cups) beef stock
15 g (½ oz) (1½ tablespoons) cornflour
60 mL (2¼ fl oz) (⅓ cup) cold water
2.5 mL (½ teaspoon) gravy browning
   (optional)
200 g (7 oz) (1 cup) long grain rice

1 Brown meat in oil in a heavy-based casserole. Add onions, pepper and celery and fry gently for 4 minutes.
2 Add tomato paste, sherry and seasoning. Stir. Add meat stock.
3 Cover and stew gently for 1½ hours on a low heat or until the meat is tender.
4 To thicken combine cornflour and water to a smooth paste. Add browning, if used, and pour into stew. Stir and simmer for 10 minutes.
5 Cook rice in boiling, salted water. Serve casserole steaming hot on a bed of rice.

Serves 6

Lamb Stew Jardiniere

75 mL (3 fl oz) (⅓ cup) oil
900 g (2 lb) leg of lamb cut into 2.5 cm
   (1 in) cubes
1 onion, chopped
25 g (1 oz) (2 tablespoons) tomato
   paste
1 beef stock cube
300 mL (½ pint) (1¼ cups) cider
900 mL (1½ pints) (3⅔ cups) water
salt and pepper
225 g (½ lb) shallots (spring onions,
   scallions)
225 g (½ lb) (2⅓ cups) peas
5 mL (1 teaspoon) sugar
15 g (½ oz) (1 tablespoon) butter
225 g (½ lb) baby carrots, quartered
225 g (½ lb) turnips, cut in strips
25 g (1 oz) (¼ cup) flour

1 Heat 50 mL (2 fl oz) (¼ cup) oil in a pan and brown lamb for 8 minutes. Place meat in a casserole.
2 In the same oil, fry chopped onion until tender. Stir in tomato paste, and cook 1 minute. Add stock cube, cider and water and season. Boil 10 minutes.
3 Pour sauce over the meat. Cover and simmer 1½ hours.
4 Boil shallots and peas until tender in water seasoned with salt, pepper and half the sugar. Drain, toss in butter and keep warm.
5 Boil carrots and turnips separately in water seasoned as for the peas and onions. Drain.
6 Mix remaining oil and flour over a low heat for 3–4 minutes. Add a little of the stew gravy, stir and simmer for 10 minutes.
7 Pour into stew and stir on a low heat for 5 minutes.
8 Pour stew into the centre of a shallow dish and surround with vegetables.

Serves 6

Lamb Stew with Celery and Pepper

Lamb Stew Jardiniere

Haricot Bean Lamb Stew

550 g (1¼ lb) stewing lamb
25 g (1 oz) (2 tablespoons) cooking oil
2 rashers bacon
8 shallots (spring onions, scallions)
1 clove garlic, crushed
25 g (1 oz) (¼ cup) flour
900 mL (1½ pints) (3¾ cups) stock
salt and pepper
bouquet garni
225 g (½ lb) (1⅓ cups) dried haricot
  beans, soaked overnight
1 carrot, chopped
1 large onion, chopped
15 g (½ oz) (1 tablespoon) tomato
  paste
15 mL (1 tablespoon) vinegar
15 mL (1 tablespoon) chopped
  parsley

1 Cut meat into cubes.
2 Heat oil in a pan and add bacon, diced (keep the bacon rind to cook with the beans) and shallots. Colour slightly and remove from pan.
3 In the same pan, brown meat. Drain off half the fat, add garlic and flour and stir for 1 minute.
4 Add stock and bring to the boil. Season, skim off any scum. Add bouquet garni, diced bacon and shallots, cover and simmer 1½ hours.
5 Preheat oven to 180°C (350°F).
6 Drain soaked haricot beans, reserving the liquid. Put beans in clean water and bring to the boil. Discard water. Put beans in an ovenproof dish with chopped carrot, onion, bacon rinds, tomato paste and vinegar. Add some of the original liquid to cover and bake for 1 hour. When the beans are tender, remove bacon rinds, and season with salt and pepper.
7 To serve, either combine the beans with the meat in one dish or serve separately, sprinkled with chopped parsley.

Serves 4

Cinnamon Lamb Stew

15 mL (1 tablespoon) flour
5 mL (1 teaspoon) cinnamon
salt and pepper
1 kg (2 lb) shoulder of lamb, cubed
25 mL (1 fl oz) (2 tablespoons) oil
225 g (½ lb) (2 cups) sliced carrots
2 small onions, quartered
2 sticks celery, chopped
550 mL (1 pint) (2½ cups) stock
20 mL (1 tablespoon) cornflour

1 Mix flour and cinnamon and season with salt and pepper. Roll cubes of lamb in the mixture.
2 Heat oil in a pan and brown meat for 8 minutes. Lift meat out of pan and keep warm.
3 Add carrots, onions and celery to pan and fry for 2 minutes. Return meat to pan, add stock and bring to the boil. Reduce heat and simmer gently for 1½ hours or until the meat is tender.
4 When ready to serve, thicken stew with cornflour mixed with 75 mL (3 fl oz) (⅜ cup) water. Check the seasoning and serve with sauteed potatoes.

Serves 6

Latin American Bean Stew

225 g (½ lb) (1⅓ cups) haricot beans,
  soaked overnight
2 litres (3½ pints) (9 cups) water
50 mL (2 fl oz) (¼ cup) oil
1 kg (2 lb) lean shoulder of lamb, cut
  in cubes
1 large onion, chopped
1 stick celery, sliced
2 eggplants (aubergines), peeled and
  cubed
1 bay leaf
3 cloves garlic, chopped
2 red chillies, sliced
50 g (2 oz) (4 tablespoons) tomato
  paste
150 mL (¼ pint) (⅔ cup) white wine
salt and pepper
15 g (½ oz) (1 tablespoon) cornflour
  (optional)

1 Place beans in a pan, add 900 mL (1½ pints) (3¾ cups) of the water and bring to the boil. Remove any scum as it rises, reduce heat and simmer 1 hour until almost tender.
2 Meanwhile, heat oil in a flameproof casserole and cook lamb for 5 minutes to brown it. Add onion and celery and cook for a further 2 minutes. Add eggplants, bay leaf, garlic and chillies and cook for 1 minute. Stir in tomato paste, the rest of the water and the wine and simmer for 1½ hours.
3 Drain haricot beans and add to stew. Season, simmer 20 minutes.
4 If liked, thicken the stew with cornflour mixed with 75 mL (2½ fl oz) (⅓ cup) water.
5 Serve the stew in the casserole dish.

Serves 6

Irish Hotpot

1 kg (2 lb) scrag end of neck, cut into
  even-sized pieces
900 mL (1½ pints) (3¾ cups) water
salt and pepper
450 g (1 lb) onions, sliced
100 g (¼ lb) leeks, sliced
1 kg (2 lb) potatoes, sliced
15 mL (1 tablespoon) chopped
  parsley

1 Preheat oven to 180°C (350°F).
2 Place meat in a flameproof casserole and add water. Season with salt and pepper and bring to the boil, removing any scum that rises.
3 Add onions, leeks and half the potatoes, cover and bake for about 1½ hours.
4 Add remaining potatoes and cook for ½ hour. If necessary, add a little more water.
5 Sprinkle hotpot with chopped parsley and serve.

Serves 4–6

Lamb Curry

1 kg (2 lb) shoulder of lamb
30 mL (2 tablespoons) oil
2 large onions, sliced
30 mL (2 tablespoons) curry powder
15 mL (1 tablespoon) turmeric
5 mL (1 teaspoon) ground ginger
150 mL (¼ pint) (⅔ cup) beef stock
salt and pepper
15 g (½ oz) (1 tablespoon) tomato
    paste
50 g (2 oz) (3 tablespoons) mango
    chutney
25 g (1 oz) (2 tablespoons) raisins
150 mL (¼ pint) (⅔ cup) yoghurt
50 g (2 oz) (⅓ cup) split almonds
½ lemon, sliced

1 Cut lamb off bone and remove fat.
Cut it into 2.5 cm (1 in) cubes.
2 Heat oil in a heavy saucepan and
fry onions until soft. Add lamb and
brown it all over.
3 Stir in curry powder, turmeric and
ginger. Cook 3 minutes.
4 Stir in stock and season with salt
and pepper. Add tomato paste and
bring to the boil, stirring all the time.
5 Add mango chutney and raisins
and simmer, covered, for 45 minutes
until the meat is tender.
6 Stir in yoghurt and most of the
almonds. Simmer gently for 10 more
minutes.
7 Arrange curry on a serving dish,
surrounded by a ring of boiled rice.
Sprinkle with remaining almonds
and decorate with slices of lemon.
Serve with sambals such as coconut,
mango chutney, sliced tomatoes,
bananas, chopped apple, cucumber
and segments of orange.

Serves 4–6

Lamb Curry

Lamb and Pineapple Curry

2 ripe bananas, peeled and sliced
1 sweet potato, peeled and diced
juice 1 lemon
1 large onion, chopped
1 green capsicum (pepper), seeded
    and chopped
25 mL (1 fl oz) (⅛ cup) oil
15 g (½ oz) (1 tablespoon) curry
    powder
15 g (½ oz) (1 tablespoon) flour
5 g (1 teaspoon) turmeric
1 clove garlic, chopped
50 g (2 oz) (2 tablespoons) fruit
    chutney
225 g (½ lb) (¾ cup) pineapple cubes
1 medium cooking apple, peeled,
    cored and diced
1 large tomato, skinned and coarsely
    chopped
100 g (¼ lb) (1 cup) corn kernels
450 mL (¾ pint) (2 cups) meat stock
350 g (¾ lb) (2 cups) diced cooked
    lamb
salt and freshly ground black pepper
275 g (10 oz) (1¼ cups) long grain rice,
    uncooked

Garnish
few lemon slices

1 Mix banana, sweet potato and
lemon juice in a bowl and set aside
for 10 minutes.
2 Lightly fry onion and green capsicum in the oil.
3 Add curry powder, flour, turmeric,
garlic, chutney, pineapple, apple,
tomato, corn kernels, and the banana
and sweet potato mixture.
4 Pour in meat stock, add cooked
lamb, and season to taste. Simmer
gently for 20 minutes.
5 Meanwhile, boil rice in salted
water until cooked. Drain and
arrange in a circle on a heated serving
dish. Spoon curry into the middle of
the rice ring and garnish with quartered lemon slices.

Serves 4

Lamb Curry with Coconut

1 large apple
rind 1 orange
1 large onion
4 cloves garlic
5 mL (1 teaspoon) each: mustard
    seed, black pepper
225 mL (8 fl oz) (1 cup) hot water
100 g (¼ lb) (1¼ cups) desiccated
    coconut
50 mL (2 fl oz) (¼ cup) oil
675 g (1½ lb) lean lamb (shoulder or
    leg) cut in 3 cm (1¼ in) cubes
5 mL (1 teaspoon) each: ground
    (powdered) fenugreek, turmeric,
    coriander, cumin
2.5 mL (½ teaspoon) each: cayenne
    pepper, ginger
10 g (2 tablespoons) chopped fresh
    parsley
salt
225 g (½ lb) (1 cup) rice
2 bananas
3 slices pineapple

1 Peel, core and dice apple. Slice orange rind into match-stick strips. Peel and chop onion and garlic.

2 Crush mustard seed and pepper and add garlic to them. Pour hot water onto the desiccated coconut and let it stand.

3 Heat oil in a heavy pan and gently fry the pieces of lamb, stirring to turn and brown them on all sides. Meanwhile boil water and coconut for 2 minutes, then strain through a clean cloth, squeezing coconut to extract all the liquid.

4 Stir in apple, onion, and all the spices, stirring to spread them over the meat. Add parsley and orange rind.

5 Pour coconut liquid into curry, add a pinch of salt and adjust seasoning to taste. Bring to boil and cover. Simmer over low heat for 40–50 minutes until lamb is cooked, stirring from time to time and adding a little water if it becomes dry.

6 Boil rice in salted water until just tender. Rinse and drain.

7 Peel and slice bananas; cut pineapple into small chunks. Put rice, bananas and pineapple into side dishes. Transfer curry to a large serving dish. Serve at once with fruit chutney and other curry accompaniments.
Serves 6

Curried Potato Pie

450 g (1 lb) potatoes
salt and pepper
25–50 g (1–2 oz) (2–3 tablespoons)
    margarine
a little milk
5 g (¼ oz) (¾ tablespoon) cornflour
150 mL (¼ pint) (⅔ cup) beef stock
40 g (1½ oz) (3 tablespoons) butter or
    margarine
100 g (¼ lb) (½ cup) onion, finely
    chopped
450 g (1 lb) (2 cups) minced cooked
    lamb or mutton
15 g (½ oz) (1 tablespoon) curry
    powder

1 Cook potatoes in boiling salted water until just tender. Mash with a fork or masher, adding margarine and milk to give a smooth consistency. Season to taste.

2 Preheat oven to 200°C (400°F). To cornflour add 60 mL (5 tablespoons) water and stir to give a smooth paste. Bring stock to the boil, add cornflour and cook until thickened.

3 Heat fat in a pan, add chopped onion and cook for 5 minutes without colouring. Add minced meat and seasoning. Stir in curry powder and add sufficient thickened stock to bind. Bring to the boil and simmer for 10–15 minutes.

4 Transfer meat to a pie dish and arrange potato on top. Make swirls on top of the potato with a fork and place in oven for 10 minutes to brown.

Serves 4

Tip: Cooked beef can also be used in this dish. When using cooked meat, care must be taken to heat the meat thoroughly.

Turkish-style Moussaka

6 small eggplants (aubergines)
salt and pepper
100 mL (4 fl oz) (½ cup) oil
450 g (1 lb) tomatoes, skinned,
    seeded and chopped
2 onions, chopped
100 g (¼ lb) (1¼ cups) sliced
    mushrooms
675 g (1½ lb) (3 cups) minced lamb
3 cloves garlic, crushed
30 mL (2 tablespoons) chopped
    parsley
2 eggs, beaten
50 g (2 oz) (½ cup) flour

1 Preheat the oven to 220°C (425°F).

2 Slice 4 of the eggplants (aubergines) in half. Make an incision around the sides with a knife. Then make a criss-cross pattern.

3 Season with salt and pepper and fry in 30 mL (2 tablespoons) oil for a few minutes. Scoop out pulp.

4 Heat 15 mL (1 tablespoon) oil in a pan and saute tomatoes.

5 Using the same amount of oil, fry onions until tender in another pan. Meanwhile, saute mushrooms in 15 mL (1 tablespoon) oil.

6 In a large bowl, mix together lamb and garlic with sauteed onions and mushrooms, and one-third of the cooked tomatoes. Mix in parsley and bind with beaten eggs, and 25 g (1 oz) (4 tablespoons) flour.

7 Peel remaining eggplants and slice thinly. Season and toss in remaining flour. Fry in the rest of the oil for 1 minute.

8 Grease a deep ovenproof dish and line the sides with eggplant skins. Fill dish with alternate layers of lamb mixture and fried sliced eggplant. Cover with more skins.

9 Bake in a bain-marie for 45 minutes. Turn out onto a serving dish and surround with remaining tomato pulp.

Serves 6

Greek-style Moussaka

2 eggplants (aubergines), peeled and
    sliced
2 zucchini (courgettes), sliced
5 mL (1 teaspoon) salt
15 g (½ oz) (2 tablespoons) flour
oil for deep frying
450 g (1 lb) potatoes, sliced
6 tomatoes, skinned and sliced
50 g (2 oz) (½ cup) grated cheese

Filling
50 mL (2 fl oz) (¼ cup) oil
1 onion, chopped
450 g (1 lb) (2 cups) minced lamb
1 clove garlic, crushed
25 g (1 oz) (4 tablespoons) flour
25 g (1 oz) (2 tablespoons) tomato
    paste
pinch each oregano and mace
salt and pepper
150 mL (¼ pint) (⅔ cup) stock

Cheese Sauce
300 mL (½ pint) (1¼ cups) white sauce
50 g (2 oz) (½ cup) grated cheese
1 egg yolk
rind and juice 1 lemon

1 Sprinkle eggplants (aubergines) and zucchini (courgettes) with salt. Leave 10 minutes, then wash and dry.

2 Parboil zucchini (courgettes) for 3–4 minutes. Coat eggplants (aubergines) with flour and deep fry for 30 seconds.

3 Make filling. Heat oil and fry onion until soft. Add lamb, garlic, flour, tomato paste, herbs and seasoning. Cook for 2 minutes. Pour in the stock, boil, then simmer for 10 minutes.

4 Blanch potatoes.

5 Preheat oven to 190°C (375°F).

6 Place alternate layers of the meat mixture, zucchini, eggplants, tomatoes and potatoes in a deep casserole.

7 Make white sauce, stir in cheese, egg yolk and lemon rind and juice. Simmer gently, then pour over the moussaka. Sprinkle with grated cheese and bake for 30 minutes.

Serves 6

Couscous

225 g (½ lb) dried chick peas
2 globe artichokes or 2 canned
    artichoke hearts, drained
1 large onion
1 green capsicum (pepper)
2 leeks, well washed
1 bulb fennel
2 carrots
3 small turnips
4 small zucchini (courgettes)
one 1¼ kg (2½ lb) chicken
450 g (1 lb) boned shoulder of mutton
    or lamb
salt
45 mL (3 tablespoons) oil
4 tomatoes, skinned, seeded and
    chopped
1 litre (1¾ pints) (4½ cups) water
2 chicken stock cubes
25 g (1 oz) (2 tablespoons) tomato
    paste
bouquet garni
1 clove garlic, crushed
6 coriander seeds
15 g (½ oz) (1 tablespoon) ground
    cumin
pinch paprika
2 cloves
6 spicy sausages
15 g (½ oz) (1 tablespoon) harissa
    paste or dash of Tabasco.

Couscous Semolina
50 g (2 oz) (⅓ cup) sultanas
450 g (1 lb) couscous semolina
75 mL (2½ fl oz) (⅓ cup) water
45 mL (3 tablespoons) oil
50 g (2 oz) (4 tablespoons) butter, cut
    in pieces

Meatballs
225 g (½ lb) (1 cup) minced lean lamb
2 sprigs parsley, chopped
1 egg, beaten
1 thick slice bread, soaked in milk
25 g (1 oz) (4 tablespoons) flour
50 mL (2 fl oz) (¼ cup) oil

1 Soak chick peas in cold water overnight. Bring to the boil and simmer for 40–60 minutes.

2 Soak sultanas in tepid water.

3 Place couscous semolina in a dish. Pour over the water and oil. Rub in gently, sprinkling on a little salt.

4 Boil water in bottom half of a steamer or large saucepan. Place semolina in top half (or in a colander over the pan) and steam 20 minutes.

5 If using fresh artichokes, peel, discard leaves and choke. Place hearts in cold, salted water. Chop onion and capsicum finely. Trim leeks and quarter the fennel. Scrape and slice the carrots, turnips and zucchini.

6 Cut chicken into 6 pieces, and mutton or lamb into cubes. Sprinkle with salt. Empty the bottom of the steamer or pan, dry, and heat oil in it. Saute chicken and mutton or lamb, covered, for 10 minutes, stirring occasionally.

7 Add onion and capsicum and fry gently for 5 minutes. Stir in tomatoes. Pour over water and crumble in the stock cubes. Add tomato paste, leeks, carrots, bouquet garni, garlic, coriander, cumin, paprika and cloves. Bring to the boil, removing scum as it rises. Simmer 45 minutes then add fennel, turnip, zucchini and drained artichoke hearts. Simmer 20 minutes. For the last 10 minutes of cooking, replace the couscous semolina and steam.

8 Now make meatballs. In a large bowl, mix minced lamb, parsley and egg. Take the bread from the milk and squeeze out excess liquid. Crumble into mixture, season, and blend well. Divide into meatballs and dust with flour. Heat oil in a pan and fry for 8 minutes. Then fry sausages in the same pan. Keep warm.

9 Place semolina in a dish. Mix in the drained sultanas and pieces of butter. Break up any lumps.

10 Strain the meat and vegetable broth into a warm serving bowl. Check seasoning. Pour a little into a sauceboat and mix with the harissa paste.

11 Serve meat and vegetables in one dish and couscous semolina on another, surrounded by chick peas and topped with meatballs and sausages. Serve with broth and hot sauce.

Serves 6

1 The ingredients for a typical North African couscous: chick peas, couscous semolina, sultanas, globe artichokes or canned artichoke hearts, onion, capsicum, leeks, fennel, carrots, turnips, zucchini, chicken, lamb, tomatoes, water, oil, stock cubes, tomato paste, garlic, sausages, chopped fresh parsley and spices.

2 Soak chick peas in cold water overnight.

3 Put chick peas in pan and bring to the boil. Simmer for 40–60 minutes.

4 Soak the sultanas in tepid water until they are swollen.

5 Pour water and oil over semolina grains.

6 Sprinkle a little salt over the semolina and rub in liquids gently with fingertips.

7 Put semolina in a perforated steamer over boiling water and cook for 20 minutes.

8 Remove the steamer of cooked semolina and keep warm.

9 If using fresh chokes remove leaves and choke. Place hearts in cold salted water.

10 Chop onion and capsicum finely, wash and trim leeks, and quarter the bulb of fennel. Scrape and slice carrots, turnips and zucchini. Tie the leeks with fine string so they do not disintegrate during cooking and can be easily lifted out.

11 Cut the chicken into 6 pieces — legs, breasts and wings. Cut the lamb into cubes of about 4 cm (1½ in) and season the pieces of chicken and lamb lightly with salt.

22

23

24

12 Empty the bottom of the steamer or the large pan, dry and heat the oil in it. Add the chicken pieces and the lamb or mutton and cook, covered, for 10 minutes, stirring occasionally.

13 Add onion and capsicum. Fry 5 minutes.

14 Stir in the tomatoes, pour in the water and crumble in the stock cubes.

15 Add tomato paste, leeks, carrots, bouquet garni, garlic, coriander, cumin, paprika and cloves. Bring to the boil and simmer 45 minutes.

16 and 17 Add fennel, turnip, zucchini and artichoke hearts. Simmer for 20 minutes. During the last 10 minutes, replace the top of the steamer or the colander containing the couscous semolina so that it is heated through.

18 Mix the minced lamb, chopped parsley and beaten egg.

Take the bread from the milk and squeeze out excess moisture. Crumble bread into mixture, season and blend well.

19 Divide mixture into balls. Dust with flour.

20 Heat oil and fry meatballs for 8 minutes.

21 Remove the meatballs, keep them warm and cook the sausages. Keep them warm.

22 Place semolina and drained sultanas in a dish. Mix in pieces of butter. Break up any lumps.

23 Strain the couscous broth into a warmed serving bowl. Pour a little into a sauce-boat and mix with the harissa paste.

24 Serve the meat and vegetables on one dish and the couscous semolina on another.

Lamb Scaloppines

1 kg (2 lb) thin slices lamb, from the
    leg
50 g (2 oz) (½ cup) seasoned flour
30 mL (1 fl oz) (2 tablespoons) oil
2 onions, finely chopped
450 g (1 lb) tomatoes, skinned,
    seeded and chopped
15 g (½ oz) (1 tablespoon) tomato
    paste
300 mL (½ pint) (1¼ cups) white wine
225 g (½ lb) (2 cups) finely sliced
    mushrooms
1 green capsicum (pepper), seeded
    and sliced

1 Beat slices of lamb with a meat
mallet or rolling pin. Dust with
seasoned flour.
2 Heat oil in a frying pan, add lamb
slices and brown quickly on both
sides.
3 Add remaining ingredients and
cook over a gentle heat for 15 minutes. Serve with boiled rice.

Lamb in Pepper Sauce

450 g (1 lb) lamb from the leg, cut in
    2.5 cm (1 in) cubes
50 g (2 oz) (½ cup) seasoned flour
oil for deep frying

Batter
1 egg
100 g (¼ lb) (1 cup + 2 tablespoons)
    flour
300 mL (10 fl oz) (1½ cups) water

Sauce
1 clove garlic, crushed
5 mL (1 teaspoon) fresh ginger,
    chopped
15 mL (1 tablespoon) vinegar
15 mL (1 tablespoon) soy sauce
150 mL (¼ pint) (⅔ cup) pineapple
    juice
15 g (½ oz) (1 tablespoon) sugar
1 small onion, chopped
90 mL (3 fl oz) (6 tablespoons) water
7 mL (½ teaspoons) cornflour

Garnish
1 red capsicum (pepper), seeded
1 green capsicum (pepper), seeded
1 small onoin
25 mL (1 fl oz) (2 tablespoons) oil
15 g (½ oz) (1 tablespoon) tomato
    paste
1 chicken stock cube
150 mL (¼ pint) (⅔ cup) water

Lamb in Pepper Sauce

1 Cook lamb in boiling water for 5
minutes, then drain. Refresh meat in
cold water. Drain and dry.
2 Prepare batter by mixing egg, flour
and water until it has a smooth consistency.
3 Roll meat in seasoned flour in
preparation for deep frying.
4 Prepare sauce by combining garlic,
ginger, vinegar, soy sauce, pineapple
juice, sugar and onion. Pour sauce
into a pan, add most of the water,
and mix the remainder with cornflour. Stir into sauce and cook until
thick. Bring to the boil and boil for
3minutes, or until it has a clear consistency.
5 Heat oil to 190°C (375°F). Dip each
cube of meat into batter and deep-fry
for 3 minutes. Drain meat and place
in a serving dish. Keep warm.

6 Prepare garnish by shredding capsicum and onion. Saute in oil. Add
tomato paste, chicken stock cube and
water and boil for 5 minutes.
7 Add garnish to sauce and boil for 3
minutes. Pour into a serving dish.
8 Serve meat immediately, accompanied with the hot pepper sauce.

Serve 4

Fried Breast of Lamb

1½ kg (3 lb) breast of lamb
oil for deep frying
175 g (6 oz) (1½ cups) flour
5 mL (1 teaspoon) dry mustard
pinch allspice
2 eggs, beaten
175 g (6 oz) (3 cups) fresh
*   breadcrumbs*

1 Remove thin skin from breast. This is easiest to do when the meat is frozen. Cut breast into rectangles including two bones. Boil for 20 minutes. The bones can then be removed easily.

2 Place pieces between sheets of kitchen paper, under a heavy weight, and cool. Chill overnight if possible.

3 When ready to cook, heat oil. Dip each piece of breast in flour, seasoned with mustard and allspice, then in beaten egg, and then in breadcrumbs.

4 Deep-fry for 3 minutes at 180°C, (350°F). Serve with Tomato Sauce as a snack for a party.   *Serves 6*

Lamburgers Capucine

725 g (1½ lb) (3 cups) minced raw
*   shoulder of lamb*
1 onion, chopped
1 egg
salt and pepper
50 g (2 oz) (1 cup) fresh breadcrumbs
25 g (1 oz) (¼ cup) flour
4 bacon rashers, scalded
50 g (2 oz) (4 tablespoons) butter
50 mL (2 fl oz) (¼ cup) oil
100 g (¼ lb) (1 cup) sliced mushrooms
1 green capsicum (pepper), sliced

1 Combine meat, onion, egg, seasoning, breadcrumbs, and flour and shape into 4 burgers. Wrap each with a rasher of bacon and secure with kitchen thread.

2 Heat butter and oil in a pan, add lamburgers, cover, and cook for 8–10 minutes, turning from time to time until golden-brown and cooked through.

3 Lift from pan, remove thread and place on a warmed serving plate. Fry mushrooms and capsicum in the same pan for 4 minutes and use to garnish the lamburgers.

Serves 4

Noisettes with Cream Cheese

1 best end of neck
salt and pepper
75 mL (3 fl oz) (⅓ cup) oil
75 g (3 oz) (½ cup) cream cheese
4 bacon rashers
1 large onion, chopped
225 g (½ lb) fresh or canned tomatoes
5 mL (1 tablespoon) chopped basil

1 Bone the best end of neck to give 4 noisettes. Fold the belly flap round and tie up with string. Season with salt and pepper. Put half the oil in a frying pan and brown noisettes on both sides. Cool.

2 Preheat oven to 190°C (375°F).

3 Spread each noisette with some cream cheese, and wrap each in a rasher of bacon, held in place with a cocktail stick.

4 Place in a roasting pan with oil from the frying pan and bake 45 minutes.

5 Put the rest of the oil in a frying pan and gently fry onion for 5 minutes. If tomatoes are fresh, skin them. Add tomatoes to pan. Season with salt and pepper. Add basil and simmer 15 minutes. Sieve the sauce, check seasoning and keep warm.

6 When ready to serve, place noisettes on a dish, having removed the string and cocktail stick. Serve sauce separately. Serve with boiled potatoes, or with noodles tossed in butter.

Serves 2

Noisettes Provencal

1 best end of neck, including the two
*   cutlets of the middle neck, to give 6*
*   noisettes*
100 mL (4 fl oz) (½ cup) oil

Provencal Sauce
225 g (½ lb) onions, sliced
1 clove garlic
5 mL (1 teaspoon) flour
15 mL (1 tablespoon) tomato paste
150 mL (¼ pint) (⅔ cup) stock
225 g (½ lb) tomatoes, skinned,
*   seeded and chopped*
bouquet garni
salt and pepper

1 Bone the noisettes of lamb by holding the best end upright and with a sharp knife gently and carefully detaching and scraping the meat from the top to the middle of the backbone until the meat is detached. Roll the belly flap round the meat and secure with cocktail sticks or string.

2 In a frying pan gently fry sliced onions and clove of garlic for 5 minutes in 25 mL (1 fl oz) (2 tablespoons) oil. Sprinkle on the flour and cook 1 minute. Stir in tomato paste and stock and simmer for 10 minutes. Add tomatoes, bouquet garni and seasoning and simmer 15 minutes until sauce is thick. Remove bouquet garni and check the seasoning.

3 Season noisettes with salt and pepper and fry 12–15 minutes in the rest of the oil. When cooked, remove the sticks or string.

4 To serve, place sauce on a dish and put noisettes on top. Serve with plain boiled potatoes.

Serves 3

Spicy Kebabs with Pear Salad

450 g (1 lb) lean lamb from the upper leg
225 g (½ lb) (1 cup) long grain rice
2 onions, quartered
2 tomatoes, quartered
30 mL (2 tablespoons) oil
salt and pepper
15 mL (1 tablespoon) chopped mint
1 lemon, quartered

Marinade
150 mL (¼ pint) (⅔ cup) yoghurt
juice 1 lemon
salt and pepper
pinch each cayenne, mustard powder, cumin
1 shallot (spring onion, scallion), grated

Salad
450 g (1 lb) fresh pears, peeled, halved and cored, or canned pears
30 mL (2 tablespoons) oil
5 mL (1 teaspoon) honey
15 mL (1 tablespoon) yoghurt
juice 1 lemon

1 Cut lamb into cubes, about 2.5 cm (1 in). Combine marinade ingredients. Soak meat pieces in marinade for at least 3 hours or overnight.

2 Boil rice in salted water until tender. Rinse and drain.

3 Drain meat pieces from marinade and place on the 4 kebab skewers; alternating with pieces of onion and tomato. Brush kebabs with oil, season with salt and pepper and sprinkle with half the chopped mint. Grill kebabs for 5 minutes or until meat is just browned, turning from time to time, and brushing with marinade to prevent meat drying out.

4 Meanwhile place pears in a dish. Mix oil, honey, yoghurt and lemon juice and season with a little salt and pepper. Pour dressing over pears and sprinkle with the rest of the chopped mint.

5 Serve kebabs on a bed of boiled rice garnished with lemon quarters, with the pear salad.

Serves 4

Sicilian-style Lamb Loaf

50 g (2 oz) (4 tablespoons) butter
3 bay leaves
6 slices very lean ham
450 g (1 lb) (2 cups) minced lamb
175 g (6 oz) (¾ cup) minced lamb's liver
50 g (2 oz) (¼ cup) texturised vegetable protein
75 mL (3 fl oz) (⅓ cup) warm water
1 egg, beaten
30 mL (2 tablespoons) dry sherry
1 small onion, chopped
1 clove garlic, crushed
50 g (2 oz) (½ cup) corn kernels
50 g (2 oz) (½ cup) cooked peas
¼ red capsicum (pepper) chopped
50 g (2 oz) (⅓ cup) diced gherkin
salt and pepper
15 mL (1 tablespoon) wine vinegar
grated rind and juice 1 lemon
1 orange, thinly sliced
12 juniper berries

1 Grease an oblong 750 mL (1¼ pint) (3 cup) ovenproof dish with butter.

2 Preheat oven to 180°C (350°F).

3 Place 3 bay leaves in bottom of dish, then line with slices of ham.

4 In a large bowl, mix lamb and liver. Soak texturised vegetable protein in warm water and add to bowl. Bind with beaten egg.

5 Mix in sherry, onion, garlic, corn kernels, cooked peas, red capsicum and gherkin. Season with salt and pepper and stir in wine vinegar and lemon rind and juice.

6 Place the filling in a lined dish and stand the dish in a shallow tray, half-filled with water.

7 Bake 1¼ hours. Remove and cool. Then chill in the refrigerator and, when cold, decorate with slices of orange and juniper berries. Serve it sliced like a meatloaf for lunch or a picnic

Serves 8

Lamb Meat Loaf

25 g (1 oz) (2 tablespoons) butter
2 onions, finely chopped
1 clove garlic, chopped
3 sticks celery, chopped
1 kg (2 lb) (4 cups) raw minced lamb
6 stuffed olives, sliced
50 g (2 oz) (1 cup) fresh breadcrumbs
5 mL (1 teaspoon) marjoram
2.5 mL (½ teaspoon) cinnamon
15 g (½ oz) (1 tablespoon) tomato paste
1 egg, beaten
50 mL (2 fl oz) (¼ cup) red wine

Garnish
1 tomato, finely sliced
30 mL (2 tablespoons) chopped parsley

1 Preheat oven to 180°C (350°F).

2 Heat butter in a frying pan and fry onion, garlic and celery until soft. Add minced lamb and fry until lightly browned (about 10 minutes). Drain and place in a bowl.

3 Add all the other ingredients to cooked lamb mixture and mix well. Place mixture in a buttered loaf tin.

4 Bake in the centre of the oven for 1 hour. Turn out of the pan and serve cold, decorated with overlapping tomato slices and chopped parsley.

Serves 6

Lamb Meat Loaf

MICROWAVE Lamb

Colonial Goose

1 × 2 kg (4 lb) leg lamb, boned

Stuffing
30 g (1 oz) butter
15 mL (1 tablespoon) honey
125 g (¼ lb) dried apricots, chopped
1 onion, finely chopped
125 g (¼ lb) white breadcrumbs
pinch lemon pepper
pinch salt
pinch dried thyme
1 egg, beaten

Marinade
1 onion, sliced
1 carrot, sliced
1 bay leaf
3 crushed parsley stalks
225 mL (8 fl oz) (1 cup) red wine
225 mL (8 fl oz) (1 cup) consomme
10 mL (2 teaspoons) arrowroot
15 mL (1 tablespoon) water

1 Combine butter and honey in a bowl and cook on high 1 minute. Blend in remaining stuffing ingredients and force prepared stuffing into boned cavity of lamb leg. Tie firmly with string and place meat in roasting dish.

2 Combine marinade ingredients, pour over meat and leave in cool place to marinate for 6 hours, turning leg occasionally. Remove from marinade. Reserve marinade.

3 Weigh leg to calculate cooking time. Place lamb on roasting rack in baking dish, fat side down. Divide cooking time in half. Cook on high 5 minutes then reduce power to medium for remaining first half of cooking time. Turn roast over and cook on medium for remaining time.

4 Let stand 10 minutes, lightly covered with foil, before carving. Arrange lamb on serving plate.

5 Remove fat from roasting dish and deglaze dish with 3 tablespoons of strained marinade and 1 extra cup consomme. Thicken lightly with extra blended arrowroot and cook on high 3-4 minutes. Strain and serve with lamb.

Serves 6–8

Shoulder of Lamb Duxelle

2 kg (4 lb) boneless rolled shoulder of lamb
1 clove garlic, quartered
15 mL (1 tablespoon) melted butter
2.5 mL (1 teaspoon) ground ginger
60 g (2 oz) (¼ cup) tasty cheese
60 g (2 oz) (¼ cup) Parmesan cheese

Stuffing
300 g (¾ lb) mushrooms, chopped
15 g (½ oz) (1 tablespoon) butter
25 g (1 oz) (¼ cup) finely chopped shallots (spring onions, scallions)
2.5 mL (½ teaspoon) dried thyme
15 mL (1 tablespoon) chopped parsley
50 g (2 oz) (½ cup) soft white breadcrumbs

1 To make stuffing, melt butter in bowl on high 1 minute. Add mushrooms and herbs and cook on high for 1 minute. Add shallots and breadcrumbs.

2 Weigh lamb. Make 4 small cuts on each side of the rolled shoulder and insert a piece of garlic in each one. Heat butter on high 1 minute and brush over lamb. Sprinkle with ginger.

3 Place lamb, fat side down, on roasting rack in baking dish and cook on high for 3 minutes. Reduce to medium and continue cooking for remaining first half of cooking time.

4 Turn shoulder over and continue cooking on medium for remaining cooking time. Remove string from shoulder. Cut three-quarters of the way through the shoulder into slices, insert stuffing between each slice and reshape. Combine tasty and Parmesan cheese. Sprinkle over top of shoulder and cook on medium for 6 minutes until cheese melts and lamb reheats. Serve with gravy.

Serves 8–10

Roasted Rosemary Leg of Lamb

1.5–2 kg (3½–4 lb) leg of lamb
30 g (1 oz) (2 tablespoons) butter
2 cloves garlic, peeled and cut in slivers
2 sprigs fresh rosemary.

1 Trim excess fat from lamb. Stud lamb with garlic slivers and sprigs of rosemary. Lightly coat with butter and place, fat side down, on a roasting rack in a shallow casserole dish.

2 Cover and cook for 35–40 minutes on high. Wrap in foil and allow to stand for 10 minutes before carving.

Serves 6–8

Lamb Burgers

500 g (1 lb) minced lamb
4 slices bacon
50 g (2 oz) (½ cup) finely chopped shallots (spring onions, scallions)
7 mL (1½ teaspoons) Worcestershire sauce
2.5 mL (½ teaspoon) lamb seasoning salt
4 slices cheese

1 Arrange bacon between two layers of white paper towel and cook on high 3 minutes.

2 Preheat browning grill on high 5 minutes. Combine lamb, shallots, sauce and seasoning and shape into 4 burgers. Place on preheated grill and cook on high 2 minutes.

3 Cut bacon slices in half and place 2 pieces on each patty. Top each slice with cheese and cook on high 2 minutes for well done. Serve on hot toasted buns.

Serves 4

Fancy Meats

Fancy meats are a highly respected and fashionable form of cuisine in most European countries, especially France and the Mediterranean. Once a bonus thrown in with the meat order, these meats are now a delicacy among gourmets. Fancy meats must be absolutely fresh when cooked as they are prone to deteriorate.

Vol-au-Vents Orleans are pastries filled with sweetbreads in a creamy sauce and make ideal party snacks. The quick and economical Brochettes of Lamb's Liver make a little meat go a long way. Easy to digest, Sweetbreads A La Creme are an excellent food for invalids and convalescents.

London-style Mixed Grill made with chicken livers and breasts.

242

American-style Barbecued Mixed Grill

4 lamb cutlets
4 lamb's kidneys, skinned
4 tomatoes
4 loin chops
4 hamburgers
4 pork or beef sausages
225 g (½ lb) (1 cup) long grain rice
salt
4 mushroom caps
50 mL (2 fl oz) (¼ cup) oil
50 g (2 oz) (4 tablespoons) butter

Barbecue Marinade
30 mL (1 fl oz) (2 tablespoons) soy
    sauce
2 cloves garlic
30 mL (1 fl oz) (2 tablespoons) oil
15 mL (1 tablespoon) vinegar
150 mL (¼ pint) (⅔ cup) tomato juice
pinch paprika
pinch ground ginger
pinch cayenne
5 mL (1 teaspoon) sugar

1 Blend all marinade ingredients.
2 Trim cutlets and remove spinal bones. Split kidneys on the rounded side, spread out flat and hold with a cocktail stick threaded through both sides. Discard any sinews or fat. Cut a cross in the top of each tomato.
3 Place all meat in an earthenware dish and cover with marinade. Leave to soak 30 minutes.
4 Cook rice in boiling salted water.
5 Drain meats and dry them. Brush meats, tomatoes and mushrooms with oil and add to the grill according to their thickness. Hamburgers and chops can be started first and cooked about 15 minutes. Add the other meats after about 5 minutes, and tomatoes and mushrooms during the last 2 minutes so that all will be ready together.
6 Drain cooked rice and mix with butter. Serve with the barbecued mixed grill.

Serves 4

Mixed Grill Kebabs

4 bacon rashers
4 lamb's kidneys, skinned, cored and
    quartered
450 kg (1 lb) lamb shoulder, cut into
    16 cubes
100 g (¼ lb) rump steak, cut into 4
    cubes
12 shallots (spring onions, scallions)
1 green capsicum (pepper), seeded
4 tomatoes, quartered
15 mL (1 tablespoon) oil
5 mL (1 teaspoon) cornflour
45 mL (1½ fl oz) (3 tablespoons) water
pinch cayenne or chilli pepper

Marinade
300 mL (½ pint) (1¼ cups) vermouth
30 mL (1 fl oz) (2 tablespoons) oil
15 mL (1 tablespoon) vinegar
6 crushed black peppercorns
1 bay leaf
pinch tarragon
pinch thyme

1 Scald bacon in boiling water for ½ minute, drain and dry.
2 Mix marinade and soak meat for 3 hours.
3 Trim shallots and cut capsicum into squares.
4 Impale meat on skewers, wrapping some of the kidney pieces in bacon, with the onions, peppers and tomatoes.
5 Brush with oil and cook under grill for 8 minutes.
6 Boil marinade for 5 minutes, thicken with cornflour and water and boil for 2 minutes. Season.
7 Serve with rice and the sauce.

Serves 4

London-style Mixed Grill

4 lamb's kidneys, skinned and cored
4 lamb cutlets
4 chipolata sausages
75 mL (3 fl oz) (⅓ cup) oil
4 × 100 g (¼ lb) pieces lamb's liver
4 bacon rashers
4 tomatoes
4 mushroom caps
few sprigs watercress

1 Cut kidneys in half and brush kidneys, cutlets and sausages with 30 mL (2 tablespoons) oil.
2 Heat remaining oil in frypan and cook liver and bacon. Place cutlets under a hot grill, cook on one side and turn. Add kidneys and sausages and cook, turning occasionally. Lastly grill tomatoes and mushrooms.
3 Serve mixed grill garnished with sprig of watercress and a pat of parsley butter on top of each kidney.

Serves 4

Tips: A mixed grill is very versatile and can be served either as a main meal, snack, or even for breakfast. It is a quick and easy way of cooking and you can vary the ingredients and quantities used. Other meats such as hamburgers, steak, pork chops and other livers and kidneys can be substituted for lamb.

Pork and Kidney Saute with Wine

15 mL (1 tablespoon) oil
15 g (½ oz) (1 tablespoon) butter
salt and pepper
4 pork chops, 225 g (½ lb) each
1 pig's kidney
15 mL (1 tablespoon) flour
5 mL (1 teaspoon) meat extract
150 mL (¼ pint) (⅔ cup) dry white
    wine
juice ½ lemon

1 Heat oil and butter in a frying pan. Season the chops and add to the pan, cover and fry over a low heat for 7 or 8 minutes on each side until cooked through. Remove chops to a warmed serving dish and keep them warm.
2 Remove fat and skin from the kidney, rinse well and slice thinly. Season with salt and pepper and roll in flour. Add to the frying pan, cover and cook lightly for 8 minutes. Arrange on the dish with pork chops.
3 Pour off fat from the pan, retaining the meat juices. Stir in meat extract and wine, and boil for about 5 minutes until reduced by half. Add lemon juice, season to taste and pour over the meat.
4 Serve with sauteed or roast potatoes, sprinkled with chopped parsley.

Serves 4

Mixed Grill Kebabs Step-by-step

1 Collect all ingredients.
2 Cut the shoulder of lamb into cubes and prepare the beef, kidneys and bacon.
3 Prepare the marinade and soak the meat for 3 hours.

Drain and dry on absorbent paper.
4 Chop tomatoes and capsicum, trim shallots.
5 Alternate ingredients on skewers.
6 Brush with oil and grill over charcoal.

Kidney Brunch

4 large potatoes
2 lamb's kidneys, skinned and cored
50 g (2 oz) (4 tablespoons) butter
1 onion, chopped
225 g (½ lb) (1⅓ cups) diced cooked
   leftover lamb
salt and pepper
pinch paprika
100 g (¼ lb) (1¼ cups) sliced button
   mushrooms
150 mL (¼ pint) (⅔ cup) stock
15 mL (1 tablespoon) soy sauce

1 Preheat oven to 190°C (375°F).
Scrub and dry potatoes, prick with a
skewer and bake 1 hour or until soft
throughout.

2 Slice kidneys in half. Saute gently
in butter for 6 minutes, turning to
cook on all sides. Remove from the
pan and keep warm.

3 Add onion to pan and fry gently
for 3 minutes. Add cooked meat and
season with salt and pepper and a
pinch of paprika. Fry for 3 minutes.

4 Stir in mushrooms and saute
gently for 2 minutes. Pour in stock
and soy sauce and bring to the boil.
Simmer 5 minutes to thicken the
sauce. Return kidneys to the pan and
cook, stirring, for 2 minutes.

5 Slice the tops off potatoes and
scoop out the centre flesh. Mix with
meat mixture and spoon back into
potato shells, topping each with a
kidney half. Serve immediately

Serves 4

Kidney Brunch

Sweet and Sour Veal Spaghetti

225 g (½ lb) spaghetti
25 g (1 oz) (2 tablespoons) butter
75 mL (3 fl oz) (⅓ cup) oil
50 g (2 oz) (½ cup) grated cheese
175 g (6 oz) veal kidneys
175 g (6 oz) veal, cut into strips
1 green capsicum (pepper), cut into
   strips
1 red capsicum (pepper), cut into
   strips
1 onion, chopped
1 clove garlic, peeled and chopped
1 canned pineapple ring, cut into
   chunks
75 mL (3 fl oz) (⅓ cup) water
150 mL (¼ pint) (⅔ cup) pineapple
   juice
30 mL (2 tablespoons) soy sauce
15 g (½ oz) (1 tablespoon) tomato
   paste
15 mL (1 tablespoon) vinegar
25 g (1 tablespoon) honey
salt and pepper
1 chicken stock cube
15 g (½ oz) (1½ tablespoons) cornflour

1 Boil spaghetti in a pan of salted
water until just tender (al dente).
Drain, then mix in the butter and
30 mL (2 tablespoons) of the oil. Place
in a shallow dish, sprinkle with
grated cheese and keep warm.

2 Heat remaining oil in the frying
pan. Trim excess fat and membranes
off the kidneys and cut into four.
Saute the kidneys and veal for 4 minutes, then add capsicums, onion and
garlic. Cover with a lid and cook for 3
minutes. Add the pineapple, water,
pineapple juice, soy sauce, tomato
paste, vinegar and honey. Season
with the salt and pepper. Crumble in
the stock cube and boil for 5 minutes.
Mix the cornflour with a little water
and stir into the sauce. Boil for 1 minute.

3 Pour the sauce over the spaghetti
and serve immediately.

Serves 4

Sweet and Sour Veal Spaghetti

Veal Kidneys in Red Wine Step-by-step

12

13

1 Dice onions, carrots, sticks of celery and parsley stalks.
2 Put some butter in a casserole, add half the onions and the rest of the vegetables and cook gently without colouring for 2 minutes. Sprinkle with flour and stir. Cook 1 minute.
3 Add half the red wine and water and stir. Bring to the boil and season with salt, the crushed peppercorns and garlic. Cook for 30 minutes until the vegetables are soft.
4 Meanwhile prepare kidney by removing the skin.
5 Cut off any fat and the hard white core from the centre.
6 Cut the kidney into 1 cm (½ in) slices with a sharp knife.
7 Heat some oil in a frying pan and brown kidneys quickly.

8 Lift out of the pan and keep hot. Discard the cooking juices and fat. Do not keep.
9 Fry the rest of the chopped onions in the butter, in another casserole.
10 Add rest of red wine and boil fast until almost evaporated.
11 Add cooked vegetables and sauce. Simmer 5 minutes.
12 Sieve the sauce through a conical strainer gently pressing the softened vegetables through the holes. Stir to a smooth sauce and check the seasoning and pour over the kidneys and reheat without boiling.
13 Place in a serving dish and sprinkle with parsley. Serve hot with vegetables.

Veal Kidneys in Red Wine

2 carrots
4 onions
6 sprigs parsley
2 celery sticks
50 g (2 oz) (4 tablespoons) butter
15 g (½ oz) (2 tablespoons) flour
300 mL (½ pint) (1¼ cups) red wine
50 mL (2 fl oz) (¼ cup) water
salt
12 peppercorns, crushed
1 clove garlic
pinch thyme
1 bay leaf
675 g (1½ lb) veal kidneys
50 mL (2 fl oz) (¼ cup) oil

1 Dice carrots, 2 of the onions, celery and parsley sprigs. Put 25 g (1 oz) (2 tablespoons) of butter in a casserole and cook the vegetables and herbs gently without colouring for 2 minutes. Sprinkle on the flour and stir 1 minute. Add 100 mL (4 fl oz) (½ cup) of the red wine, and the water. Bring to the boil. Season with salt, crushed peppercorns, crushed garlic, thyme and bay leaf. Simmer 30 minutes until the vegetables are tender.

2 Prepare the kidneys by removing the skin from the outside. Cut off fat, and the central hard white core. Slice.

3 Heat the oil in a frying pan, and saute the slices of kidney briefly. Lift out of the pan, discarding the cooking fat and juices.

4 Heat remaining butter in a casserole, gently fry the rest of the onions, chopped finely. Add remaining wine and boil until almost evaporated.

5 Add the cooked vegetables and sauce and simmer for 5 minutes.

6 Sieve the sauce through a conical strainer, pressing the cooked vegetables through the holes.

7 Pour over the kidneys and reheat without boiling.

8 Put in a serving dish and sprinkle with chopped parsley.

Serves 4

Sauteed Kidneys and Mushrooms

450 g (1 lb) veal kidneys
salt and pepper
50 g (2 oz) (4 tablespoons) butter
225 g (½ lb) (3 cups) button mushrooms
100 mL (4 fl oz) (½ cup) white wine
150 mL (¼ pint) (⅔ cup) Demi-glace Sauce (see recipe)
juice ½ lemon

1 Trim kidneys, removing the fat and membranes and cut into pieces. Season with salt and pepper.

2 Heat the butter in a frying pan and saute the kidneys for about 5 minutes. Remove and keep warm.

3 Add the button mushrooms and saute for 3 minutes. Add the wine and boil to reduce it, then add the Demi-glace Sauce. Boil it for a few minutes, stirring from time to time. Stir in the kidneys and lemon juice. Serve with plain boiled rice, zucchini and grilled tomatoes

Serves 4

Brochettes of Lamb's Liver

225 g lamb's liver
12 cocktail sausages or 12 × 5 cm (2 in) chunks of sausage
4 tomatoes, halved
4 slices lightly toasted bread, quartered
salt and pepper
125 g (5 oz) (½ cup) butter
1 clove garlic, crushed
5 mL (1 teaspoon) chopped parsley
5 mL (1 teaspoon) chopped marjoram

1 Trim liver and cut into 3 cm chunks.

2 Thread liver, sausage, tomato halves and toast quarters alternately onto 4 kebab skewers. Sprinkle with salt and pepper.

3 Soften butter in a bowl and mix crushed garlic, parsley and marjoram into it. Brush some on brochettes.

4 Cook brochettes under a hot grill, turning frequently and basting with herb butter, until liver and sausage are browned.

Serves 4

Liver and Bacon Casserole

1 large onion
3 large tomatoes
450 g (1 lb) ox liver
salt and pepper
225 g (½ lb) (2 cups) flour
8 rashers bacon
2 g (1 teaspoon) dried oregano
1 stock cube
225 mL (8 fl oz) (1 cup) water
50 g (2 oz) (4 tablespoons) tomato paste

1 Slice onion, tomatoes and liver. Season liver and dip in 50 g (2 oz) (½ cup) of the flour.

2 Arrange half the floured liver in casserole, with half the onion on top. Lay half the bacon above and repeat the layers of liver, onion and bacon. Lay sliced tomatoes on top and sprinkle with oregano.

3 Preheat oven to 180°C (350°F).

4 Mix stock cube with 150 mL (¼ pint) (⅔ cup) of the water. Stir in tomato paste and pour into casserole.

5 Make a firm paste from the rest of the flour and water and press around the edge of the casserole.

6 Put lid on and press firmly to make an airtight seal.

7 Bake 1½ hours.

8 Carefully chop away the cooked paste, and serve.

Serves 4

Liver in Cointreau

4 × 180 g (6 oz) slices liver
50 g (2 oz) (½ cup) flour
salt and pepper
5 mL (1 teaspoon) dried marjoram
70 mL (2½ fl oz) (⅓ cup) oil
2 onions, chopped
100 mL (4 fl oz) (½ cup) red wine
30 mL (1 fl oz) (2 tablespoons) orange
   juice
30 mL (1 fl oz) (2 tablespoons)
   Cointreau
15 mL (1 tablespoon) brandy

1 Roll liver in flour seasoned with
salt, pepper and marjoram. Shake off
excess and reserve 15 mL (1 tablespoon) of the flour.

2 Heat oil in a pan and cook onions
until soft. Remove and drain. Fry
liver on both sides for 4 minutes and
keep warm.

3 Gradually whisk wine, reserved
flour, orange juice, Cointreau and
brandy into pan. Add onions and
continue to stir over a low heat until
sauce thickens. Pour over liver.

Serves 4

Sweetbreads a la Creme

4 calf's sweetbreads
pinch salt
juice 2 lemons
15 g (½ oz) (2 tablespoons) seasoned
   flour
40 g (1½ oz) (3 tablespoons) butter
100 g (¼ lb) (1 cup) mushrooms, diced
1 egg yolk
30 mL (1 fl oz) (2 tablespoons) cream

1 Soak sweetbreads in cold, salted
water for about 3 hours, changing the
water from time to time. Place in a
pan, cover with cold water and add a
pinch of salt and the juice of 1 lemon.
Bring to the boil, then simmer gently
for 8 minutes. Cool the sweetbreads
under running water and when cold,
carefully pick out the gristle and
membranes. Dry on absorbent
paper.

2 Slice across each sweetbread to
make 4 thin slices. Dredge with the

flour. Heat the butter in a frying pan,
add the sweetbreads and fry lightly
until they are golden-brown on each
side. Add the mushrooms and fry for
2 minutes more, then lower the heat,
cover and cook for 15 minutes, until
tender. Remove and keep hot.

3 Place the egg yolk and cream in a
bowl and beat well together. Pour
the juice of the second lemon onto
the pan and heat through for 2 minutes, scraping the bottom of the pan
with a wooden spoon to incorporate
the sweetbread and mushroom
juices. Take off the heat, stir in the
cream mixture, check seasoning and
pour over the sweetbreads.

Serves 4

Fried Sweetbreads

4 sweetbreads
salt
juice 2 lemons
25 g (1 oz) (2 tablespoons) flour
5 mL (1 teaspoon) made mustard
1 egg, beaten
50 g (2 oz) (½ cup) chopped cooked
   ham
100 g (¼ lb) (1½ cups) dried
   breadcrumbs
2 sprigs parsley, chopped
50 g (2 oz) (4 tablespoons) butter

1 Soak sweetbreads in cold, salted
water. Place in a pan, cover with cold
water and add a pinch of salt and
lemon juice. Bring to the boil and
simmer gently for 8 minutes.

2 Cool sweetbreads under cold tap.
Carefully pick out gristle and membranes, lay between 2 plates and
place a heavy weight on top to press
them for 1–2 hours.

3 Cut into slices and dredge in flour.
Dilute mustard with an equal quantity of water and mix with beaten
egg. Mix together ham, breadcrumbs
and parsley.

4 Coat sweetbreads with egg and
mustard mixture and roll in ham,
breadcrumbs and parsley. Heat butter in a frying pan and fry sweetbreads gently on both sides until
brown.

Serves 4

Vol-au-vents Orleans

4 puff pastry vol-au-vent cases, about
   10 cm (4 in) wide
2 sweetbreads
salt
600 mL (1 pint) (2½ cups) water
1 chicken stock cube
30 mL (1 fl oz) (2 tablespoons) wine
   vinegar
1 onion, sliced
1 carrot, sliced
bouquet garni

Sauce
50 g (2 oz) (3 tablespoons) butter
50 g (2 oz) (½ cup) flour
300 mL (½ pint) (1¼ cups) milk
100 mL (4 fl oz) (½ cup) dry vermouth
100 g (¼ lb) (1 cup) diced mushrooms

Scrambled Eggs
25 g (1 oz) (2 tablespoons) butter
2 eggs, beaten
30 mL (1 fl oz) (2 tablespoons) cream
pinch paprika

1 Place the prepared vol-au-vent
cases on a greased baking sheet.

2 Soak the sweetbreads in cold
salted water for about 3 hours,
changing the water occasionally.

3 Bring the water to the boil in a
pan. Crumble in the stock cube and
add the vinegar, onion, carrot and
bouquet garni. Season to taste. Add
sweetbreads and simmer 45 minutes.

4 When the sweetbreads are tender,
take them out of the cooking liquor
and pick out the gristle and membrane. Cut into small pieces. Strain
the liquor and reduce to 300 mL (½
pint) (1¼ cups).

5 Make a roux with 50 g (2 oz) (3
tablespoons) butter and the flour.
Over a low heat stir in first the milk,
then the reduced stock until the mixture thickens. Check the seasoning.
Meanwhile heat the oven to 180°C
(350°F) and place the vol-au-vent
cases in the oven to reheat. Heat the
vermouth in a pan, add the mushrooms and sweetbreads and simmer
gently for 5 minutes. Stir into the
sauce.

6 To make the scrambled eggs, heat 25 g (1 oz) (2 tablespoons) butter in a pan and stir in the eggs and cream. Season with salt and a pinch of paprika. Take off the heat as soon as soon as they become fluffy and add to the sauce. Take the vol-au-vent cases out of the oven, fill with the mixture and serve immediately.

Serves 4

Tip: This mixture can be used to fill small bouchee cases for a buffet party, as shown in the photograph.

Vol-au-vents Orleans

Ox Tongue Casalinga

1 pickled ox tongue, about 2 kg (4 lb)
1 carrot, sliced
1 onion, chopped
bouquet garni
6 peppercorns
30 mL (1 fl oz) (2 tablespoons) oil
100 g (¼ lb) streaky bacon, cut in
   strips
2 shallots (spring onions, scallions),
   sliced
100 g (¼ lb) (1¼ cups) sliced button
   mushrooms
150 mL (¼ pint) (⅔ cup) flat light beer
15 mL (1 tablespoon) tomato paste
15 mL (1 tablespoon) chopped fresh
   parsley
salt and pepper
15 mL (3 teaspoons) cornflour

1 Soak the tongue in cold water for 3 hours. Drain and place in a pan with carrot, onion, bouquet garni and peppercorns. Cover with water and simmer 3 hours, skimming occasionally.

2 Heat oil in a pan and fry bacon pieces for 3 minutes, stirring. Add shallots and fry 3 minutes. Add mushrooms and fry 2 minutes. Stir in the flat beer, tomato paste, parsley and seasoning. Bring to the boil and simmer for 10 minutes.

3 Drain tongue and remove the skin and tubes. Cut into thick slices and arrange on a heated serving dish.

4 Thicken sauce if necessary with cornflour dissolved in a little water. Pour over the tongue and garnish the dish with garden peas. Serve hot.

Serves 6–8

MICROWAVE Fancy Meats

Tongue

1.5–1.75 g (3–3½ lbs) ox tongue
300 mL (½ pint) (1½ cups) water
2.5 mL (½ teaspoon) salt
pinch pepper
2 bay leaves
1 onion, quartered

1 Wash tongue and trim off fat. Place into a 2 litre casserole with water, salt, pepper, bay leaves and onion.

2 Cover and cook on high 3 minutes. Reduce power to medium and cook 70–80 minutes, or until tender, turning tongue halfway through cooking. Let stand 5 minutes before removing skin.

Serves 4–6

Calf's Liver and Bacon

375 g (¾ lb) calf's liver
4 large bacon rashers
1 small onion, finely chopped
2.5 mL (½ teaspoon) freshly ground
   pepper
pinch salt
50 mL (2 fl oz) (4 tablespoons) sweet
   vermouth
15 mL (1 tablespoon) tomato paste
5 mL (1 teaspoon) Gravox powder
50 mL (2 fl oz) (4 tablespoons) beef
   consomme or stock

Mustard Cream
225 mL (1 cup) sour cream
45 mL (3 tablespoons) French
   mustard

1 Soak liver in cold, salted water for 10 minutes. Remove skin and cut liver into thin slices. Derind bacon rashers and cut each rasher into 2.5 cm lengths.

2 Place bacon and onion in casserole and cook on high 4 minutes, stirring after 2 minutes. Add liver and cook on high 2 minutes. Add freshly ground pepper and salt, vermouth and tomato paste.

3 Blend in Gravox and consomme. Cover and cook on medium 10 minutes, stirring and rearranging liver every 3 minutes.

4 Serve with mustard cream — made by blending sour cream and French mustard.

Serves 4

Calf's Liver and Bacon

Pastry Savouries

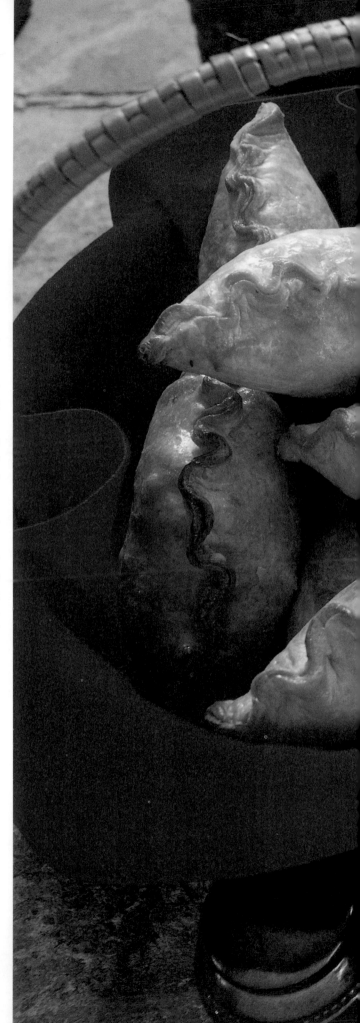

Meat served in pastry is a delicious combination which can radically alter the appearance of a familiar meat dish. Pies, pasties, flans or vol-au-vents are welcome additions at any stage of a meal. Savoury pastry dishes are tasty and satisfying served hot or cold.

Country Pork Pie is easily made and an excellent alternative to the commercial varieties. Ham and Egg Flan is quickly prepared because the filling, mixed with mayonnaise, needs no cooking. Steak and Kidney Pie, one of the great British dishes, deserves its international reputation for hearty goodness.

Cornish Pasties

Basic Hot Water Crust

150 mL (5 fl oz) (⅔ cup) water
pinch salt
75 g (3 oz) (6 tablespoons) margarine
75 g (3 oz) (6 tablespoons) butter
450 g (1 lb) (4½ cups) flour
1 egg, beaten

1 Place the water, salt and fats in a pan and bring to the boil — the fats should now have melted.
2 Add the flour and stir to a thick dough. Allow dough to cool a little, then transfer to a mixing bowl. Stir in beaten egg and cool.
3 Knead the pastry and roll into a ball. It is now ready to use.

Makes 675 g (1½ lb)

Basic Shortcrust

225 g (½ lb) (2¼ cups) flour
good pinch salt
50 g (2 oz) (4 tablespoons) butter
50 g (2 oz) (4 tablespoons) margarine
  or butter
45 mL (1½ fl oz) (3 tablespoons) water

1 In a mixing bowl, sift flour and salt.
2 Cut fats into small pieces. Rub into flour lightly but thoroughly until mixture looks like breadcrumbs.
3 Pour over the water and bind together to make a stiff dough.
4 With your fingertips, lightly roll dough into a ball. Let it rest for 10 minutes.
5 Roll out dough on a floured board. Take care not to stretch it. Let it rest 10 minutes before using.

Makes 350 g (¾ lb)

Steak and Kidney Pie

Steak and Kidney Pie

30 mL (2 tablespoons) oil
450 g (1 lb) lean chuck steak, cubed
225 g (½ lb) calf's kidneys (or lamb or
  ox), trimmed and quartered
1 onion, chopped
25 g (1 oz) (4 tablespoons) flour
salt and pepper
350 mL (12 fl oz) (1½ cups) water
1 beef stock cube
1 bouquet garni
100 g (¼ lb) (¾ cup) broad beans,
½ lb flaky pastry
1 egg, beaten

1 Heat oil in a large pan and saute the pieces of steak and kidney for 5 minutes until light brown. Lower heat, add the onion and cook gently for 5 minutes. Stir in flour and cook for a few more minutes. Season.

2 Pour over the water and crumble in the stock cube. Add the bouquet garni and bring to the boil. Turn the heat down, put a lid on the pan and simmer for 1½ hours or until meat is tender. Add broad beans and transfer to a medium-sized pie dish.
3 Preheat oven to 220°C (425°F).
4 Roll out the flaky pastry on a floured surface until it is 5 cm (2 in) wider all round than the dish. Prick all over with a fork. Cut out a 2.5 cm (1 in) strip of pastry and place on the rim of the dish. Brush with water. Then place the pastry lid on top and press edges together. Cut the pastry trimmings into leaf shapes and decorate the pie with them. Brush with beaten egg.
5 Leave in a cool place for 20 minutes.
6 Bake for 30 minutes. Serve hot.

Serves 4

Spanish Pie

675 g (1½ lb) stewing beef cut in
  1.5 cm (¾ in) cubes
25 g (1 oz) (4 tablespoons) flour
5 g (1 teaspoon) salt
good pinch pepper
40 g (1½ oz) (3 tablespoons) butter
2 large onions, finely sliced
2 sticks celery, sliced
150 mL (¼ pint) (⅔ cup) water
½ beef stock cube
225 g (½ lb) (¾ cup) tomatoes,
  skinned, seeded and chopped
15 g (½ oz) (1 tablespoon) tomato
  paste
20 green olives, stuffed
350 g (¾ lb) puff pastry dough
1 egg, beaten

1 Preheat oven to 170°C (325°F).
2 Coat beef cubes with flour seasoned with salt and pepper. Heat fat in a frying pan and quickly brown the meat. Remove and place in a casserole. Fry onion and celery in the fat for 3 minutes, then add to meat. Boil the water in a pan and crumble in the ½ stock cube. Pour into the casserole and stir in the tomatoes and tomato paste. Cover and cook for 2 hours or until the meat is tender. Remove from oven, add olives and check the seasoning. Turn into a 1.4 litre (2½ pint) pie dish and leave to cool.

3 Turn oven heat up to 220°C (425°F).
4 Roll out the puff pastry dough to a thickness of 3 mm (⅛ in) on a floured board. Place over the pie dish, trim and seal the edges. Brush with beaten egg. Make 2 small slits in the centre of the pie and bake for 45 minutes.

Serves 6

Beef and Eggplant (Aubergine) Pie

2 eggplants (aubergines), sliced
salt and pepper
150 g (5 oz) (⅝ cup) butter
2 onions, peeled and chopped
450 g (1 lb) minced beef
1 beef stock cube, dissolved in
  200 mL (7 fl oz) (⅞ cup) hot water
25 g (1 oz) (4 tablespoons) flour
225 g (½ lb) puff pastry
225 g (½ lb) tomatoes, sliced
15 mL (1 tablespoon) chopped
  parsley
2.5 mL (½ teaspoon) oregano
milk to glaze

1 Sprinkle eggplant slices with salt and leave for 30 minutes. Rinse.
2 Preheat the oven to 190°C (375°F).

3 Melt 100 g (¼ lb) (½ cup) of the butter in a frying pan and fry eggplants on both sides until golden-brown. Drain. Melt remaining butter and fry onion and minced beef gently for 15 minutes. Add stock and seasoning and simmer gently for 15 minutes.
4 Blend flour with a little water, add to beef and simmer 2 minutes, stirring constantly.
5 Roll out two-thirds of the pastry to line the base and sides of a 450 g (1 lb) aluminium foil loaf tin. Cover the base with half the eggplant slices. Spoon over half the beef and top with half the tomato slices. Sprinkle over with herbs. Cover with remaining eggplant slices, beef and tomato.
6 Roll out the remaining pastry to form a 'lid'. Dampen edge of the pastry base, cover with 'lid' and press edges together. Trim and 'knock up' with the back of a knife. Decorate with leaves made from the pastry trimmings and brush the top with milk.
7 Bake for 50 minutes. Serve the pie hot with a green salad.

Serves 4–6

Beef and Eggplant (Aubergine) Pie

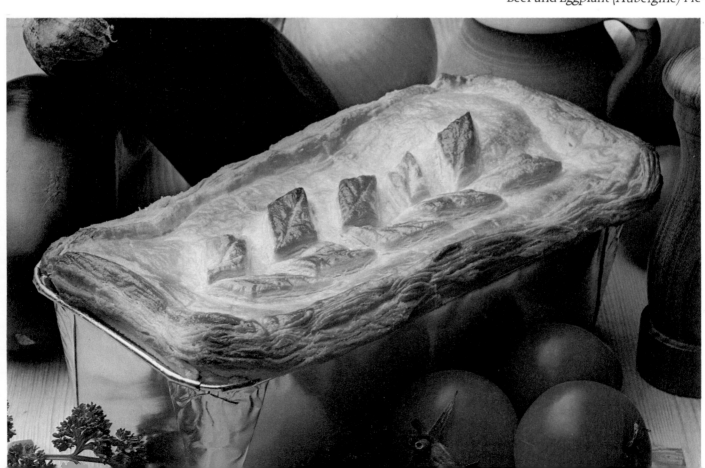

Farmer's Pie

450 g (1 lb) shortcrust
1 egg, beaten
225 g (½ lb) (1 cup) beef sausage meat
150 g (6 oz) (1½ cups) mushrooms, diced
1 onion, chopped
1 egg
5 g (1 tablespoon) chopped fresh parsley
1 clove garlic, peeled and chopped
salt and pepper
pinch ground mace
75 g (3 oz) (½ cup) chopped gherkin
30 mL (2 tablespoons) port wine

1 Preheat oven to 180°C (350°F). Roll out two-thirds of the dough to 5 mm (¼ in) thick on a floured board. Cut a 23 cm (9 in) circle to line a 20 cm (8 in) flan case greased. Brush the inside of the dough with beaten egg.

2 In a mixing bowl, combine the other ingredients with a wooden spoon to form a smooth mixture. Spread mixture evenly over the flan.

3 Roll out the remaining one-third of dough and cut a circle of 20 cm (8 in) diameter. Cover the filled flan shell. Pinch edges together to seal, brushing with beaten egg if necessary. Use the dough trimmings to make leaves or twisted strips to decorate the top of the pie. Brush the top with the remaining beaten egg. Bake for 1 hour. Serve hot, cut in wedges, with fresh tomatoes and a potato salad.

Serves 6

Boeuf en Croute

15 mL (1 tablespoon) oil
1.5 kg (3 lb) beef topside
25 g (1 oz) (2 tablespoons) butter
1 onion, chopped
100 g (¼ lb) button mushrooms, finely chopped
30 mL (2 tablespoons) chopped parsley
salt and pepper
275 g (10 oz) puff pastry
few sprigs watercress

1 Preheat oven to 200°C (400°F). Heat oil in a large pan and fry meat quickly on all sides to seal the juices. Transfer oil and meat to a roasting pan for 45 minutes. Leave to cool.

2 Melt butter and fry the onion for 5 minutes until soft. Add mushrooms, parsley and seasoning. Cover and fry for 5 more minutes.

3 Roll out the pastry to a rectangle large enough to completely cover the meat. Spread ⅓ of the stuffing over the centre of the pastry and place the meat on top. Spread the rest of the stuffing over the meat. Dampen edges of the pastry and fold up over the meat like a parcel. Trim.

4 Place meat, join downwards, in a roasting pan. Roll out pastry trimmings and cut them into 'leaves' to decorate the top. Brush the top with a little milk. Increase the oven temperature to 220°C (425°F) and cook the beef for 40–45 minutes until the pastry is crisp and golden.

5 Transfer the meat to a serving dish and garnish with watercress.

Serves 6–8

Cornish Pasties

350 g (¾ lb) shortcrust
225 g (½ lb) lean chuck steak
1 swede, coarsely grated
2 potatoes, coarsely grated
1 large onion, finely chopped
salt and freshly ground black pepper
50 g (2 oz) (4 tablespoons) butter
1 egg, beaten

1 Preheat oven to 200°C (400°F).

2 Roll out the dough to a thickness of 5 mm (¼ in). Using a small plate about 15 cm (6 in) in diameter as a pattern, cut out 4 circles with a knife. Leave them to rest in a cool place.

3 With a sharp knife, cut the beef into small cubes, and then into tiny dice.

4 Sprinkle grated swede over the centre of each round of dough, then sprinkle over grated potato. Repeat with diced beef, then onion. Season generously with salt and freshly ground black pepper. Top each pastry with 15 g (½ oz) (1 tablespoon) butter.

5 Dampen edges of the pastry with water and fold them together. Press to seal and twist the edges to make a fluted pattern.

6 Glaze with beaten egg. Place on a baking tray and bake for 15 minutes. Then reduce heat to 180°C (350°F) and bake for 30 minutes. Serve hot or cold.

Serves 4

Tip: This is the traditional Cornish way of making pasties. However, if you prefer, you can dice the potatoes and swede.

Florentine Rolls

30 mL (1 fl oz) (1 tablespoon) oil
1 onion, chopped
350 g (¾ lb) sausage meat
150 g (¼ lb) (1 cup) mushrooms, chopped
salt and pepper
100 g (¼ lb) (¼ cup) spinach, cooked and drained
2 eggs, beaten
5 g (1 tablespoon) chopped parsley
pinch ground nutmeg
450 g (1 lb) flaky pastry

1 Heat oil in a frying pan and gently fry the chopped onion and sausage meat until lightly browned. Add mushrooms, season, and cook for 5 minutes more.

2 Take off heat and pour away excess fat. Mix in chopped spinach, beaten egg, chopped parsley and nutmeg. Mince to form a smooth paste.

3 Roll out pastry to a thickness of 3 mm (⅛ in). Prick all over with a fork. Cut into 6 equal strips. Place a sausage-shaped piece of filling along the length of each strip. Fold pastry over and seal the edges. With a sharp knife, make a decorative pattern on top of each roll.

4 Brush with the second beaten egg and leave to rest for 30 minutes in a cool place. Meanwhile heat the oven to 220°C (425°F).

5 Place on a greased baking tray and bake for 15 minutes on the middle shelf.

Serves 6

Florentine Rolls (see previous page)

Curry Vol-au-vent

350 g (¾ lb) puff pastry
1 onion, chopped
25 mL (1 fl oz) (2 tablespoons)
  cooking oil
1 clove garlic, chopped
5 g (¼ oz) (1 teaspoon) curry powder
225 g (½ lb) (1 cup) minced beef
25 g (1 oz) (2 tablespoons) tomato
  paste
150 mL (¼ pint) (⅔ cup) beef stock
50 g (2 oz) (½ cup) cooked peas
salt and pepper
15 g (½ oz) (1 tablespoon) cornflour

1 Make and bake a triangular vol-au-vent.

2 Brown onion in oil for 5 minutes, add garlic and curry powder and cook for ½ minute. Stir in meat and brown it for 5 minutes. Add all other ingredients except cornflour and simmer 15 minutes.

3 Dilute cornflour with a little water and stir it into the meat mixture. Cook 4 minutes until the sauce is thickened. Fill the vol-au-vent case with meat and serve immediately.

Serves 4

Beef and Vegetable Vol-au-vent

1 × 15 cm (6 in) vol-au-vent shell
225 g (½ lb) Basic Economy Beef (see
  recipe)
50 g (2 oz) (½ cup) frozen peas
2 zucchini (courgettes), peeled and
  sliced
1 tablespoon fresh grated Parmesan
  cheese

1 Preheat oven to 220°C (425°F). Bake the vol-au-vent shell for 20–25 minutes, or until golden-brown. Keep warm.

2 Meanwhile prepare Basic Economy Beef (see recipe). While it is cooking, add the peas to boiling, salted water. Bring back to boil, add zucchini, and cook 4 minutes.

3 When the beef is cooked, stir in the peas and zucchini and pour the mixture into the vol-au-vent case. Serve immediately sprinkled with the cheese.

Serves 4

Curry Vol-au-vents Step-by-step

1 Roll out the pastry to 1 cm (3/4 in) deep. With a pastry cutter 15 cm (6 in) make 2 rounds.
2 In the middle of one round cut a lid.
3 Put complete round on baking sheet moistened with water. Brush edges of the round with beaten egg and stick the hollow circle on it.
4 Another method is to cut one 2 cm (⅝ in) deep round and press in smaller cutter to half depth.
5 Other shapes such as a triangle can be cut.
6 Crimp the edges of the triangle with a knife.

7 Use up spare pastry to make crescents for garnishing fish dishes.
8 Glaze the pastry with beaten egg.
9 Cut the lid of the triangle with a knife.
10 Decorate the surface by scoring lightly.

11 Bake in a hot oven: 220°C (425°F).
12 Lift off the lids and remove the soft middle layers, leaving a base about 1 cm (¾ in) thick.
13 Spoon the filling into the vol-au-vent case.
14 Top with pastry lid, and serve.

Country Pork Pie

675 g (1½ lb) hot water crust
1 egg, beaten

Filling
225 g (½ lb) (1 cup) pork sausage meat
225 g (½ lb) (1 cup) cooked ham, diced
50 g (2 oz) (½ cup) flour
1 egg, beaten
1 onion, chopped
salt and pepper
2 g (1 teaspoon) sage
pinch mace
2 g (1 teaspoon) marjoram
5 g (1 tablespoon) chopped parsley

Aspic Jelly
15 g (½ oz) (2 tablespoons) gelatine
150 mL (¼ pint) (⅔ cup) stock, heated
15 mL (1 tablespoon) sherry

1 Mix filling ingredients and chill for 1 hour before using.

2 Roll out ¾ of the dough, 5 mm (¼ in) thick. Use remainder for lining the base of the tin and making a lid and leaves for decoration.

3 Grease a 17.5 cm (7 in) pie tin. Roll out a little dough and line the base. Cut out a strip of dough to the depth of the wall of the tin, about 10 cm (4 in), and use to line the greased tin wall.

4 Place filling inside and wet the top edge of the pastry with water.

5 Preheat the oven to 180°C (350°F).

6 Roll out the remainder of the dough 5 mm (¼ in) thick and cut out a round lid. Place lid on top, pressing firmly around the edge, and brush with beaten egg.

7 Cut remaining dough into shapes and, using a sharp knife or the prong of a fork, make a leaf-pattern. Arrange on top of the pie and brush with beaten egg. Put the pie aside for 15 minutes.

8 Bake pie in the oven for 1½–2 hours, then cool for several hours.

9 Meanwhile, make the aspic jelly. Mix the gelatine and hot stock together. Cool a little but do not allow it to set, then make hole in top of pie and pour in jelly. Freeze the pie for 20 minutes until the jelly sets completely. Serve cold with salad.

Serves 4

Oaty Pork Pie

675 g (1½ lb) pork spare rib joint
50 g (2 oz) (4 tablespoons) oil
2 large onions, sliced
3 sticks celery, sliced
3 carrots, thickly sliced
30 mL (1 fl oz) (2 tablespoons) Worcestershire sauce
300 mL (½ pint) (1¼ cups) flat light beer
salt and pepper
1.25 mL (¼ teaspoon) nutmeg
1 chicken stock cube
15 mL (1 tablespoon) cornflour

Pie Crust
225 g (½ lb) (2 cups) flour
100 g (4 oz) (8 tablespoons) butter
50 g (2 oz) (⅔ cup) rolled oats
about 50 mL (2 fl oz) (¼ cup) flat light beer
a little milk to glaze

1 Remove the bone and excess fat from the pork and cut meat into cubes. Heat oil in a large pan and fry onions, celery and carrots for 3 minutes. Add pork and brown.

2 Stir in Worcestershire sauce, beer, seasoning and nutmeg, crumble in the stock cube and bring to the boil. Cover and simmer gently for 30 minutes.

3 Blend cornflour with a little water and stir into the pork mixture. Simmer for 3 minutes. Transfer to a 900 mL (1½ pint) (3¾ cup) pie dish and allow to cool.

4 Preheat oven to 200°C (400°F). Make the pie crust: sieve flour with a pinch of salt and rub in the lard and butter. Stir in the oats and bind with the beer.

5 Roll out the dough, slightly larger than the pie dish. Cut 2 cm (¾ in) wide strips from the edge and place around the rim of the dish. Moisten with water and top with the dough lid. Press the edges together, trim, and knock up with the back of a knife. Make a small hole in the centre and decorate with dough leaves. Brush the pie with milk and bake for 10 minutes. Reduce the heat to 180°C (350°F) and bake for a further 45 minutes, covering the pie with aluminium foil if necessary to prevent overbrowning. Serve hot.

Serves 5

Chicken and Ham Pie

675 g (1½ lb) hot water crust dough
150 g (5 oz) thin slices of pork fat
1 egg, beaten

Filling
1 kg (2 lb) roasting chicken, skinned and boned
450 g (1 lb) lean pork
225 g (½ lb) stewing veal
salt and pepper
pinch mace and paprika
2 g (1 teaspoon) mixed herbs
1 egg, beaten
150 mL (¼ pint) (⅔ cup) medium sherry
225 g (½ lb) ham, cut in strips
25 mL (1 fl oz) (2 tablespoons) brandy
150 g (5 oz) (¾ cup) liver sausage

1 Remove flesh from chicken breasts and legs.

2 Coarsely mince chicken, pork and veal. Blend with half the seasonings, spices and herbs. Add the beaten egg and 75 mL (3 fl oz) (⅓ cup) sherry. Refrigerate overnight.

3 Place ham in a shallow dish and cover with the remaining seasonings, sherry and the brandy. Soak overnight.

4 Wrap the liver sausage in a thin strip of pork fat.

5 Roll out the hot water crust dough and line a greased, hinged mould. Cover with pork fat slices.

6 Place a layer of minced meat inside and then layer of ham. Pour in the leftover sherry and brandy.

7 Place the liver sausage in the half-filled pie and cover with ham and minced meat.

8 Cover with pork fat and brush with beaten egg. Lay a dough lid on top.

9 Preheat oven to 180°C (350°F).

10 Decorate with pastry leaves and brush with beaten egg. Make a small hole in the top and insert a cardboard funnel.

11 Bake 1½–2 hours. Cool for several hours before serving.

Serves 6

Country Pork Pie

Veal and Ham Pie

675 g (1½ lb) hot water crust
1 egg, beaten

Filling
150 g (5 oz) (⅔ cup) pork sausage meat
150 g (5 oz) (⅔ cup) minced pie veal
150 g (5 oz) (¾ cup) cooked ham,
  diced
150 g (5 oz) (¾ cup) cooked veal, diced
1 onion, chopped
50 g (2 oz) (½ cup) flour
5 g (1 tablespoon) chopped parsley
salt and pepper
pinch mace
2 g (1 teaspoon) basil or oregano
1 egg, beaten

1 Mix ingredients for the filling and bind with beaten egg.
2 Roll out the dough 5 mm (¼ in) thick and line a greased pie mould (as described in the Country Pork Pie recipe). Add filling and cover with a pastry lid. Decorate with leaves of dough and brush with beaten egg.
3 Put pie aside for 15 minutes to rest. Meanwhile, preheat oven to 180°C (350°F).
4 Bake pie for 1½–2 hours, then cool. Make a small hole in the lid and pour in the aspic jelly (see Country Pork Pie recipe).
5 Freeze 20 minutes until the jelly has completely set and serve.

Serves 4

Easter Pie

450 g (1 lb) (4½ cups) flour
9 eggs
225 g (1 lb) (1 cup) butter or
  margarine, softened
675 g (1½ lb) (3 cups) pork sausage
  meat
15 mL (1 tablespoon) chopped
  parsley
2.5 mL (½ teapoon) salt
pinch freshly ground black pepper
5 mL (1 teaspoon) allspice
pinch cayenne pepper
1 egg yolk, beaten
25 g (1 oz) (2 tablespoons) butter

1 Form the flour into a ring on the work surface. Break in 2 eggs and add the softened butter. Mix together with the fingers, adding 15–30 mL (1–2 tablespoons) water, and knead dough for 2–3 minutes until smooth. Roll dough into a ball and place in a cool place or in the refrigerator for 30 minutes.
2 Cook 5 of the eggs in boiling water for 10 minutes, drain and cover them with cold water to cool.
3 In a bowl, combine the sausage meat with 2 of the eggs and the parsley, salt, pepper, allspice and cayenne. Mix well.
4 Shell the hard-boiled eggs to prevent them discolouring; cover them with cold water until needed.
5 Halve the dough and roll out each piece to form a circle about 5 mm (¼ in) thick.
6 Place half the meat mixture along the centre of one piece of dough and arrange hard-boiled eggs along the top of the meat. Cover eggs with the rest of the meat mixture, making sure they are well covered at the sides.
7 Brush the border of dough round the meat with the egg yolk and lay the second piece of dough over the top. Trim off excess dough and crimp the edges of the parcel with the fingers to seal. Pinch together at intervals to produce a fluted edge. Preheat the oven to 180°C (350°F).
8 Brush the whole parcel with more egg yolk. Roll out dough trimmings to 3 mm (⅛ in) thickness and cut out decorative leaf shapes. Arrange some into roses and place the roses and the leaves on the top of the Easter Pie. Brush the decorations with more beaten egg yolk.
9 Grease a baking sheet with the butter and place the pie on the sheet. Bake for 1 hour. Allow to cool and decorate with sprigs of parsley. Serve cold.

Serves 8

Dickens Pies

100 g (¼ lb) (½ cup) mincemeat
225 g (½ lb) cooked pork sausages,
  skinned and chopped
2 eggs
350 g (¾ lb) puff pastry

1 Preheat oven to 220°C (425°F). Combine mincemeat, sausages and 1 egg.
2 Roll out pastry to 3 mm (⅛ in) thickness and cut into 12 × 7.5 cm (3 in) rounds. Place a spoonful of the mixture in the centre of 6. Roll remaining rounds to enlarge them to 10 cm (4 in). Dampen edges of the filled rounds with water and cover with the larger pieces. Press edges to seal and place on a greased baking sheet. Brush with remaining egg, beaten, and allow to rest for 20 minutes.
3 Bake for 20 minutes and serve hot or cold.

Makes 12 pies

Ham and Egg Flan

450 g (1 lb) shortcrust dough
175 g (6 oz) (2 cups) boiled potatoes,
  diced
100 g (¼ lb) (¾ cup) cooked ham,
  diced
100 mL (4 fl oz) (½ cup) mayonnaise
salt and pepper
5 g (1 tablespoon) chopped fresh
  parsley
4 hard-boiled eggs
50 g (2 oz) (¼ cup) anchovy fillets

1 Preheat oven to 200°C (400°F). Roll out the pastry to line a flan case of 20 cm (8 in) diameter. Bake blind for 20 minutes until the shell is crisp and light golden then cool.
2 In a mixing bowl, combine potatoes and ham with mayonnaise. Season to taste with salt and pepper, stir in the chopped parsley.
3 Spoon the mixture into the flan shell. Cut the hard-boiled eggs into quarters and arrange them on top of the flan. Decorate with anchovy fillets. Serve cold with a mixed salad.

Serves 4

Bacon Braid

225 g (½ lb) bacon rashers
225 g (½ lb) potatoes
100 g (¼ lb) onions
100 g (¼ lb) carrots
25 g (1 oz) (2 tablespoons) butter
5 mL (1 teaspoon) dried mixed herbs
15 mL (1 tablespoon) fresh chopped
*   parsley*
pepper
375 g (13 oz) puff pastry,
1 egg, beaten

1 Discard rind and cartilage from bacon and cut into small pieces.
2 Peel and dice potatoes. Peel and chop onions. Scrape and dice carrots.
3 Fry bacon and vegetables in the butter for about 8 minutes. Add dried herbs, parsley, and pepper to taste. Leave to cool.
4 Roll pastry out on a floured board to make a rectangle of about 28 × 33 cm (11 × 13 in). Trim off any uneven edges.
5 Arrange the cooked vegetable mixture in a row down the middle of the pastry, leaving 2 cm (¾ in) at the ends and about 10 cm (4 in) bare at each side. Make several slanted cuts in the uncovered side pieces from the edge to near the filling, about 2.5 cm (1 in) apart.
6 Fold the cut pieces over the filling alternately, to form a plaited effect. Tuck the ends up neatly. Brush beaten egg over the top of the braid. Preheat the oven to 220°C (425°F). Place the braid on a greased baking sheet and bake for 20 minutes. Reduce heat to 180°C (350°F) and cook for 15 minutes. This dish can be served hot or cold.

Serves 4

Bacon Braid

Lamb Cobbler

50 mL (2 fl oz) (¼ cup) oil
1 onion, chopped
675 g (1½ lb) (3 cups) minced lamb
100 g (¼ lb) (½ cup) chopped lamb's
*   liver*
25 g (1 oz) (4 tablespoons) flour
50 g (2 oz) (4 tablespoons) tomato
*   paste*
300 mL (½ pint) (1¼ cups) stock
salt and pepper
pinch rosemary
5 mL (1 teaspoon) made mustard
25 g (1 oz) (2 tablespoons) chopped
*   gherkin*

Topping
350 g (¾ lb) (3 cups) self-raising flour
pinch salt
100 g (¼ lb) (½ cup) butter
75 mL (3 fl oz) (⅓ cup) water
15 mL (1 tablespoon) milk

1 Heat oil in a pan and fry onion until soft. Add lamb and liver and cook for 5 minutes.
2 Stir in flour and tomato paste and cook 2–3 minutes. Pour in stock and add salt, pepper and rosemary.
3 Preheat oven to 190°C (375°F).
4 Mix mustard and gherkin into lamb mixture and pour into a shallow ovenware dish. Leave to cool.
5 Meanwhile, make the topping. Sift flour and salt together and rub in butter. Add enough water to form a stiff dough.
6 Knead dough a little on a floured board and roll out ½ cm (¼ in) thick. With a round pastry cutter cut dough into rounds. Arrange these, overlapping each other, around the top of the casserole dish. Brush with milk.
7 Bake for 30 minutes.

Serves 6

Lamb Cobbler

Lamb Capriccio Pie

450 g (1 lb) shortcrust
225 g (½ lb) (1 cup) minced cooked
  lamb
175 g (6 oz) (¾ cup) pork sausage meat
100 g (¼ lb) (½ cup) minced cooked
  lamb's liver
1 small onion, chopped
8 stuffed olives, sliced
2 eggs, beaten
150 mL (¼ pint) (⅔ cup) dry sherry
75 g (3 oz) (1½ cups) fresh
  breadcrumbs
salt and pepper
pinch curry powder

1 Preheat oven to 200°C (400°F).
2 Roll out the shortcrust dough, 3 mm (⅛ in) thick and 40 × 20 cm (16 × 18 in).
3 Cut pastry into 2 squares and use 1 to line the base and sides of a greased square cake tin. Prick pastry all over with a fork and bake blind for 15 minutes. Remove from oven and cool.
4 Meanwhile, mix the other ingredients together in a large bowl. Reserve a little beaten egg for glazing the pie.
5 Fill the baked pastry case with the filling and cover with the uncooked square of dough. Crimp the edges of the pie together and glaze with beaten egg.
6 Bake for 20 minutes. Serve cold with salad.

Serves 6–8

Lamb Picnic Pie

675 g (¾ lb) (1¾ cups) diced lamb
15 g (½ oz) (1 tablespoon) butter
1 onion, finely chopped
50 g (2 oz) (½ cup) sliced button
  mushrooms
300 mL (½ pint) (1½ cups) meat stock
salt and pepper
pinch chopped dried sage
50 g (2 oz) (1 cup) fresh breadcrumbs
225 g (½ lb) shortcrust
1 egg, beaten

1 Brown diced lamb in the butter. Add onion and cook gently for 5 minutes. Add mushrooms and cook for 3 minutes.

2 Pour in stock and season with salt, pepper and sage. Bring to the boil and simmer for 30 minutes. Remove from heat and add breadcrumbs, stirring them in to form a smooth mixture. Allow to cool.
3 Preheat the oven to 200°C (400°F). Roll out the pastry to fill a 20 cm (8 in) flan case and to cut a circle of the same size for the pastry lid. Fill pastry shell with the mixture and cover with the pastry lid, binding the edges with a little of the beaten egg. Bake for ½ hour or until the pastry is golden-brown. Serve hot or cold.

Serves 4

Lamb Braid

450 g (1 lb) (2 cups) minced lamb
2 onions, chopped
25 g (1 oz) (½ cup) fresh breadcrumbs
15 g (½ oz) (1 tablespoon) tomato
  paste
15 mL (1 tablespoon) Worcestershire
  sauce
2 eggs, beaten
salt and pepper
225 g (½ lb) puff pastry

1 Mix together minced lamb, onions, breadcrumbs, tomato paste, Worcestershire sauce and one of the beaten eggs. Season with salt and pepper.
2 Roll out pastry on a floured surface, 3 mm (⅛ in) thick, into an oblong.
3 Place lamb mixture in the centre, and with a knife, cut diagonal strips from the centre to the edges along each side. Dampen edges with a little water.
4 Fold pastry at each end and then fold the strips over alternately so that they meet in the centre.
5 Preheat oven to 220°C (425°F).
6 Place the Lamb Braid on a greased baking tray and brush with remaining beaten egg. Bake for 15 minutes, then reduce the temperature to 180°C (350°F). Cook for a further 30 minutes. Serve hot with fresh vegetables.

Serves 4

Tip: To make this dish more economical and to give it a smoother tex-

ture, try mixing pork sausage meat with the minced lamb. For a different flavour, why not add a little chopped liver? The addition of herbs such as rosemary, or even spices, make the Lamb Braid taste delicious.

Lamb en Croute (1)

225 g (½ lb) (1 cup) lean, minced lamb
2 onion, finely chopped
50 g (2 oz) (½ cup) mushrooms, finely
  chopped
25 g (1 oz) (½ cup) fresh white
  breadcrumbs
15 g (½ oz) (1 tablespoon) tomato
  paste
15 mL (½ fl oz) (1 tablespoon)
  Worcestershire sauce
2 eggs, beaten
salt and pepper
225 g (½ lb) flaky pastry

1 Preheat oven to 220°C (425°F).
2 In a bowl, blend lamb, onions, mushrooms, breadcrumbs, tomato paste, Worcestershire sauce and 1 beaten egg. Season.
3 Roll out pastry to an oblong, about 30 × 23 cm (12 × 9 in). Prick all over with a fork. Place lamb mixture along the centre, leaving a margin of 7.5 cm (3 in) pastry on either side.
4 Make diagonal cuts of 7.5 cm (3 in) down both outside strips of pastry. Brush edges with water.
5 Fold pastry strips over the meat mixture, alternating left and right in a braiding motion. Brush with the second beaten egg and rest for 20 minutes.
6 Bake for 15 minutes at the preheated temperature, then turn the heat down to 180°C (350°F) and cook for a further 20 minutes. Serve hot or cold.

Serves 4

Lamb Capriccio Pie

Lamb en Croute (2)

1.75 kg (3½ lb) leg of lamb, boned
5 mL (1 teaspoon) each chopped
*   fresh rosemary and sage*
salt and pepper
50 mL (2 fl oz) (¼ cup) oil
450 g (1 lb) puff pastry
1 egg, beaten

1 Preheat oven to 180°C (350°F). Rub the outside of the leg of lamb with the herbs, salt and pepper. Baste the lamb with oil and roast for 20–25 minutes per 450 g (1 lb). Remove and cool.

2 Roll out the pastry to ½ cm (¼ in) thick. Place the leg of lamb on it and roll pastry around the meat to cover it closely on all sides, sealing edges with a little of the beaten egg. Decorate the top of the pastry with shapes cut from the pastry offcuts. Brush with beaten egg.

3 Raise the oven heat to 220°C, (425°F) and bake the meat for about 15 minutes until the pastry is golden-brown. Serve, cut in slices, with glazed carrots.

Serves 8

Tip: To give extra flavour, and to fill the slight gap left between the meat and the pastry as they cook, the meat may be coated with a thin layer of stuffing before being encased in the crust. Duxelles of mushroom is excellent, or try a stuffing containing lamb's liver pate and herbs.

Lamb en Croute (2)

Lamb Cutlets en Croute

4 lamb cutlets
25 g (1 oz) (2 tablespoons) butter
15 mL (1 tablespoon) oil
1 small onion, chopped
25 g (1 oz) (¼ cup) chopped
    mushrooms
15 g (½ oz) (¼ cup) fresh breadcrumbs
5 mL (1 teaspoon) mixed herbs
salt and pepper
1 egg, beaten
225 g (½ lb) puff pastry
few sprigs parsley

1 Trim cutlets to expose 5 cm (2 in) bone at the narrow end. Melt butter and oil in a frying pan and brown cutlet on both sides. Drain on absorbent kitchen paper and cool.

2 Cook onions and mushrooms in the same butter and oil until soft. Place in a bowl with the breadcrumbs and herbs and mix well. Season with salt and pepper and bind with some of the beaten egg.

3 Preheat oven to 220°C (425°F).

4 Roll out pastry on a floured surface into a large oblong, 3 mm (⅛ in) thick. Cut into 4 strips.

5 Season cutlets with salt and pepper and spread each with the stuffing mixture on one side only. Wrap a strip of pastry around each cutlet, working from one end to the other and seal the ends well.

6 Brush with remaining beaten egg and place on a baking tray. Bake for 15 minutes, then reduce the heat to 180°C (350°F). Continue cooking for another 15 minutes until golden-brown, then remove and arrange on a serving dish. Garnish with sprigs of parsley and serve with buttered peas, carrots and roast potatoes.

Serves 4

Curried Lamb Pasties

1 onion, chopped
15 mL (1 tablespoon) oil
225 g (½ lb) (1 cup) minced lamb
15 g (½ oz) (3 teaspoons) flour
5 mL (1 teaspoon) curry powder
25 g (1 oz) (2 tablespoons) raisins
    (optional)
salt and pepper
150 mL (¼ pint) (⅔ cup) meat stock
5 mL (1 teaspoon) tomato paste
1 large green apple, peeled, cored
    and chopped
225 g (½ lb) shortcrust
1 egg, beaten

1 Fry onion gently in the oil until soft. Add the lamb, stir to brown, add the flour and curry powder and cook for about 3 minutes.

2 Mix in raisins if used, season with salt and pepper, and stir in the stock and tomato paste. Bring to the boil and simmer for ½ hour to make a thick mixture. Add a little more water if it becomes too dry. When it is cooked, remove from heat and stir in the chopped apple.

3 Preheat oven to 200°C, (400°F). Roll out dough to ½ cm (¼ in) thick and cut 4 circles of about 15 cm (6 in) diameter.

4 Place dough circles on a greased baking tray. Spoon ¼ of the meat mixture into the middle of each dough circle. Fold over one end to encase the meat mixture, binding the edges with a little of the beaten egg and crimping them with a fork.

5 Brush the top of the pasties with the beaten egg and bake for about 20 minutes or until pastry is crisp and golden-brown. Serve hot or cold.

Serves 4

Lamb Turnovers

225 g (½ lb) puff pastry
150 g (5 oz) (⅔ cup) minced cooked
    lamb
25 g (1 oz) (1 tablespoon) apple
    chutney
25 g (1 oz) (2 tablespoons) diced apple
15 mL (1 tablespoon) grated onion
1 egg, beaten
salt and pepper
pinch cumin

1 Roll out pastry on a floured surface, 3 mm (⅛ in) thick and, using a saucepan lid, cut out 4 circles.

2 Preheat oven to 200°C (400°F).

3 In a large bowl, mix minced lamb, chutney, diced apple and grated onion. Bind with most of the beaten egg (put a little aside to glaze the pastry). Season with salt, pepper and a pinch of cumin.

4 Divide mixture into 4 portions and place 1 in the centre of each pastry circle. Wet the edges of the pastry with water and fold over, pressing the edges firmly together. Then crimp the edges.

5 Place the turnovers on a greased baking tray and bake on the middle shelf of the oven for 20 minutes until well-risen and golden-brown.

Serves 4

Lamb Vol-au-vent Pascaline

4 × 10 cm (4 in) vol-au-vent cases
50 g (2 oz) (4 tablespoons) butter
1 onion, chopped
100 g (¼ lb) (1 cup) diced mushrooms
225 g (½ lb) (1⅓ cups) diced cooked
    lamb
50 mL (2 fl oz) (¼ cup) sherry
salt and pepper
4 stuffed olives, sliced
25 g (1 oz) (4 tablespoons) flour
300 mL (½ pint) (1¼ cups) milk
pinch nutmeg

1 Preheat oven to 200°C (400°F). Bake vol-au-vent cases for 15 minutes until cooked.

2 Melt half the butter and fry the onion for 4 minutes until soft. Add mushrooms and cook for 1 minute. Stir in the lamb and fry for 4 minutes. Pour in sherry, season and add olives; simmer gently for 5 minutes.

3 In another pan melt the rest of the butter. Stir in flour and cook for 1 minute. Remove from heat, blend in milk and season with salt, pepper and a pinch of nutmeg. Stir over heat until thick and creamy.

4 Add white sauce to the meat mixture, stir well and simmer gently for 10 minutes, stirring frequently. Pour the mixture into the vol-au-vent cases. Serve immediately.

Serves 4

Sausage Pie

450 g (1 lb) shortcrust
25 g (1 oz) (2 tablespoons) butter
225 g (½ lb) beef and pork chipolata
 sausages
3 eggs
100 g (¼ lb) (½ cup) pork sausage
 meat
15 mL (1 tablespoon) chopped
 parsley
1 onion, chopped
45 mL (3 tablespoons) fresh white
 breadcrumbs
30 mL (1 fl oz) (2 tablespoons) brandy
 or sherry
salt and pepper
pinch paprika
pinch mace or nutmeg
pinch garlic salt

1 Preheat oven to 190°C (375°F). Roll
out dough to 3 mm (⅛ in) thickness
and divide into two. Grease a 20 cm
(8 in) pie tin with the butter and line
the bottom with 1 piece of the dough.
Trim, and prick the base with a fork.
2 Grill sausages for 3 minutes to
brown the outsides. Cut into thick
chunks and allow to cool.
3 Beat 2 of the eggs and combine
with the sausage meat, parsley,
onion, breadcrumbs, brandy or
sherry, salt, pepper, paprika, mace or
nutmeg, and garlic salt. Blend in the
chunks of sausage and place mixture
in the pie tin.
4 Cover with the remaining piece of
dough. Beat remaining egg and use to
glaze the surface of the pie. Decorate
with pastry trimmings and brush
again with the beaten egg. Flute the
edges of the pie with a fork to seal.
5 Bake for 40 minutes and serve hot
or cold.

Serves 6

Sausage and Mushroom Pie

Sausage and Mushroom Pie

450 g (1 lb) pork sausages
50 g (2 oz) (¼ cup) butter
2 onions, sliced
40 g (1½ oz) (6 tablespoons) flour
300 mL (½ pint) (1¼ cups) milk
300 mL (½ pint) (1¼ cups) stock
salt and pepper
100 g (¼ lb) (1 cup) sliced button
 mushrooms
350 g (¾ lb) puff pastry
1 egg, beaten

1 Preheat oven to 200°C (400°F).
2 Prick sausages and grill them until
golden.
3 Heat butter in a pan and gently fry
the onions for 5 minutes. Stir in the
flour and cook another minute.
4 Gradually blend in the milk and
stock and bring to the boil. Stir until
thickened and then add seasoning
and mushrooms.
5 Place sausages in a pie dish and
pour over the mushroom sauce. Roll
out the puff pastry, cover the dish
with it and trim off any excess. Brush
top with the beaten egg and bake the
pie for 40 minutes. Serve piping hot.

Serves 6

Tip: This pie can be stored in the
freezer. Freeze it uncooked, and
when ready to use, cook in an oven
preheated to 220°C (425°F) for 45–50
minutes.
Vary the vegetables used in the sauce
— try sweetcorn kernels, carrots or
peas.

Sausage Rolls

450 g (1 lb) (2 cups) pork sausage
meat
450 g (1 lb) puff pastry
1 egg, beaten

1 Preheat oven to 220°C (425°F).

2 Roll sausage meat into a long strip 60 cm (24 in) long.

3 Roll out the pastry to 3 mm (⅛ in) thickness and cut it into 2 strips 30 cm × 10 cm (12 in × 4 in). Cut sausage meat in half and place one half on each strip of pastry. Brush the edge of the pastry with beaten egg and fold over. Crimp the edge with a fork. Cut into pieces about 6.5 cm (2½ in) long and brush all over with beaten egg.

4 Place the rolls on a greased baking sheet and bake for 15 minutes. Serve hot.

Makes 10 sausage rolls

Sausage Cheese Flan

225 g (½ lb) shortcrust
225 g (½ lb) beef and pork chipolata
sausages
150 mL (¼ pint) (⅔ cup) white sauce
2 eggs
salt and pepper
pinch cayenne pepper
50 g (2 oz) (½ cup) grated Cheddar
cheese

1 After making the shortcrust, allow it to rest for 20 minutes.

2 Prick sausages and grill them for 4 minutes to brown the outsides.

3 Preheat oven to 200°C (425°F). Grease a 20 cm (8 in) flan tin. Roll out the dough to 3 mm (⅛ in) thickness and use it to line the flan tin. Prick dough with a fork and bake blind for 12 minutes. Cool. Reduce oven temperature to 180°C (350°F).

4 Combine white sauce and eggs, season to taste and add half the cheese. Pour mixture into flan and arrange sausages on top. Sprinkle with the rest of the cheese and bake for 30 minutes.

Serves 4

Sausage Cheese Flan

MICROWAVE Pastry Savouries

Fillet of Beef Wellington

Fillet of Beef Wellington

1.5 kg (3 lb) middle cut fillet in one
   piece
2 cloves garlic, peeled
50 mL (2 fl oz) (¼ cup) brandy
30 mL (2 tablespoons) oil
30 mL (2 tablespoons) French
   mustard
2 sheets puff pastry
1 egg, beaten

1 Cut each clove of garlic in four.
Make 4 small cuts in each side of beef
and insert garlic. Tie roast at 5 cm
intervals with kitchen string. This
holds the beef in shape while browning. Cook in browning casserole on
high 6 minutes.

2 Remove beef, add oil and cook on
high 2 minutes. Return beef to casserole and cook on high 4 minutes, turning fillet four times during cooking
for even browning. Cook on medium
20 minutes. Remove string.

3 Place brandy in jug and cook on
high 15–20 seconds to warm. Ignite
with flaming taper. Pour over fillet
and let stand 5 minutes, turning beef
twice.

4 Place beef onto sheet of puff
pastry. Spread top and sides with
French mustard. Brush edges of
pastry with beaten egg and shape
second sheet of pastry over beef. Seal
edges and cut off excess pastry. Brush
pastry with beaten egg and decorate
with excess pastry.

5 Bake in convection microwave
200°C until pastry is well risen and
golden. Serve with demi-glace sauce.

Serves 6–8

1 Turn beef 4 times while cooking.

2 Pour warmed brandy over beef.
3 Cover beef with puff pastry.

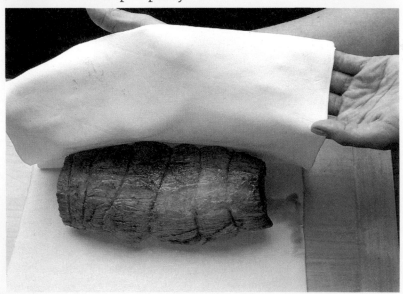

Scrumptious Salads

S alads are becoming ever more popular and original and can be served as hors d'oeuvres or as main meals in themselves. Depending on whether you plan the dish for a family meal or a dinner party, the amount of meat used can be varied. Ideal if you are slimming or health-conscious, salads contain very little carbo-hydrate or fat and are rich in vitamins and roughage.

Melon Ball and Tongue Salad is an unusual combination which will intrigue your guests. Lentil and Salami Salad with Artichoke Hearts makes a delicious starter and is easy to prepare well in advance.

Cold meats add flavour and flair to vegetable salads.

Lamb, Apple and Rice Salad

450 g (1 lb) cooked shoulder of lamb
225 g (½ lb) (1 cup) long grain rice
1 onion, finely chopped
100 mL (4 fl oz) (½ cup) mayonnaise
15 mL (1 tablespoon) lemon juice
salt and pepper
2 eating apples
½ lettuce
50 g (2 oz) (⅓ cup) salted peanuts

1 Cut lamb into cubes.
2 Cook rice in boiling salted water for 20 minutes, drain and refresh in cold water. Cool.
3 When rice is cold, mix lamb and rice in a bowl with chopped onion. Mix mayonnaise with lemon juice, season and stir into lamb and rice. Chill for 1 hour.
4 When ready to serve, finely dice apples. Arrange lamb and rice on a bed of lettuce leaves, and garnish with apples and peanuts.

Serves 6

Lamb Salad with Almonds

225 g (½ lb) (1 cup) rice
2 sticks celery
1 red or green capsicum (pepper), seeded
450 g (1 lb) (2⅔ cups) lamb, cooked and diced
salt and pepper
100 mL (4 fl oz) (½ cup) mayonnaise
½ lettuce
50 g (2 oz) (½ cup) flaked almonds

1 Cook rice in boiling salted water for 20 minutes. Drain and refresh in cold water. Place in a bowl and cool.
2 Chop celery and capsicum and add with lamb to rice.
3 Season mayonnaise and stir into bowl. Chill.
4 When ready to serve arrange lettuce leaves on a shallow dish and put lamb mixture on top. Garnish with almonds.

Serves 6

Beef Coleslaw

450 g (1 lb) hard white cabbage
60 mL (2½ fl oz) (4 tablespoons) vinegar
15 mL (1 tablespoon) sugar
salt and pepper
2 carrots, grated
15 mL (1 tablespoon) snipped chives
1 green capsicum (pepper) cut in strips
225 g (½ lb) (1⅓ cups) cooked beef, cut in strips
90 mL (3 fl oz) (6 tablespoons) mayonnaise
50 mL (¼ pint) (⅔ cup) sour cream

1 Shred cabbage finely and placed in salted, cold water in the fridge for 1 hour. Drain and dry.
2 Mix vinegar, sugar, salt and pepper in a bowl. Add cabbage and leave for 1 hour.
3 Add grated carrots, chives, capsicum and beef.
4 Mix together mayonnaise and sour cream and pour over salad.

Serves 4

Beef Ravigotte Salad

225 g (½ lb) (1⅓ cups) cooked beef
225 g (½ lb) (2 cups) cooked potatoes

Sauce Ravigotte
30 mL (1 fl oz) (2 tablespoons) oil
15 mL (1 tablespoon) vinegar
½ hard-boiled egg, chopped
15 mL (1 tablespoon) capers
15 mL (1 tablespoon) chopped shallots (spring onions, scallions) or onions
salt and pepper
4 gherkins

1 Dice beef and potatoes and place in bowl.
2 Make sauce by combining oil and vinegar. Add egg, capers, shallots or onions and seasoning.
3 Pour over beef and potatoes. Decorate with sliced gherkins.

Serves 4

Belgian Salad

4 chicory (Belgian endives)
225 g (½ lb) (1⅓ cups) diced ham
16 walnuts

Dressing
30 mL (1 fl oz) (2 tablespoons) oil
15 mL (1 tablespoon) vinegar
30 mL (1 fl oz) (2 tablespoons) cream
salt and pepper

1 Make dressing by mixing oil, vinegar, cream, salt and pepper.
2 Wash the chicory and separate leaves. Cut in half.
3 Combine with diced ham and walnuts. Toss in dressing, and serve.

Serves 4

Country Salad

450 g (1 lb) (4 cups) diced, cooked potatoes
70 mL (2½ fl oz) (⅓ cup) dry white wine
salt and pepper
225 g (½ lb) (1⅓ cups) diced ham
2 frankfurts, sliced
15 mL (1 tablespoon) chopped parsley
15 mL (1 tablespoon) snipped chives

Dressing
50 mL (2 fl oz) (¼ cup) oil
juice 1 lemon
5 mL (1 teaspoon) made mustard
2 shallots (spring onions, scallions), chopped

1 Place potatoes in bowl and pour the wine over them. Season.
2 Mix together dressing ingredients and tip dressing, ham and frankfurts over potatoes.
3 Mix well and sprinkle with chopped herbs.

Serves 4

Belgian Salad

Ham Espagnole Salad

225 g (½ lb) ham
1 onion
4 tomatoes
1 green capsicum (pepper)
30 mL (1 fl oz) (2 tablespoons) oil
15 mL (1 tablespoon) vinegar
2 cloves garlic, crushed
salt and pepper

1 Cut ham into strips.
2 Slice onions into rings.
3 Cut tomatoes into quarters, and capsicum in rings, discarding seeds.
4 Make a dressing by mixing oil and vinegar. Add crushed garlic and season with salt and pepper.
5 Toss onions, tomatoes, capsicum and ham in dressing and arrange in bowl.

Serves 4

Ham and Cabbage Salad

225 g (½ lb) white cabbage
100 g (¼ lb) (⅔ cup) chopped ham
8 black olives
50 g (2 oz) (½ cup) chopped walnuts
2 hard-boiled eggs, cut in chunks

Dressing
50 mL (2 fl oz) (¼ cup) oil
15 mL (1 tablespoon) wine vinegar
5 mL (1 teaspoon) made mustard
1 clove garlic, crushed
salt and pepper
2 anchovy fillets, chopped
15 mL (1 tablespoon) cream

1 Wash cabbage thoroughly, drain and shred it finely.
2 Place in a bowl with chopped ham, black olives and walnuts.
3 Make dressing by mixing together oil and vinegar. Stir in mustard till well blended. Add garlic, seasoning and anchovy fillets. Then stir in the cream.
4 Toss salad in the dressing and decorate with chunks of hard-boiled egg. Serve as an appetiser, or make extra quantities for a main meal.

Serves 4

Eggplant (Aubergine) and Ham Salad

1 large eggplant (aubergine)
pinch salt
2 red capsicums (peppers)
2 pickled cucumbers
50 mL (2 fl oz) (¼ cup) vinegar
salt and pepper
50 g (2 oz) (½ cup) flour
50 mL (2 fl oz) (¼ cup) oil
½ lettuce, washed and separated
225 g (½ lb) (1⅓ cups) chopped ham
15 mL (1 tablespoon) chopped dill

1 Cut eggplant into 'chips'. Sprinkle with salt and leave for ½ hour.
2 Dice capsicums and cucumbers and put in a bowl with vinegar and seasoning.
3 Dry the eggplant 'chips' and roll in flour. Fry in hot oil for 2–3 minutes until crisp. Add to salad. Leave to cool for a few hours.
4 Serve on a bed of lettuce leaves, with chopped ham arranged on top. Sprinkle with dill.

Serves 4

Ham and Cabbage Salad

Ham and Pineapple Salad

100 g (¼ lb) (⅔ cup) diced ham
100 g (¼ lb) (1 cup) diced cooked
  potatoes
100 g (¼ lb) (1 cup) diced Gruyere
  cheese
100 g (¼ lb) seedless green grapes,
  washed
100 g (¼ lb) (½ cup) canned pineapple
  chunks
200 mL (6 fl oz) (¾ cup) mayonnaise
30 mL (1 fl oz) (2 tablespoons)
  pineapple juice
salt and pepper
30 mL (1 fl oz) (2 tablespoons) sour
  cream
15 g (½ oz) 3 tablespoons chopped
  parsley

1 Combine together ham, potatoes, Gruyere, grapes and pineapple chunks in a bowl.

2 Mix in mayonnaise and pineapple juice so that all ingredients are well coated. Season with salt and pepper and stir in the sour cream.

3 Serve in an attractive dish, sprinkled with chopped parsley.

Serves 4

Ham and Egg Salad

1 apple
100 g (¼ lb) ham, diced
100 g (¼ lb) boiled new potatoes,
  diced
15 mL (1 tablespoon) snipped chives
150 mL (¼ pint) (⅔ cup) mayonnaise
4 lettuce leaves
4 hard-boiled eggs
5 mL (1 teaspoon) chopped parsley

1 Peel and core apple and dice finely. Combine with ham, potatoes and chives. Pour over mayonnaise, reserving a little for later, and toss.

2 Wash, dry and shred lettuce. Place a quarter of the lettuce in the bottom of each of 4 glasses. Top with ham and potato mixture.

3 Cut each egg into 8 wedges and arrange like the spokes of a wheel on each serving. Dot yolks with a little mayonnaise and sprinkle with chopped parsley.

Serves 4

Smoked Ham Salad

1 small melon
½ cucumber
4 large lettuce leaves
225 g (½ lb) smoked ham, cut in very
  thin slices

Dressing
15 mL (1½ fl oz) (3 tablespoons) plain
  yoghurt
juice ½ lemon
salt and pepper

1 Remove seeds from melon and cut off rind. Cut flesh into 2 cm cubes.

2 Peel cucumber and remove seeds. Dice flesh.

3 Place a lettuce leaf on each plate and arrange ¼ of the ham on top of each leaf. Mix melon and cucumber and divide between each plate, beside ham. Serve slightly chilled.

4 To make dressing, beat yoghurt and lemon juice together until well blended. Season lightly and serve separately.

Serves 4

Meat and Corn Salad

100 g (¼ lb) cooked ham
100 g (¼ lb) tongue
1 small red capsicum (pepper)
1 small green capsicum (pepper)
3 shallots (spring onions, scallions)
100 g (¼ lb) (1 cup) corn kernels
salt and pepper
150 mL (¼ pint) (⅔ cup) mayonnaise
few sprigs parsley

1 Cut ham and tongue into 1 cm cubes.

2 Seed capsicum and dice flesh. Mix with meats in a salad bowl.

3 Slice shallots thinly, including some of the green parts.

4 Mix ingredients in a salad bowl, season, and stir in the mayonnaise until well-coated. Decorate with sprigs of parsley.

Serves 4

Tongue Salad

8 shallots (spring onions, scallions)
bunch radishes
1 lettuce, washed
225 g (½ lb) luncheon meat
225 g (½ lb) cooked, salted ox
  tongue, sliced
2 hard-boiled eggs, sliced
225 g (½ lb) green cabbage, shredded
2 sticks celery, chopped
½ cucumber, sliced

Dressing
45 mL (1½ fl oz) (3 tablespoons) oil
15 mL (1 tablespoon) cider vinegar
5 mL (1 teaspoon) made mustard
5 mL (1 teaspoon) honey
salt and pepper

1 Split green part of shallots down to bulbs. Make cuts in the tops of radishes to resemble the petals of a rose. Place shallots and radishes in iced water until radishes open and the shallots curl.

2 Place lettuce leaves on a serving platter and arrange luncheon meat and tongue in the centre with slices of hard-boiled eggs.

3 Decorate the edge of the dish with shredded green cabbage, chopped celery and sliced cucumber. Arrange radishes and shallots around the border.

4 Combine ingredients for dressing and either sprinkle dressing over salad or serve separately.   *Serves 6*

Melon Balls and Tongue Salad

1 medium-sized melon
1 large grapefruit
225 g (½ lb) tongue
30 mL (1 fl oz) (2 tablespoons) oil
15 mL (1 tablespoon) vinegar
salt and pepper
pinch paprika

1 Cut melon in half and remove seeds. Scoop out flesh with a melon baller and place in a bowl.

2 Cut grapefruit into segments.

3 Cut tongue into thin strips.

4 Make dressing by mixing oil, vinegar, salt and pepper, and toss the melon, grapefruit and tongue into it.

5 Place in a bowl and sprinkle with paprika. Chill until served.   *Serves 4*

Corned Beef and Cucumber Salad

100 g (¼ lb) (⅔ cup) diced corned beef
225 g (½ lb) (2 cups) diced, cooked new potatoes
50 g (2 oz) (½ cup) chopped dill pickle
50 mL (2 fl oz) (¼ cup) mayonnaise
4 large lettuce leaves

1 Mix together beef, potato and chopped dill pickle. Stir in mayonnaise until all ingredients are well coated.
2 Place lettuce leaves on 4 salad dishes. Divide meat and potato mixture evenly between them, piling mixture on top of lettuce leaves and serve.

Serves 4

Corn and Lentil Salad

250 g (½ lb) corn kernels
250 g (½ lb) cooked lentils
250 g (½ lb) cooked, diced corned beef

Dressing
50 mL (2 fl oz) oil
15 mL (3 teaspoons) vinegar
15 mL (3 teaspoons) made mustard
salt and pepper
15 mL (3 teaspoons) chopped pickled cucumber
15 mL (3 teaspoons) chopped onion

1 Mix the corn, lentils and beef in a bowl.
2 Blend together dressing ingredients and pour over the corn, lentils and beef. Serve either hot or cold.

Serves 4

Tip: The flavour can be enhanced by adding chopped shallots (spring onions, scallions) and capsicum (peppers).

Salami Salad

150 g (5 oz) (¾ cup) diced salami
150 g (5 oz) (¾ cup) diced ham
150 g (5 oz) (¾ cup) diced Gruyere cheese
1 bunch watercress
6 black olives
6 anchovy fillets, cut in strips

French Dressing
30 mL (1 fl oz) (2 tablespoons) oil
15 mL (1 tablespoon) vinegar
salt and pepper
5 mL (1 teaspoon) made mustard

1 Make French dressing by mixing oil, vinegar, seasoning and mustard.
2 Place diced salami, ham, and Gruyere cheese in a bowl and toss in dressing.
3 Arrange watercress around bowl, and decorate with strips of anchovy fillets and black olives.

Serves 6

Lentil and Salami Salad with Artichoke Hearts

225 g (½ lb) (1⅓ cups) brown lentils
2 red capsicums (peppers)
225 g (½ lb) salami
6 canned artichoke hearts
60 mL (2¼ fl oz) (4 tablespoons) oil
30 mL (1 fl oz) (2 tablespoons) wine vinegar
5 mL (1 teaspoon) mild mustard
salt and pepper
30 mL (2 tablespoons) chopped fresh parsley and chervil

1 Boil lentils in water without salt for about 1 hour or until tender.
2 Meanwhile seed capsicum and cut into thick strips. Boil for about 10 minutes until soft. Drain and cool.
3 Cut salami into thin slices. Drain artichoke hearts. Beat together oil, vinegar, mustard, salt and pepper.
4 Mix together lentils and capsicum and toss lightly in the dressing. Arrange on a large serving dish. Place artichoke hearts in a row down the middle, and salami slices around the sides. Sprinkle the whole dish with chopped fresh herbs.

Serves 6

Salami Salad

Lentil and Salami Salad with Artichoke Hearts

Tasty Toppings

An imaginative sauce can transform a simple dish into something special. Once you have mastered the basic sauces — Brown, Bechamel and Hollandaise — you have the key to countless variations. Save time by making a quantity of very thick base sauce which can be kept covered in the refrigerator and used as desired.

Add spice to your cooking with Mexican Barbecue Sauce or Hot Chilli Tomato Sauces. Try flavoured butters such as Herb or Garlic Butter for a garnish with a difference or add them to sauces to enhance flavour and colour.

Basic Brown Sauce is a delicious accompaniment for meat dishes.

Hollandaise and Bearnaise Sauces Step-by-step

Hollandaise Sauce
1 Melt butter in deep pot or bain marie. Skim off froth which forms.
2 Place egg yolks, vinegar and water in metal bowl. Rest bowl over deep pan of boiling water ensuring that bowl does not touch water.
3 Beat lightly until thick and creamy.
4 Remove from heat and continue stirring while gradually adding melted butter in a thin stream. Add the lemon juice and seasoning.

Bearnaise Sauce
5 Place shallots, peppercorns, half the tarragon and the vinegar in a small pan. Boil briskly until vinegar has almost evaporated.
6 Make hollandaise sauce and add melted butter. Then add shallot mixture.
7 Strain sauce through fine muslin over bowl or through a conical sieve.
8 Sprinkle in the rest of the tarragon, stir and check the seasoning.

The Hollandaise family

Basic Hollandaise Sauce

4 egg yolks
60 mL (4 tablespoons) cold water
15 mL (1 tablespoon) white vinegar
225 g (½ lb) (1 cup) butter, melted
juice 1 lemon
salt and white pepper
pinch cayenne

1 Whip egg yolks, water and vinegar in a stainless steel bowl (a metal bowl is the best conductor of heat).
2 Place bowl over a deep pan of boiling water, making sure the bottom of the bowl does not touch the water — egg yolks coagulate at 60°C (140°F), a temperature which is lower than that of boiling water. Beat lightly until eggs are cooked to the consistency of a custard sauce. Mix well, stirring up from the bottom of the bowl and scraping down any sauce that adheres to the sides.
3 Remove bowl from the heat. Stir for 5 minutes while gradually pouring in all the melted butter, whisking all the time to obtain a thick emulsion.
4 Add lemon juice and season to taste. This sauce should be served immediately and will not keep for longer than 2 or 3 hours.

Makes about 300 mL (½ pint) (⅝ cup)

Conil Sauce

1 In a pan mix 10 g (2 tablespoons) mixed chopped parsley, tarragon, chervil and mint, 30 mL (2 tablespoons) dry vermouth, 5 mL (1 teaspoon) tomato paste and 1 peeled clove garlic. Bring to the boil and simmer for 1 minute.
2 Rub mixture through a sieve or mix in a blender and add puree to 300 mL (½ pint) (1¼ cups) basic hollandaise sauce.
Serve with grilled steaks and beef kebabs.

Makes 300 mL (½ pint) (1¼ cups)

Rosalie Sauce

1 To 300 mL (½ pint) (1¼ cups) Conil sauce, add 15 mL (¼ pint) (⅔ cup) veloute or white sauce.
2 Fold in 150 mL (¼ pint) (⅔ cup) whipped cream.
Serve with grilled veal chops.

Makes 300 mL (½ pint) (1¼ cups).

Choron Sauce

1 To 300 mL (½ pint) (1¼ cups) basic hollandaise sauce, add 15 mL (1 tablespoon) tomato sauce and 5 mL (1 teaspoon) tarragon vinegar.
Serve with grilled meat and tournedos.

Makes 300 mL (½ pint) (1¼ cups).

The Bearnaise family

Bearnaise Sauce

15 mL (1 tablespoon) chopped shallots (spring onions, scallions)
pinch chopped tarragon
6 finely crushed white peppercorns
45 mL (3 tablespoons) tarragon vinegar
300 mL (½ pint) (1¼ cups) basic hollandaise sauce
pinch chopped parsley

1 Place shallots, half the tarragon, peppercorns and vinegar in a small pan. Boil briskly until vinegar has almost evaporated. Remove from heat.
2 Add mixture to hollandaise sauce and then strain sauce through muslin into a bowl. Add the rest of the tarragon and the chopped parsley and mix.
Serve with grilled meat.

Makes 300 mL (½ pint) (1¼ cups)

Bechamel Sauce Step-by-step

1 Collect the ingredients.
2 Heat the butter gently in a pan until melted.
3 Draw pan off heat. Add flour and make a roux.
4 Return to the heat and cook the roux until it bubbles and has the appearance of wet sand. Stir all the time with a wooden spoon.
5 Draw pan off heat and blend in milk.
6 The sauce is heated again for a few minutes, then seasoned and poured into a sauce-boat to serve.

The Bechamel family

Bechamel Sauce

The quantity below makes a panada or thick paste-like mixture which can be stored, covered, in a refrigerator for up to 1 week. For a flowing or pouring sauce, add up 450 mL (¾ pint) (2 cups) liquid — 300 mL (½ pint) (1¼ cups) is usually sufficient; reheat gently, stirring all the time, until smooth.

1 small onion, studded with 2 cloves
500 mL (1 pint) (2 cups) milk
50 g (2 oz) (4 tablespoons) butter or
   margarine, or mixture of both
50 g (2 oz) (½ cup) flour
salt and pepper
pinch nutmeg
pinch thyme

1 Place onion in a saucepan with the milk. Bring gently to the boil, remove pan from heat and allow to cool. Cover with a lid and leave the milk to infuse and absorb the flavour of the onion.
2 Melt fat in a pan and stir in the flour. Cook the roux over a low heat without letting it colour, for about 1 minute, stirring with a wooden spoon. Gradually pour in the milk, stirring continuously until a smooth sauce forms.
3 Add onion and simmer sauce 5 minutes. Remove onion and add salt, pepper, nutmeg and thyme.

   Makes 500 mL (1 pint) (2½ cups)

Hint: The liquid used can be milk, cream, stock or water, according to the recipe.

Asparagus Sauce

1 To 300 mL (½ pint) (1¼ cups) of basic bechamel sauce, add 50 g (2 oz) cooked asparagus, blended with 300 mL (½ pint) (1¼ cups) of the water in which the asparagus was cooked.
2 After the sauce is cooked, remove pan from heat and add 50 mL (2 fl oz) (4 tablespoons) sour cream or natural yoghurt to give sauce a piquant flavour. Check seasoning.
Serve with veal.

Carrot Sauce

1 To 300 mL (½ pint) (1¼ cups) of basic bechamel sauce, add a puree of 50 g (2 oz) cooked carrots, liquidised with 150 mL (¼ pint) (⅔ cup) of their cooking water.
2 Add 50 mL (2 fl oz) (¼ cup) cream or sour cream and reheat. Flavour sauce with a pinch of paprika, 2.5 mL (½ teaspoon) liquid honey and 30 mL (2 tablespoons) lemon juice. Check the seasoning.
Serve with boiled beef.

Mustard Sauce

1 To 300 mL (½ pint) (1¼ cups) butter sauce, add, with pan off the heat, 15 mL (1 tablespoon) made English mustard according to taste.
2 Thin sauce to required consistency with 300 mL (½ pint) (1¼ cups) white stock and season to taste.
Serve with pork.

Parsley Sauce

1 To 300 mL (½ pint) (1¼ cups) basic bechamel sauce, add 5 g (1 tablespoon) freshly chopped parsley.
2 Thin sauce to required consistency with 300 mL (½ pint) (1¼ cups) white stock and season to taste.
Serve with white meat, calf's head and tongue.

Soubise Sauce

1 To 300 mL (½ pint) (1¼ cups) basic becamel sauce, add 100 g (¼ lb) cooked onion, liquidised with 200 mL (6 fl oz) (¾ cup) cold milk and blend. Flavour with a pinch of sage.
2 Add 100 mL (4 fl oz) (½ cup) cream and boil for 5 minutes. Season to taste.
Serve with roast or boiled mutton or veal.

The brown family

Basic Brown Sauce

75 g (3 oz) (good ¾ cup) flour
100 g (¼ lb) (½ cup) margarine
2 medium carrots, coarsely sliced
2 medium onions, coarsely sliced
2 sticks celery and trimmings,
   coarsely sliced
100 g (¼ lb) bacon rashers, chopped
1 bouquet garni
1 clove garlic
50 g (2 oz) tomato paste
1 litre (1¾ pints) (5 cups) brown stock
   or other liquid
salt and pepper
pinch mace

1 Brown flour on a baking sheet for 15 minutes at 200°C (400°F). Remove. Heat half the margarine in a heavy-bottomed pan and stir in baked flour. Cook roux for 3 minutes to a sandy texture. Cool.
2 In another pan heat remaining margarine and brown vegetables and bacon for 8 minutes, keeping the lid on the pan throughout. Add the bouquet garni, garlic and tomato paste. Drain off surplus fat, pour in the brown stock and boil for 1 hour. This reduces the stock and concentrates its flavour; skim from time to time.
3 Stir the cold roux into the boiling stock, then whisk to avoid lumps. Simmer for another hour, skimming occasionally, until sauce is clear.
4 Strain sauce and season with salt, pepper and mace. Thin down with 300 mL (½ pint) (1¼ cups) of brown stock, or beer, wine, cider or fruit juice if preferred, and boil for another 30 minutes, adjusting seasoning at the last moment.

   Makes ½ litre (1 pint) (2½ cups)

Demi-glace Madeira Sauce

1 Thin down ½ litre (1 pint) (2½ cups) basic brown sauce with 150 mL (¼ pint) (⅝ cup) brown stock and 150 mL (¼ pint) (⅝ cup) Madeira, stirring in 5 mL (1 teaspoon) beef extract.
2 Boil sauce for 15 minutes to reduce by one-third, to give a thinner, glossier and more aromatic mixture than the basic brown sauce.
Serve with meat.

Makes about 1 litre (1½ pints) (4 cups)

Demi-glace Sherry Sauce

1 Use the same ingredients as for demi-glace Madeira sauce but substitute medium sherry for Madeira and flavour with a sprig of mint and sage.
Serve with meat.

Makes about 1 litre (1½ pints) (4 cups)

Chasseur Sauce

25 g (1 oz) (2 tablespoons) butter mixed with 25 mL (1 fl oz)(⅛ cup) oil
50 g (2 oz) (½ cup) chopped shallots (spring onions, scallions) or onions
50 g (2 oz) (⅔ cup) mushrooms
150 mL (¼ pint) (⅔ cup) dry white wine
½ litre (1 pint) (2½ cups) demi-glace or basic brown sauce
150 g (5 oz) (½ cup) tomatoes, skinned, seeded and coarsely chopped
salt and pepper
15 mL (1 tablespoon) chopped parsley and tarragon leaves

1 Heat butter and oil mixture in a saute pan and simmer shallots for 2 minutes without colouring them. Add mushrooms and cook a further minute.
2 Strain and add the wine. Reduce sauce by boiling for 4 minutes, then stir in the demi-glace sauce and tomatoes and simmer for 15 minutes. Season.
3 Add chopped parsley and tarragon before serving.
Serve with veal escalopes or chops or lamb noisettes.

Makes about ½ litre (1 pint) (2½ cups)

Basquaise Sauce

1 Halve 1 red and 1 green capsicum (pepper), seed and shred finely.
2 Scald and drain, add to ½ litre (1 pint) (2½ cups), chasseur sauce and simmer for 10 minutes. Season with salt, pepper and garlic salt.
Serve with veal and pork chops.

Makes about ½ litre (1 pint) (2½ cups)

Bordelaise Sauce

50 g (2 oz) (¼ cups) onions or shallots (spring onions, scallions), finely chopped
6 black peppercorns, crushed
1 sprig thyme
1 bay leaf
150 mL (¼ pint) (⅔ cup) red wine (claret)
½ litre (1 pint) (2½ cups) demi-glace Madeira or sherry sauce

1 Place onion in saucepan with peppercorns, thyme, bay leaf and wine. Boil 5 minutes, then add demi-glace sauce.
2 Boil a further 30 minutes and pass through a fine sieve. Serve with Steak Bordelaise

Makes ½ litre (1 pint) (2½ cups)

Tip: This sauce can also include diced or sliced poached beef marrow, but this does tend to make the sauce richer and greasy.

Burgundy Sauce

150 g (5 oz) button mushrooms
50 g (2 oz) (4 tablespoons) margarine
150 g (5 oz) chopped shallots (spring onions, scallions)
½ litre (1 pint) (2½ cups) bordelaise sauce, substitute Burgundy for claret
salt and pepper
15 mL (1 tablespoon) brandy

1 To prepare garnish: wash mushrooms and remove stalks (these can be used to make a mushroom-flavoured stock). Heat margarine and brown shallots for approx 4 minutes. Drain.

2 Pour in bordelaise sauce and boil 10 minutes until onions are almost soft. Strain.
3 Reheat sauce and add mushroom caps. Boil 3 minutes. Check seasoning, adding salt and pepper to flavour, then pour in the brandy. Serve with veal and beef dishes.

Makes ½ litre (1 pint) (2½ cups)

Piquant Sauce

50 g (2 oz) (¼ cup) onions or shallots (spring onions, scallions), peeled and chopped
50 mL (2 fl oz) (¼ cup) vinegar
½ litre (1 pint) (2½ cups) demi-glace or basic brown sauce
50 g (2 oz) gherkins, chopped
15 g (½ oz) pickled capers
5 g (1 tablespoon) chopped parsley and tarragon leaves, mixed
salt and pepper

1 Boil onions in the vinegar for 4 minutes to reduce liquid by half, then stir in the sauce and simmer for 15 minutes.
2 Add gherkins, capers, parsley and tarragon, and season with salt and pepper to taste.
Serve with made-up cooked meat dishes, boiled beef, ham and pork

Makes about ½ litre (1 pint) (2½ cups)

Robert Sauce

Use the same ingredients as for Piquant Sauce but omit gherkins and capers; at the last moment, draw the pan off the heat and mix in 5 g (1 teaspoon) made English mustard to prevent curdling.

Serve with grilled pork chops and any other fatty meat.

Makes about ½ litre (1 pint) (2½ cups)

The tomato family

Tomato Sauce

25 mL (1 fl oz) (⅛ cup) oil
25 g (1 oz) (2 tablespoons) margarine
50 g (2 oz) celery, diced
50 g (2 oz) (½ cup) carrots, diced
50 g (2 oz) (¼ cup) onions, diced
50 g (2 oz) (⅓ cup) unsmoked bacon
　　trimmings and bones, diced
25 g (1 oz) (4 tablespoons) flour
75 g (3 oz) (5 tablespoons) tomato
　　paste
1 litre (1¾ pints) (4 cups) chicken
　　stock
1 bouquet garni
1 sprig mint
salt and pepper
pinch paprika
15 g (½ oz) (½ tablespoon) sugar

1 Heat oil and margarine in a large saucepan and fry vegetables and bacon trimmings for 15 minutes.
2 Add flour, cook 5 minutes, stir in tomato paste and cook another 5 minutes.

3 Stir in stock, add bouquet garni and mint, and bring to the boil. Simmer 1 hour.
4 Season with salt, pepper, paprika and sugar, then strain through a fine sieve.
Serve with hamburgers.

Makes about 900 mL (1½ pints)
(4½ cups)

Spicy Tomato Sauce

450 g (1 lb) tomatoes
225 g (½ lb) cooking apples
1 onion, chopped
150 mL (¼ pint) (⅔ cup) white vinegar
100 g (¼ lb) (½ cup) sugar
6 cloves
2 pieces root ginger, chopped
12 peppercorns
5 mL (1 teaspoon) salt
2 chillies, seeded and chopped
30 mL (2 tablespoons) tomato paste

1 Chop tomatoes and apples roughly, including peel, pips and cores. Place in a pan with the onion, cover and simmer gently over low heat until soft.

2 Add remaining ingredients and simmer, covered, for 30 minutes. Sieve tomato mixture, return to pan and simmer until thick (approx 15 minutes).
3 Pour tomato sauce into warm sterilised jars and stand in a large pan of simmering water for 30 minutes. Water level should be half-way up the sides of the jars.
4 Remove jars and seal in the usual way.

Makes approximately 1 kg (2 lb)

Tomato Sauce

Roman Sauce

30 mL (2 tablespoons) oil
50 g (2 oz) (⅔ cup) chopped, white mushrooms
30 g (1 oz) (¼ cup) chopped shallots (spring onions, scallions) or onions
60 g (2 oz) chopped ham
150 g (5 oz) (½ cup) fresh tomatoes, skinned, seeded and chopped
1 clove garlic, peeled and chopped
30 mL (2 tablespoons) tomato paste
½ litre (1 pint) (2½ cups) demi-glace sauce
salt and pepper
15 mL (1 tablespoon) chopped parsley, mint, tarragon

1 Heat oil in a pan and cook vegetables for 5 minutes. Add ham, tomatoes and garlic and cook another 10 minutes.
2 Stir in tomato paste and sauce and simmer 10 minutes. Season with salt and pepper and add parsley, mint and tarragon.
Serve with escalopes or steaks.

Makes about ½ litre (1 pint) (2½ cups)

Portuguese Sauce

1 To 600 mL (1 pint) (2½ cups) tomato sauce, add 150 g (5 oz) (½ cup) skinned, seeded and chopped tomatoes, and 2 chopped cloves of garlic.
2 Bring sauce back to the boil for 10 minutes. Season to taste with salt and pepper.
Serve with meat.

Makes 600 mL (1 pint) (2½ cups)

Neapolitan Sauce

1 To 300 mL (½ pint) (1¼ cups) tomato sauce, add 225 g (½ lb) of fresh, skinned, seeded and chopped tomatoes.
2 Season with salt and pepper and reboil for 5 minutes. Add mint or oregano to flavour.
Serve with meat.

Makes 600 mL (1 pint) (2½ cups)

Other favourite sauces

Hot Chilli Tomato Sauce

50 g (2 oz) (4 tablespoons) tomato paste
2 cloves garlic, peeled and chopped
1 green chilli, sliced
1 red chilli, sliced
1 onion, chopped
30 mL (2 tablespoons) vinegar
30 mL (2 tablespoons) soy sauce
15 g (½ oz) (1 tablespoon) sugar
150 mL (⅔ cup) (¼ pint) water
15 mL (1 tablespoon) oil
1 chicken stock cube
pinch salt, oregano and basil

To thicken the Sauce
15 g (½ oz) (1½ tablespoons) cornflour
75 mL (2½ fl oz) (⅓ cup) water

Garnish
4 tomatoes, skinned, seeded and chopped
25 g (1 oz) (2 tablespoons) corn kernels, cooked or canned

1 Blend all ingredients and marinate steaks for 30 minutes.
2 After removing steaks, boil marinade for 4 minutes.
3 Mix cornflour with water and add to marinade. Boil 1 minute to thicken.
4 Add garnish and reheat. Pour over steaks, or serve separately.

Makes 300 mL (½ pint) (1¼ cups)

Mexican Barbecue Sauce

3 red capsicums (peppers) grilled, skin removed and chopped
3 small fresh green chillies, seeded and chopped
salt
6 cloves garlic, peeled
300 mL (½ pint) (1¼ cups) olive oil
6 onions, peeled and finely chopped
1½ kg (3 lb) ripe tomatoes, skinned, seeded and diced
50 g (2 oz) (3 tablespoons) (¼ cup) sugar
45 mL (3 tablespoons) vinegar
1 bouquet garni
5 g (¼ oz) saffron

1 Put chopped capsicum (pepper) and chilli in a mortar, with a pinch of salt and the garlic.
2 Pound these ingredients, adding some of the oil dry by drop until it has acquired a very smooth, paste-like consistency. Set aside.
3 Heat 15 mL (1 tablespoon) olive oil in a frying pan, add the onions and cook until golden-brown then sprinkle with sugar.
4 Leave to caramelise, watching that the sugar does not burn. Remove from heat, add vinegar and diced tomatoes.
5 Add bouquet garni and cook over a low heat for about 20 minutes, stirring frequently with a wooden spoon, to make a thick tomato mixture.
6 Remove bouquet garni and rub through a sieve or blend to a puree. Chilli paste can be blended at the same time if desired.
7 Tip mixture into a small saucepan and add saffron and chilli paste, if not already included. Cook for 2 minutes, beating with a whisk. Remove pan from the heat and cool.
8 Before serving, gradually whisk the rest of the oil into the sauce. Serve cold or chilled with grilled meat.

Makes about 300 mL (½ pint) (⅝ cup)

To Prepare Chillies

Fresh Chillies: soak in cold salted water for 1 hour to help temper their hot flavour, then drain. Cut in half and discard stem, seeds and pith. Avoid handling chillies as much as possible as their pungent oils can burn and irritate your skin.

Canned Chillies: rinse under cold running water, then drain. Use as required.

Pineapple Barbecue Sauce

Marinade
150 mL (¼ pint) (⅔ cup) pineapple juice
30 mL (2 tablespoons) soy sauce
15 mL (1 tablespoon) Worcestershire sauce
3 cloves garlic, peeled and chopped
10 g (1 tablespoon) freshly peeled ginger root, chopped
1 small onion
30 mL (2 tablespoons) vinegar
15 mL (1 tablespoon) honey
pinch salt
pinch cayenne pepper

Stock
100 mL (4 fl oz) (½ cup) water
1 beef stock cube
15 g (½ oz) (1½ tablespoons) cornflour
75 mL (2½ fl oz) (⅓ cup) water

1 Blend ingredients and marinate the steaks to be barbecued for 30 minutes.
2 When steaks are removed, add water and beef stock cube and boil the marinade for 5 minutes.
3 Thicken with cornflour mixed with water. Pour over the steaks or serve separately.

Makes 300 mL (½ pint) (1¼ cups)

Mint Sauce

25 g (1 oz) fresh mint leaves
25 g (1 oz) (2 tablespoons) brown sugar
150 mL (¼ pint) (⅔ cup) malt vinegar

1 Wash mint and drain; coat with sugar and chop finely.
2 Place mint in a basin, add vinegar and mix.

Makes 150 mL (¼ pint) (⅔ cup)

Bolognese Sauce

50 mL (2 fl oz) (¼ cup) oil
1 onion, chopped
1 stick celery, chopped
1 clove garlic, chopped
225 g (½ lb) (1 cup) minced beef
50 g (2 oz) (¼ cup) minced chicken or calf's liver
25 g (1 oz) (4 tablespoons) flour
25 g (1 oz) (2 tablespoons) tomato paste
1 beef stock cube
300 mL (½ pint) (1¼ cups) water
50 mL (2 fl oz) (¼ cup) sherry or Marsala
pinch each oregano, paprika and mace
salt and pepper

1 Heat oil in pan and saute onion, celery and garlic for 5 minutes until lightly browned.
2 Add minced beef and liver and cook a further 5 minutes.
3 Sprinkle in flour and cook for 1 minute. Stir in tomato paste and cook for another minute. Dissolve the beef stock cube in water and add to pan with sherry or Marsala. Add oregano, paprika, mace and seasoning and simmer a further 15 minutes.

Makes 500 mL (1 pint) (2½ cups)

Cumberland Sauce

25 g (1 oz) shallots (spring onions, scallions), finely chopped
grated rind and juice of 1 lemon and 1 orange
450 g (1 lb) redcurrant jelly
225 mL (8 fl oz) (1 cup) port
5 g (1 teaspoon) made English mustard
pinch ground ginger

1 Boil shallots with strained fruit juices for 5 minutes.
2 Boil rind in a little water for 5 minutes, rinse, drain and add to shallots with the redcurrant jelly and port. Simmer for 10 minutes.
3 Cook, add mustard to taste, and season with ginger.
Serve with cold ham and pressed beef.

Makes about 150 mL (¼ pint) (⅔ cup)

Horseradish Cream

75 g (3 oz) fresh horseradish root, peeled and washed
45 mL (3 tablespoons) white vinegar
75 mL (2½ fl oz) (⅓ cup) water
salt and pepper
pinch sugar
300 mL (½ pint) (1¼ cups) cream, lightly whipped
25 g (1 oz) (½ cup) fresh breadcrumbs

1 Soak grated horseradish in vinegar for 1 hour. Season with salt and pepper and a pinch of sugar.
2 Fold whipped cream into horseradish mixture, then stir in the breadcrumbs. Store covered in the refrigerator. Turn into a sauce-boat or dish and serve when required.
Serve with roast beef, or joints of hot and cold salted meat.

Makes about 300 mL (½ pint) (1¼ cups)

Horseradish Sauce

75 g (3 oz) fresh horseradish root, peeled and washed
45 mL (3 tablespoons) wine vinegar
pinch sugar
salt and pepper
300 mL (½ pint) (1¼ cups) milk
75 g (3 oz) (1½ cups) fresh white breadcrumbs

1 Grate horseradish and soak in wine vinegar for 1 hour. Season with salt, pepper and sugar.
2 Heat milk in a saucepan and bring to the boil. Stir in breadcrumbs and soak for 10 minutes. Blend in horseradish mixture and serve the sauce with roast beef.

Makes about 300 mL (½ pint) (1¼ cups)

Tip: As a change, make the horseradish sauce in the Hungarian way by mixing the horseradish and vinegar mixture into 300 mL (½ pint) (1¼ cups) white sauce.

Gravies and garnishes

Plain Brown Gravy

*450 g (1 lb) bone trimmings from
   cooked joints of meat
50 g (2 oz) (4 tablespoons) margarine
1 medium onion, peeled and
   coarsely chopped
1 medium carrot, peeled and
   coarsely chopped
2 celery sticks, peeled and coarsely
   chopped
1 bouquet garni
1 litre (1¾ pints) (4 cups) water
1 beef stock cube or 2 teaspoons
   meat extract
salt and pepper*

1 Preheat oven to 200°C (400°F). Chop bones into small pieces and place in a roasting pan with margarine. Roast in preheated oven for 30 minutes. Remove from pan, reserving liquid.

2 Put liquid into a frying pan, add chopped vegetables and fry for 5 minutes until brown.

3 Drain off liquid and place the bones and vegetables in a large saucepan with the bouquet garni, water and stock cube or meat extract. Bring to the boil and simmer for 1 hour.

4 Check seasoning and strain. Serve with any roast meat.

Makes 1 litre (1¾ pints) (4 cups)

Thickened Gravy

In professional kitchens this is made from a rich veal and beef stock which is reduced by half and then thickened with starch in the form of arrowroot or cornflour.

You will need 25 g (1 oz) (4 tablespoons) cornflour or arrowroot for each 750 mL (1¼ pints) (3 cups) gravy. Mix thickening agent with a little cold water to a smooth paste, add some of the hot gravy and return mixture to the main gravy. Boil for 5 minutes until the starch clears. Season to taste.

If you wish to give gravy extra flavour, add 100 mL (4 fl oz) (½ cup) port, Madeira or sherry to each 750 mL (1¼ pints) (3 cups) of gravy.

Orange Bigarade Gravy

*3 oranges
3 sugar lumps
15 mL (1 tablespoon) butter or
   margarine
45 mL (3 tablespoons) distilled wine
   or vinegar
½ litre (1 pint) (2½ cups) thickened
   gravy
small sprig mint
salt and pepper
60 mL (4 tablespoons) orange
   Curacao or 5 drops orange essence*

1 Remove zest of the oranges, making sure that no white pith is included, and cut the skin into thin julienne strips. Squeeze and strain juice from the oranges.

2 Place sugar and margarine in a pan and heat until sugar caramelises. Add vinegar and orange juice and boil for 3 minutes to concentrate the liquid.

3 Add gravy and mint, cover with a lid and simmer for 5 minutes.

4 Meanwhile, put the strips of orange rind in a pan, cover with cold water and boil for 10 minutes. Drain and refresh in cold water, drain again and add strips to the gravy. Remove mint and check the seasoning. Add the orange liqueur or essence. Serve with pork, bacon and lamb.

*Make about ½ litre (1 pint) (2½ cups)
gravy.*

Tip: To improve the aroma, add thin julienne strips of lemon peel (½ lemon will be sufficient).

Herb Butter

*100 g (¼ lb) (½ cup) butter, softened
2 sprigs tarragon
2 sprigs parsley
15 mL (1 tablespoon) lemon juice
salt and pepper*

1 Cream butter in a bowl.

2 Chop tarragon and parsley finely and mix into butter. Add lemon juice and salt and pepper to taste. Serve with grilled meat.

Garlic Butter

*2–8 cloves garlic
100 g (¼ lb) (½ cup) butter, softened
salt and pepper to taste*

1 Pound the garlic to a smooth paste by using a garlic press or a pestle and mortar, or by firmly crushing the peeled cloves, sprinkled liberally with salt, with the flat blade of a knife until a pulp is obtained.

2 Cream butter in a bowl, mix it with the garlic and season to taste with salt and pepper.

Serve with grilled steaks, hamburgers and lamb chops.

Bercy or Bordelaise Butter

*15 g (½ oz) (⅛ cup) chopped shallots
   (spring onions, scallions)
150 mL (¼ pint) (⅔ cup) dry white
   wine
100 g (¼ lb) (½ cup) softened butter
salt and pepper
15 mL (1 tablespoon) lemon juice
5 g (1 tablespoon) chopped parsley*

1 Put shallots in a pan, add white wine and bring to the boil. Boil for 5 minutes and cool.

2 When shallot mixture is cold, blend it with the butter, adding the rest of the ingredients. Cream well.

Use to garnish Steak Bordelaise or for blending into Bordelaise Sauce (see recipe).

Yorkshire Pudding

*2 eggs
150 g (5 oz) (1¼ cups) flour, sifted
300 mL (½ pint) (1¼ cups) water, or
   milk and water mixed
pinch salt*

1 Beat eggs well, then stir in flour. Add liquid and beat for 3–4 minutes to obtain a smooth batter. Season with salt and leave the batter for 1 hour.

2 Preheat oven to 190°C (375°F).

3 Place a teaspoon of the meat juices in the bottom of each patty tin and heat in oven for 5 minutes. Half-fill them with batter and bake for 15–20 minutes until well-risen and golden.

Makes 6–8

Weights and Measures

Quantities are given in Metric, Imperial and US cup/avoirdupois measures. Rarely do exact conversions from Imperial/US measures to Metric measures give convenient working quantities, and so Metric measures have been rounded off to a more handy unit: 1 ounce (oz) = 25 grams (g) (28.5 g is the exact conversion of 1 oz). The tables below show recommended equivalents:—

As a general rule 1 kilogram (kg) (1000 g) = about 2 pounds (lb) 3 oz (2.2 lb); 1 litre (1000 millilitres (mL) = about 1¾ pints (1.75 pints). However, in some recipes a more exact conversion has been used to maintain the balance between ingredients.

Notes for Australian Users
Ingredients are given in Metric/Imperial/US cup/avoirdupois measures. In Australia the American 8 oz measuring cup is used in conjunction with the Imperial pint — 20 fluid ounces (fl oz). Also in this book, remember that the tablespoon measure used in these recipes differs from the Australian tablespoon, e.g.:

1 British standard tablespoon holds 17.7 mL
1 Australian tablespoon holds 20 mL.
However 1 teaspoon holds 5 mL in both systems.

Remember: follow only one set of quantities for any single recipe, as Metric/Imperial/US measures are not interchangeable.

WEIGHT		VOLUME			LINEAR MEASURE		Equivalent Oven Temperatures			SPOONS (level unless otherwise stated)	
Metric	Imperial	Metric	Imperial	US Cup	Metric	Imperial	°C	°F	Gas Mark	Metric	Imperial
15 g	½ oz	50 mL	2 fl oz	¼	3 mm	⅛ in	110	225	¼	1.25 ml	¼ teasp.
20 g	¾ oz	75 mL	2½ fl oz	⅓	5 mm	¼ in	130	250	½	2.5 ml	½ teasp.
25 g	1 oz		3 fl oz	⅜	1 cm	½ in	140	275	1	5 ml	1 teasp.
40 g	1½ oz	100 mL	4 fl oz	½	2.5 cm	1 in	150	300	2	15 ml	1 tablesp.
50 g	2 oz	150 mL	5 fl oz		4 cm	1½ in	170	325	3	30 ml	2 tablesp.
75 g	3 oz		(¼ pint)	⅝	5 cm	2 in	180	350	4		(1 fl oz)
100 g	4 oz (¼ lb)	200 mL	6 fl oz	¾	6.5 cm	2½ in	190	375	5		
150 g	5 oz		7 fl oz	⅞	7.5 cm	3 in	200	400	6		
175 g	6 oz	225 mL	8 fl oz	1	10 cm	4 in	220	425	7		
200 g	7 oz	275 mL	9 fl oz	1⅛	12.5 cm	5 in	230	450	8		
225 g	8 oz (½ lb)	300 mL	10 fl oz	1¼	15 cm	6 in	240	475	9		
250 g	9 oz		(½ pint)		18 cm	7 in					
(¼ kg)			11 fl oz	1⅜	20 cm	8 in				3 teasp.	1 tablesp.
275 g	10 oz		12 fl oz	1½	23 cm	9 in				2 tablesp.	1 fl oz
300 g	11 oz	400 mL	14 fl oz	1¾	25 cm	10 in				16 tablesp. (US)	1 cup (US)
350 g	12 oz		16 fl oz	2 = 1 pint (US)	30 cm	12 in (1 ft)					
	(¾ lb)	½ litre			35 cm	14 in					
375 g	13 oz	(500–600mL	20 fl oz	2½	38 cm	15 in					
400 g	14 oz	see recipe)	(1 pint)		45 cm	18 in					
425 g	15 oz	750 mL	1¼ pints	3	60 cm	24 in					
450 g	16 oz	(¾ litre)			92 cm	36 in					
	(1 lb)	900 mL	1½ pints	—							
		1 litre	1¾ pints	—							
900–1000g	2 lb										
(1 kg)											
1½ kg	3 lb	**BAR MEASURES**		Pony/liqueur glass	1 fl oz						
2 kg	4 lb			Jigger	1½ fl oz						
2½ kg	5 lb	Dash 4–6 drops		Wineglass	4 fl oz						
3 kg	6 lb	Teaspoon ⅙ fl oz		Cup	8 fl oz						
3½ kg	7 lb	Tablespoon ½ fl oz									
4 kg	8 lb										

Index

References to *microwave* recipes are in *italic* type.